UNDERSTANDING
CENTRAL AMERICA

SIXTH EDITION

UNDERSTANDING CENTRAL AMERICA

Global Forces, Rebellion, and Change

John A. Booth
UNIVERSITY OF NORTH TEXAS

Christine J. Wade
WASHINGTON COLLEGE

Thomas W. Walker
OHIO UNIVERSITY

WESTVIEW
PRESS

A Member of the Perseus Books Group

Westview Press was founded in 1975 in Boulder, Colorado, by notable publisher and intellectual Fred Praeger. Westview Press continues to publish scholarly titles and high-quality undergraduate- and graduate-level textbooks in core social science disciplines. With books developed, written, and edited with the needs of serious nonfiction readers, professors, and students in mind, Westview Press honors its long history of publishing books that matter.

Westview Press books are available at special discounts for bulk purchases in the United States by corporations, institutions, and other organizations. For more information, please contact the Special Markets Department at the Perseus Books Group, 2300 Chestnut Street, Suite 200, Philadelphia, PA 19103, or call (800) 810-4145, ext. 5000, or e-mail special.markets@perseusbooks.com.

Designed by Linda Mark

Library of Congress Cataloging-in-Publication Data
    Booth, John A., 1946–
    Understanding Central America: global forces, rebellion, and change / John A. Booth, Christine J. Wade, Thomas W Walker. — Sixth edition.
        pages cm
    Includes bibliographical references and index.
    ISBN 978-0-8133-4958-9 (paperback) — ISBN 978-0-8133-4959-6 (e-book)
1. Central America—History—1951–1979. 2. Central America—History—1979–
3. Political stability—Central America—History—20th century. 4. Democratization—Central America—History—20th century. 5. Social conflict—Central America—History—20th century. 6. Revolutions—Central America—History—20th century.
I. Wade, Christine J. II. Walker, Thomas W., 1940– III. Title.
    F1439.B66 2014
    972.805'2—dc23
                                                                    2014005228

10 9 8 7 6 5 4 3 2 1

To Patti,
to Greg, and
to Anne

CONTENTS

TABLES AND FIGURES

TABLES

FIGURES

PREFACE TO THE SIXTH EDITION

FOR THIS, THE TWENTY-FIFTH ANNIVERSARY OF *Understanding Central America's* first edition in 1989, we have again extensively updated the volume. For the fourth and fifth editions, multiple transformations of the region—the formal democratization of several countries, the end of several civil wars, and the adoption of new, neoliberal economic development models—required a major rearrangement of the book. This sixth edition follows the same organization as the fourth and fifth but contains extensively updated country chapters to incorporate developments up through early 2014, including elections in Honduras (2013), and Costa Rica and El Salvador (early 2014). Chapter 9, on political participation and public opinion, integrates new survey data on the region from 2012, and traces trends in behavior and attitudes from the 1990s. We have added new figures and updated tables on trends in politics, economics, social conditions, and election outcomes through March of 2014.

ACKNOWLEDGMENTS

WE OWE MANY PEOPLE AND INSTITUTIONS IN CENTRAL AMERICA and the United States our sincerest thanks for their time, support, and encouragement. For fieldwork support over the decades while our book was written and repeatedly updated, we thank the Latin American Studies Association; the Advisory Council on Church and Society of the United Presbyterian Church, USA; the Inter-American Dialogue; the International Human Rights Law Group; the Washington Office on Latin America; Hemispheric Initiatives; Alice McGrath; the University of North Texas; the Heinz Foundation, University of Pittsburgh; Ohio University; Washington College and the Louis L. Goldstein Program in Public Affairs; and the Carter Center. For collaboration in Central America we gratefully acknowledge the assistance of the Facultad Latinoamericana de Ciencias Sociales and the Centro Superior Universitaria Centroamericana in Costa Rica, the Asociación y Estudios Sociales (ASIES) in Guatemala, and the Confederación Nacional de Profesionales Héroes y Mártires in Nicaragua. We thank the United Presbyterian Church, USA, for granting Thomas Walker the right to reuse some material he originally wrote for a Presbyterian Church publication (incorporated into Chapters 1 through 3 and 10). We acknowledge the cooperation of the US Agency for International Development, the Latin American Public Opinion Project (LAPOP), and Professor Mitchell A. Seligson, of Vanderbilt University, for access to various surveys employed in Chapter 9, and most recently the 2012 AmericasBarometer surveys. For the underwriting acquisition of the 2008 AmericasBarometer surveys we thank Professor T. David Mason, the Elizabeth Rhodes Peace Research Fund, and the Johnie Christian Family Peace Professor Endowment of the University of North Texas.

Dozens of kind Central Americans have granted us interviews and helped us collect data on their countries. Without them this book would have been impossible to write. E. Bradford Burns, Richard E. Clinton Jr., Sung Ho Kim, Harold Molineu, Mitch Seligson, and several anonymous reviewers read portions of the manuscript at different stages in its evolution through all six editions and made valuable suggestions. Our thanks to Cece Hannah for typing the first-edition manuscript, to Steve Lohse for research assistance on the second edition, to Mehmet Gurses and Nikolai Petrovsky for research assistance on the fourth edition, and to Brittany Weaver for research assistance on the sixth edition. Ryan Salzman provided valuable bibliographic research assistance for the fifth edition. Over time several editors at Westview Press encouraged us along the way. We especially thank Miriam Gilbert and Barbara Ellington for their assistance and guidance during work on the first two editions, Karl Yambert and Jennifer Chen for their efforts on the third, Steve Catalano and Kay Mariea for their help with the fourth, Karl Yambert and Sandra Beris for their support on the fifth, and Kelli Fillingim for assistance with the sixth.

John A. Booth
Christine J. Wade
Thomas W. Walker

ACRONYMS

Abbreviations of countries:
CR = Costa Rica; ES = El Salvador; G = Guatemala; H = Honduras; N = Nicaragua

ACC	Civil Society Association (Asociación de la Sociedad Civil) (G)
AID	Agency for International Development
AL	Liberal Alliance (Alianza Liberal) (N)
ALBA	Bolivarian Alliance for the Americas (Alianza Bolivariana para las Américas); until 2009 Bolivarian Alternative (Alternativa)
ALIPO	Popular Liberal Alliance (Alianza Liberal Popular) (H)
ALN	Nicaraguan Liberal Alliance (Alianza Liberal Nicaragüense)
AMNLAE	Luisa Amanda Espinosa Nicaraguan Women's Association (Asociación de Mujeres Nicaragüenses Luisa Amanda Espinosa)
AMPRONAC	Association of Women Confronting the National Problem (Asociación de Mujeres Frente a la Problemática Nacional) (N)
ANEP	National Association of Private Enterprises (Asociación Nacional de Empresas Privadas) (ES)
APRE	Alliance for the Republic (Alianza para la República) (N)
ARDE	Revolutionary Democratic Alliance (Alianza Revolucionaria Democrática) (Costa Rican–based Contra forces)
ARENA	Nationalist Republican Alliance Party (Alianza Republicana Nacionalista) (ES)
ASC	Assembly of Civil Society (Asamblea de la Sociedad Civil) (G)
ATC	Rural Workers' Association (Asociación de Trabajadores del Campo) (N)
BPR	Revolutionary Popular Bloc (Bloque Popular Revolucionario) (ES)

CACM	Central American Common Market
CAFTA	Central merican Free Trade Agreement
CARSI	Central America Regional Security Initiative
CBI	Caribbean Basin Initiative
CC	Court of Constitutionality (Corte de Constitucionalidad) (G)
CD	Democratic Change (Cambio Democrático) (ES)
CD	Democratic Convergence (Convergencia Democrática) (ES)
CDC	Civil Defense Committee (Comité de Defensa Civil) (N and H)
CDS	Sandinista Defense Committee (Comité de Defensa Sandinista) (N)
CDU	United Democratic Center (Centro Democrático Unido) (ES)
CEB	Christian base communities (*comunidades eclesiales de base*)
CEH	Historical Clarification Commission (Comisión de Esclarificación Histórica) (G)
CGUP	Guatemalan Committee of Patriotic Unity (Comité Guatemalteco de Unidad Patriótica)
CIA	Central Intelligence Agency
CICIG	International Commission Against Impunity in Guatemala (Comisión Internacional Contra la Impunidad en Guatemala)
CN	National Conciliation (Conciliación Nacional) (ES)
CODEH	Human Rights Committee of Honduras (Comité de Derechos Humanos de Honduras)
COSEP	Superior Council of Private Enterprise (Consejo Superior de la Empresa Privada) (N)
COSIP	Superior Council of Private Initiative (Consejo Superior de la Iniciativa Privada) (N)
CPC	Citizens' Power Councils (Consejos del Poder Ciudadano) (N)
CPI	consumer price index
CREO	Commitment, Renewal and Order Party (Compromiso, Renovación y Orden) (G)
CRIES	Regional Coordinating Body for Economic and Social Research (Coordinadora Regional de Investigaciones Económicas y Sociales) (N)
CRM	Revolutionary Coordinator of the Masses (Coordinadora Revolucionaria de Masas) (ES)
CSE	Supreme Electoral Council (Consejo Supremo Electoral) (N)
CSJ	Supreme Court of Justice (Corte Supremo de Justicia) (G and N)
CST	Sandinista Workers' Federation (Central Sandinista de Trabajadores) (N)
CUC	Peasant Unity Committee (Comité de Unidad Campesina) (G)
DC	Christian Democratic Party (Partido Demócrata Cristiano) (G)

DINADECO	National Community Development Directorate (Dirección Nacional de Desarrollo de la Comunidad) (CR)
DNC	Joint National Directorate (Dirección Nacional Conjunta) (N)
DNU	National Directorate of Unity (Dirección Nacional de Unidad) (H)
ECLAC	Economic Commission for Latin America and the Caribbean (Comisión Económica para América Latina y el Caribe)
EG	Encounter for Guatemala (Encuentro por Guatemala)
EGP	Guerrilla Army of the Poor (Ejército Guerrillero de los Pobres) (G)
EPS	Sandinista People's Army (Ejército Popular Sandinista) (N)
ERP	Revolutionary Army of the People (Ejército Revolucionario del Pueblo) (ES)
ERP27	Army of Patriotic Resistance (Ejército de Resistencia Patriótica) (H)
ESAF	Enhanced Structural Adjustment Facility
EXA	export agriculture
FAL	Armed Forces of Liberation (Fuerzas Armadas de Liberación) (ES)
FAO	Broad Opposition Front (Frente Amplio Opositor) (N)
FAPU	United Popular Action Front (Frente de Acción Popular Unida) (ES)
FAR	Revolutionary Armed Forces (Fuerzas Armadas Revolucionarias) (G)
FARC	Revolutionary Armed Forces of Colombia (Fuerzas Armadas Revolucionarias de Colombia)
FARN	Armed Forces of National Resistance (Fuerzas Armadas de Resistencia Nacional) (ES)
FDCR	Democratic Front Against Repression (Frente Democrático Contra la Represión) (G)
FDN	Nicaraguan Democratic Force (Fuerzas Democráticas Nicaragüenses)
FDNG	New Guatemala Democratic Front (Frente Democrático Nueva Guatemala)
FDR	Revolutionary Democratic Front (Frente Democrático Revolucionario) (ES)
FGEI	Edgar Ibarra Guerrilla Front (Frente Guerrillera Edgar Ibarra) (G)
FMLH	Morazán Front for the Liberation of Honduras (Frente Morazanista para la Liberación de Honduras)
FMLN	Farabundo Martí National Liberation Front (Frente Farabundo Martí de Liberación Nacional) (ES)

FNT	National Workers' Front (Frente Nacional de Trabajadores) (N)
FOL	Forward Operating Location
FOSALUD	Fund for Health Solidarity (Fondo Solidario para la Salud) (ES)
FP13	January 13th Popular Front (Frente Popular 13 de Enero) (G)
FPL	Popular Forces of Liberation (Fuerzas Populares de Liberación) (ES)
FPN	National Patriotic Front (Frente Patriótico Nacional) (N)
FPR	Lorenzo Zelaya Popular Revolutionary Forces (Fuerzas Populares Revolucionarias "Lorenzo Zelaya") (H)
FRG	Republican Front of Guatemala (Frente Republicano de Guatemala)
FRNP	National Popular Resistance Front (Frente Nacional de Resistencia Popular) (H)
FSLN	Sandinista National Liberation Front (Frente Sandinista de Liberación Nacional) (N)
FUR	United Front of the Revolution (Frente Unido de la Revolución) (G)
FUSEP	Public Security Forces (Fuerzas de Seguridad Pública) (H)
GANA	Grand National Alliance (Gran Alianza Nacional) (G)
GANA	Grand Alliance for National Unity (Gran Alianza por la Unidad Nacional) (ES)
GDP	gross domestic product
HIPC	(World Bank's) Heavily Indebted Poor Countries
IAD	Inter-American Development Bank
ICE	Costa Rican Electrical Institute (Instituto Costarricense de Electricidad)
ICJ	International Court of Justice
IIRIRA	Illegal Immigration Reform and Immigrant Responsibility Act
IMF	International Monetary Fund
INE	National Statistical Institute (Instituto Nacional de Estadística) (G)
LIBRE	Liberty and Refoundation Party (Partido Libertad y Refundación) (H)
LIDER	Renewed Democratic Liberation Party (Libertad Democrática Renovada) (G)
LP28	28th of February Popular Leagues (Ligas Populares 28 de Febrero) (ES)
MAS	Solidarity Action Movement (Movimiento de Acción Solidaria) (G)
MINUGUA	United Nations Mission in Guatemala (Misión de las Naciones Unidas en Guatemala)

MLN	National Liberation Movement (Movimiento de Liberación Nacional) (G)
MLP	Popular Liberation Movement (Movimiento de Liberación Popular) (ES)
MNR	National Revolutionary Movement (Movimiento Nacional Revolucionario) (ES)
MPL	Popular Movement for Liberation (Movimiento Popular de Liberación) (H)
MPU	United People's Movement (Movimiento Pueblo Unido) (N)
MR13	13th of November Revolutionary Movement (Movimiento Revolucionario del 13 de Noviembre) (G)
MRPIxim	People's Revolutionary Movement Ixim (Movimiento Revolucionario del Pueblo Ixim) (G)
MRS	Sandinista Renovation Movement (Movimiento de Renovación Sandinista) (N)
NAFTA	North American Free Trade Agreement
OAS	Organization of American States
OPEC	Organization of Petroleum Exporting Countries
ORDEN	Nationalist Democratic Organization (Organización Democrática Nacionalista) (ES)
ORPA	Organization of the People in Arms (Organización del Pueblo en Armas) (G)
PAC	Anti-Corruption Party (Partido Anti-Corrupción) (H)
PAC	Citizen Action Party (Partido de Acción Ciudadana) (CR)
PAC	Civil Self-Defense Patrols (Patrullas de Autodefensa Civil) (G)
PAN	National Advancement Party (Partido de Avance Nacional) (G)
PARLACEN	Central American Parliament (Parlamento Centroamericano)
PASE	Accessibility without Exclusion Party (Partido Accesibilidad sin Exclusión) (CR)
PCH	Honduran Communist Party (Partido Comunista de Honduras)
PCN	National Conciliation Party (Partido de Conciliación Nacional) (ES)
PCS	Communist Party of El Salvador (Partido Comunista de El Salvador)
PDC	Christian Democratic Party (Partido Demócrata Cristiano) (ES)
PDCG	Christian Democratic Party of Guatemala (Partido Demócrata Cristiano de Guatemala)
PDCH	Christian Democratic Party of Honduras (Partido Demócrata Cristiano de Honduras)
PES	Party of Hope (Partido de la Esperanza) (ES)

PGT	Guatemalan Labor Party (Partido Guatemalteco del Trabajo)
PID	Institutional Democratic Party (Partido Institucional Democrático) (G)
PINU	Innovation and Unity Party (Partido de Inovación y Unidad) (H)
PLC	Liberal Constitutionalist Party (Partido Liberal Constitucionalista) (N)
PLH	Honduran Liberal Party (Partido Liberal de Honduras)
PLN	Liberal Nationalist Party (Partido Liberal Nacionalista) (N)
PLN	National Liberation Party (Partido de Liberación Nacional) (CR)
PML	Libertarian Movement Party (Partido Movimiento Libertario) (CR)
PMOP	Military Police of Public Order (Policía Militar y de Orden Público) (H)
PN	The National Party (Partido Nacional) (H)
PNC	National Civil Police (Policía Nacional Civil) (ES)
PNDH	National Plan for Human Development (Plan Nacional para el Desarrollo Humano) (N)
POLSEPAZ	Policy for Integral and Sustainable Citizen Security and Promotion for Peace (Política Integral y Sostenible de Seguridad Ciudadana y Promoción de la Paz Social para Costa Rica) (CR)
PP	Patriot Party (Partido Patriota) (G)
PR	Revolutionary Party (Partido Revolucionario) (G)
PRTC	Revolutionary Party of Central American Workers (Partido Revolucionario de Trabajadores Centroamericanos) (CR)
PRTCH	Revolutionary Party of Central American Workers of Honduras (Partido Revolucionario de Trabajadores Centroamericanos de Honduras)
PRTCS	Revolutionary Party of Central American Workers (Partido Revolucionario de Trabajadores Centroamericanos) (ES)
PRUD	Revolutionary Party of Democratic Unification (Partido Revolucionario de Unificación Democrática) (ES)
PSD	Democratic Socialist Party (Partido Socialista Demócrata) (G)
PTS	The Political Terror Scale
PUSC	Social Christian Unity Party (Partido de Unidad Social Cristiano) (CR)
RN	Nicaraguan Resistance (Resistencia Nicaragüense)
SAA	structural adjustment agreements
TPS	temporary protected status

TSE	Supreme Electoral Tribunal (Tribunal Supremo Electoral) (CR, ES, and G)
UCN	National Union of Change (Unión del Cambio Nacionalista) (G)
UCN	Union of the National Center (Unión del Centro Nacional) (G)
UDEL	Democratic Liberation Union (Unión Democrática de Liberación) (N)
UDN	Democratic Nationalist Union (Unión Democrática Nacionalista) (ES)
UFCO	United Fruit Company
UN	United Nations
UNAG	National Union of Farmers and Ranchers (Unión Nacional de Agricultores y Ganaderos) (N)
UNDP	United Nations Development Program
UNE	National Unity of Hope (Unidad Nacional de la Esperanza) (G)
UNIDAD	Unity Movement (Movimiento Unidad) (ES)
UNO	National Opposition Union (Unión Nacional Opositora) (N and ES)
URNG	Guatemalan National Revolutionary Union (Unidad Revolucionaria Nacional Guatemalteca)
USAID	US Agency for International Development
USDEA	US Drug Enforcement Agency
USSR	Union of Soviet Socialist Republics
VCE	Let's Go with Eduardo (Vamos con Eduardo [Montealegre]) (G)
ZEDE	Employment and Economic Development Zones (Zonas de Empleo y Desarrollo Económico) (H)

UNDERSTANDING
CENTRAL AMERICA

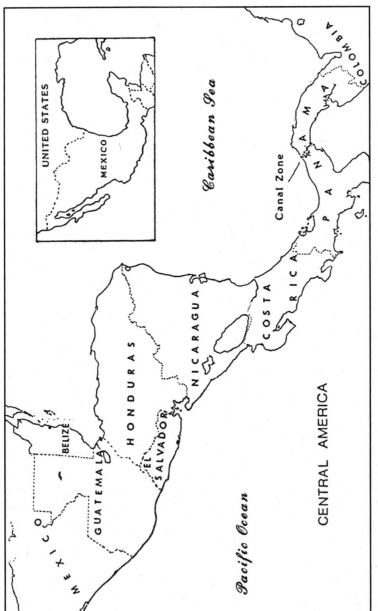

MAP OF CENTRAL AMERICA. Reprinted from Harold Molineu, *U.S. Policy Toward Latin America: From Regionalism to Globalism*, 2nd ed. (Boulder, CO: Westview Press, 1990), p. 4. Copyright © Westview Press, 1990.

1

CRISIS AND TRANSFORMATION

CENTRAL AMERICA LIES SO CLOSE TO THE UNITED STATES THAT from Miami or Houston one can fly to Managua or Guatemala City more quickly than to Chicago or Boston. The region's five countries, each profoundly shaped by proximity and trade with the United States, had roughly 20 million people in 1975 and attracted little of the world's attention, but that soon changed. For two decades after World War II, the area had seemed a placid geopolitical backwater of the United States. Despite its mostly despotic regimes, Central America was poor but friendly to US interests. The region was making moderate progress under an economic strategy that gave development-planning roles to its governments and the regional common market. Yet in the early 1960s revolutionary groups appeared, followed by economic crises and political unrest in the 1970s. Central America then surged into world headlines as its governments, aided by the United States, cracked down on rapidly multiplying opposition movements. By the late 1970s waves of state terror, revolutionary insurrection, counterrevolution, and external meddling engulfed the region, taking over 300,000 lives, turning millions into refugees, and devastating economies and infrastructures.

By the first decade of the twenty-first century, the region had calmed remarkably from the politically turbulent 1980s. Constitutional, elected civilian governments had become the norm. US policy makers' geopolitical concerns had waned, and political news from the region became scarce in the US media.

But economic problems remained grave in several countries. Poor economic performance, low evaluations of some Central American governments by their citizens, and high political participation levels marked Honduras and Guatemala as having an elevated potential for political instability. In a shocking reversal of the region's democratic progress, the Honduran army and Congress ousted President Manuel Zelaya from office. Though a new government was soon elected, Honduras had become the region's first democratic breakdown of the new century. Criminal violence related to gangs and drugs rose sharply in several countries.

The first two editions of *Understanding Central America* focused on the tidal wave of political violence during the 1970s and 1980s and why great revolutionary movements wracked three Central American countries while the other two remained relatively politically stable.[1] We argued, based on scholarly theories of revolution, that grievances arose from regionwide economic problems and from the political repression of mobilized demands for reform. When regimes in Nicaragua, Guatemala, and El Salvador violently refused to accommodate these demands, their opponents and would-be reformers coalesced and radicalized into revolutionary political opposition. In Nicaragua insurrection culminated in a rebel victory and eleven years of social revolution under the Sandinistas. In El Salvador and Guatemala civil war resulted in protracted stalemates eventually followed by negotiated peace and a significant alteration of the status quo. In striking contrast, political stability—although threatened— prevailed in Honduras and Costa Rica. Their governments undertook modest economic and political reforms and kept repression at moderate levels.

External actors, especially the United States, struggled to shape these events by providing political and material resources to the political actors. The United States expended enormous diplomatic and political energy and several billion dollars trying to determine winners and losers locally and affect institutions and policy. This outside manipulation of Central American politics profoundly affected all five countries by intensifying and prolonging their conflicts.

In the third edition of this book we expanded our focus to explain regime changes in the region—whether arising from revolutionary impulses or those managed by elites to prevent revolution. By the late 1990s each Central American nation, following sharply divergent paths, had arrived at one common regime type—a sort of minimalist electoral democracy. While hardly ideal democracies in execution, these civilian-led, constitutional, electoral regimes were sharply different from and less abusive than most governments in place in the 1970s.[2] This convergence on governance style in five adjacent countries was no coincidence. The regime-change process regionwide resulted from the interaction of global economic and political forces with local politico-economic realities and actors.[3] Certain contextual forces and actors had pushed Central America's key players to settle on formal electoral democracy as their new preferred regime type, rather than returning to their traditions of military or personalistic authoritarianism.

By 2004, as we wrote the fourth edition, Central America's political violence and repression were well below their civil war levels, human rights performance was somewhat better than in prior decades, and the region's five major nations practiced at least a minimalist formal electoral democracy. The Cold War had ended and US fears of Communist expansion in the hemisphere had subsided below crisis pitch. This persuaded the United States to live with leftist parties participating openly in governance, despite a strong preference that they not win actual control anywhere. Neoliberalism, a new strategy of economic development, exposed Central America to the larger world economy more openly than ever. With its political systems moving toward electoral democracy, its economies liberalized, and the anti-Communist geopolitical imperative receding, Central America gradually faded from the world's headlines.

By 2012 Central America had developed new problems. Counter-narcotics efforts made drug smuggling harder elsewhere in Latin America, so smugglers shifted trafficking routes to Central America. Gang violence developed and escalated to horrific levels in several isthmian countries, linked in part to US deportation of gang members back to the region and to domestic narcotics trafficking. The US, Mexican, and Central American governments developed a regional counter-narcotics and police-assistance program known as Plan Mérida to address these troubles, but much of it focused on strengthening armed forces. Meanwhile, leftist leaders came to power in Nicaragua and El Salvador, organized crime spread, the Honduran coup shocked regional and hemispheric governments, and political corruption scandals roiled several countries. Democratization had clearly not solved Central America's problems.

This, the revised and updated sixth edition, tracks and seeks to explain how evolving global forces affect Central America. These waves of shared turmoil and change across several nations allow us to understand certain great forces beyond the nation-state. These forces compelled diverse sets of such apparently independent actors as the local elites of five Central American nations to reach common outcomes by following shared plans not entirely of their own devising. Although there is much worth knowing about Central America in its own right, the region's experience with these greater metanational forces tell us much about how individual nations and groups of nations interact with the world environment.

Another reason why Central America should retain our attention resides in its ongoing poverty. An estimate for 2009 put the number of direly poor Central Americans (living on US$2 per day or less) at around 9.5 million— almost one-fourth of the region's populace.[4] Despite improvement of the region's economies in the first decade of the 2000s, misery and dismal prospects remained for millions unable to escape from grinding poverty. Some old sources of poverty persisted, and new ones had developed as Central America's economies opened themselves up to the world. Examining how both global and local forces had affected Central America's poor will tell us something about how capitalism had evolved and how it continues to function in Latin America and the developing world.

A third reason to study Central America is its population growth and migration. Central America's combined population had risen to 40 million by 2012, and a quarter of the region's citizens faced limited economic opportunity. One result of this was migration. The 2010 US Census revealed that approximately 4 million Central Americans lived in the United States.[5] Many of these Central American–born residents of the United States had, of course, fled from the civil wars of the 1980s and, over the longer term, came seeking to alleviate their poverty and escape crime. The trend continued well into the twenty-first century as hundreds of thousands of Central Americans sought economic opportunity as migrant workers or as residents of Mexico and Costa Rica.

Understanding how global economic forces interact with local ones will also help us determine the impact on Central America of the major world economic slowdown of 2008–2009. Only Guatemala escaped an economic contraction in 2008–2009. Fortunately all the region's economies returned to positive economic territory by 2010.[6] A fourth reason to study Central America is that, as if persistent poverty and migration were not problems enough, its societies and political systems must cope with daunting new and old social and political pathologies. The end of civil wars and military and police reforms, paradoxically, failed to improve the security of many citizens. Police reform in Guatemala and El Salvador caused crime waves, as cashiered and corrupt former policemen became well-organized gangsters, while the reformed, new police lacked the resources to counter them effectively. Youths repatriated to Central America from inner cities in the United States brought with them an eruption of criminal gangs that scourged several countries. Security forces responded to youth gangs and to impoverished street children alike with draconian violence. Assassinations of political figures remained disconcertingly common in several countries. Newspapers regionwide reported a stream of political-corruption scandals. Examining these problems can illumine the local and global forces behind them and the raft of difficulties that the region's civilian political leaders must overcome for democracy to consolidate and for economic development to ameliorate poverty.

A shorthand term for these big forces that act on Central America is *globalization*. Globalization refers to compelling systemic forces that act above and beyond the level of the nation-state, and above and through international institutions, penetrating into local affairs. Global forces press the political and economic actors of Central America and have often pushed them in similar directions and at the same times. What are these global forces? World-scale economic forces generate markets, commodity price cycles, and market crises that shape domestic economies and subpopulations for good or ill. Changes in the structure of the global economy, licit and illicit trade, and class systems force realignments of domestic economic organization and classes. New ways of organizing the world economic and political arenas produce new ideologies and operating policies for institutions. These constrain local actors by favoring some, weakening others, and reshaping institutions to fit global needs and preferences. We believe Central America's revolutions, regime changes, economic development strategies, evolving classes, social problems, and persistent poverty in recent decades all reveal the impact of the global upon the local.

The "Central America" upon which we focus in this book consists of Guatemala, El Salvador, Honduras, Nicaragua, and Costa Rica.[7] We do not address Belize and Panama individually. Although Belize is geographically Central American, that English-speaking microstate only became independent from Great Britain in 1981; its history is distinct from the region's other countries. Panama is outside Central America historically. Its pre-Columbian indigenous cultures were South American. From 1821 until 1903, Panama formed part of the South American republic of Colombia. "The five," however, share a common political heritage from the colonial period, during which Spain administered them as a unit. During the national period (1823 to 1838) they formed a single state called the United Provinces of Central America. In the late nineteenth century, several ill-fated attempts at reunification occurred. In the 1960s the five joined to form a common market. More recent unification efforts include a common regional parliament and shared trade agreements with the United States. Out of this history comes a sense of Central American national identity and, among some, a hope that someday the larger homeland might be reunited.

Central America, as defined above, is small. Its combined landmass of 431,812 square kilometers is barely larger than that of California (404,975 square kilometers). Moreover, its estimated total 2012 population of around 40.1 million was only slightly larger than California's. The country with the smallest surface area, El Salvador, is smaller than Maryland. The largest, Nicaragua, is barely larger than Iowa. In population, the five varied in 2013 between a low of 4.9 million in Costa Rica (similar to the population of Alabama) and a high of 15.4 million in Guatemala (somewhat larger than Illinois).[8] Central America's population has more than doubled since the 1970s, but the rates of population growth have diminished in recent decades due to rapid urban growth and out-migration to the United States and elsewhere (see Appendix, Table A.2). Central America's natural resources are modest. However, had different political systems and economic models prevailed across Central America during the nineteenth and twentieth centuries, there certainly would have been enough arable land to provide adequate sustenance for the present population, while at the same time producing some primary products for export. Yet responses to international market demands by the region's elite led to land-ownership concentration, an overemphasis on export, and inadequate production of consumer food staples. Instead of growing beans, corn, rice, plantains, and cassava for local consumption, big landholders normally concentrated on lucrative exports such as coffee, cotton, sugar, and beef. Central America also possesses varied but not abundant mineral resources. One possible recent exception is Guatemala, with its nickel and its modest oil reserves. Historically, Nicaragua has been viewed as the logical site for a future trans-isthmian waterway. As we write this in 2014, Nicaragua had begun off-shore oil exploration, and a new canal-building initiative was developing.

Central America's main resource is clearly its people. Contrary to the ethnic stereotypes often held by North Americans, Central Americans are as hardworking as most other humans on this planet. To verify that statement, one need only observe the bustle of Central American cities at daybreak, or follow the activity of a typical Central American through the long hours of his or her daily routine. Central Americans are also remarkably resilient. The strength with which they have faced more than their share of hardship— including intense repression, occasional civil war, foreign occupation, and such frequent natural disasters as volcanic eruptions, earthquakes, hurricanes, mudslides, and floods—impresses outside observers, especially those used to safer natural and political environments.

Despite their similarities of geography and juxtaposition to the world outside the isthmus, there are some sharp differences among the Central American nations (see Table 1.1). For example, in economic development, Costa Rica in 2012 had a gross domestic product (GDP) per capita—a comparative measure of overall economic activity per citizen—of $5,725. (For comparison, US GDP per capita in 2010 was almost four times higher than Costa Rica's—the ratio having declined considerably from 2007 because of Costa Rica's fast-rising prosperity.)[9] Costa Rica's GDP per capita was over $2,500 greater than that of its nearest rival in the region, El Salvador. And with 3.6 and 4.2 times more GDP per capita than Honduras and Nicaragua, respectively, the Costa Rican economy in 2012 far outperformed its poorer neighbors. Are such stark economic differences inevitable in the region? Not at all. In 1950, the countries of Central America had much more similar levels of economic activity than they do today; the richest (El Salvador) had only 1.8 times the GDP per capita of the poorest (Nicaragua). But as Table 1.1 reveals, overall national economic activity changes from 1950 to 2007 differed enormously. Whereas Costa Rica's GDP per capita rose 301 percent over this period and Guatemala's rose 114 percent, Nicaragua's grew by only 19 percent. Masked by the data's 50-year span is something that makes this startling fact even worse: Nicaragua's GDP per capita actually doubled from 1950 to the early 1970s but was subsequently beaten back to pre-1950 levels by war, revolution, a US-imposed economic embargo, and disinvestment by its elites. During these same five decades Costa Rica's government, a politically stable democracy, pursued development by investing more in its citizens (especially in social programs of education and health care) than any other country in the isthmus. Thus Costa Ricans weathered the half-century's storms much better and emerged in better shape than their neighbors. They now enjoy much greater prosperity and literacy, and much lower rates of infant mortality and working children than their neighbors. Recent economic-growth rates somewhat mirror the five-decade history of economic development, with more prosperous Costa Rica growing fastest. From 1990 to 2012 Costa Rica's GDP per capita increased by 79 percent. El Salvador's rate of growth followed at 67 percent, whereas the other three ranged between 32 and 44 percent (Table 1.1).

These comparisons of economic change strongly argue against the inevitability of poverty, at least within Central America itself. Even starting out poor and with scarce resources, Costa Rica relied on a development strategy and democratic government that produced great success. And Honduras, the second-poorest country in the region in 1950 and governed largely by its armed forces until 1985, achieved the region's second-highest levels of overall investment and government spending on social programs. Thus by 2000 Honduras more than doubled its average economic activity level and did so despite a fourfold population increase.[10]

In dismaying contrast, Nicaragua, the nation most torn by political violence, boomed economically until the early 1970s but then regressed through the ravages of insurrection, revolution, economic embargo, and a second civil war. Table 1.1 reveals that choices made by Guatemala's leaders over five decades have left only 75 percent of its population over the age of 15 literate, kept infant mortality the highest in the region (Table 1.1), and created the circumstances in which over a quarter of children 10 to 14 years old work (Table 2.1). These developments have occurred despite a 114 percent increase in Guatemala's GDP per capita between 1950 and 2007. Thus local political and economic elites, even though constrained by global forces and their own resources, had much to say about economic development and human welfare outcomes.

Even well-intentioned Central American elites, however, now face tough domestic and global obstacles. Table 1.1 highlights other characteristics of the populations of some Central American countries that pose problems. Guatemala struggles with how to integrate its 41 percent indigenous population, much of which speaks little or no Spanish. El Salvador continues to confront an enormous social headache posed by the country's high density of population (approximately 320 persons per square kilometer in 2013—eight times more concentrated than Nicaragua, and ten times more than the United States).[11]

8

TABLE 1.1 Basic Socioeconomic Data on Central American Countries

	Costa Rica	El Salvador	Guatemala	Honduras	Nicaragua
Population 2013 (estimated, in millions)	4.86	6.33	15.42	8.08	6.07
Gross domestic product (GDP) per capita 1990 (in constant 2005 US $)	3,198	1,815	1,726	1,147	937
GDP per capita 2012 (in constant 2005 US $)	5,725	3,023	2,322	1,575	1,353
Percent change in GDP per capita from 1990 to 2012[a]	79	67	32	37	44
Percent change in GDP per capita from 1950 to 2007[a]	301	67	114	84	19
Percent growth rate of GDP per capita 2012	3.7	1.1	0.5	1.3	3.7
Percent of self-reported Afro-origin population in 2012[b]	7	5	0	4	8
Percent of self-reported indigenous population in 2012[b]	1	4	41	4	4
Literacy of population aged 15 and older (2005)	96	85	75	85	78
Literacy of population aged 15 and older (1970)	88	58	45	51	54
Internet users (%) within previous year as of 2012[b]	52	35	44	33	24
Life expectancy at birth (2012)	79	72	72	73	73
Infant mortality per 1,000 live births (2012)	9	13	24	18	22
Infant mortality 1990–1995	15	40	55	43	48
Change in infant mortality from 1990–1995 to 2012	-6	-27	-31	-25	-26
Mean annual percentage growth in population 2000–2013	1.8	NA	2.2	1.5	1.8
Percent urban population 2012	66	60	57	51	58

[a]Authors' estimate from ECLAC (2008 and 2013).
[b]Drawn from the 2012 AmericasBarometer surveys of each country by the Latin American Public Opinion Project (LAPOP), www.LapopSurveys.org.
SOURCES: United Nations Economic Commission for Latin America and the Caribbean (ECLAC), *Statistical Yearbook for Latin America and the Caribbean 2007*, http://websie.eclac.cl/anuario_estadistico /anuario_2008, accessed July 29, 2008; United Nations Economic Commission for Latin America and the Caribbean (ECLAC), http://estadisticas.cepal.org/cepalstat/WEB_CEPALSTAT/estadisticas Indicadores.asp?idioma=i, accessed August 28, 2013.

8

By the late twentieth century, a powerful global constraint known as *neoliberalism* confronted all Central American governments with important new rules and policy preferences promoted by powerful international economic actors. Under pressure from abroad in the 1980s and 1990s, all isthmian nations adopted neoliberal development strategies. No country in the region could deviate much from this austere capitalist development model, which stingily discouraged governmental social spending and human-capital investment. At the beginning of the twenty-first century, no isthmian country could fully embrace even the social-democratic development model that Costa Rica followed from 1950 to 1985, much less a revolutionary development model like Nicaragua's in the early 1980s. For example, when concerns about a loss of domestic control over social spending in Costa Rica held up ratification of the Central America Free Trade Agreement from 2004 to 2007, the United States exerted great diplomatic pressure to secure eventual ratification.

It is true that, despite institutional barriers to human development that we will detail in later chapters, the human resources of the region are a very positive factor. The dignity, determination, and remarkable humor of the Central American people must be taken as a cause for hope. Poverty in Central America has not always been inevitable. But poverty remains quite difficult for isthmian governments to reduce—even assuming national leaders and other elites might acquire a new determination to move in that direction. Despite an encouraging recent economic upturn, for example, Nicaragua fell further behind the rest of Latin America in its rate of economic and social development.[12]

In sum, Central America remains small in size and population, poor in resources, and beset by problems. Early in the twenty-first century, these problems affected mostly the region's own people, although emigration, elevated levels of violence, and an increase in drug trafficking concerned the region's Latin American neighbors and the United States. Its small nation-states, once riven by severe internal strains, had quieted as the twenty-first century began, but were pushed and pulled anew by international economic and political pressures that intensified domestic strains as often as reduced them. The deepening US involvement in the region during the 1980s and the efforts that numerous Latin American and European nations made to promote negotiated settlements to the various open and latent conflicts in the region at that time made these strains and conflicts worthy of serious study. Globalization and its contemporary effects on the region underscore our need to understand Central America and its place in the world.

US interests and involvement in the isthmus have fluctuated widely over the past century. Protracted US inattention to Central America after World War II contrasted with intense US concern in the late 1970s when Nicaraguans rebelled against the Somoza regime. Although they lavished attention on Central America, the Carter and Reagan administrations treated and described the region so differently as to bewilder many observers—including academic and policy experts, and especially Central Americans themselves. The first Bush administration remained powerfully involved in Central America but gave the region much less noisy public attention than had its predecessors.[13] With the Cold War clearly over and problems looming in the Balkans and Middle East, the Clinton and second Bush administrations paid much less visible attention to Central America. But not having forgotten the isthmus entirely, they labored assiduously to keep neoliberal economic policies on track and to block leftist parties from winning national elections in El Salvador and Nicaragua. Despite US efforts during the second Bush administration, two leftists won Central American presidencies anyway—Nicaragua's Daniel Ortega Saavedra in 2006, and El Salvador's Mauricio Funes Cartagena in March 2009. The incoming Obama administration encountered the Honduran coup of 2009 and had to deal with tensions over migration, narcotics trafficking, and the influence on Central America of Venezuela under the late President Hugo Chávez and his successor Nicolás Maduro. Venezuela has used economic aid to counter American influence.

The waning of frontline US attention as geopolitical winds changed did not eliminate Central America's endemic poverty, its problems with development strategies and political order, its constant need to adjust to evolving global forces, or pressures from the United States. In our effort to help the reader understand Central America, we examine these issues and consider the relative importance of evolving domestic and external influences on the region.

Central Americans (photo of baby in hammock by John Booth; other photos by Steve Cagan).

Recommended Readings and Resources

Lehoucq, Fabrice. 2012. *The Politics of Modern Central America: Civil War, Democratization, and Underdevelopment.* New York: Cambridge University Press.

Sánchez-Ancochea, Diego, and Salvador Martí i Puig, eds. 2013. *Handbook of Central American Governance.* London: Routledge.

Notes

1. John A. Booth and Thomas W. Walker, *Understanding Central America,* 1st and 2nd eds. (Boulder, CO: Westview Press, 1989 and 1993).

2. We except Costa Rica from this generalization. It has had civilian constitutional government since the 1950s. In 2004 Freedom House ranked Costa Rica as "free" and the remaining four countries of the region "partly free" (source: Freedom House, *Freedom in the World 2004,* www.freedomhouse.org/template.cfm?page=363&year=2004, accessed August 13, 2009). In 2013 El Salvador had moved into Freedom House's "free" category, leaving Guatemala, Nicaragua, and Honduras in the "partly free" category (Freedom House, *Freedom in the World 2013,* http://www.freedomhouse.org/report/freedom-world/2013/el-salvador, accessed September 1, 2013.

3. Booth and Walker, *Understanding Central America,* 3rd ed. (Boulder, CO: Westview Press, 1999), Ch. 5.

4. Calculated by the authors from data from World Bank, Data, "Poverty headcount ratio at $2 a day (PPP) (% of population)," http://data.worldbank.org/indicator/SI.POV.2DAY, accessed August 25, 2013. See Table 2.1.

5. See Chapter 10 for details.

6. Inter-American Development Bank, Latin American and Caribbean Macro Watch Data Tool, http://www.iadb.org/Research/LatinMacroWatch/lmw.cfm?lang=en, accessed August 27, 2013.

7. Here, and in certain other parts of this volume, much of the wording is from Thomas W. Walker's unsigned contribution to: Presbyterian Church USA, *Adventure and Hope: Christians and the Crisis in Central America: Report to the 195th General Assembly of the Presbyterian Church* (Atlanta, 1983), pp. 57–91, 97–101. The authors thank the Presbyterian Church for its permission to publish this material (which Walker wrote in 1982 while he was part of the United Presbyterian Church USA Task Force on Central America) here.

8. Population estimates for Central America for 2013 from Table 1.1; population estimates for US states based on United States Census Bureau, "US and World Population Clock," http://www.census.gov/popclock/, accessed August 30, 2013.

9. Alan Heston, Robert Summers, and Bettina Aten, Penn World Table Version 7.1, Center for International Comparisons of Production, Income and Prices at the University of Pennsylvania, July 2012. Accessed on August 19, 2012. Note: GDP per capita data are "PPP Converted GDP Per Capita, average GEKS-CPDW, at current prices (in I$)," labeled as variable "cgdp2."

10. The first datum refers to investment from all sources as percent of GDP, from Heston et al., Penn World Table; social spending datum from David E. Ferranti et al., *Inequality in Latin America and the Caribbean: Breaking with History? Advance Conference Edition* (Washington, DC: International Bank for Reconstruction and Development/The World Bank, October 2003), Table 4.1. See also John A. Booth, Christine J. Wade, and Thomas W. Walker, *Understanding Central America: Global Forces, Rebellion, and Change,* 4th ed. (Boulder, CO: Westview Press, 2006), Table 2.2.

11. "List of Sovereign States and Dependent Territories in North America by Population Density," Wikipedia, http://en.wikipedia.org/wiki/List_of_North_American_countries_by_population_density, accessed September 1, 2013.

12. John A. Booth and Mitchell A. Seligson, *The Political Culture of Democracy in Nicaragua, 2010: Democratic Consolidation in the Americas in Hard Times* (Nashville, TN: Vanderbilt University, Latin American Public Opinion Project), 2011, Ch. 1.

13. Although it is outside the purview of our study, the United States invaded Panama in 1989 to oust its dictator and install in power the true victors of the 1989 election. Though this is an example of intense attention, the US government's focus on the other five nations during this later period was much less overtly public and confrontational than had been the case under President Reagan.

2

GLOBAL FORCES AND SYSTEM CHANGE IN CENTRAL AMERICA

THIS CHAPTER FOCUSES ON EXPLANATIONS FOR CENTRAL AMERICA'S two principal problems of the recent past and likely future—political and economic system change. They are interrelated, driven by common forces, which we sketch below and illustrate in subsequent chapters. Despite certain differences among them, Central American nations have marked commonalities of history, global context, and political and economic development. These similarities reveal that much that affects Central America is part of a larger world dynamic. We show that common forces led to Central America's rebellions and shaped the regime changes that led from authoritarianism toward electoral democracy and new economic development strategies.[1]

Our theory about system change in Central America comes from simple premises. First, the economic and political arenas of human activity are entangled. Much of what occurs in the political world stems from economic forces, and political decisions in turn affect economic outcomes. Second, nations—their governments, economies, and citizens—exist within an evolving international or global environment. Local problems can quickly become global problems and cycle back to the local. For example, political unrest in Syria (a local problem) can elevate oil-price futures (a world problem), which in turn can raise fuel costs for consumers in localities around

15

the globe. A third premise is that inequality exists within and between societies and that outcomes usually follow power. Within nations there exist hierarchies of minorities of elites (those who control resources and institutions) and large majorities of non-elites (ordinary citizens, who are poorer and less powerful). In the world of nations, there are hierarchies of more powerful and weaker states. Elites from different societies often cooperate across national boundaries for mutual benefit, whereas non-elites find this more difficult. Elites from large nations often successfully cooperate with each other as individuals, through organizations, or through governments and multilateral institutions to promote their interests and those of their nations. The elites of small nations sometimes promote small-nation cooperation, but tend not to be as successful at getting what they desire as are the elites of powerful nations. Small nations' elites often find it very advantageous to cooperate with external elites representing large and powerful interests, whether governmental or private. Increasingly over the last half of the twentieth century, private global economic elites operating above the level of the nation-state forged a world economy with new rules that favored global capital above the interests of even powerful nation-states.

Small nations, such as those of Central America, tend to be very sensitive to powerful global forces and actors. Their sensitivity to the political and economic world outside their borders derives from the very limits of their wealth, resources, populations, and military capacities. Central Americans depend very heavily on what their countries export (commodities) and import (manufactured goods and energy). They also have large, powerful, and often pushy neighbors. In this globalized world, problems move across borders quickly, and powerful actors—bigger states, international organizations, or even global non-state elites—can often compel the compliance or cooperation of others.

After World War II, Central American economies faced economic stagnation and deep poverty. The region's leaders feared possible leftist revolutions. Isthmian governments thus collaborated on a regional economic-integration scheme to promote capitalist economic growth and to preserve their regimes. Although successful for a while, that system crashed in world economic and domestic political crises during the 1970s and 1980s. Struggling to recover and under heavy pressure from outside political and economic actors, Central American states eventually adopted a new, common economic development model. We seek to understand the region's persistent poverty, what governments have done and are doing about it, and how the region's economies fit into and move with the world economy.

The region has also experienced political transformations directly related to the economic changes just mentioned. The political regimes prior to the 1970s, all but one of them authoritarian coalitions, passed through a long spasm of violence to become by the late 1980s and 1990s electoral democracies. Ironically, the economic development programs designed to prevent leftist rebellions and preserve regimes in place circa 1960 actually promoted the violence that helped forge several new electoral democracies and change their ruling coalitions. Thus we need to understand the region's political turmoil and its roots in economic change. We seek to explain the emergence of and threats to electoral democracy, and to explore its quality.

We begin by examining Central America's poverty and its causes, with special attention to the economic situation of Central Americans at the beginning of the twenty-first century. We then examine Central America's political regime changes from 1970 onward and offer a theory to explain them.

POVERTY AND ITS CAUSES

Commonsense interpretations of the causes of Central America's 1970s and 1980s turmoil often stress poverty. Indeed, poverty has always been a serious problem in the region. Even in relatively prosperous Costa Rica many suffer severe economic difficulties. Poverty constitutes a persistent crisis of great human cost and cries out for social and economic reforms.

Common sense betrays us, however, if we attempt to explain Central America's 1970s and 1980s rebellions as simply the product of poverty. Most of the world's population lives in poverty, yet the poor rarely rebel. Poverty alone cannot account for the revolts in Nicaragua, El Salvador, or Guatemala. Indeed, if poverty were sufficient to cause rebellions, Honduras should have exploded with popular fury long before Nicaragua or El Salvador. We thus encounter the paradox that among Central America's five nations, the poorest historically (Honduras) and the richest (Costa Rica) have been the most stable, whereas those that had the most rapid industrialization and economic growth in the 1960s and 1970s became the most unsettled.

To affirm that poverty alone did not cause Central America's rebellions, however, is not to say that poverty did not contribute. In fact, there is an important link between *becoming* impoverished and popular unrest. Large segments of Central America's poor and middle classes *became* much worse off during the 1970s and early 1980s. It was not the grinding deprivation of persistent poverty, but this change—impoverishment and declining living conditions—that motivated much of the region's unrest. This section examines Central America's long-standing deprivation that affects large segments of the population and what it means for contemporary Central Americans. The country chapters that follow examine how impoverishment contributed to popular unrest and rebellion in the 1970s and 1980s.

Poverty Measured

The human condition in Latin America generally falls between the extreme deprivation of parts of Africa and the relative prosperity of North America, Europe, and Japan. Within Latin America, Central America's economic indicators fall well below the median for the entire region. Latin America in 2007 had a gross domestic product (GDP) per capita (in current 2012 US dollars) of roughly $9,493. Only the relatively wealthy Costa Rica, with a GDP per capita of $9,402, approached that figure. The other four ranged from El Salvador, with a 2012 per capita GDP of $3,783, down to Nicaragua, with $1,761.[2]

GDP per capita figures require some explanation and context. First, for comparison, per person economic activity in the United States in 2012 (GDP per capita), at $49,965, was over fifteen times that of the average for Central America ($3,175).[3] Second, remember that the "average" indicated in GDP per capita figures distorts reality. GDP per capita divides annual total value of goods and services produced in a given country by the total population. In Central America, where a small minority controls most of the resources and earns most of the income, averaging the income of the wealthy in with that of the rest of the population gives per capita GDP values that overstate the real condition of most people. Indeed, the real income per capita of the poorer half of the population in most of Central America probably runs between $500 and $1,000 per year. Finally, while "average" Salvadorans thus struggled to make do on roughly one-thirteenth of what the average US citizen had to work with, they and other Central Americans faced prices for many consumer products—food, clothing, health care—similar to those in the United States.

Table 2.1 presents dramatic data about poverty's dynamics. Low income and poor living standards afflict many Central Americans. The income ratios of the wealthiest 10 percent of the people to the poorest 10 percent in 2000 revealed extreme inequality—a low of 25.1 for Costa Ricans rising to a high of 63.3 among Guatemalans. A general measure, the Gini index of income inequality, in 2004 was lower (indicating lower inequality) in El Salvador and Costa Rica than in Honduras and Nicaragua, and was highest in Guatemala. Put concretely, if we estimate that the poorest Guatemalans eked out a living on $500 per year in 2000, the wealthiest tenth of Guatemalans would have enjoyed a comfortable $31,500 each.

More recently, a measure of household living standard calculated from the 2012 survey of the AmericasBarometer revealed that the richest 10 percent of Costa Ricans had 2.7 times more of the measured family-wealth indicators than the poorest 20 percent—a modest level of inequality. The ratio rose to 4.7 in El Salvador, 10.9 in Honduras, and 22.7 in Nicaragua (extreme inequality). Households without the basic services of sewers, indoor toilets, and potable water were scarce at 2.1 percent in Costa Rica in 2012. In contrast, households without these services ranged from Guatemala's 10.6 percent to Nicaragua's 34.1 percent.

Data on the share of citizens below the regional poverty line from the 1990s and mid-2000s reveal that the region's economies had improved since the early 1990s. Twenty-six percent of Costa Ricans had incomes below the regional poverty line in the early 1990s; that figure improved to 20.5 percent in 2004. In the early 1990s, from 54 to 81 percent of the rest of Central Americans' incomes were below the poverty line. Modest improvement by 2004 left the number in poverty in those countries ranging from 48 to 75 percent. In four countries in the early 1990s almost two-thirds of the population lived on less than US$2 a day.[4] This figure improved substantially by 2012, declining to about one-quarter of the population of those four countries (Table 2.1). Only 3 percent of Costa Ricans fell below the $2 per day line in 2012.

Education can provide one way out of poverty. Data reveal both the difficulties that Central Americans confront and the progress made in recent decades. Elite-dominated systems have long placed scant emphasis on public education, but Table 2.1 provides evidence that more Central Americans are presently attending school than in the past. Literacy among those 15 years and older in 2005 ran from a high of 96 percent in Costa Rica to a low of 75 percent in Guatemala (see Table 1.1). The percentage of the population over age 25 with no schooling at all in 2012 ranged from a low of 2.8 percent in Costa Rica to between 12.6 and 16.3 percent in the other four countries (Table 2.1). Except for Nicaragua, the population 25 and older with no schooling declined between 2000 and 2012, indicating progress in educating younger Central Americans. Another positive sign is the rise in the average years of education for the population over 25 between 1960 and 2012. Costa Rica's average more than doubled from 3.9 to 8.3 years over this fifty-two-year span, while the other four countries more than tripled their averages to between 6.2 and 6.8 years of schooling. The average years of education for the 18- to 25-year-old group in 2012 was about 10 years in both Costa Rica and El Salvador, but only between 8.5 and 8.9 years elsewhere.

An index of inequality of education among those between 25 and 65 years of age in 2000 reflected great distortions in access to education. On a scale running from zero (everyone having equal education) to 100 (very unequal education), Costa Rica had a low score of 30; Nicaragua, Honduras, and El Salvador scored in the high 40s, and Guatemala a highly unequal 62. Table 2.1 divides the populations aged 18 or older into quintiles (fifths) by country according to levels of education attained as of 2012. For each quintile the table reports the mean years of education, allowing us to compare education inequalities. Costa Rica's lead across all the quintiles stands out clearly. El Salvadorans are approaching Costa Ricans averages among the third and fourth quintiles, but they still lag 1.6 years of schooling behind the most-educated Costa Ricans. Guatemalans, Hondurans, and Nicaraguans lag between one and 2.3 years behind Costa Ricans in every quintile of education achieved.

For the region as a whole, therefore, one may fairly say that the typical Central American is poorly fed, housed, inadequately educated, and with little or no access to medical care or cultural and recreational opportunities.[5] Improvements in income and education occurred in the 1990s and early 2000s, but it may take decades of continued investment in education to lift Guatemala, Honduras, and Nicaragua to the living standards of El Salvador, and for those of El Salvador to approach the living standards of Costa Rica.

Basic food production illustrates some of the problems stemming from greater economic inequality. Land in the region is very inequitably distributed. The rich and powerful control the best land and on it grow export products rather than food staples. In a capitalist economy, this makes good sense to landowners because export products earn greater profits than domestically marketed staples. But over time this process has allowed export producers to progressively buy up and concentrate land in fewer hands, and so countries produced fewer staples in relation to population. Meanwhile, the prices of these scarcer staples rose inexorably with population growth and thus forced the common citizen to make do on less and cheaper food. Recently, this

TABLE 2.1 Dynamics of Poverty in Central America

	Costa Rica	El Salvador	Guatemala	Honduras	Nicaragua
EDUCATIONAL INEQUALITY					
Mean years of education by national education quintiles (20% of population in least-to-most order of education)[a]					
Quintile					
1	2.9	0.8	0.6	0.5	0.6
2	6.0	3.9	3.7	3.8	3.8
3	8.4	7.5	6.6	6.1	6.3
4	10.7	10.8	9.7	9.3	8.9
5	15.2	13.6	13.0	13.6	12.9
Mean years of schooling (population over 25)					
in 1960[b]	0.9	1.7	1.4	1.7	2.1
in 2012[a]	8.3	6.8	6.3	6.2	6.7
Mean years of schooling population aged 18 to 25					
in 2012[a]	10.0	9.8	8.9	8.5	8.6
Percent of population over 25 with no schooling, c. 2000					
c. 2000[b]	9.4	35.0	47.1	25.9	18.0
In 2012[a]	2.8	12.6	16.0	14.9	16.3
Gini index of education inequality,[a] among population ages 25–65, c. 2000[b, c]					
	29.7	47.3	61.8	47.7	48.3

TABLE 2.1 *(continued)*

	Costa Rica	El Salvador	Guatemala	Honduras	Nicaragua
INCOME INEQUALITY					
Percent below poverty line, early 1990s					
	26.2	54.0	64.6	80.5	73.6
Percent below poverty line, 2004					
	20.5	47.5	56.0[b]	74.6	69.3
Percent of families with female heads of household, 2004 (% change since 1990)					
	27.6	32.2	19.3	25.7	32.2
	(+8.7)	(+5.5)	(+2.4)	(+4.3)	(+4.1)
Percent of children ages 10–14 who work					
	3.5	8.4	27.7	15.5	12.2
Percent of individuals living on less than US$2 per day, c. 2009					
	3	17	26	30	32
Ratio of incomes of wealthiest 10% to poorest 10% of population, c. 2000					
	25.1	47.4	63.3	49.1	56.2

Household living standard measured by mean number of 14 services and artifacts present in home (ranging from potable water to luxury appliances, vehicles, computers, and internet service)[a] by deciles (10% segments of population in least-to-most order of living standard)

Deciles					
1+2	4.89	2.33	1.45	1.09	0.42
10	13.31	10.95	12.11	11.39	9.52
Ratio of deciles 10 to 1+2	2.72	4.70	8.35	10.92	22.67

Households (percent) without sewer service, indoor bathroom, or potable water service[a]

	2.1	19.0	10.6	16.1	34.1
Gini index of income inequality,[a] c. 2004					
	0.46	0.46	0.62b	0.55	0.56

[a]Data drawn from 2012 national sample AmericasBarometer surveys of each country by the Latin American Public Opinion Project (LAPOP), www.LapopSurveys.org.
[b]Other sources: United Nations Economic Commission for Latin America and the Caribbean (ECLAC), *Statistical Yearbook for Latin America and the Caribbean 2007,* http://websie.eclac.cl/anuario_estadistico/anuario_2008, accessed July 29, 2008; United Nations Economic Commission for Latin America and the Caribbean (ECLAC), http://estadisticas.cepal.org/cepalstat/WEB_CEPALSTAT/estadisticasIndicadores.asp?idioma=i, accessed August 28, 2013; David E. de Ferranti et al., *Inequality in Latin America: Breaking with History?* (Washington, DC: The World Bank, 2004), http://www-wds.worldbank.org/external/default/WDSContentServer/WDSP/IB/2004/06/22/ 000160016_20040622141728/Rendered/PDF/28989.pdf, accessed July 29, 2008; Matthew Hammill, "Growth, Poverty, and Inequality in Central America," *Serie Subregional de la CEPAL en México,* United Nations, Economic Commission for Latin America, Social Development Unit, Mexico, D.F., 2007.
[c]The Gini index is a measure of inequality that ranges from 0 (perfect equality) to 1.00 (perfect inequality); the higher the index score, the greater the inequality among members of a population.

problem has been compounded by climate change, as floods and droughts have resulted in crop loss. Many Central Americans still eat little animal protein; instead, they derive their essential amino acids from corn and beans. But even these foods are expensive because costly imported staples have replaced insufficient domestic production. USAID estimates that 1.8 million Guatemalans suffer from food insecurity. Guatemala has the highest rate of chronic malnutrition in the hemisphere. Nearly half of all Guatemalans suffer from malnutrition, and the problem is concentrated in indigenous populations.

Conditions and trends are somewhat better in public health. Especially since World War II, improved weapons against communicable diseases have allowed international health organizations and Central American governments to curtail several killer diseases. This has lowered death rates and raised life expectancies, which for 2012 ranged from a regional mean of around 72.5 years for four countries, but was a respectably high 79 in Costa Rica (Table 1.1). Costa Rica, whose governments excelled for decades in providing decent, low-cost health care to much of the populace, widely beat out its neighbors in reducing infant mortality. Costa Rica for 2012 experienced nine infant deaths per 1,000 live births (similar to advanced industrial countries). El Salvador improved dramatically between 1990 and 2012, when infant deaths per 1,000 live births were only 13 compared to 40 some 22 years earlier. The other three countries also improved infant-mortality rates between 1990 and 2012, but rates there still remained relatively high in Nicaragua at 22, Honduras at 18, and Guatemala at 24 infant deaths per 1,000.

Improved preventive medicine has extended the life span of Central Americans, but most still faced serious health problems in the early twenty-first century. Local hygiene is often poor. Most rural and many urban houses lack interior plumbing, and many lack even backyard latrines (Table 2.1). Except for Costa Rica, the curative medical system was inadequate and scarce for the rural population. Expensive private medical care lay beyond the reach of most. Hospitals, doctors, and pharmaceuticals in most countries remained consistently available only to the wealthy and a part of the urban middle class. As a result, good health was largely a matter of privilege or luck. That said, Table 1.1 reveals that that national efforts to provide better health services were having beneficial effects. Between 1990–1995 and 2012 all Central American nations reduced infant-mortality rates; Guatemala made the most progress.

High natural population-growth rates exacerbate poverty. From 2010 to 2013, annual population-growth rates ranged from 0.6 percent in El Salvador to 2.4 percent in Guatemala (Table 1.1). Growth rates declined significantly over the last two decades, and urban populations of Central America are growing much faster than rural areas. If Central America's current rates of growth persist, its population will reach 65 million by 2040—an increase of 59 percent.[6] The region's population grows rapidly for several reasons. Advances in public health have reduced death rates. Second, the median age of the population for four of the five countries is around twenty-four (compared to thirty-seven in the United States). Thus much of the female population is of childbearing age. Costa Rica's median age is the highest, at 29.5.[7]

Finally, high fertility is normally related to high poverty and low urbanization. Although poverty persists, much of Central America has significantly urbanized in recent decades. As Table 1.1 shows, Costa Rica in 2012 was the most urban (66 percent urban population), followed by El Salvador at 60 percent down to Honduras at 51 percent. Guatemala's urban population was growing fastest in 2012, up 7 percent since 2005. Urbanization makes education more widely available to women and encourages wider use of birth control. Persistent high population growth makes efforts to reduce social inequities and improve living conditions more difficult, but some progress has occurred. The much higher population-growth rates of previous decades have begun to tail off across the region as urbanization has increased and the median age has risen.

The Causes of Poverty

Poverty in Central America is neither completely natural nor inevitable. Foreigners once argued that Central Americans were poor because they were racially inferior. For instance, one geography text used widely in US primary schools in the 1920s claimed that "except where white men have established plantations, the resources [of Central America] are poorly developed. Most of the Indians, *mestizos*, and negroes are poor and ignorant . . . few care to work hard. More white men are needed to start plantations and to fight tropical diseases."[8] Today we recognize such statements, once found in prominent encyclopedias, to be racist nonsense. Likewise, one cannot maintain that the region lacks sufficient resources to support its human population. El Salvador *is* overpopulated. But Central America as a whole has enough good land not only to produce some primary products for export and foreign exchange but also to grow sufficient staples to feed its people. And though not exceptionally blessed in this regard, the region also has some mineral resources and significant hydroelectric-energy resources and potential.

In fact, much of Central America's poverty is a human artifact—produced by exploitation of the many by the region's powerful upper classes as they operate within the larger world economic system. Powerful foreign interests often joined and supported Central America's local elites in this exploitive behavior. Evidence that human volition caused much of the region's poverty leaps out of some of the data in Tables 1.1 and 2.1. In these facts, one repeatedly finds that Costa Rica has done better than its neighbors in economic growth, economic equality, poverty reduction, providing education and literacy, and promoting its citizens' health. Moreover, Costa Rica accomplished these things while exporting agricultural commodities and having only modest resources. It did so despite starting the second half of the twentieth century ranked behind El Salvador in per capita income. How did Costa Rica do so much better by its citizens than its four northern neighbors since 1950? The answer, we contend, stems from the political will of Costa Rican leaders. Even though they shared the same disadvantageous economic context of the rest of Central America, Costa Rica's leaders adopted and kept democracy, abolished the armed forces, moderated income inequality, and invested in education and health over the long haul. The leaders of the other nations did not make these choices, at least not consistently enough to do the job.

Dependency. What developed over time and accounts for much of the Central American economic system was *dependency.*[9] Though some disagree on specifics, most experts view dependency as a complex political, economic, and social phenomenon that retards the human development of the majority in certain privilege-dominated Third World countries with heavily externally oriented economies. In such countries, even during periods of rapid economic growth, the benefits of growth normally do not meaningfully "trickle down" to the majority of the people. The *dependistas* (dependency theorists) argue that dependent countries' social stagnation derives from the combination of an income-concentrating, externally oriented, externally conditioned form of capitalism with political systems controlled by privileged minorities who benefit from such poorly distributed growth.

We emphasize that for the *dependency syndrome* to exist, a country needs *both* an externally oriented economy (specializing in commodity exporting) *and* a socially irresponsible political elite. External economic orientation, though essential, is not sufficient to cause the socially regressive dependency. Korea and Japan are both heavily externally oriented, but their elites have demonstrated a greater sense of social responsibility than Latin America's and have allowed growth to promote generally improved living standards. Cuba from 1959 to the collapse of the Soviet Union and the Socialist bloc in 1989 provides another example of dependence without the poverty-generating dependency syndrome. Critics of Cuba argue that the island republic's revolutionary government simply replaced dependence on the United States with dependence on the Socialist bloc. Quite so. However, a crucial difference was that the Cuban political elite distributed the income from its externally dependent economy so as to significantly improve general levels of public health, education, and nutrition. Thus while dependent on the Soviet bloc for aid, Cuba for a time avoided the dependency syndrome per se.

Capitalist development in dependent countries such as those of Central America differs sharply from what occurred in the industrialized countries. In the Western industrial nations common citizens became crucially important to the economy as consumers. In the United States for much of the twentieth century, for instance, domestic consumers absorbed much of the industrial production. So for at least a century it was not in the US ruling class interest to exploit ordinary citizens to the extent that they could no longer consume. In an internally oriented economic system like that of the United States, income redistribution through the graduated income tax, social-welfare programs, and a free-labor movement actually served the interest of the moneyed elite as well as that of the common citizen. However, in dependent Third World countries, the tiny upper and middle classes that control the political systems derive most of their income from exports or from the products manufactured by multinational corporations that the upper and middle classes—but not the masses—consume. In such a system the common citizen becomes important not as a consumer but as a vulnerable source of cheap labor.

Under this type of system, average citizens have little opportunity to lift themselves by the bootstraps because they lack either the means of production or the riches that flow therefrom. By its nature, elite-run dependency produces an inexorable concentration of property and income. In rural areas, stimulated by the growing lure of high profits through export, the rich and the powerful simply buy out or drive poor peasants from the land. In the cities, local elites and foreign enterprises dominate the usually modest industrial production. Foreign firms enjoy huge advantages in technology and brand recognition that retards the formation of locally based industry. Nevertheless, the local elites benefit from contracts, services, and employment for the educated few, as well as occasional payoffs and bribes. Meanwhile, only limited advantages accrue to a host country from the foreign firms that export both profits and earnings from licenses, patents, and materials sold at inflated prices by parent companies. They tend to use capital-intensive rather than labor-intensive technology, thus draining foreign exchange for the purchase of costly industrial equipment and providing limited "trickle-down" in the form of wages. And finally, by obtaining much of their capital locally, they dry up domestic capital that might otherwise be available to native entrepreneurs.

This system privileges a local elite and its foreign associates while ignoring the interests of the vast majority. Powerful economic disincentives discourage elites from improving the miserable condition of the masses. Adopting a more socially responsible, mixed economic system could involve economic dislocation and personal sacrifice that many among Central America's dominant elites would not accept without a fight. Indeed, the two main Central American experiments with such a more socially responsible, state-led development model only arose at least in part from violent political conflicts—the Costa Rican civil war of 1948 and the Nicaraguan revolution of 1979.

At this point, one might reasonably ask why the dependency system developed in Central America while a consumer-driven economy arose in North America. And why has the great bulk of the Central American people proven unable to alter a system so contrary to their interests? Much of the answer to the first question lies in the distinct ways in which North America and Central America were colonized. European nonconformists originally settled North America seeking a new life and greater freedom. These people tamed the land with their own labor and eventually developed into a large class of freeholders. North America did develop an aristocracy of sorts, but it never completely dominated the common citizen.

In Central America, the conquistadores sought quick riches. They superimposed their administration over that of the indigenous peoples and immediately began exacting tribute in gold and slaves. Within decades, the Spaniards plundered the region's gold and decimated much of its native population by slavery and contagion with European diseases. The Spanish steadily drained resources from the region. Subjugated masses of indigenous *peones* (workers and peasants), mestizos (people of mixed white and Indian descent), and eventually black slaves and mulattoes (people of mixed white and black descent) supplied most of the labor. Only in Costa Rica, with few easily exploitable resources and few native peoples, did many Spaniards come to till the soil. Costa Rican economic and political elites, absent a coercible indigenous workforce, learned to co-opt and cajole their working classes.

Small wonder, then, that over five centuries later, the four northern countries of Central America had severe mass poverty and class disparities, whereas Costa Rica had developed a relatively more democratic, egalitarian, and socially just system. Evidence that elite decisions underlie these within-region differences stands out in certain facts. After 1950 Costa Rica's governments directed far more of their national budgets to social spending (health, education, and welfare) than other Central American governments. Costa Rica consistently dedicated more of its budget to social welfare partly because, after 1949, it had no armed forces to support. The Costa Rican government's overall spending and social spending as a percentage of GDP were nearly always greater than those in other isthmian countries.[10] Even after sharp curtailment under international pressure in the 1990s, for example, Costa Rica in 1998 spent 16.8 percent of GDP on social welfare, compared to Nicaragua's next-best effort at 12.7 percent.[11] In contrast, the Salvadoran government's social spending—a crude measure of elite commitment to reducing poverty—was 4.3 percent of GDP in 1998, the region's least, but exceeded only modestly by Guatemala (6.2 percent) and Honduras (7.4 percent). By 2012 Costa Rica's social spending as a percentage of GDP had increased over 1998 by nearly one-third to 22.9 percent (Table 2.2). El Salvador's social spending nearly tripled from 1998 to reach 13 percent, a major increase in its effort. The other three countries' social spending rose slightly between 1998 and 2012. Even having increased since 1998, Guatemala's relative social expenditures in 2012 lagged well behind the other countries.

TABLE 2.2 Recent Economic Data on Central American Governments

	Costa Rica	El Salvador	Guatemala	Honduras	Nicaragua
Government spending over-all as percentage of gross domestic product in 2012	18.8	17.5	14.0	22.8	15.9
Government social spending as percentage of gross domestic product, c. 2011	22.9	13.0	8.1	12.0	13.0
External debt as percentage of gross domestic product in selected years, 1982–2012					
1982	110.3	42.0	17.6	69.4	121.5
1991	73.0	36.7	29.8	118.9	649.1
2007	13.8	24.5	11.1	41.7	93.8
2012	30.1	50.8	13.6	26.1	40.8

SOURCES: Economic Commission for Latin America and the Caribbean, CEPALSTAT/Databases and Statistical Publications, http://estadisticas.cepal.org/cepalstat/WEB_CEPALSTAT/perfilesNacionales .asp?idioma=e, accessed December 5, 2013; Inter-American Development Bank, www.iadb.org/gl/, accessed January 25, 2009; Inter-American Development Bank, *Economic and Social Progress in Latin America, 1983 Report* (Washington, DC, 1983), country profiles; Inter-American Development Bank, *Economic and Social Progress in Latin America, 1992 Report* (Washington, DC, 1992), country profiles.

This also leads to the explanation for why the mass of citizens did not improve these systems for so long. Rather than docilely accept their imposed and sorry lot, numerous groups have revolted when things got rapidly worse. Indigenous peoples resisted the conquistadores. Peasants revolted against land concentration caused by the late nineteenth-century Liberal reforms and the spread of coffee cultivation. Peasants and workers united under Nicaraguan nationalist Augusto C. Sandino to resist US occupation from 1927 to 1933. Workers led by El Salvador's homegrown Communist Agustín Farabundo Martí revolted in 1932. Nicaraguans successfully rebelled against the Anastasio Somoza Debayle regime in 1978–1979. Mass-based insurrections took place in El Salvador and Guatemala beginning in the late 1970s.

Such struggles between popularly based movements and those in power have usually been very unequal. Entrenched elites typically enjoyed huge advantages in military, economic, and propaganda resources. And the elites usually also counted on the support of foreign powers—Spain in the colonial period and the United States in the twentieth century. During the Cold War, Central America's ruling classes learned that merely by labeling their opposition "Communist" they could usually win US support from direct armed intervention to economic and military aid. From 1946 through 1992 the

United States provided US$1.8 billion in military assistance to the region (98 percent of it to Guatemala, El Salvador, Honduras, and prerevolutionary Nicaragua) to shore up authoritarian regimes against challenges from the left (see Appendix, Table A.3).

During the 1960s the United States assisted Central American governments with the Alliance for Progress. From 1962 through 1972 the Alliance provided US$617 million (Appendix, Table A.3) to help build Central America's roads, ports, schools, and service infrastructures. This complemented the five-nation Central American Common Market's (CACM) effort to promote a common state-directed, import-substitution industrialization program and customs union. Intended to advance economic development and security objectives, the CACM stimulated rapid economic growth, but national elites mismanaged the distribution of its benefits. Rejecting the strategy of Costa Rican leaders, the regimes of Guatemala, El Salvador, and Nicaragua resisted sharing the benefits of growth with most citizens.

Afflicted by rising oil prices and falling commodity prices in the mid-1970s, the Common Market development model failed spectacularly. For every isthmian country this crisis brought high inflation, unemployment, and foreign debt while sharply lowering productivity and real wages. Worsening circumstances mobilized many citizens in protest, and some to violence, destabilizing several governments. Despite US$5.6 billion in economic aid from 1977 to 1988 (Appendix, Table A.3) and assistance from other nations, turmoil blocked Central America's economic recovery. Eventually the United States and the major world multilateral lending organizations such as the International Monetary Fund pressured all five countries into adopting a new economic model known as *neoliberalism* and enacting programs of *structural adjustment,* economic reforms mandated by foreign lenders.

Neoliberalism complemented regional and international political efforts to end the civil wars and promote electoral democracy. That outside elites and Central American leaders pushed together for peace, democratization, and neoliberal economic reform is no accident. Robinson summarizes:

> As the transnational ruling bloc emerged in the 1980s and 1990s it carried out a "revolution from above," involving modifications in global social and economic structures through the agency of [transnational system] apparatuses aimed at promoting the most propitious conditions around the world for . . . the new global capitalist production system. This global restructuring, the so-called "Washington consensus," [or] neo-liberalism, is a doctrine . . . [that calls for] worldwide market liberalization, . . . the internal restructuring and global integration of each national economy . . . [and] an explicitly political component . . . [that] revolved around the promotion of "democracy."[12]

The transnational organizations pushing the neoliberal model in Central America included the US Agency for International Development (USAID) and multilateral lenders the International Monetary Fund and Inter-American Development Bank. Together they exacted internal political and economic "reforms" from debt-ridden Central American nations in exchange for critically needed loans to keep their economies functioning.

Promoted by international lenders, the United States, and Europe, this neoliberal development model advocated certain basic changes: (1) downsizing government by laying off public employees; (2) balancing public budgets by cutting programs and subsidies to food, transport, and public services; (3) privatization of state-owned enterprises; (4) deregulation of private enterprise; (5) currency devaluations to discourage imports and encourage investment; and (6) sharp reduction of tariff barriers to foreign trade. Neoliberalism's advocates argued such measures would eliminate inflation, increase productivity, stimulate international trade (especially exports), and lay a foundation for future economic growth. Although many would be dislocated and suffer in the short run, long-term economic growth would in theory eventually "trickle down" to everyone.

For Central Americans with a sense of history, neoliberalism portended mixed blessings. It resembled the raw economic liberalism of the region's late-nineteenth- and early-twentieth-century economic models. Peace, democracy, and neoliberalism's monetary and price stability brought economic recovery to parts of the region through improved growth, investment, and trade. Operating under the new rules mandating economic austerity for the state, Central American governments by 2007 had reduced the foreign debt they had accumulated by the early 1990s (see Table 2.2). On the other hand, because these policies, including debt repayment, reduced governments' capacity to protect and assist their citizens, they also increased disparities between the rich and poor, and hurt the small middle class. Ironically, then, after achieving hard-fought political reforms, Central Americans found their governments still pursuing (or in Costa Rica's case, newly pursuing) economic policies that might aggravate economic and social inequality—one of the central problems that contributed to the violence of the 1970s and 1980s.

The Great Recession of 2008–2009 left major nations and international lending institutions divided over neoliberal versus Keynesian stimulative recovery policies. This argument relieved external pressure on Central American governments as their economies experienced renewed aggregate economic growth. Regional governments responded differently to the recession, recovery, and external lenders' divided policy preferences. Costa Rica and El Salvador doubled their ratios of external debt to GDP between 2007 and 2012 and increased their social-program spending (Table 2.2). Guatemala, consistently conservative in its external borrowing, changed little over this period. Meanwhile Nicaragua and Honduras saw external-loan forgiveness programs lower their international debts sharply by 2012.

Whether the newly democratic institutions born of the struggles of the 1970s and 1980s would allow Central American nations to curtail poverty remains to be seen. Costa Rica and El Salvador considerably increased government spending on social programs after 2007, and the other nations increased their efforts somewhat. But a long-prevailing regional pattern persisted— Costa Rica invested roughly double its share of national GDP in its citizens' well-being compared to the other four (Table 2.2). This left two major questions: Would, or could, the other nations' elites attempt to balance growth with equity, as Costa Rica had for six decades? And would foreign lenders continue to allow relaxation of neoliberal strictures to accommodate greater social equity? The quality of life of the poor majority of the region's people depends on the answer to these questions.

REGIME CHANGE IN CENTRAL AMERICA

We turn now to the transformations of Central America's political regimes in the 1980s and 1990s. We believe regional political transformations and the economic processes just discussed are related and largely driven by common forces.

Regimes are coherent systems of rule over mass publics established among a coalition of a nation's dominant political actors. The *coherence of a system of rule* refers to a persistent and identifiable set of political rules determining access to power and decision making.[13] Political regimes thus stand distinct from the particular governments or administrations that operate under the same general rules. For instance, Costa Rica has had a single civilian democratic regime since the 1950s, consisting of a series of constitutionally elected presidential administrations. Likewise, Guatemala in the 1970s had a military authoritarian regime, subdivided into governments headed by various president-generals.

A new regime differentiates itself from its precursor (a regime shift), when change occurs in *both the fundamental rules of politics and the makeup of its ruling coalition.* We identify eight basic regime types in Central America between 1970 and 2013:

1. *Military authoritarian*, dominated by a corporate military establishment in coalition with a narrow range of civilian sectors.
2. *Personalistic military*, the only case of which was Nicaragua, dominated by the Somoza family and military in coalition with segments of the Liberal and Conservative parties and key financial sectors.

3. *Military transitional,* dominated by reformist military elements and willing to liberalize or democratize the political system.
4. *Civilian transitional,* with elected civilian rulers backed by a strong military and mainly incorporating center and rightist parties.
5. *Civilian democratic,* which have freely and fairly elected, civilian, constitutionally restrained governments, broad ruling coalitions, and political competition open to parties from left to right.
6. *Revolutionary,* dominated by a weakly restrained revolutionary party with a center-left coalition.
7. *Revolutionary transitional,* civilian-dominated and moving toward accommodating the revolutionary party and toward constitutional restraints; has occurred only in Nicaragua.
8. *Semi-democratic,* defined by Peter Smith as a regime in which "elections are free but not fair, . . . [or] elections are free and fair, but effective power does not go to the winner . . . [but] resides outside the realm of elective offices."[14] To this we add one additional characteristic: serious deviations from constitutional rule.

Table 2.3 displays Central America's political regimes since 1970 according to this scheme. Over the more than four decades since 1970 only Costa Rica has remained politically stable. Among the other four countries we count fourteen regime shifts (changes between categories).[15] Nicaragua's 1978–1979 insurrection culminated in a four-and-a-half-year period of revolutionary rule until internationally observed elections took place in 1984. With new members in the ruling coalition and National Assembly and top public officials separated from the revolutionary armed forces, the new revolutionary-transitional regime's National Assembly drafted a new constitution (1985–1987),

TABLE 2.3 Central American Regime Types, 1970–2013

Costa Rica	El Salvador	Guatemala	Honduras	Nicaragua
CD[a]	MA	MA	MA	PM
	MT (1979)	MT (1982)	MT (1980)	Rev (1979)
	CT (1984)	CT (1985)	CT (1982)	RevT (1984)
	CD (1992)	CD (1996)	CD (1996)	CD (1987)
			SD (2009)	SD (c. 2006)

NOTE: Explanation of regime-type notations: CD = civilian democratic, CT = civilian transitional, MA = military authoritarian, PM = personalistic military, MT = military transitional, Rev = revolutionary, RevT = revolutionary transitional, and SD = semi-democratic. See text for fuller explanation of types. Date of inception of new regimes is in parentheses.
[a]Uninterrupted from 1949 to the present.

the promulgation of which instituted constitutional civilian democracy in 1987. El Salvador and Guatemala traversed three similar stages after military-authoritarian rule. In both, a military-led transitional regime during civil war engineered changes that led to a civilian transitional regime; the settlement of each war eventually ushered in a more inclusive civilian democratic government. Honduras' military regime, anxiously eyeing neighboring Nicaragua's revolutionary turmoil at the end of the 1970s, moved quickly toward transitional civilian democratic rule. The military retained veto authority for a long time—full civilian democracy came only in 1996. Hopes for consolidation of full civilian democracy proved vain.

Following constitutional and election-system changes and the collapse of the Liberal family of opposition parties in the mid-2000s, Nicaragua became a semi-democracy under President Daniel Ortega and the dominance of the Sandinista National Liberation Front (FSLN). In mid-2009, Honduras shifted from a civilian democracy to semi-democracy when the Congress, Supreme Court, and armed forces ousted President Manuel Zelaya from office. Despite the late 2009 election that put an elected president in office, Honduras clearly had a new regime in which effective power "resides outside the realm of elective offices."[16] Both Nicaragua and Honduras since these changes have also experienced serious deviations from constitutional rule.

How and why did these regime shifts occur? We examine both what caused the changes and the mechanisms or processes of change.

Causes of Regime Change

Several interacting factors drove most regime change: Rapid economic growth in the 1960s followed by severe reversals in the 1970s impoverished many and generated widespread mobilization and demands for political and economic reform. Economic crisis bred mass unrest and helped undermine authoritarian coalitions. Violent repression of those demanding reform by several governments drove opposition unification, radicalization, and revolutionary insurrection. Fear of a revolution like Nicaragua's prompted the militaries of other nations, some with US aid, to initiate gradual political changes and eventually to accept transitional civilian regimes with liberalized rules. During the wars themselves, the failure of the armed forces to defeat the insurgents added impetus to calls from international actors (neighboring Latin American states, Europe, and the Catholic Church) to accept negotiated regime change. Finally, the end of the Cold War convinced the United States in the early 1990s that it was now in its interest to accept or promote rather than resist the negotiated settlements all Central American regimes had agreed to in principle in 1987.

As the twenty-first century began, new factors arose to influence events in Central America. First, US influence over Latin America declined. Larger, resource-rich, or economically successful nations such as Brazil, Mexico, Argentina, Venezuela, and Chile gained economic and political influence within the hemisphere. Hugo Chávez's election to Venezuela's presidency in 1999 escalated expressions of anti-imperialist views. Venezuela aligned with and supported left-leaning and populist governments in Cuba, Bolivia, and Ecuador, along with Honduras and Nicaragua. New regional organizations arose to promote regional cooperation outside US influence. These included the Union of South American nations, the Bank of the South, and the Bolivarian Alliance for the Americas (known by its Spanish acronym ALBA), which distributed economic assistance to poorer nations and counterbalanced US aid. Another new factor was that the United States turned much of its attention away from Latin America after the terrorist attacks of September 11, 2001. The United States also lost credibility as a promoter of democracy in the region when US officials endorsed the failed coup against President Chávez in early 2002.

Finally, shifting political alignments and elite attitudes within some Central American countries weakened electoral democracy. Key elites in Honduras and Nicaragua had failed to embrace fully the constitutional democratic rules of the political game. Their deviation from these norms to their narrow advantage came at great cost to democracy. In Nicaragua, the several parties within the Liberal movement dissolved into a bitter factionalism that allowed the FSLN's Daniel Ortega to win back the presidency in 2006, consolidate power, and win reelection to another term in 2011.

Processes of Regime Change

If these were the likely causes of regime transformation, how did the changes occur? A widely based mass insurrection initiated the revolutionary regime in Nicaragua by defeating the authoritarian Somoza regime in 1979. The Nicaraguan revolutionary government enacted party and electoral laws similar to those of Western Europe and Costa Rica in 1983 and won internationally observed elections in 1984. In the ensuing revolutionary transitional period the National Assembly wrote a new constitution that took effect in 1987, ushering in the civilian democratic regime.

The overthrow of Somoza and beginning of the Nicaraguan revolution in 1979 were political earthquakes that motivated regime change elsewhere in the isthmus. Military coups d'état ushered in transitional military regimes in El Salvador, Guatemala, and Honduras. At first the new Salvadoran and Guatemalan military regimes kept repression high. Their critics rightly doubted that meaningful changes in political rules had occurred. But gradually the military transitional leaders produced new constitutions (some exculpating the military for their crimes while in power). They then allowed elections that brought civilians to nominal power while permitting at least some formerly excluded centrist and center-left civilian groups back into the political arena. Eventually all of the region's transitional regimes allowed full civilian electoral democracy to operate (see Table 2.3). But these regimes were not fully consolidated. After civilian democratic regimes had operated for a while, the post-2000 vacuum of US attention to the region contributed to democratic backsliding by some countries. Honduras and Nicaragua became semi-democracies.

Isthmian nations have much of their history, global contexts, and political and economic development in common. As noted, these common attributes demonstrate that Central America exists within a larger world dynamic that similarly constrains its component states. Just as common forces caused Central America's three great national revolts in the 1970s, the same forces influenced the overall process of regime change leading from authoritarianism toward electoral democracy. In fact, the revolutionary movements were key steps in the process of regime change that led to the region's formal democratization.

THREE LITERATURES ON REGIME CHANGE IN CENTRAL AMERICA

Our explanatory argument integrating Central America's insurrections and other regime changes employs elements of regime-change theory and the dependency and world-system theories already discussed. We briefly review the political science literatures on regime change, revolution, and democratization and show how they overlap and inform each other. These common features lead us toward a more general explanation of the remarkable transformations of Central American politics since the 1970s.

Causes, Processes, and Outcomes of Regime Change

Students of regime change examine the causes, processes, and outcomes of regime change. Barrington Moore explored how the characteristics of several established regimes and the interaction of their various social classes shaped the particular characteristics of new regimes.[17] Guillermo O'Donnell examined the role of military–middle class coalitions as bureaucratic authoritarianism replaced civilian governments in Argentina and Brazil.[18] The contributors to Guillermo O'Donnell et al.'s *Transitions from Authoritarian Rule* examined the nature of authoritarian regimes and the causes and processes involved in the breakdown of authoritarian governments of southern Europe and Latin America.[19] Mark Gasiorowski has employed quantitative analysis to account for factors that contribute to regime change.[20] Dietrich Rueschemeyer and Evelyne and John Stephens' *Capitalist Development and Democracy* contends that regimes shift toward democracy when organized working- or middle-class groups have sufficient power to undermine the wealth of entrenched elites. In essence, threatened elites use political reform to co-opt those below.[21]

Carles Boix takes a slightly different tack, contending that democratic regimes arise when pressed by masses from below if key elites have mobile capital (for example, industrial or financial assets) rather than fixed assets (extensive landholdings or mineral deposits). Capital mobility, he believes, makes elites more flexible and willing to negotiate concessions to those pressing them for change.[22]

In sum, despite the difference among these theories, the regime-change literature clearly views regimes as systems of rule over mass publics established among a coalition of a nation's dominant political actors. Regime-coalition members benefit from inclusion in the regime. Social and especially economic change can generate and mobilize new political actors who seek inclusion into the ruling coalition and its benefits. They may or may not be admitted by those within the regime (details of why concessions occur are disputed). Contented, indifferent, unorganized, or effectively repressed populations and groups do not seek inclusion in the regime, nor do they violently rebel. Strong, flexible regimes with satisfied allies rarely collapse or wage war against their populations.

Charles Anderson's classic work explains that Latin American regimes have corporatist tendencies, meaning that new actors usually win admission to the regime coalition only when they prove themselves capable, if excluded, of destabilizing the existing regime. Regime transformations in the region therefore often involve conflict because excluded forces must fight for inclusion.[23] This view accounts for the well-documented case of Costa Rica's last regime shift. The narrowly based coffee grower–dominated semi-democracy of the 1930s was disrupted first by emergent Communist-led unions, who made a pact with the reformist president to enact key social protections in the early 1940s. Six years later, middle-class actors and elements of the coffee elite coalesced to rebel in a brief but violent civil war in 1948. The latter forces forged a new regime after winning the civil war.[24]

Political Violence, Revolution, and Regime Change

The second relevant literature concerns political violence and revolution, part of which concerns regime change.[25] First, for a rebellion to occur, a fundamental basis of conflict must exist that defines groups or categories of affected persons that provide "recruiting grounds for organizations."[26] What bases of conflict are most likely to lead citizens to widespread rebellion, a phenomenon that John Walton usefully designates the *national revolt*?[27] Walton, Theda Skocpol, Jeffrey Paige, Mancur Olson, David Mason, and others argue that rapid economic change and evolving class relations typically drive the mobilization required for a violent challenge to a regime.[28] For agrarian societies, inclusion into the world capitalist economy through a shift to heavy reliance upon export agriculture may harm huge sectors of the peasantry, urban poor, and middle sectors and thus provide large numbers of aggrieved citizens.

Once motivated, groups must organize and focus their struggle for change upon some target, most likely the regime in power. Rod Aya and Charles Tilly have shown that effective organization for opposition requires the mobilization of resources. They emphasize the key role of the state in shaping rebellion. The state is not only the target of the rebels, but it also reciprocally affects the revolt as it represses rebels and promotes change.[29] Walton, Skocpol, Jack Goldstone, and Ted Gurr concur that once a contest over sovereignty begins, political factors such as organization and resource mobilization by both sides eventually determine the outcome.[30] Goldstone, James DeFronzo, and Bill Robinson particularly emphasize the contribution to successful revolutionary movements of both external actors and inter-elite competition, elite alienation, and factors that may weaken the state's capacity to act.[31] Perhaps the most satisfactory explanation is that offered by Timothy Wickham-Crowley.[32] Rejecting single-factor theories, he argues from recent Latin American history that successful insurrection requires a combination of four factors: the right social conditions in the countryside; an intelligent and flexible guerrilla movement; a despicable target regime ("mafiacracy"); and the right international conditions. The last of these can include economic forces (e.g., falling international commodity prices that impoverish and thus mobilize local actors) and political ones (e.g., something that distracts a hegemonic actor from its normal clients, new international power configurations, or overt decisions not to intervene on behalf of a regime).

Democratization and Regime Change

The third literature is the growing body of scholarship on democratization, the process of moving from an authoritarian to a democratic regime. The main explanations focus respectively on political culture, political processes, social structures and forces (both domestic and external), and elites.

The cultural approach argues that the ideal of political democracy can evolve within a society or spread among nations by cultural diffusion among elite and mass political actors.[33] Elite and mass preferences for democracy promote its adoption and help sustain it. Like regime-change theory, process approaches to democratization also examine the mechanics of and paths toward democratic transition.[34]

Structural theories emphasize how shifts in the distribution of critical material and organizational resources among political actors can lead to democracy.[35] Democratic regimes emerge when the distribution of political and economic resources and the mobilization of actors permit formerly excluded actors to disrupt the extant authoritarian coalition. Elites are more likely to allow democratization when they enjoy capital mobility rather than capital rigidity (such as having wealth-based large landholdings). Another structural approach examines the imposition of democracy by external actors.[36]

The fourth approach examines the roles of leaders.[37] Key societal elites must engineer specific democratic arrangements (elite settlements) and agree to operate by them. The broader the coalition of political forces involved, the more stable and consolidated a democratic regime will be. Weak elite commitment to constitutional democratic norms can undermine a democratic regime as opportunistic elites act undemocratically to seek their narrow advantage. Robinson's explanation of the emergence of what he calls *polyarchy*, a minimalist variant of formal electoral democracy, encompasses aspects of structural democratization theory (global economic and political forces and institutions impinge on the local) and elite democratization theory (external, international, and global elites cooperate with and impose democratic rules on local elites).[38]

These three literatures have much in common. All concern regime change or efforts to promote it, although the democratization literature emphasizes transition in one particular direction. Elements of all three envision polities with many actors, whose makeup and roles can evolve. All treat political regimes as coalitions of actors that survive by successful mobilization of resources in and around the state or governmental apparatus. All recognize that regimes can experience crisis, whether challenges from without, deterioration from within, or erosion of state capacity. All have causal explanations for change, although the approaches disagree somewhat over the importance of such factors as psychology, political culture, leaders and elites, masses, and social structures. However, the more sophisticated treatments in the revolution/violence and democratization literatures tend to treat causality as both complex and multiple.

Finally, each of these fields and a substantial literature on foreign policy recognize that international constraints can shape regime change.[39] Foreign governments, international institutions, and other actors from outside a nation can act as players in domestic economics and politics. They can support a prevailing regime, withhold support, or overtly oppose it. External resources given to domestic actors can alter their capacities to act and their relative strengths. Key external actors can pressure domestic actors to adopt certain policies or regime types using the inducements of money, trade, arms, and political cooperation. The international context can also constrain a nation's regime type by demonstration effect—having mostly democratic neighbors makes it easier to adopt or retain a democratic regime.

A THEORY OF REGIME CHANGE IN CENTRAL AMERICA

We draw from these elements to propose our theory of regime change: Political systems are nation-states with defined populations and territorial boundaries. Political systems exist within an international context of various types of actors: nation-states, formal and informal alliances among nations, corporations, the world political economy, international organizations, and political and ideological groupings. A political regime consists of a coherent system of rule over a mass public established by a coalition of the nation's dominant political actors. Political actors include individuals, organized groups, factions, ideological groupings, parties, interest sectors, or institutions, each pursuing objectives within the political system and each with resources to bring to bear. Actors may or may not constitute part of the *regime coalition*, which is the group of actors who dominate and benefit most from the state, its resources, and its policy-making capacity.

Political regimes persist based upon two things: They must constantly manage the state and economy well enough to retain coalition members' loyalty. And they must continuously keep actual and potential outside-the-regime actors (both domestic and external) content or indifferent or, failing those, keep them disorganized, uninterested, distracted, or effectively repressed. Many factors can potentially destabilize a regime. International or domestic economic forces may disrupt the political economy or the security of regime-coalition members or other actors. Such forces may include rapid economic growth followed by a sharp downturn, or a sharp recessive episode by itself. Powerful external actors may withdraw support and resources from a regime, or shift from tacit support to active opposition, and thus create a permissive external environment for opponents. Ideologies or different real-world examples may suggest alternative system rules (for example socialism instead of capitalism, or civilian democracy instead of military authoritarianism) to key actors within or outside the regime coalition.

A *regime crisis* occurs when such forces (1) undermine the loyalty and cooperation of some or all of the coalition members, (2) undermine the resource base and capacity of the regime to respond to challengers, and/ or (3) mobilize external actors against the regime. Crises can take various forms based upon the severity of the challenge and distribution of resources among actors. Regime-coalition members may renegotiate the regime's political rules and benefits and deny significant adjustments to outside actors. Regimes may also make policy changes to mollify aggrieved outside actors. Reforming extant political rules and payoffs and incorporating new coalition members can quell a disruptive challenge. Outside-the-regime actors may initiate a violent challenge to the regime's sovereignty by coup d'état, insurrection, or even invasion. Inside-the-regime actors may employ a coup to displace incumbents or initiate a new regime. Leaders of a regime may voluntarily institute regime change on their own terms, even absent a regime crisis, although most likely in response to anticipated challenges to the regime or polity. (Whatever the motivation, we consider this combination of alterations—change in the coalition membership plus an adjustment of the rules—to constitute a regime change.)

The evolution and outcome of a regime crisis will depend upon the ability of the regime and its challengers to mobilize and deploy their respective resources. The closer the contenders are to resource parity and the stronger they are, the longer and more violently they will struggle over power. A dominant actor (such as the military) in a weak to moderately strong regime, confronted with a significant but potentially growing opposition, might initiate a regime change (co-optative reform by including new actors to minimize expected damage to its interests). The military-transitional regime type discussed above provides an example. Other things equal, a strong, flexible, resource-rich regime will be likely to reform, or to successfully repress or exclude its opponents, and thus to survive. A weak regime confronting a strong opposition coalition may be overthrown and replaced by a revolutionary regime, likely then to exclude some of the old regime's coalition. A protracted crisis, especially a lengthy civil war, eventually increases the prospects for a negotiated settlement and regime transformation with new political and economic rules, redistributed benefits, and the inclusion into the political game of both former challengers and old-regime actors.

The settlement upon a new regime will derive from the resolution of forces among the various actors, and may, in turn, depend heavily upon the role of external actors. A single regime shift may not bring enough change to permit political stability. Military reformism (a transitional military regime), for instance, although intended to pacify a polity by including certain new actors and by enacting policy reforms, may fail to satisfy violent, ideologically antagonistic opponents. Despite establishing a new coalition, new rules, and new policies, a revolutionary regime may quickly attract direct or indirect external opposition. If important actors (internal or external) remain unsatisfied or unsuccessfully repressed, the new regime may be unstable. Protracted instability for a newly constituted regime, we believe, increases the likelihood of its failure and further regime shifts.

EXPLAINING REGIME CHANGE IN CENTRAL AMERICA

From the common elements of the theories examined above we offer the following propositions to account for regime change in Central America since the 1970s. We discuss two phases of regime change. In the first, the evolving world economic and geopolitical context interact with domestic forces in the 1970s. The interplay of domestic and external forces and their respective resources shaped the ultimate outcomes in electoral democracy. In the second phase, during the first decade of the 2000s, domestic actors in Nicaragua and

Honduras took advantage of shifts in external pressures to degrade democracy in Nicaragua and Honduras.

Phase I: 1970–1996

The Evolving US Viewpoint. The geopolitics of the Cold War set the context for Central American geopolitics in the 1970s. US policy focused on perceived threats of expanded Soviet and Cuban influence in the Western Hemisphere. The United States therefore regarded most of the region's political and economic reformists and opponents of Central America's US-friendly, anti-Communist, authoritarian regimes as unacceptable potential allies of Communist subversion. Civilian democracy, though an ideological preference of the United States, remained secondary to security concerns in this tense world environment. US policy makers viewed the promotion of civilian democracy as risky because it might encourage leftists.

Central America's authoritarian regimes thus usually enjoyed political, military, and economic support from the United States. US military personnel trained Latin American officers during the Cold War using special manuals that explicitly advocated the use of illegal detention, torture, and murder (state-sponsored terror) against a wide spectrum of groups opposed to pro-US regimes.[40] This behavior created a profound contradiction between the proclaimed values of the United States and the reality of its policy in the region. It also caused some Central Americans in the center and on the left to doubt the potential virtues of formal electoral "democracy" as practiced against a backdrop of state terror under pro-US regimes.

US views of the ideological geopolitics of Central America evolved from the 1970s through the early 2000s. In the latter half of the 1970s, Congress and the Carter administration came to view the inhumane, anti-Communist, authoritarian regimes of Nicaragua, Guatemala, and El Salvador as unacceptable. This policy change encouraged Central America's reformists and revolutionaries and briefly opened the international environment toward regime change. After the Sandinistas' victory in 1979, however, US human rights policy in Central America was "put on the back burner,"[41] and Washington once again encouraged Central American regimes to clamp down on "subversives." When that posture encountered congressional opposition in the first few years of the Reagan administration, US diplomats again began stressing democracy by insisting on formal elections in pro-US countries, albeit against a background of state terror. This policy continued under the first President Bush until the end of the Cold War in 1989. After that Washington's second-order preference for civilian democracy came to the fore, allowing US support for the peace process and the emergence of cleaner, more inclusive elections in El Salvador and Guatemala.

Evolving Central American Viewpoints. Prior to 1979 many leftists in Central America distrusted electoral "democracy" as practiced by the US-sponsored regimes that repressed them. However, from the time of their victory in 1979, many Sandinistas viewed electoral democracy as compatible with the economic/participatory democracy it sought to construct. The FSLN (Frente Sandinista de Liberación Nacional, or Sandinista National Liberation Front) also viewed electoral democracy as a stratagem to enhance their revolution's acceptability to the openly hostile United States and among their Central American neighbors. Thus in 1983 and 1984 they enacted a well-designed electoral system to replace their revolutionary government.

However it was that they initially envisioned their ideal post-victory government, the insurgents in El Salvador (by 1982) and Guatemala (by 1986) ultimately decided not to fight for all-out victory but for a negotiated settlement including demilitarization and civilian rule in which they could openly participate. Eventually, with the Cold War waning and the US opposition to negotiated settlements having ended, the armed forces of each nation—exhausted by the long civil wars—decided they could accept electoral rules of the game, with the leftists included, in exchange for peace and institutional survival.

Certain emergent capitalist sectors sympathetic to trade liberalization, involved in nontraditional exporting and linked to transnational capital, emerged to challenge traditional economic elites for control of private-sector organizations and rightist parties. These groups embraced electoral democracy as a key to peace, neoliberal economic reforms, and revitalized economies. Operating both through business-dominated organizations and political parties, and supported by powerful external actors like USAID and the IMF, these transnationally oriented groups eventually played major roles in negotiating peace and running transitional governments and post-settlement governments. They became powerful ruling-coalition members across the region, heavily involved in setting economic policy.

Other Actors' Views. European nations, other Latin American countries, and such international organizations as the United Nations and the Organization of American States once largely deferred to US influence in Central America. However, during the 1980s they became increasingly fearful that the isthmian civil wars and US intervention could escalate. These actors therefore embraced and promoted electoral democracy as the best mechanism to promote peace in Central America. The preference for formal democratization at first put Europe at odds with the strenuous US military and diplomatic efforts to contain Central American leftist movements. With the Cold War's waning, the shared concern of major industrial powers for a healthy global capitalist environment operating along neoliberal lines contributed to the emergence of the Washington consensus favoring formal democracy (and neoliberal economic policies).

The Catholic Church in the isthmus was influenced by liberation theology in the 1960s and 1970s, a phenomenon that encouraged social mobilization, which in some cases contributed to insurrection. By the 1980s, however, the institutional Church reined in liberation theology and emphasized formal democratization and improved human rights as means toward social justice. Catholic hierarchs on balance became more politically conservative. Some local variation in practice and policy remained, as indicated by performance differences among Church human rights offices in the region. With the main exception of Nicaragua in the 1970s, evangelical Protestants (growing rapidly in number since the 1960s) tended to either eschew politics or identify during elections with conservative and sometimes antidemocratic forces.

The 1970s Regimes. In the early 1970s only Costa Rica among the region's nations had a broadly inclusive, constitutional, civilian-led democratic regime. It had evolved from that country's 1948 civil war and 1948–1949 revolution.

The other four nations had military-dominated authoritarian regimes: Nicaragua's was a personalistic-military regime dominated by the Somoza clan, a narrow coalition of key business interests and parts of the two major parties. Guatemala and El Salvador had corporately run military-authoritarian regimes, allied with some business and large-scale agricultural interests and with the collaboration of weak political parties. Honduras had a military-authoritarian regime that incorporated one of the two strong traditional political parties and tolerated a strong but anti-Communist labor sector.

Causes of Regime Crises. A wave of economic problems afflicted all Central American countries in the late 1970s and early 1980s. Rapidly escalating oil prices and resultant inflation, the deterioration of the Central American Common Market (in the mid- and late 1970s), and natural or economic catastrophes (e.g., the 1972 Managua earthquake and 1978–1979 Common Market trade disruptions) greatly reduced real income and employment among working-class and some white-collar sectors.

The grievances caused by increasing inequalities, declining real income, economic/natural catastrophes, and the political dissatisfactions of would-be competing elites led in the mid- and late 1970s to various events: the development of opposition parties; the rapid growth of agrarian, labor, neighborhood, and community self-help organizations; and reformist demands upon the state and protests of public policy. Regime coalitions experienced defections, and the economic resources of all five regimes eroded.

Regime Responses to Crisis. In both the short and long term, Central American regimes responded very differently to unrest, mobilization, and demands for change. Where regimes responded to demands with ameliorative policies to ease poverty and permit the recovery of real wages, with political reform, and with low or modest levels of repression, protests failed to escalate further or subsided.

Costa Rica's regime did not shift. Honduras' military-authoritarian regime voluntarily returned nominal control to civilians, and the armed forces gradually reduced military tutelage of national politics. In contrast, regimes in Nicaragua, El Salvador, and Guatemala in the short run rejected ameliorative policies and, with US assistance, sharply escalated repression by public security forces. Waves of protest ensued, and oppositions stepped up organization and resource mobilization. In the longer run, the regimes that responded with violent repression and refusal to ameliorate the effects of economic crisis faced violent, broadly based insurrections. They struggled to mobilize their economic and political resources to resist the revolts, including seeking more aid from the United States. They also eventually made extensive policy changes in their struggles to manage, repress, divide, and isolate their violent challengers. Nicaragua under Somoza was the least flexible. Military-authoritarian regimes in El Salvador and Guatemala were overthrown from within by military reformers. The resulting military transitional regimes gradually adopted policy reforms and, unable to crush their armed opponents, eventually moved toward civilian transitional regimes.

Outcomes. The outcomes of Central America's regime crises depended upon the relative success of each regime in mobilizing and maintaining domestic and external material support and organization. Failure to placate or repress enough outside-the-regime actors eventually led to regime shifts.

In Nicaragua, Somoza lost direct US and regional support and vital economic resources, enabling the Sandinistas to oust him and establish the revolutionary regime. The Somoza wing of the old Liberal Party was discredited and Somoza's National Guard was defeated and disbanded. The Sandinistas formed a center-left coalition and governed by revolutionary rules for several years. Top FSLN leaders dominated the executive, and the Sandinista armed forces replaced all security forces. Center and right-wing political forces grew increasingly unhappy with the regime. The FSLN itself contained ideologically rigid, less-democratic "vanguardists," as well as more genuine and pragmatic democrats. Likely because the revolutionary regime found itself in the world-media spotlight and needed to retain as much international support as possible, the more democratic faction prevailed. Somocista Liberals and an increasing number of other disaffected economic and political elements formed various outside-the-regime forces, including the US-backed Contra rebels. The revolutionary regime's response to this challenge and the counterrevolutionary war included nearly continuous economic and political reform, including adopting democratic electoral rules, holding the 1984 election, and writing a new constitution. We consider the adoption of the constitution in early 1987 the beginning of civilian democratic rule in Nicaragua because it formalized the rules of the political game along traditional liberal-democratic lines, with a clear division of powers and checks on executive authority.[42]

In 1979, facing domestic turmoil and the Nicaraguan revolution next door, the Honduran military regime preemptively initiated transition to civilian democracy. The traditional Liberal and National parties dominated the civilian transitional regime. However, flush with massive political, economic, and military resources, earned by cooperating with US efforts to defeat the revolutionary left in Nicaragua and El Salvador, the armed forces retained great power and influence. This delayed transition to civilian democracy until after the military's power was eventually trimmed by further reforms in the mid-1990s. A 1979 coup d'état in El Salvador and another in Guatemala in 1982 instituted ostensibly transformation-oriented military regimes (although early on their reformist intentions appeared questionable). These governments at first repressed moderates and centrists who remained outside the regime coalitions, while also attempting to defeat leftist rebel coalitions. The failure of this strategy and pressure from the United States (a major resource supplier to the Salvadoran regime) led the transitional military regimes to complete the transfer of nominal power to civilian transitional governments. These transitional civilian regimes, although weak, governed with broader coalitions and liberalized rules. This tactic won over some of the political center in each country, deprived the rebel coalitions of important allies and resources, and contributed to the stagnation of both civil wars. The Central American Peace Accord of 1987 provided a mechanism for eventual negotiations between the parties to the stalemated conflicts. Military exhaustion, US exasperation with the Central American quagmires, the rise of new domestic transnational elites, and the Cold War's end moved all actors' positions. The United States, other outside actors, national militaries, the civilian reformist regimes, and the rebels all eventually embraced more inclusive civilian democracy and some economic reforms, position changes that helped settle both wars.

Phase II: 2000–2013

Evolving US Policy and Behavior. After the United States was attacked by al Qaeda in 2001, US policy swiftly veered toward enhancing national security and prosecuting two wars in the Middle East. This undermined President George W. Bush's wish to improve relations with Latin America and to reform immigration policy. US deportations of Central Americans with criminal records pushed populations of decultured members of US urban gangs into several countries in Central America. US promotion of democracy in Latin America stumbled in 2002 when the White House applauded the attempted (but unsuccessful) coup against constitutionally elected Venezuelan president Hugo Chávez. The United States also interfered in elections in Brazil, Bolivia, El Salvador, and Nicaragua by telling voters there that electing leftist candidates would be viewed negatively and could result in unspecified US sanctions.

Other Actors' Views. European powers joined the United States in the Iraq and Afghanistan wars and efforts to curtail terrorism, and thus provided less of a counterbalance for US policy in Central America during the 1980s. The Hugo Chávez–inspired rise of Latin American international cooperative organizations, combined with Venezuelan economic assistance, encouraged Central America's leftist and populist governments and provided them assistance that filled gaps in US aid.

Evolving Central American Viewpoints. The main change within the region in this phase involved key elites in Honduras and Nicaragua who demonstrated weak commitment to democratic rule, possibly responding to weakened US and European pressure on democracy's behalf and to a lull in US attention to the region. Moreover, Venezuela provided material support to partially offset US influence and support for left-populist leaders including Nicaragua's Daniel Ortega and Honduras' Manuel Zelaya.

Nicaragua's slide toward semi-democracy involved many steps in which elites demonstrated weak allegiance to democratic rules of the game. First came FSLN leader Daniel Ortega and former Liberal president Arnoldo Alemán, both legislative leaders, who forged a pact that degraded election quality and undermined smaller parties. Sandinistas on the Supreme Court later invalidated a constitutional provision against re-election of former officeholders, allowing Ortega and many FSLN mayors to return to office. Meanwhile the FSLN purged reformists and anti-Ortega elements, leaving the "Danielistas" dominant. An unresolved split among the multiple Liberal parties divided the electoral opposition to the FSLN. These actions permitted FSLN nominee Ortega to narrowly regain the presidency in the 2006 election. Irregularities marred the 2008 municipal election. The Liberals failed to unite by 2011, effectively collapsing, and President Ortega comfortably won a new term in 2011.

In Honduras, President Zelaya attempted to call a referendum on whether to amend the constitution, a move the courts blocked as unconstitutional and which legislative leaders of both major parties rejected. Opposing elites demonstrated their lack of commitment to democratic rules when the Honduran Congress and Supreme Court collaborated with the military to oust Zelaya from office and unconstitutionally exile him. The crisis dragged on for months as the de facto government and its elite backers resisted international mediation seeking to restore President Zelaya to power. The Obama administration stated its opposition to the coup and imposed sanctions upon the resulting de facto government. This may have encouraged the de facto government to hold regularly scheduled elections in late 2009.

The June 2009 Honduran coup and various less-than-democratic actions by Sandinista elites in Nicaragua demonstrate that, just as elites can embrace democracy because it is useful to them, they can also turn away from it if domestic or external constraints weaken.

DISCUSSION

What has regime change actually meant? Many observers have expressed doubts about the quality of the new regimes in Central America, deriding them as "democracy light" or "low-intensity democracy" to emphasize their shortcomings. Robinson uses the term *polyarchy* to describe these civilian electoral regimes that remain dominated by elites and unresponsive to the interests of mass publics despite the rupture with open authoritarianism.

We share many of these misgivings but nevertheless disagree that regime change toward or away from democracy means little for the ordinary citizen. The authors have seen much evidence that democracy, however flawed, makes life safer from state violence for Central Americans. Citizens express more support for their governments than they did in the 1980s (see Chapter 9). Evaluations by outside observers as summarized in Figure 2.1 show that trends in democracy levels have evolved since the early 1980s. The line for each country represents a composite democracy measure ranging from 0 (the lowest) to 10 (the highest possible score) in 1973–1974 to 2012–2013, measured at roughly decade intervals.[43] Starting at the highest possible level of democracy

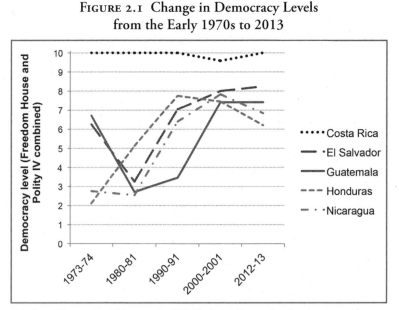

FIGURE 2.1 Change in Democracy Levels
from the Early 1970s to 2013

Freedom House, Freedom in the World, http://www.freedomhouse.org/report-types/freedom-world, accessed September 10, 2013; and Monty G. Marshall and Keith Jaggers, Polity IV Country Reports, http://systemicpeace.org/polity/polity06.htm, accessed September 10, 2013.

registered by the rating agencies in the early 1970s, Costa Rica's score changed only negligibly during the 40-year period. In contrast, real change stands out in the scores for the other four nations. Guatemala's and El Salvador's scores plunged during their civil wars during the 1980s. Honduras' democracy score rose quickly between 1973–1974 and 1990–1991 as the military passed power to elected civilian governments, then eroded between 2001 and 2013 (the graph misses the 2008–2009 coup period). Nicaragua's low scores of the Somoza regime and early revolutionary years improved sharply through 2001, later eroding by 2012–2013. All four moved from well in the nondemocratic range of the scale (below 5.0) to scores above 7.0, in the democratic range.

What about security and human rights? Figure 2.2 presents the Political Terror Scale, a measure ranging from one (very low violence and few human rights abuses) to five (generalized violence and severe human rights abuses). Levels of violence and repression rose sharply in Guatemala, El Salvador, and Honduras from the mid-1970s to 1980–1981 (Figure 2.2). The end of the civil wars in Guatemala and El Salvador brought political violence sharply down by 2000–2001. Political violence in Nicaragua, horrific in the late 1970s, declined gradually over the next three decades. In contrast, Costa Rica's score remained near 1.0, the lowest across the entire period. That four of five countries have violence and repression scores of 2.5 or higher in the early

**FIGURE 2.2 Evolution of Political Violence
and Repression over Time**

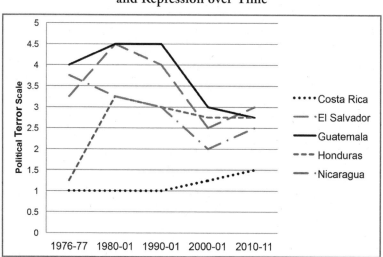

Gibney, M., Cornett L., Wood, R., and Haschke, P., *Political Terror Scale 1976–2012*. http://www.politicalterrorscale.org/, accessed October 31, 2013. (1 = very low…5 = very high; values are means for each period for the Political Terror Scale)

2000s and early 2010s testifies to the failure of their governments on several scores. They have not managed criminal behavior (gangs, narcotics trafficking) rooted in social pathologies (extreme poverty, gang members deported from the United States, homeless children in urban areas), and police have responded heavy-handedly to such crime and problem. Nevertheless, four of five Central American nations had much less political violence in 2010–2011 than they did in 1980–1981.

These dry statistics have real meaning for Central Americans. The repression scores and democracy indexes represent political murders and rights abuses by government. Improved democracy scores reflect enhanced freedom to exercise rights and liberties. Lower violence scores mean that fewer Central Americans are being murdered and repressed by their governments. Many flaws remain in these performances. Even Costa Rica could do better on civil liberties (Figure 2.1). The other four nations obviously have considerable room to improve. But regime change, even to civilian transitional rule or semi-democracy, left the glass of political freedom at least partway filled, if not to the brim. The glass may of course empty quickly, as the Honduran coup of 2009 vividly demonstrated, or more slowly, as in Nicaragua.

Since the 1970s, Central American polities have undergone dramatic transformations. Rapid, inequitable economic development drove mass mobilization and protest that shattered several seemingly stable, US-backed authoritarian regimes. These authoritarian breakdowns occurred variously through military-led transformation, violent insurrection, and revolutionary transition. From such disparate initial outcomes, however, a new and coherent pattern emerged in the late 1980s and 1990s—all of Central America's governments became civilian electoral democracies. That outcome brought measurable improvements in the freedom and political lives of citizens of at least three of the region's five countries, opportunities for further progress notwithstanding. Democratic regimes can also deteriorate into semi-democracy, as the Honduran and Nicaraguan cases demonstrate. Chapters 4 through 8 discuss these changes in detail by country.

RECOMMENDED READINGS AND RESOURCES

Anderson, Charles W. 1967. *Politics and Economic Change in Latin America: The Governing of Restless Nations*. New York: Van Nostrand Reinhold.

Booth, John A. 1998. *Costa Rica: Quest for Democracy*. Boulder, CO: Westview Press.

Chilcote, Ronald H., and Joel C. Edelstein. 1986. *Latin America: Capitalist and Socialist Perspectives of Development and Underdevelopment*. Boulder, CO: Westview Press.

Economic Commission for Latin America and the Caribbean (ECLAC). www.eclac.cl/default.asp?idioma=IN.

Ferranti, David E. 2004. *Inequality in Latin America: Breaking with History?* Washington, DC: International Bank for Reconstruction and Development/The World Bank.

Freedom House. 2004. *Freedom in the World 2004.* www.freedomhouse.org/research /freeworld/2004/table2004.pdf.

Gasiorowski, Mark J. 1995. "Economic Crisis and Regime Change: An Event History Analysis." *American Political Science Review* 89:882–897.

Gibney, Mark, Linda Cornett, and Reed Wood. 2009. *Political Terror Scale 1976– 2006.* www.politicalterrorscale.org/.

Haerpfer, Christian W., Patrick Bernhagen, Ronald F. Inglehart, and Christian Welzel. 2009. *Democratization.* Oxford: Oxford University Press.

Heston, Alan, Robert Summers, and Bettina Aten. 2006. *Penn World Table Version 6.2.* Philadelphia: Center for International Comparisons at the University of Pennsylvania.

Higley, John, and Michael Burton. 1989. "The Elite Variable in Democratic Transitions and Breakdowns." *American Sociological Review* 54 (1):17–32.

Linz, Juan J., and Alfred Stepan. 1978. *The Breakdown of Democratic Regimes.* Baltimore, MD: Johns Hopkins University Press.

Mason, T. David. 2004. *Caught in the Crossfire: Revolutions, Repression, and the Rational Peasant.* Lanham, MD: Rowman & Littlefield.

Moore, Barrington. 1966. *Social Origins of Dictatorship and Democracy.* Boston: Beacon Press.

O'Donnell, Guillermo. 1973. *Modernization and Bureaucratic Authoritarianism: Studies in South American Politics.* Los Angeles: University of California Press.

O'Donnell, Guillermo, Philippe C. Schmitter, and Laurence Whitehead. 1986. *Transitions from Authoritarian Rule.* Baltimore, MD: Johns Hopkins University Press.

Peeler, John. 1985. *Latin American Democracies.* Chapel Hill: University of North Carolina Press.

Polity IV Project: Political Regime Characteristics and Transitions, 1800–2007. www .systemicpeace.org/polity/polity4.htm.

Robinson, William I. 1996. *Promoting Polyarchy: Globalization, US Intervention, and Hegemony.* Cambridge: Cambridge University Press.

Sánchez-Ancochea, Diego, and Salvador Martí i Puig, eds. 2003. *Transnational Conflicts: Central America, Social Change and Globalization.* London: Verso.

———. 2013. *Handbook of Central American Governance.* London: Routledge.

Wiarda, Howard J. 1992. *Politics and Social Change in Latin America: Still a Distinct Tradition?* Boulder, CO: Westview Press.

Yashar, Deborah J. 1997. *Demanding Democracy: Reform and Reaction in Costa Rica and Guatemala, 1870s–1950s.* Stanford, CA: Stanford University Press.

NOTES

1. William I. Robinson discusses the forces and processes of regime change in *Transitional Conflicts: Central America, Social Change, and Globalization* (London: Verso, 2003), especially Ch. 1, and *Promoting Polyarchy: Globalization, US Intervention, and Hegemony* (Cambridge: Cambridge University Press, 1996).

2. Latin American GDP per capita drawn from the United Nations Economic Commission for Latin America and the Caribbean, Economic Indicators and Statistics, http://interwp.cepal.org/sisgen/ConsultaIntegrada.asp?idIndicador=2205 &idioma=i, accessed September 2, 2013.

3. US GDP per capita data from the World Bank, Data by Country, http://data .worldbank.org/indicator/NY.GDP.PCAP.CD, accessed September 2, 2013. Authors' calculations and comparisons drawn from this source and from note 2.

4. Matthew Hammill, "Growth Poverty and Inequality in Central America," Serie Subregional de la CEPAL en México, United Nations, Economic Commission for Latin America, Social Development Unit, Mexico, D.F., 2007.

5. For an extended overview of data on Central America's social welfare and inequality within the larger Latin American context, see David E. Ferranti et al., *Inequality in Latin America: Breaking with History? Advance Conference Edition* (Washington, DC: International Bank for Reconstruction and Development/The World Bank, October 2003).

6. Calculated by the authors based on United Nations Economic Commission for Latin America, http://websie.eclac.cl/sisgen/ConsultaIntegrada.asp?idAplicacion =1&idTema=1&idIndicador=1&idioma=i, accessed March 25, 2009.

7. Median-age data drawn from the Central Intelligence Agency's country reports in the *World Factbook*, https://www.cia.gov/library/publications/the-world-factbook /geos/us.html, accessed September 12, 2013.

8. Wallace W. Atwood and Helen Goss Thomas, *The Americas* (Boston: Ginn and Co., 1929), p. 45.

9. For an overview, see, for instance, Ronald H. Chilcote and Joel C. Edelstein, *Latin America: Capitalist and Socialist Perspectives of Development and Underdevelopment* (Boulder, CO: Westview Press, 1986).

10. For evidence see the Appendix, Table A.5. The exception to this came during the Nicaraguan revolution in the 1980s, during parts of which state spending exceeded half of GDP. Because of the Contra war, however, the revolutionary government dropped many social programs in order to finance defense spending.

11. The 1998 data are drawn from Table 2.2, fifth edition of our *Understanding Central America*.

12. Robinson, *Transitional Conflicts*, pp. 50–53.

13. This concept of political regimes draws upon Charles W. Anderson, "The Latin American Political System," in Charles W. Anderson, *Politics and Economic Change in Latin America: The Governing of Restless Nations* (New York: Van Nostrand Reinhold,

1967). It also owes something to the conceptualization of John Higley and Michael Burton, "The Elite Variable in Democratic Transitions and Breakdowns," *American Sociological Review* 54, No. 1 (1989), pp. 17–32; and to Gary Wynia's use of the term *political game,* in his *Politics of Latin American Development* (Cambridge: Cambridge University Press, 1990), pp. 24–45.

14. Peter H. Smith, *Democracy in Latin America: Political Change in Comparative Perspective* (Oxford: Oxford University Press, 2005), pp. 10–11.

15. Note that any such categorization of regimes is somewhat arbitrary, but we undertake the effort in Table 2.3 to illustrate the extent and the high number of regime changes in Central America. The authors discussed and to some extent disagreed about labeling the regime types and dates of change, especially for Nicaragua, without straying from the regime-change criterion (new rules and new coalition) laid out above.

16. Smith, *Democracy in Latin America*, p. 11.

17. Barrington Moore, *Social Origins of Dictatorship and Democracy* (Boston: Beacon Press, 1966).

18. Guillermo O'Donnell, *Modernization and Bureaucratic Authoritarianism: Studies in South American Politics* (Los Angeles: University of California Press, 1973).

19. Guillermo O'Donnell, Philippe C. Schmitter, and Laurence Whitehead, eds., *Transitions from Authoritarian Rule* (Baltimore, MD: Johns Hopkins University Press, 1986).

20. Mark J. Gasiorowski, "Economic Crisis and Regime Change: An Event History Analysis," *American Political Science Review* 89 (1995), pp. 882–897; Mark J. Gasiorowski, "An Overview of the Political Regime Dataset," *Comparative Political Studies* 21 (1996), pp. 469–483.

21. Dietrich Rueschemeyer, Evelyne Huber Stephens, and John D. Stephens, *Capitalist Development and Democracy* (Chicago: University of Chicago Press, 1992).

22. Carles Boix, *Democracy and Redistribution* (Cambridge: Cambridge University Press, 2003).

23. Charles W. Anderson, "Toward a Theory of Latin American Politics," in Howard J. Wiarda, ed., *Politics and Social Change in Latin America: Still a Distinct Tradition?* (Boulder, CO: Westview Press, 1992), pp. 239–254.

24. See John Peeler, *Latin American Democracies* (Chapel Hill: University of North Carolina Press, 1985); Deborah J. Yashar, *Demanding Democracy: Reform and Reaction in Costa Rica and Guatemala, 1870s–1950s* (Stanford, CA: Stanford University Press, 1997); John A. Booth, *Costa Rica: Quest for Democracy* (Boulder, CO: Westview Press, 1998); Iván Molina Jiménez, *Demoperfectocracia: La democracia pre-reformada en Costa Rica (1885–1948)* (Heredia, Costa Rica: Editorial Universidad Nacional, 2005), Ch. 8–10; and John A. Booth, "Democratic Development in Costa Rica," *Democratization* 15, No. 4 (August 2008), pp. 714–732.

25. For an excellent integrated overview of why and how revolutions occur, see T. David Mason, *Caught in the Crossfire: Revolutions, Repression, and the Rational Peasant*

(Lanham, MD: Rowman & Littlefield, 2004). See also John A. Booth and Thomas W. Walker, *Understanding Central America*, 2nd ed. (Boulder, CO: Westview Press, 1993), Ch. 5.

26. Louis Kriesberg, *Social Conflicts*, 2nd ed. (Englewood Cliffs, NJ: Prentice-Hall, 1982), p. 29.

27. John Walton, *Reluctant Rebels: Comparative Studies in Revolution and Underdevelopment* (New York: Columbia University Press, 1984), p. 13.

28. Ibid. See also Theda Skocpol, *States and Social Revolutions* (Cambridge: Cambridge University Press, 1979); Mancur Olson, "Rapid Growth as a Destabilizing Force," *Journal of Economic History* 23, No. 4 (1963), pp. 529–552; and Jeffrey M. Paige, *Agrarian Revolution: Social Movements and Export Agriculture in the Underdeveloped World* (New York: Free Press, 1975). For specific applications to Central America, see Charles Brockett, *Land, Power, and Poverty: Agrarian Transformation and Political Conflict in Central America* (Boston: Unwin Hyman, 1988); Timothy P. Wickham-Crowley, *Guerrillas and Revolution in Latin America* (Princeton, NJ: Princeton University Press, 1992); Robert Williams, *Export Agriculture and the Crisis in Central America* (Chapel Hill: University of North Carolina Press, 1986); John A. Booth, "Socioeconomic and Political Roots of National Revolts in Central America," *Latin American Research Review* 26, No. 1 (1991), pp. 33–73; Edelberto Torres Rivas, *Crisis del poder in Centroamérica* (San José, Costa Rica: Editorial Universitaria Centroamericana, 1981); and Mason, *Caught in the Crossfire*.

29. Kriesberg, *Social Conflicts*, pp. 66–106; Charles Tilly, *From Mobilization to Revolution* (Reading, MA: Addison-Wesley, 1978); Rod Aya, "Theories of Revolution Reconsidered: Contrasting Models of Collective Violence," *Theory and Society* 8 (June–December 1979), pp. 39–100; Mason, *Caught in the Crossfire*.

30. Jack A. Goldstone, "An Analytical Framework," in Jack A. Goldstone, Ted Robert Gurr, and Farrokh Moshiri, eds., *Revolutions of the Late Twentieth Century* (Boulder, CO: Westview Press, 1991), pp. 37–51; Ted Robert Gurr, *Why Men Rebel* (Princeton, NJ: Princeton University Press, 1970); Walton, *Reluctant Rebels*; Skocpol, *States and Social Revolutions*.

31. Goldstone, "An Analytical Framework"; James DeFronzo, *Revolutions and Revolutionary Movements* (Boulder, CO: Westview Press, 1991), pp. 7–25; Robinson, *Promoting Polyarchy* and *Transitional Conflicts*.

32. Wickham-Crowley, *Guerrillas and Revolution*.

33. Ronald Inglehart, "The Renaissance of Political Culture," *American Political Science Review* 82 (November 1988), pp. 1203–1230; Mitchell A. Seligson and John A. Booth, "Political Culture and Regime Type: Evidence from Nicaragua and Costa Rica," *Journal of Politics* 55 (August 1993), pp. 777–792; Edward N. Muller and Mitchell A. Seligson, "Civic Culture and Democracy: The Question of Causal Relationships," *American Political Science Review* 88 (September 1994), pp. 645–652; Larry Diamond, "Introduction: Political Culture and Democracy," and "Causes and

Effects," both in Larry Diamond, ed., *Political Culture and Democracy in Developing Countries* (Boulder, CO: Lynne Rienner Publishers, 1994).

34. Dankwart Rustow, "Transitions to Democracy: Toward a Dynamic Model," *Comparative Politics* 2 (April 1970), pp. 337–363; Adam Przeworski, "Some Problems in the Study of the Transition to Democracy," in O'Donnell, Schmitter, and Whitehead, eds., *Transitions from Authoritarian Rule*; Samuel P. Huntington, *The Third Wave: Democratization in the Late Twentieth Century* (Norman: University of Oklahoma Press, 1991); Mitchell A. Seligson and John A. Booth, eds., *Elections and Democracy in Central America, Revisited* (Chapel Hill: University of North Carolina Press, 1995).

35. Seymour Martin Lipset, "Social Requisites of Democracy: Economic Development and Political Legitimacy," *American Political Science Review* 53 (March 1959), pp. 69–105; Tatu Vanhanen, *The Process of Democratization* (New York: Crane Russak, 1990); Rueschemeyer et al., *Capitalist Development and Democracy*; Robert D. Putnam, "Bowling Alone: America's Declining Social Capital," *Journal of Democracy* 7 (Summer 1996), pp. 38–52; Boix, *Democracy and Redistribution*; and Robert D. Putnam, *Making Democracy Work: Civic Traditions in Modern Italy* (Princeton, NJ: Princeton University Press, 1993).

36. Laurence Whitehead, "The Imposition of Democracy," in Abraham F. Lowenthal, ed., *Exporting Democracy: The United States and Latin America* (Baltimore, MD: Johns Hopkins University Press, 1991).

37. Peeler, *Latin American Democracies*; Larry Diamond, "Introduction: Politics, Society, and Democracy in Latin America," in Larry Diamond, Juan Linz, and Seymour Martin Lipset, *Democracy in Developing Countries,* Volume 4: *Latin America* (Boulder, CO: Lynne Rienner Publishers, 1989); John Higley and Richard Gunther, eds., *Elites and Democratic Consolidation in Latin America and Southern Europe* (Cambridge: Cambridge University Press, 1992); and Huntington, *The Third Wave*.

38. Robinson, *Promoting Polyarchy and Transitional Conflicts*. Robinson's interpretation is similar to Boix's explanation but is richer because it examines the dimension of international capital's influence on domestic economic elites.

39. For example, Lowenthal, ed., *Exporting Democracy*; Thomas Carothers, *In the Name of Democracy: US Policy Toward Latin America in the Reagan Years* (Berkeley: University of California Press, 1991); Huntington, *The Third Wave*; Dario Moreno, "Respectable Intervention: The United States and Central American Elections," in Seligson and Booth, eds., *Elections and Democracy in Central America, Revisited*; Thomas W. Walker, "Introduction: Historical Setting and Important Issues," in Thomas W. Walker, ed., *Nicaragua without Illusions: Regime Transition and Structural Adjustment in the 1990s* (Wilmington, DE: Scholarly Resources, 1997); Gary Prevost and Harry E. Vanden, eds., *The Undermining of the Sandinista Revolution* (New York: St. Martin's, 1997); Wickham-Crowley, *Guerrillas and Revolution*; and DeFronzo, *Revolutions and Revolutionary Movements*.

40. Seven training manuals used between 1982 and 1991 were disclosed by the Department of Defense. See US Department of Defense, "Fact Sheet Concerning Training Manuals Containing Materials Inconsistent with US Policy" (Washington, DC: September 1996). See also Dana Priest, "US Instructed Latins on Execution, Torture—Manuals Used 1982–1991, Pentagon Reveals," *Washington Post*, September 21, 1996, pp. A1, A9; Lisa Haugaard, "How the US Trained Latin America's Military: The Smoking Gun," *Envio* 16, No. 165 (October 1997), pp. 33–38.

41. The words of a State Department official who appeared with coauthor Walker on a panel on Central America at California State University, Los Angeles, on April 20, 1979.

42. The Contra war and conflict with the United States would continue during the first three years of the new civilian democratic regime and three remaining years of Daniel Ortega's first presidential term, at that time obscuring the profound import of these changes. The 1987 Central American Peace Accord eventually facilitated a negotiated end to the war. In the 1990 election Nicaragua's voters, disillusioned by a collapsing economy and the Contra war, replaced the FSLN administration with the opposition.

43. The measure in Figure 2.1 combines both parts of the Freedom House one-to-seven scale (1 = high levels, 7 = low levels of rights and liberties) into a single scale and reverses its polarity. It also takes the twenty-one-point Polity IV scale (-10 = most authoritarian, 10 = most democratic). Each is mathematically standardized into a scale ranging from 0 (least democratic) to 10 (most democratic) and the two are averaged to provide the measure used here. Measures drawn from Freedom House, Freedom in the World, http://www.freedomhouse.org/report-types/freedom-world, accessed September 10, 2013; and Monty G. Marshall and Keith Jaggers, Polity IV Country Reports, http://systemicpeace.org/polity/polity06.htm, accessed September 10, 2013. Freedom House (FH) scores on political rights and liberties, Polity IV scores on authoritarianism-democracy, and the Political Terror Scale data cited below provide useful comparative measures. However, they must be viewed with some caution because they are compiled by evaluators who attempt systematically to glean evidence over time from press coverage of incidents of political violence (PTS) or political rights and liberties (FH). Accordingly, they reflect the biases and fluctuating intensity of coverage of the US newspapers from which they are drawn and their manipulation by US foreign-policy makers. Such bias appears in 1980s Freedom House scores for relatively rights-respectful ("enemy") Nicaragua, which are practically as poor as those for massively rights-abusive ("friends") El Salvador and Guatemala in the same period. That said, we still find these indexes useful in illustrating change over time within individual countries, especially El Salvador, Guatemala, and Honduras. In those instances they help us to draw reasonably valid inferences about evolving liberties and levels of political violence.

3

THE COMMON HISTORY

ONE TRUTH ABOUT CENTRAL AMERICA IS THAT, ALTHOUGH MANY similarities exist among the five countries, there are also significant differences. Both similarities and differences arose largely from the early history of the region as it experienced conquest, the colonial period, independence, union with Mexico, and fifteen years of common political identity as part of the United Provinces of Central America.[1] The five also share similar positions in the global economy and political system that have constrained them in similar ways.

CONQUEST TO 1838

Spanish conquest profoundly affected the nature of Central America's present-day societies. Spain conquered the territories that are today Nicaragua, Honduras, El Salvador, and Guatemala in the two decades following the first Spanish penetration in 1522. Spain imposed its rule upon those indigenous peoples lucky enough to survive the tremendous depopulation of the region caused by enslavement and exposure to Old World diseases. Costa Rica's experience soon set it apart from the other four countries. Spaniards did not settle there until the 1560s because, unlike the other areas, it offered no easily exploitable resources in either gold or native slaves. Indeed, the hostile indigenous inhabitants resisted European encroachment. In the end, the Spanish neither pacified nor conquered Costa Rica's original inhabitants, but either exterminated them or pushed them into remote areas. Thus the population of the Central Valley of Costa Rica became heavily Iberian, and a racially distinct and exploited underclass never developed.

In the rest of Central America, however, the Spaniards imposed their dominion despite active and passive resistance by the native people. Although this period meant annihilation for many, some original populations survived. When the Spaniards came they encountered millions of indigenous people in what are today the four northernmost countries of Central America. By co-opting and controlling native *caciques* (chiefs), the bearded foreigners proved adept at extracting local riches in the form of gold and native slaves. In addition, the conquistadores unwittingly brought several diseases to which Old World populations had become partially immune or resistant. Lacking such natural immunity, though, the native people perished in large numbers.

In western Nicaragua alone, a population of over 1 million declined to a few tens of thousands by the end of the conquest. It is unlikely that the Spaniards killed very many natives outright. Rather, careful historical research indicates that the Spanish exported as many as half a million indigenous Nicaraguans to Panama and Peru as slaves. Most subsequently died either in passage or in slavery within a year or two thereafter. Much of the rest of the populace succumbed to disease.[2] Only in Guatemala did large numbers of indigenous peoples survive, perhaps partly because the conquistadores found it harder to completely subjugate the relatively more advanced societies they encountered there. Perhaps, too, the cooler climates of the mountainous parts of Guatemala presented a less congenial environment for the spread of disease.

The drastic reduction in the native population was not the only change wrought by the conquest in northern Central America. Prior to the conquest, labor-intensive agriculture typified this area. The common people grew corn, beans, peppers, and squash on land consigned to them by their caciques. Although obliged to turn over part of the crop to the chief as tribute, the rest they controlled for home consumption, barter, or sale in local markets. By the end of the conquest, depopulation had converted most of the indigenous farmlands back to jungle. The economy then became externally oriented. Spaniards controlled the region's human and natural resources to produce articles for trade among the colonies and with Spain. The remaining indigenous population (still outnumbering their white masters) supplied the labor that produced the gold, silver, timber, and cattle products (hides, tallow, and dried beef) for export. Most of the wealth that this economy produced went to the white elite. The culture and process of dependent underdevelopment had begun.

Many aspects of culture changed practically overnight as the conquistadores sought to impose their religion, language, and ways on the conquered. Of course, nowhere was native culture completely obliterated. In Guatemala, where hispanicization was least effective, the indigenous peoples retained their languages and hid many aspects of their old religion under a patina of Catholicism. Even in El Salvador, Honduras, Nicaragua, and Costa Rica, where the native populations were the most decimated, some indigenous traits remained. For instance, to this day, everywhere in the region, corn and beans (native staples) constitute the heart of local cuisine. Moreover, many indigenous place names remain, as do the names of hundreds of common objects, from peppers and turkeys to grindstones. Yet, by and large, Central America was hispanicized. Spanish became the lingua franca except in rural Guatemala and certain remote regions elsewhere. A mystical, elite-supporting, pre-Reformation version of Catholicism became the nearly universal religion. Even the cities, often built on or next to the sites of pre-Columbian centers, eventually took on Spanish characteristics, with the typical Iberian arrangement of plazas, cathedrals, and public buildings.

The conquest established new class patterns. The larger pre-Columbian societies of Central America had been ordered hierarchically, with chiefs and associated elites dominating the masses. That may have facilitated the Spaniards superimposing themselves on the system. But what changed most after the conquest was a new racial configuration of class. With the exception of Costa Rica, what emerged was a highly unequal, two-class society, with people of Spanish birth or descent constituting the ruling upper class and everyone else composing a downtrodden lower class. Within the lower class, there eventually evolved a subsystem of stratification as the biological union between Spaniards and native women produced mestizos, who, never considered equals by the Spaniards, nonetheless held higher social status than persons of pure indigenous origin.

From the late sixteenth century to 1821, the Viceroyalty of New Spain (Mexico) nominally ruled over the Kingdom of Guatemala, which included the territory of today's five modern countries of Central America (plus Chiapas in present-day Mexico). In fact, however, the viceroyalty exercised little control over the kingdom, which in practice was administered directly by Spain. In turn, the nominal capital, Guatemala, only loosely controlled the other provinces of Central America. Underpopulated, geographically isolated, and economically insignificant, the tiny Costa Rican colony became a neglected backwater and began its distinctive evolution. Elsewhere, resentment grew between the provinces and the central administration in Guatemala as the newly emerging system of dependency inevitably brought the greatest development to that administrative center. Even within individual provinces, such as Nicaragua, regional differences and rivalries developed and festered. Therefore, while Central Americans shared a common experience, seeds of division germinated.

Besides these political factors, other important economic and social patterns that emerged during the conquest persisted into the colonial era. Costa Rica's relative isolation led to a more self-contained economy. A persistent labor shortage, relatively equal land distribution, access to unclaimed crown lands for poor farmers, and the lack of an easily exploitable indigenous population produced a large class of free farmers unused to subjugation by the colony's leading families. Though such factors can easily be overvalued, they appear to have contributed to Costa Rica's development into a fairly successful liberal, democratic political system by the mid-twentieth century—decades before its neighbors.

In contrast, in the rest of Central America, an externally oriented, elite-controlled, dependent pattern of economic activity became more entrenched. The Spanish first exploited the region's human and material resources to produce cacao, silver, gold, timber, and cattle products for export. Later, export production expanded to include indigo and cochineal for the blue and red dyes, respectively, needed by a growing European textile industry. As in present-day Central America, fluctuations in external demand produced periods of boom and bust in the local dependent economies. New groups joined the population. The colonies imported black slaves to replace some of the labor supply lost with the decimated indigenous population, and later there arose mulatto offspring of white–black unions. The social and economic gap between the European and *criollo*[3] elite and the non-European majority remained wide. With the premium placed on export and maximizing profits for the elites, the masses were generally allowed to consume only at a subsistence level. It is small wonder that the four republics of northern Central America are typified to this day by wide social and economic disparities generated by centuries of control by socially irresponsible economic elites.

Central America passed from colonial rule to formal independence with almost no violence. When Mexico broke from Spain in mid-1821, Central America also declared its independence. In January 1822, it joined the Mexican empire of Agustín de Iturbide. El Salvador resisted union with Mexico but was incorporated by force of arms. However, by mid-1823, soon after the abdication of Agustín the First, Central America declared its independence from Mexico. Only the former Central American province of Chiapas chose to remain a part of the larger country to the north. From then until 1838, the isthmus was fused—legally, at least—into a federation called the United Provinces of Central America, or the Central American Republic.

At first Central Americans felt enthusiasm about this union. The idea made good sense. Clearly, a federated republic could be stronger politically and economically than five tiny independent nations. Yet from the start, several factors undermined the success of the United Provinces. First was the outlying provinces' long history of resentment of Guatemala. This grew when Guatemala, the largest province, received 18 of the 41 seats in the Congress (by proportional representation) and therefore dominated policy making. Second, although the constitution of 1824 declared the states to be "free and independent" in their internal affairs, it also contained nationalist and centrist features that undermined the provinces' autonomy. Finally, rivalry between emerging Liberal and Conservative factions of the ruling elite generated conflict within each province and across provincial boundaries. Meddling in their neighbors' affairs became commonplace among Central American leaders. These problems saddled the union with constant tension and recurrent civil war. The experiment finally collapsed in 1838, as first Nicaragua and later the other countries split from the federation. Despite reunification efforts later in the nineteenth century, the bitterness and rivalries that destroyed the United Provinces in the first place also blocked its resurrection.

1838 TO THE PRESENT

Continuing hardship for most of the region's people has prevailed since the disintegration of the federation. The patterns of dependency and elite rule that took firm root in each of the republics except Costa Rica during the colonial period continued through the nineteenth century and into the twentieth century. Costa Rica, too, eventually developed debilitating external economic dependencies as it integrated into the world economy in the nineteenth century. Overall, despite bringing occasional surges of development, dependency and elite rule seldom benefited the majority of Central Americans.

After independence, Central America's tiny, privileged elites—those who had inherited economic power and social standing—continued to use their control of government to repress popular demands. They perpetuated for their own benefit an essentially unregulated, externally oriented, "liberal" economic system. Except in Costa Rica, the continued existence of Liberal–Conservative factionalism, relatively large indigenous communities to supply forced labor, and the emergent hacienda system all helped strengthen the military's political role. Armies (at first belonging to individual strongmen, or *caudillos*) fought civil wars, subdued peasants who had been forcibly deprived of their land, and implemented forced-labor laws against these new "vagrants." This heavy military involvement in national life retarded the development of civil political institutions and spawned both military rule and political violence. Central American nations spent most of the period from 1838 until 1945 under civilian or military dictatorships. Even Costa Rica showed little democratic promise. Although less turbulent than its neighbors, it experienced elite rule, militarism, dictatorship, and political instability into the mid-twentieth century.

Politics

In the nineteenth century, the basic conflict among elites was between Conservatives and Liberals. Before independence and in the first decades afterward, the Conservatives advocated authoritarian, centralized government (sometimes even monarchy), greater economic regulation, and a continuation of special privileges for the Catholic Church. Liberals espoused limited representative democracy, decentralized government, free trade, reduced economic regulation, and separation of church and state. Conservatives tended to come from more traditional large-scale landholders who had benefited from crown licenses and export monopolies. Liberals tended to include both disgruntled large landowners who lacked crown licenses to export their crops and urban elites concerned with commerce.

One important difference was that whereas Conservatives generally remained wedded to more traditional economic practices, the Liberals—who by the late nineteenth century had come to dominate all the Central American nations—advocated "modernization" within an externally oriented, laissez faire economic framework. Specifically, Liberals championed new export products—such as coffee and bananas—and development of government institutions and material infrastructure (highways, railroads, and ports) to facilitate growth in the export economy. Liberals also worked to reduce the role of the Catholic Church in some countries. To promote exports, the Liberals enacted legislation that stripped most indigenous communities of lands once reserved for them by the Spanish crown. Despite such early contrasts and after considerable warfare between the two factions, by the late nineteenth century, ideological and policy differences between Liberals and Conservatives largely vanished. Liberals, when in power, ruled as authoritarians and eventually reached accommodations with the Church, thus eliminating a long-standing difference between the parties. Conservatives eventually supported laissez faire economics and expanded coffee production.

The Liberals and Conservatives degenerated over time into ideologically indistinguishable clan-based political factions. Conservatives generally ruled in the mid-nineteenth century, but Liberal regimes eventually supplanted them. Liberal hegemony in Central America thereafter lasted well into the twentieth century. As it died, it spawned an extreme right-wing form of militarism that plagued Guatemala, El Salvador, and Honduras until the 1990s.

One should not confuse the Central American meaning of *Liberal* with the vernacular meaning of that word in the United States. Central American Liberals were exponents of classical liberal economic policies (capitalism) and republican government. They held elitist attitudes, advocated essentially unregulated free enterprise, and generally believed the precept that "that government is best which governs least." Indeed, in the US political system today, modern conservatives would likely find themselves very much at home with the economic policies of nineteenth-century Central American Liberals. The modernization that liberalism brought tended to accelerate the concentration of wealth and income in the hands of the elite and to increase the external dependency of local economies.

Eventually, however, Central American liberalism drew fire from more popularly oriented political movements motivated by the Great Depression and World War II's economic dislocations. In Costa Rica, challenges to Liberal dominance and political reforms began in the late nineteenth century, and a labor movement developed early in the twentieth. In the mid-1940s, the government of Rafael Calderón Guardia allied with Communist-dominated labor unions and the Catholic Church to curtail liberalism with labor and social security legislation. In 1948 and 1949, a social-democratic revolution went even further by retaining Calderón's reforms, abolishing the army, and giving the state important economic regulation and planning roles. In El Salvador during the 1930s, local Liberals responded to depression-driven labor and peasant discontent by ruling through the military. An abortive labor and leftist uprising in 1932 gave the army and landowners a pretext to massacre 30,000 peasants. The military controlled the presidency for the next five decades, and by the 1970s sometimes acted independently on economic policy and ignored the wishes of its former Liberal masters.

In Guatemala in 1944, social democrats overthrew a "modernizing" dictator, Jorge Ubico, and began a mild democratic revolution that accommodated indigenous groups and organized labor. A successful CIA-sponsored counterrevolution took place in 1954, and soon the military took power and ruled the country into the 1980s. In Nicaragua, US armed intervention favored Conservatives between 1909 and 1927. The United States then switched sides and helped put the Liberals back in power, which led to the establishment of the Somoza family dictatorship. The Somozas ruled Nicaragua from 1936 until a mass-based insurrection brought the social-revolutionary Sandinista National Liberation Front (Frente Sandinista de Liberación Nacional, FSLN) to power in 1979. Many Nicaraguan Liberals exiled themselves in the United States and waited for the Sandinista revolution to end in 1990 before returning to national politics. In traditional Honduras, Liberals and Conservatives (the National Party) alternately held formal office under the watchful eye of the military from the 1980s into the 1990s. It was only in the mid-1990s that Honduras' civilian leaders came to effective power.

Interestingly, the "neoliberalism" that would come to dominate the region in the late twentieth and early twenty-first centuries would, in many ways, recall the crude liberalism prevalent at the turn of and into the twentieth century.

Like its forerunner, neoliberalism promoted free trade, largely unregulated capitalism, and a role for government limited mainly to "housekeeping" activities and promotion of trade. And, like nineteenth-century liberalism, it tended to accentuate inequitable distribution of income and property even as it achieved sometimes impressive economic growth.

External Involvement

International pressures battered Central America after 1850 as great powers pursued economic, political, and security interests there. Britain carved British Honduras from the Guatemalan territory and the Miskito Protectorate from Nicaragua, to promote and protect British mining, timber, and geopolitical interests. British influence was greatest during the first half of the nineteenth century, but thereafter US influence increasingly supplanted the British. Foreign intervention exacerbated the Central American nations' established penchant for interfering in each other's affairs and led to international disputes within the region and overt and covert military and political intervention by outsiders. Tennessean William Walker undertook the most flagrant (but not the only) intervention into Nicaragua. Contracted by business partners of Cornelius Vanderbilt to hijack Vanderbilt's transit route across the isthmus, Walker brought mercenaries to Nicaragua in 1855 in an unofficial military expedition, or filibuster. In league with out-of-power Liberals, he formed an army and toppled the Conservative government. The United States quickly recognized the fledgling Liberal government of Walker, who announced his intention to reinstitute slavery, make English the official language, and seek US statehood.

Conservative governments in the other four Central American nations agreed to send troops to oust Walker. War ensued in 1856, with Conservative forces partly financed by the British and by Vanderbilt. Walker capitulated in 1857 and fled Nicaragua under US protection. He attempted another filibuster in 1859, bound once again for Nicaragua, but was captured by the British after occupying the Honduran town of Trujillo. They handed Walker over to the Hondurans, who executed him. This 1856–1857 National War against Walker's takeover of Nicaragua briefly rekindled interest in reunifying Central America, reinforced Conservative political hegemony in Nicaragua for decades, and contributed to anti-US nationalism among Central Americans.[4]

By 1900 the dominant outside power in the isthmus, the United States, energetically promoted its economic and security interests. US diplomats served US banks by peddling loans to the region's governments. US customs agents seized Central American customs houses to repay the loans, and US marines intervened in domestic politics in Honduras, Nicaragua, and Panama. Transit across the narrow isthmus via a ship canal especially motivated Washington. When President Theodore Roosevelt could not win agreement from either Colombia or Nicaragua for a proposed canal lease agreement, he sent US troops in 1903 to ensure that local and foreign insurgents could "liberate" Colombia's province of Panama. This intervention secured for the United States the right to build a canal through what then became the Republic of Panama. When Nicaragua's president José Santos Zelaya contemplated a canal deal with Germany in 1909, the United States helped foment a Conservative rebellion against him and landed US troops to back it up. Zelaya resigned, and the new government gave the United States a treaty for canal rights that effectively guaranteed that Nicaragua would never have a canal. US marines returned to Nicaragua in 1912 and remained there most of the period until 1933.

The United States under Franklin Roosevelt flirted with good-neighborliness toward Central America during the 1930s. During World War II, security interests led to heavy US assistance to train and modernize Central America's armies. During the Cold War that developed after 1945, the United States emphasized containment of Communism by backing anti-Communist regimes. It enlisted other Central American governments to help oust the reformist civilian government of Guatemala in 1954 and to reinforce the Somoza regime after Managua's catastrophic earthquake of 1972.

The Cuban revolution in 1959 reinforced the US tendency to concentrate its Central American policy upon containment of Communism. US economic and military assistance strengthened the region's armies, pursued counterinsurgency against leftist rebels, promoted regional economic integration and development, worked to divide organized labor, and undermined political reformers of the left and center. The Carter administration's novel emphasis on human rights (1977 to 1979) led to aid cutoffs for abusive military governments in Guatemala and El Salvador and to reduced US support for Nicaragua's Somoza regime.

When the FSLN led a popular rebellion that toppled Anastasio Somoza Debayle from power in 1979, however, US policy in Central America shifted sharply back toward the thirty-year tradition of containment. Washington lifted its military aid ban for El Salvador and involved itself deeply in trying to block the growing rebellion there. The US tactic of allying openly with military despots was modified under the Reagan and subsequent administrations, which found it useful, in dealing with a very reluctant Congress, to appear to promote electoral democracy as the best model for the isthmus. The United States policy had two prongs: It encouraged elections and nominal transition to civilian rule. It also promoted and financed a large counterrevolutionary force to fight Nicaragua's Sandinista government; devoted massive economic, military, and political aid to bolster nominally civilian governments (under military tutelage) in El Salvador and Honduras; and invaded Panama to overthrow its military government in 1989. Even after the Cold War ended in 1989, the Sandinistas lost power, and the Salvadoran and

Guatemalan insurgents signed peace accords, the United States still remained unable to transcend habitual Cold War attitudes in Central America.[5] US diplomats repeatedly interfered in Central American elections to discourage voting for leftist parties. The practice continued into the 2000s.

Economic and Social Change

In the economic arena, Central America has specialized in exporting agricultural commodities since 1838. After 1850 coffee gradually became a major export throughout the region (except Honduras). During the twentieth century, other commodity export production developed (bananas, cacao, cotton, sugar, and beef), and like coffee, each of these products was subject to great world market price swings. Cyclical recessions and depressions in the international economy hit Central America hard. Industrialization was slow, the extreme inequalities in the class systems intensified, and dependency upon imported food and manufactures grew.

Coffee production wrought major socioeconomic changes in the late nineteenth century. It concentrated landownership in the hands of major coffee growers, millers, and exporters; in several countries these constituted new national economic elites who advanced their interests by controlling (or sharing control of) the state.[6] Other export crops had regional importance with similar effects on the distribution of wealth and political power.

The agro-export elites eventually had to enlist the national armed forces to suppress popular discontent. Together they opposed socioeconomic reform so tenaciously that their rule has been labeled "reactionary despotism."[7] Writing about the 1970s and 1980s, Baloyra described the reactionary coalitions of Central America as

> bent on the preservation of privilege [and their] monopoly of public roles and of the entrepreneurial function. . . . The dominant actors of the reactionary coalitions of Central America do not believe in suffrage, do not believe in paying taxes, and do not believe in acting through responsible institutions. Their basic ideological premise is that the government exists to protect them from other social groups in order to continue to accumulate capital without the restraints created by labor unions, competition, and government regulation.[8]

During the 1950s and 1960s Central American investors began the extensive cultivation of grains for the regional market and cotton for the international market. Except for Honduras,[9] each Central American nation by the mid-1970s had reduced its smallholding and subsistence agricultural sectors (small farmers) and had expanded migrant wage labor forces. A large rural labor surplus developed, urban migration by unemployable *campesinos* (peasants) swelled, domestic food production shrank, and landownership and agricultural production became more concentrated in fewer hands. National dependency upon imported foodstuffs rose throughout the region, as did the number of citizens directly affected by imported inflation.

Following the 1959 overthrow of Fulgencio Batista in Cuba,[10] Central American governments despaired of the region's slow growth rates. In 1960 they formed the Central American Common Market (CACM) to spur regional economic integration, foreign investment, intraregional trade, and industrialization. A stated rationale was to diversify and increase production so that wealth might "trickle down" to the poor and undercut the potential appeal of socialism. The CACM's objectives converged in 1961 with those of the US Alliance for Progress, which sought to bolster the capitalist development model. The Alliance sought to undercut the left by greatly increasing public development aid to Central America and thus encouraging private investment. During the 1960s, to varying degrees in each nation, the CACM and Alliance stimulated considerable domestic and foreign investment in the capital-intensive production of consumer goods, manufactured mainly with imported raw materials and fuel. Gross domestic products—both overall and per capita—grew rapidly into the early 1970s because of rapidly increasing industrial production, while input prices remained stable.[11]

Students of the CACM agree, however, that industrialization failed to absorb the rapidly growing labor supply and in some nations shifted wealth and income away from working-class groups. Industrialization and economic diversification expanded factory and middle-class jobs until the early 1970s, but rural and urban unemployment simultaneously rose throughout the region. The CACM's development model also began to exhaust its growth potential in the 1970s. Imported industrial, raw materials prices rose 150 percent from 1968 to 1976. Higher costs eroded investment, productivity, output growth, and the competitiveness of regional products.[12] In Nicaragua, El Salvador, and Guatemala, the industrial sector's share of exports declined about 6 percent from the 1970–1974 to the 1975–1979 periods. Balance-of-payments pressures afflicted all the Central American economies in the 1970s because of declining terms of trade (the relative costs of imports versus exports), a recession in the world economy, and higher foreign interest rates. According to Weeks, "each government in effect decided to pursue a separate strategy to weather the crisis, rather than a collective one."[13] By the late 1970s the CACM accord began to break down, and in the 1980s the breakdown became complete.

Socioeconomic change accelerated in Central America after World War II. Population almost doubled between 1960 and 1980, and high growth rates persisted. The expanding commercial agricultural sector and the increasing concentration of landownership forced peasants off the land and swelled agricultural labor migration and urbanization. Enhanced educational programs increased school attendance, literacy, and participation in higher education throughout the isthmus. Ownership of radio and television receivers spread and broadcasters multiplied. Roads were improved and means of transportation developed. As communication became easier and faster, public awareness of national problems grew. Economic activity shifted away from agriculture and toward manufacturing and services. Overall economic activity (measured as GDP per capita) more than doubled between 1960 and 1980. However, this growth was unevenly distributed, and as noted, a sharp recession reduced production regionwide in the late 1970s and the 1980s.

The wrenching economic strains of the 1970s caused cascading political and economic difficulties that are detailed in the country chapters of this volume. At the macro-social level, Central American nations tried to borrow their way through recession and political crisis. All multiplied their foreign debt several-fold while their economies eroded. The resulting interest payments undermined economic recovery, increased government dependency on foreign lenders, and eventually forced the Central American countries to undergo neoliberal structural adjustment programs in the late 1980s and 1990s. By 2000, under neoliberal policies, Costa Rica and El Salvador had found new sources of growth in assembly plant production, nontraditional exports, and tourism, such that their economic growth resumed and their foreign debt shrank. During the 1990s El Salvador and Costa Rica had recovered enough to surpass their 1980 levels of GDP per capita, and some analysts believed trade liberalization had "been an effective means to bring growth and development to the Central American region."[14] The benefits were uneven, however. Between 1980 and 2004 neither Guatemala, Honduras, nor Nicaragua had experienced real net economic growth. Tragically, Nicaragua's 2004 per capita GDP was only 56 percent of its per capita GDP in 1970. Still reeling from a decade of externally financed civil war and economic destabilization, Nicaragua had become one of the hemisphere's historically most dramatic cases of economic collapse.[15]

The second great consequence was political turmoil that exacerbated economic crisis throughout the 1980s by disrupting production and frightening away capital. At the microsocial level, the living conditions of rural and urban lower-class citizens deteriorated while they witnessed the rapid enrichment of economic elites. This impoverishment and growing inequality stimulated regionwide mobilization of protest, opposition, and demands for economic and political reform. Some governments violently repressed such mobilization, which brought about revolution in Nicaragua and lengthy civil wars in El Salvador and Guatemala. These, combined with deepening economic crises and escalating foreign interventions in Central American affairs, sparked a series of regime changes in the region's governments between 1979 and 1996. Only Costa Rica—the sole democracy in the region in the 1970s—escaped regime change.

In summary, the rapid but inequitable economic growth of the 1960s and 1970s caused economic policies and class conflict that transformed Central America both politically and economically in the 1980s and 1990s. Political change was generally toward electoral democracy and less repression and violence. The economic results varied widely, however. All countries suffered in the crisis of the 1970s and 1980s, and all eventually adopted the neoliberal economic model as their best hope for development. It worked best in Costa Rica, whose economy recovered and began to grow again. But the other four nations either remained stagnant or steadily lost ground in comparison to developed economies. Lehoucq summarizes that since 1990 "most of the isthmus has a GDP per capita rate that, by the late 2000s, is less than 20 percent of the Western European average."[16]

Between 2008 and 2012 most of Central America experienced real economic growth that somewhat alleviated poverty. El Salvador's performance was the weakest, with negative 2.3 percent gross national income (GNI) per capita change in 2009 and finishing the five-year span with only a 6 percent net increase in GNI per capita. Already the region's wealthiest country, and going counter to the world recession with a 6.9 percent per capita GNI change in 2009, Costa Rica ended the 2008–2012 period with a net output increase per head of 44 percent. Honduras, Nicaragua, and Guatemala fell in between: each registered five-year GNI per capita increases of 18 to 19 percent.[17] Corbacho and Davoodi trenchantly summarize the economic situation in Central America for the 1990s as follows: "Poverty and inequality are higher in Central America than in Latin America. Latin America, in turn, is the most unequal region of the world. While poverty declined modestly in the 1990s, inequality in Central America has risen and continues to be high and persistent."[18] More recently, the economic growth of the early 2000s appears to have slightly reduced income inequality in every country but Honduras, where it rose somewhat.[19]

As we write this in 2014, Central Americans enjoy more freedom and democracy than in the 1970s. However, backsliding on democratic practices in Nicaragua after the early 2000s and the 2009 coup d'état in Honduras revealed weak elite commitment to democratic rules of the game. These events offered a strong caution to those who hoped democracy had consolidated in the isthmus. Nicaraguans are also still on average poorer than four decades before, but Costa Rica's peace, stability, and human capital investments have left its citizens better off over the same period. New threats to democracy and stability have also emerged in the last decade, as El Salvador, Guatemala, and Honduras struggle with the highest levels of violence in the world. These governments increasingly deal with these problems by relying on their militaries in an attempt to restore order in their countries, a tactic the region's history proves to carry great risks.

Recommended Readings and Resources

Bulmer-Thomas, Victor. 1987. *The Political Economy of Central America Since 1920.* Cambridge: Cambridge University Press.

Brignoli, Hector Pérez. 1989. *A Brief History of Central America.* Berkeley: University of California Press.

Danielson, Anders, and A. Geske Dijkstra, eds. 2001. *Towards Sustainable Development in Central America and the Caribbean.* New York: Palgrave-Macmillan.

Dunkerley, James. 1988. *Power in the Isthmus: A Political History of Modern Central America.* London: Verso.

LeHoucq, Fabrice. 2012. *The Politics of Modern Central America: Civil War, Democratization, and Underdevelopment.* Cambridge: Cambridge University Press.

Rennhack, Robert, and Erik Offerdal, eds. 2004. *The Macroeconomy of Central America.* New York: Palgrave-Macmillan.

Schneider, Aaron, "The Great Transformation in Central America: Transnational Accumulation and the Evolution of Capital." In Diego Sánchez-Ancochea and Salvador Martí i Puig, eds., 2013. *Handbook of Central American Governance.* London: Routledge.

Weeks, John. 1985. *The Economies of Central America.* New York: Holmes and Meier.

Woodward, Ralph Lee, Jr. 1985. *Central America: A Nation Divided,* 2nd ed. New York: Oxford University Press.

Notes

1. Good histories are Ralph Lee Woodward Jr., *Central America: A Nation Divided,* 2nd ed. (New York: Oxford University Press, 1985); and Mario Rodríguez, *Central America* (Englewood Cliffs, NJ: Prentice-Hall, 1965). The best short history is Hector Pérez Brignoli, *A Brief History of Central America* (Berkeley: University of California Press, 1989). For a longer treatment, see James Dunkerley, *Power in the Isthmus: A Political History of Modern Central America* (London: Verso, 1988). See also John A. Booth, *Costa Rica: Quest for Democracy* (Boulder, CO: Westview Press, 1998), Ch. 3. On the twentieth century to the present, see Fabrice LeHoucq, *The Politics of Modern Central America: Civil War, Democratization, and Underdevelopment* (Cambridge: Cambridge University Press, 2012).

2. See David Richard Radell, "An Historical Geography of Western Nicaragua: The Spheres of Leon, Granada, and Managua, 1519–1965," Ph.D. dissertation, University of California, Berkeley, 1969, pp. 66–80.

3. Criollos (creoles) were people of European origin born in the colonies. As descendants of the conquerors and land grantees, many had wealth, but the colonial system restricted their political and administrative power.

4. On the Walker filibuster and its aftermath, see Karl Bermann, *Under the Big Stick: Nicaragua and the United States Since 1848* (Boston: South End Press, 1986).

5. For an inside perspective on US intervention in Nicaragua and El Salvador during the 1980s and 1990s, see Todd Greentree, *Crossroads of Intervention: Insurgency and Counterinsurgency Lessons from Central America* (Westport, CT: Praeger Security International, 2008).

6. Honduras never really developed a landowning aristocracy; economic and political power remained in the hands of regional hacendados and newer urban industrial-commercial-financial entrepreneurs.

7. Enrique A. Baloyra, "Reactionary Despotism in Central America," *Journal of Latin American Studies* 15 (November 1983), pp. 295–319.

8. Ibid., pp. 309–310.

9. In Honduras, agrarian colonization and expanding employment in the modern capitalist sector of agriculture continued to absorb much of the growth of the rural labor force.

10. Victor Bulmer-Thomas, *The Political Economy of Central America Since 1920* (Cambridge: Cambridge University Press, 1987), pp. 177–180.

11. See Appendix, Tables A.1 and A.2 of John A. Booth and Thomas W. Walker, *Understanding Central America*, 3rd ed. (Boulder, CO: Westview Press, 1999).

12. John Weeks, "The Industrial Sector," in Thomas W. Walker, ed., *Nicaragua: The First Five Years* (New York: Praeger, 1985), pp. 281–296; John Weeks, *The Economies of Central America* (New York: Holmes and Meier, 1985), pp. 101–151.

13. Weeks, *The Economies of Central America*, p. 284.

14. Guillermo Perry, Daniel Lederman, and Rodrigo Suescún, "Trade Structure and Policy," in *The Macroeconomy of Central America*, Robert Rennhack and Erik Offerdal, eds. (New York: Palgrave-Macmillan, 2004).

15. Per capita GDP trends are in constant-dollar terms. Alan Heston, Robert Summers, and Bettina Aten, Penn World Table Version 6.2 (Center for International Comparisons at the University of Pennsylvania [CICUP], September 2006), http://pwt.econ.upenn.edu/php_site/pwt62/pwt62_retrieve.php, accessed April 27, 2009.

16. LeHoucq, *The Politics of Modern Central America,* Kindle edition, location 2328.

17. Values are calculated for GNI per capita, Atlas method, as reported by the World Bank, Country Data, http://data.worldbank.org/country, accessed September 15, 2013.

18. Ana Corbacho and Hamid R. Davoodi, "Public Expenditure and Governance," in Rennhack and Offerdal, eds., *The Macroeconomy of Central America.* See also Trevor Evans, "The Fruits of Interest: Financial Liberalization and Banking in Central America," in *Towards Sustainable Development in Central America and the Caribbean*, Anders Danielson and A. Geske Dijkstra, eds. (New York: Palgrave-Macmillan, 2001).

19. Leonardo Gasparini, Guillermo Cruces and Leopoldo Tornarolli, "Recent Trends in Income Inequality in Latin America," Society for the Study of Economic Inequality, Working Paper Series, 2009, http://www.development.wne.uw.edu.pl/uploads/Courses/DW_inequality_latin.pdf, accessed December 4, 2013.

4

COSTA RICA

A SLOGAN ON A POPULAR T-SHIRT SOLD TO TOURISTS IN COSTA RICA
proclaims "¡Costa Rica es diferente!" (Costa Rica is different). Alluding in part
to the country's stable democracy and high levels of social development, the
slogan evokes the myth of Costa Rican exceptionalism. Schools, the media,
and popular tradition inculcate Costa Ricans in the belief that their country
stands apart from the rest of Central America's record of dictatorship, political
violence, and underdevelopment.[1] Costa Rica's record is indeed distinctive, yet
in the early twenty-first century there was less to the myth than met the eye.
For most of the nineteenth and twentieth centuries Costa Rica differed from
its neighbors in important ways, but its economy always experienced the same
commodity price swings and dependent development as its neighbors. From
the 1950s on, however, Costa Rica's governments managed these economic
problems better, easing their impact on citizens and masking underlying similarities to neighbors.

But as the twentieth century ended, Costa Rica had become more like its
neighbors politically and economically. As formal electoral democracy and
improved human rights spread, Costa Rica became less politically distinct
from other isthmian regimes. But in the economic arena, Costa Rica evolved
toward a model common across Central and Latin America. Global economic
changes compelled Costa Rica to abandon a post–civil war development strategy that served its people well for decades. Forced like its neighbors to adopt a

neoliberal economic development model, Costa Rica opened up to the world economy and changed domestic welfare policies. Some observers believed neoliberalism began pushing Costa Rica toward the human development levels of other Central American nations,[2] although Costa Rica eventually widened its wealth gap over other isthmian nations.

As we argued in Chapter 2, shifting global political and economic forces have shaped the region from the 1500s on. Local conditions, resources, and actors have shaped these common external pressures to produce divergent local effects. Costa Rica's evolution through these forces has been the most distinctive almost from the outset, but one should not lose track of the similarities in the pressures that drive change.

HISTORICAL BACKGROUND

Costa Rica deviated from certain patterns in the rest of Central America during the colonial period and often remained an exception to social, economic, and political norms until the present. Rather isolated from the rest of Central America because of distance and rugged terrain, Costa Rica remained more racially and economically homogeneous than its neighbors. This does not mean that Costa Rica lacked social disparities or that it remained economically self-contained. Rather, its social inequities never allowed one class or race to completely dominate others to the detriment of the majority, as occurred elsewhere in the isthmus. Despite embracing export agriculture, Costa Rica never fully developed the dependency system prevalent elsewhere in the isthmus, with its tremendous human costs.

The roots of eventual Costa Rican democracy were planted in the nineteenth century, although true democratic rule would not materialize until the 1950s. From 1824 to 1899, one Costa Rican government in five ended by coup d'état. The military ruled the country 44 percent of the time.[3] During most of that epoch, moneyed rural families governed the country. The elections that occurred were indirect, were confined to a tiny, literate elite, and were often rigged. However, certain economic trends and political reforms prevented a total domination of Costa Rican national politics by a landed oligarchy. The first dictator president, Braulio Carrillo (1835 to 1842), for instance, increased the already fairly large number of small farmers by distributing municipal lands to the inhabitants. He also promoted coffee cultivation and included small farmers in coffee cultivation, in contrast to elsewhere in Central America. This helped form a class of smallholding yeoman farmers that continuously renewed itself by expanding the agricultural frontiers.

The incipient landed elite continued to rule the country until it lost its control to the military, which greatly expanded after the 1857 Central American war. The military's leader, Liberal dictator Tomás Guardia (1870–1882), took power, confiscating some of the properties of the wealthy and exiling some of their leaders. Guardia contracted foreigners to construct new roads and railways to move coffee to market. A late-nineteenth-century labor shortage kept rural wages high as coffee production spread. By then market forces in the rapidly growing coffee industry had begun to concentrate land ownership and had pushed many smallholders off the land. In order to secure the labor essential to the nation's wealth, large coffee farmers had to pay decent wages and the government had to pass reformist public policies. Costa Rican peasants and workers therefore generally experienced less exploitation and repression than common elsewhere in Central America.

Despite the militarization of politics during the Guardia dictatorship, precursors of democracy developed in the second half of the nineteenth century. Elections, though indirect, elite-dominated, and often rigged, became important by the 1840s. The growth of commerce, government, transport, immigration, and urban centers swelled the number of people available for political activity. The modernizing Liberals (Guardia and his civilian successors) greatly increased education spending and thus literacy by 1900. Because literacy was a key criterion for voter eligibility, its increase expanded suffrage.[4]

By 1889 an economic slowdown and the Liberals' anti-clericalism generated support for an opposition Catholic Union Party and its presidential candidate José J. Rodríguez. Backed by the Catholic Church, Rodríguez won the vote among the electors, but the army tried to block him from taking office. Incited by the Church, angry citizens took to the streets and forced the army to back down. Often incorrectly cited as the birth of Costa Rican democracy, this election nevertheless forced the military to respect an opposition victory and mobilized ordinary citizens to defend an election. After Rodríguez, however, authoritarian elite rulers and election fraud returned.[5]

From 1905 to 1914, presidents Cleto González Víquez and Ricardo Jiménez Oreamuno further broadened suffrage, established direct popular election of public officials, and permitted free and open opposition campaigns. A military regime led by the Tinoco brothers seized power in 1917 during the recession caused by World War I. In 1919 popular protest and an invasion by exiled elites toppled the Tinoco regime, Costa Rica's last military government. Civilian, constitutional rule continued thereafter, and the Costa Rican electorate expanded continuously.

The Atlantic railroad's completion led to an additional export crop, bananas. The foreign-owned banana industry, concentrated in the sparsely populated Atlantic coastal lowlands, had little effect on Costa Rican politics in the early twentieth century. As hard times developed later, labor organizers led by Communists organized the banana plantations. Union influence and political power grew. By the 1940s, the Great Depression and World War II had caused severe social dislocations. This pitted against one another factions representing variously the political-economic elite, the working classes and unions, and an emerging middle class. In the early 1940s, President Rafael Calderón Guardia, a medical doctor and reformist coffee aristocrat, broke with the rest of the coffee-growing political class. Bidding to dominate the government, he allied with the Communist unions and the Catholic Church. Assisted by Communist legislators, Calderón enacted and began implementing Costa Rica's first labor and social security laws.

Calderón's alliance with the Communists and, in 1948, electoral fraud and legislative tampering with the presidential election results provided pretexts for a brief but violent civil war. A coalition between elite politicos angry at Calderón and middle-class elements, dominated by a junta of social democrats led by José "Pepe" Figueres Ferrer, rebelled. The rebels defeated the government within a few months. From that time to the 1990s, the country's social democrats—the National Liberation Party (Partido de Liberación Nacional, PLN), led for three decades by Figueres—set the tone of Costa Rican political life. In keeping with a well-established tradition of political accommodation, the victorious National Liberation junta retained Calderón's social reforms for workers. The junta went even further by nationalizing the banking and insurance industries. A constituent assembly rewrote the constitution in 1949, enfranchising women and blacks and abolishing the army. The latter act ensured future political stability. In late 1949, the junta turned the presidency over to the rightful winner of the 1948 election, Otilio Ulate, who was not a part of the National Liberation movement.

When the PLN and Figueres first won the presidency in 1954, they expanded the social legislation initiated under Calderón. Increasing segments of the populace received health and social security coverage. Even the conservative coalition governments that periodically replaced the PLN in power preserved and expanded these social benefits. After 1949, successive governments held regular and scrupulously honest elections administered by the powerful and independent Supreme Electoral Tribunal. When defeated at the polls, the PLN willingly relinquished control of the presidency and the Legislative Assembly to a conservative opposition coalition. The PLN won the presidency nine times and the opposition won it seven times between 1949 and 2010. Opinion surveys showed strong citizen support for democratic civil liberties and alternation in power by the competing parties.

In sum, Costa Rica's center-left social democratic PLN governments took power and consolidated a new political and economic regime in the 1940s and 1950s despite countervailing trends elsewhere in the isthmus. Similar post–World War II movements favoring democracy appeared in Guatemala, Honduras, Nicaragua, and El Salvador, but all failed. Instrumental in this failure of pro-democracy mobilization elsewhere were US anti-Communist policies that aided and encouraged national armed forces and rightist elites to block the left's struggle for reform. In contrast, in Costa Rica the pro-democracy reformers had defeated the Communists in the 1948 civil war and thereafter contained their influence. This put Costa Rica's new regime on the good side of the United States and helped it survive where others nearby would not.

Despite developing and consolidating a constitutional electoral democracy, not all remained well in Costa Rica. From the 1970s forward commodity price shifts, great power geopolitics, civil war in neighboring nations, and an evolving international economy repeatedly disturbed Costa Rica, challenged its institutions and its citizens' confidence in them, and forced frequent adjustment to changing realities.

WEATHERING GLOBAL FORCES

Costa Rica experienced the same global economic forces as its neighbors during the 1970s and 1980s, generating some internal unrest. Nevertheless, it escaped the violent strife that afflicted much of the isthmus without regime change. This relative stability was no accident—it resulted from elites' decisions in the 1970s and 1980s to alleviate some of the erosion of popular living standards and to avoid political repression. These decisions stemmed partly from late-nineteenth-century rulers and landowners accommodating peasants to secure a labor supply. At mid-twentieth century both Calderón Guardia and later PLN leaders employed political and economic reforms to placate and stabilize mobilized working and middle classes. This tradition of elites accommodating mobilized lower sectors, we believe, provided Costa Rica's leaders a model that allowed them to preserve stable electoral democracy in the 1970s and 1980s despite grave challenges.

The government's task proved difficult over the longer term. Costa Rica's post–civil war, social-democratic development model relied on state-led development projects and Central American Common Market (CACM)–coordinated import substitution industrialization that enlarged the government's payroll and economic role. Costa Rica's social welfare programs, ambitious for a developing country, grew during the 1950s and 1960s. Industrialization aside, in the 1970s the economy and national budget still depended heavily on international market prices for its exports (coffee, bananas, and goods sold to the CACM) and its imports (especially vital petroleum). Problems arose, however, when skyrocketing oil costs after 1973 and simultaneously falling export prices caused inflation, layoffs, and a public revenue crunch.

Sources of Class Conflict. How did the Costa Rican variant of the Central American crisis of the 1970s arise? The CACM accelerated economic growth and industrialization in the 1960s and early 1970s. Costa Rican per capita gross domestic product (GDP) rose at an annual average of 3.4 percent from

1962 through 1971, and at 2.6 percent from 1972 through 1979. Per capita GDP in constant 1986 dollars almost doubled from 1960 to 1980. Among Central American nations, Costa Rica had more of its workforce (16 percent) in manufacturing by 1983. By 1987, Costa Rica (at 23 percent) ranked second in the isthmus in manufacturing's contribution to domestic production. The agricultural sector's workforce shrank from 51 percent to 29 percent between 1960 and 1980.[6] Commerce, services, and government all expanded as the nation rapidly modernized and urbanized.

The prevailing theory about the onset of rebellion in Central America in the 1970s contends that severe declines in real working-class wages and living conditions mobilized many people into labor, political, and protest organization and activity.[7] Because many urban and rural wage earners in Central America had little or no margin of safety, a drop in their real earnings (wages corrected for inflation) could catastrophically reduce their ability to survive. Such a rapid erosion of life chances provided a powerful impetus to join political or labor groups seeking redress of such problems.

Data on Costa Rica reveal that wage workers lost ground relative to other income earners in the mid-1970s, but recovered much of their purchasing power by 1978 or 1979. An index of working-class wages shows that Costa Rican workers' real pay rates fell in 1975 and 1976, but recovered and then began to exceed earlier levels by the late 1970s. Wages fell again in 1982 but began an immediate recovery in 1983–1984 and remained relatively high through the rest of the 1980s.[8] Although working-class earnings and living standards declined in Costa Rica during the mid-1970s, the losses were less severe and sustained than those in Guatemala, Nicaragua, and El Salvador, because the Costa Rican government found ways to let real wages recover much of their earlier purchasing power.[9] From 1982 until the late 1990s Costa Rican workers fairly steadily gained ground against inflation.

Income Distribution. Another insight into economic disparity in Costa Rica comes from shifts in the distribution of income among classes. One measure of changing income inequality during the 1970s is the share of national income paid out as employee compensation; decreasing employee compensation would suggest a shift of income away from salaried and wage-earning workers and toward investors and entrepreneurs. Data reveal that between 1970 and 1975, the employee-compensation share of all national income fluctuated but tended to increase.[10] During the 1960s and early 1970s, Costa Rican public policy redistributed income toward the middle three-fifths of the populace, mainly at the expense of the richest fifth.[11] In both relative and absolute income trends, Costa Rica clearly contrasts with what the evidence will later show for Nicaragua, El Salvador, and Guatemala. In Costa Rica, wages fluctuated during the 1970s and early 1980s, but generally recovered after short-term declines. In the three other countries, wages declined but did not recover, increasingly aggrieving those losing out.

Wealth. During the 1970s Costa Rica also avoided sharp increases in class inequality observed in Nicaragua, El Salvador, and Guatemala. Although Costa Rica was in the CACM and was also hit by rapid energy-driven consumer price increases of the mid-1970s, data reveal that in Costa Rica these factors affected wealth distribution less than elsewhere in the isthmus.

Costa Rica's social-democratic economic development model and low military expenditures brought that nation into the 1970s with a social-welfare system and economy that attenuated inflation's impact on popular living conditions. Data comparing Costa Rica's spending on social programs to other isthmian nations' appear in Table A.5 (see Appendix). In the 1970s and early 1980s Costa Rica's ratio of spending for social services versus defense was between four and five times greater than that of its nearest competitor in Central America. The benefits of these policies became manifest in Costa Rica's higher literacy, greater longevity, and lower mortality rates.[12] As noted above, income distribution in Costa Rica actually became modestly more egalitarian during the 1960s and 1970s, helping prevent the rapid movement of wealth toward the upper classes observed in Nicaragua, Guatemala, and El Salvador.

In Costa Rican agriculture, concentration of land ownership grew steadily in the 1960s and early 1970s, but the availability of some land that could still be colonized until the late 1960s and the still-growing banana industry absorbed much of the surplus agricultural workforce. Moreover, during the 1974 to 1978 period, Costa Rica aggressively distributed land to numerous peasants and staved off the deterioration of living standards for many.[13] Additionally, employment growth in urban services and manufacturing absorbed much of the surplus agricultural population and prevented the sharp growth of rural unemployment and poverty through the late 1980s.[14]

Popular Mobilization. The Costa Rican government carefully managed citizen mobilization in one critical arena—labor—but encouraged it in others. On the one hand, following the 1948 civil war, the government worked to fragment the national union movement (including industrial workers, service workers, and white-collar public employees) among competing, party-affiliated confederations in order to curtail union power.[15] On the other hand, during the 1960s and early 1970s the government employed social promoters to help organize communal self-help organizations. Hundreds of community-development associations, largely uncoordinated among themselves, worked on local projects and made small demands to legislators for funds for local improvements. The state-promoted community-development movement was at first fairly docile and easier to co-opt than leftist-led unions had been in the 1930s and 1940s.

By the 1970s, however, union membership began expanding.[16] Then the oil-price and inflation shocks from the global economy stirred popular mobilization.[17] Unions became more militant. Industrial disputes rose sharply during 1975 and 1976, when real wages declined, but subsided when wages recovered in the late 1970s. Wage disputes rose again in 1982 after real wages fell again, then leveled off in 1983 and 1984 when earnings once again recovered purchasing power. Austerity measures included public-employee layoffs, service cuts, and sharp consumer-price increases in the late 1980s and early 1990s.[18] Civil society, including government-promoted community organizations, became more restive. Hard times brought numerous strikes and demonstrations, but wage and policy concessions eventually quelled them.[19]

Costa Rica's system of political parties remained stable in the 1960s and 1970s; the social democratic National Liberation Party (PLN) alternated in power with a coalition of moderately conservative parties under the Unity banner. The traditional Unity coalition of conservative parties reorganized and institutionalized itself into the Social Christian Unity Party (Partido de Unidad Social Cristiano, PUSC) in 1985. Radical-left parties won a few seats to the Legislative Assembly during the 1970s, but they were weak outside the union movement. As living standards of most Costa Ricans declined during the 1980s, mobilization of demands by a broad array of interest groups increased and public approval of government declined. Organized labor unsuccessfully tried to forge a militant general confederation. Voting for leftist parties—long considered a bellwether of protest—declined in the 1982 and 1986 national elections. Costa Rica's more radical parties and labor became increasingly estranged and divided in the early and mid-1980s. Polls revealed that even in the midst of a severe recession, most citizens remained loyal to the regime.

In sum, Costa Rica experienced increased organization and protest, but no dramatic increase in anti-regime organization or coalitions from the late 1970s through the early 1990s.[20] Unlike Nicaragua, Guatemala, and El Salvador, Costa Rica experienced no significant challenge to the sovereignty of the state.

Government Response to Popular Mobilization. Central American regimes all experienced popular mobilization during the 1970s and 1980s, but responded very differently. In contrast to Costa Rica, the Salvadoran, Guatemalan, and prerevolutionary Nicaraguan regimes reacted violently to popular organization and protest. In contrast, Costa Rica (a democracy) and Honduras (a military government) each addressed popular mobilization relatively moderately. This prevented the mobilization of new opponents to the government angered by repression and thus avoided escalating conflict.

Costa Rica kept an open, constitutional regime with clean elections and considerable popular access to public officials. Costa Rican officials typically responded to mobilized demands by accommodating rather than repressing them. Even when demands escalated into civil disobedience, demonstrations, strikes, and riots, the government usually responded with moderate force and used study and compromise to defuse conflict. For instance, rulers met violent civil disturbances—land invasions in the early 1970s; the Limón riot of 1979; banana workers' strikes in 1980, 1981, and 1982; and street vendors' strikes in 1991—with moderate official force so that deaths among protesters were rare.[21] Different PLN and PUSC administrations sought to accommodate demand-makers by negotiating with them, forming panels of inquiry, or making conciliatory policies.

As later chapters will spell out, Central America's major national revolts of the 1970s and 1980s (Nicaragua, El Salvador, Guatemala) arose from sharp increases in inequality and decreases in popular living standards during the mid-1970s. These grievances drove popular mobilization that demanded redress of the working majorities' wages and living standards. Costa Rica experienced this mobilization but responded to it by allowing workers' wages to recover, along with other ameliorative policies and typically with low repression. This combination of amelioration of grievances and low repression defused popular anger, demobilized much protest, and prevented rising conflict that in three neighboring nations caused open rebellions. Thus Costa Rica's regime survived the onslaught of globally driven economic uncertainty and turmoil by following the national elite's long-standing accommodative traditions. But the global strains of the 1970s and 1980s nonetheless left marks on Costa Rica—not of political regime change but transformations in its economic development model and political party system.

THE ECONOMIC DEVELOPMENT MODEL TRANSFORMED

As noted above, simultaneously declining export revenues and rising energy costs pushed Costa Rica into a severe economic crisis. Rapid inflation drove down demand and real wages, which further reduced consumer demand. The governments of the mid- and late 1970s and early 1980s, rather than curtailing public spending to address shrinking state revenues, borrowed abroad to finance the growing public deficit. In the short term this lightened the impact of the crisis on the Costa Rican public, but it disastrously affected national financial health. Foreign debt as a share of GDP rose from 12 percent in 1970 to 147 percent in 1982. Foreign-interest payments consumed a third of export earnings and further weakened the public and private sectors. Similar difficulties and escalating civil wars elsewhere in Central America combined to collapse Costa Rica's regional markets and drive away tourists and foreign capital. In 1981 the administration of Rodrigo Carazo Odio found its foreign-reserve coffers empty and defaulted on Costa Rica's foreign debt. This pushed the currency (the *colón*) into a ten-year slide that eroded 90 percent of its value.[22]

When the PLN's Luis Alberto Monge became president in 1982, these economic predicaments forced him to seek international assistance that would come with high costs. One source of help sprang from US wishes to secure a southern base for its efforts to unseat Nicaragua's Sandinista revolution. The Reagan administration pressured Costa Rica, and Monge agreed to collaborate with the Nicaraguan counterrevolutionaries (the Contras) and their American helpers. In exchange the United States compensated Costa Rica with over US$1.1 billion in aid during the mid-1980s, much of it in the unusual form of outright grants instead of loans. These funds delayed Costa Rica's reckoning with its sick economy while addicting it ever more to external aid. By 1985 a second source of international help had to be invoked.

The flow of US grants for pro-Contra activities ended when Monge's successor, PLN president Oscar Arias Sánchez, in 1987 successfully advanced the Central American Peace Accord and sharply reduced Costa Rica's cooperation with the Contras. Although Costa Rican peace initiatives would soon win Arias the Nobel Peace Prize, the Reagan administration opposed them and retaliated with sharp aid cuts that reduced economic output and increased inflation.

Costa Rica's second source of external aid, borrowing from intergovernmental lenders and individual nations, also came heavily conditioned. As Robinson details, the emergence of "global" capitalism in the late twentieth century had begun to draw Central America into the evolving global economy and society.[23] This involved replacing the previous epoch's traditional agro-exports and import-substitution industrialization (ISI) development orientation with a neoliberal economic model emphasizing free-market capitalism, a smaller public sector, liberalization of markets, privatization of public-sector enterprises, and reorientation of production toward nontraditional exports. Promoters of the new style of global capitalism included the US government, other major capitalist countries, and international lenders (the Inter-American Development Bank, the International Monetary Fund, the Paris Club). These institutions, heavily influenced by the United States' heavy voting weight on their policy boards, shared and promoted a neoliberal agenda for economic reform in developing countries.

These states and organizations combined to effectively force Costa Rica into three structural adjustment agreements (SAAs) in 1985, 1989, and 1995, with the Monge, Arias, and Figueres Olsen administrations, respectively. In exchange for the credit essential to restructure Costa Rica's foreign debt and keep the deeply indebted, foreign reserve–starved state and economy afloat, the United States, International Monetary Fund, Paris Club, and Inter-American Development Bank forced Costa Rica to enact neoliberal economic policies that revolutionized its development model. Supported by conservative domestic economic interests and by the neoliberal

PUSC (which fortuitously avoided having to sign any of the SAAs), Costa Rica trimmed its public-sector payroll, social-service programs (education, health), and infrastructure investment; privatized most of the nation's many publicly owned enterprises and banking; and cut subsidies to agricultural-commodity producers, utility consumers, and housing. The government energetically promoted nontraditional exports, reducing trade barriers and integrating Costa Rica into the global economy.[24]

Successive governments in San José used legislation and executive decrees to implement public-sector wage cuts and layoffs, privatization, and reductions in public services—major departures from the development model in place since the 1950s.[25] These policy changes mobilized protest, but, as in the 1970s, again the government responded with amelioration. Repression remained low, real wages were kept up, and social-assistance and housing-subsidy programs rose sharply. Income distribution among classes remained fairly stable into the 1990s despite the economic turmoil. Voting for leftist parties remained low. Besides protests, there were three significant signs that economic difficulties and the change of economic model angered Costa Ricans: Voters ousted the governing party in successive elections in 1990, 1994, and 1998. Turnout in 1998 dropped from the usual level above 80 percent to only 73 percent and then to 59 percent in 2002. Turnout recovered slightly to 64 and 62 percent in the 2006 and 2010 elections, respectively. As turnout fell, the two-party system in place since the rise of the PUSC began to change rapidly.[26]

In contrast to these political discontents, the new development model's short- and middle-run economic successes made Costa Rica a poster child for neoliberalism. Economic liberalization, particularly with regard to non-traditional exports, along with the settlement of the region's civil conflicts in the 1990s and Costa Rica's significant human-capital advantages, stimulated a period of rapid economic growth. During the 1990s Costa Rica's combined rate of investment between government and private-sector sources was high for the region. Government spending on social services far exceeded any other country in the area. GDP per capita grew by nearly 25 percent between 1990 and the early 2000s, driven by a tourism boom, domestic and foreign investment, new computer-assembly and online-services industries, and expanded textile manufacturing.[27]

In the early 2000s, the effects of the new Costa Rican development model were still unfolding. According to Robinson, they included the following: Deregulation allowed a new private banking system dominated by international capital and deepening integration into the world economy. Investment in traditional agriculture and agricultural-extension services had declined along with domestically consumed agricultural production, pushing rural populations toward urban areas to seek employment. Investment in industry, however, had lost ground to investment in the commercial and service sectors. The informal sectors (petty commerce and services—often street vendors, unlicensed taxis, etc.) had grown rapidly, drawing those unable to find formal-sector employment. Female participation in the workforce had risen sharply without a proportionate accompanying public investment in family social services and childcare. Large numbers of Nicaraguan immigrants had flooded Costa Rica to assume lower-skilled jobs in nontraditional agriculture, construction, and domestic service. Nicaraguan immigrant workers, vulnerable to police and immigration authorities, experienced employer victimization while exerting downward pressure on wages and undermining Costa Rican worker organization and mobilization efforts.[28]

The publication of data on income, inequality, and poverty lags behind social change, so we could not at this writing fully assess whether these negative trends would continue in Costa Rica. The evidence is conflicting. Inequality worsened measurably in the 1990s and early 2000s, but then diminished slightly by a 2008 estimate only to increase again in 2009.[29] On the other hand, the share of people living in poverty in the early 1990s was 26.2 percent, a level reduced to 20.5 percent in 2004 (Table 2.1). Only three percent of Costa Ricans lived on less than $2 per day in 2009, by far the lowest in the region (Table 2.1). In 2012 Costa Rica's GDP per capita was 79 percent higher than in 1990 (see Table 1.1), the best economic performance in the region.

In sum, external forces used the debt crisis of the 1980s to force Costa Rica to adopt a neoliberal development model. Even when forced to adopt its distributively stingy policies, Costa Rican governments found ways to cushion some of the economic blows to citizens, managed a short-term macroeconomic turnaround, and found new industries to bolster economic output over the longer run. As of 2013 the model seemed to be "floating all boats" by raising macroeconomic output while inequality remained much lower than in other countries (Table 2.1). Throughout this difficult period, the overarching framework of the constitutional democratic regime established in the late 1940s and early 1950s remained solidly in place.

CHANGES IN POLITICS AND PARTIES

Despite the long life of Costa Rica's political regime, the country's economy affected the political party system.[30] Scholars believe globalization and neoliberalism had two main impacts on Latin American political parties: At the macro level, neoliberalism's structural constraints undermined ruling social-democratic parties by undercutting their preferred redistributive and protectionist public policies. This alienated their working- and middle-class supporters and boosted other parties more amenable to neoliberal reforms. At the micro level, social-democratic parties divided ideologically and lost programmatic focus, as they could neither campaign on their traditional programs nor embrace the required but unpopular neoliberal reforms. This turned campaigns into personalistic or populist appeals to distract voters from unpalatable economic options.[31] Costa Rican parties experienced this, harming the long-dominant social-democratic PLN and for a while benefiting the newer PUSC. (See Appendix, Tables A.6 and A.7, for selected presidential and legislative election results.)

The PLN. Neoliberalism harmed the social-democratic National Liberation Party because PLN presidents had to sign and implement all three structural-adjustments accords. As Costa Rica's leftist parties declined in the 1970s and early 1980s, popular-sector interests within the PLN lost importance relative to the party's emerging advocates of neoliberalism. The neoliberal imperative drove wedges between traditionalist social democrats and the PLN's neoliberal reformers. Having to govern while implementing structural adjustment also drove a wedge between the party's office-holding neoliberal technocrats and its aspiring presidential candidates.[32]

By the late 1980s the PLN's messages to its longtime supporters and activists became muddled as its actions in power conflicted with traditional Liberación ideology and policies. The PLN lost its perennial control of the Legislative Assembly from 1990 on and won the presidency only once during the 1990s. The PLN presidential vote share shrank steadily after 1986, when Arias captured 52.3 percent. The struggling party in 1994 nominated for president José Maria Figueres Olsen, son of PLN founder and two-time president, José Figueres Ferrer. The family name helped the party win the presidency in 1994 but not an Assembly majority. Figueres Olsen had to implement the unpopular 1995 structural-adjustment agreement, and his administration experienced several scandals. This record further eroded Liberación's support in elections, including the defection of some core voters. Turnout in the 1997 PLN presidential primary election fell sharply because of "the negative weight of an unpopular Liberación administration, . . . [and] a very fragmented party."[33]

Other factors also divided the party and reduced its discipline and appeal. First, technocrats gained control over policy making while the party was in power, displacing long-term party loyalists and activists. Second, the PLN opened presidential primary elections to non-PLN members. Third, presidential campaign organizations rose to dominate the traditional party apparatus. Fourth, a rapid shift to retail campaigning via television in the 1980s combined with the presidential primary nominating election to collapse the PLN's tradition of face-to-face, grassroots organization.

By the twenty-first century, Liberación seemed in dire straits. In the 2002 election the party split, and many voters and top leaders defected to the new Citizen Action Party (Partido de Acción Ciudadana, PAC). As a result the PLN took only 31 percent of the presidential vote and captured only 30 percent of the Legislative Assembly, its worst performance in five decades.[34] The PLN staged a comeback in 2006 with 40 percent of the vote, although much of the PLN's success in the 2006 elections could be attributed to the candidacy of former president Oscar Arias. The PLN also increased its share of the Assembly seats to 37 percent. In 2010 PLN presidential nominee Laura Chinchilla did better still with 47 percent of the national vote.

PUSC. While globalist pressures for neoliberalism harmed the PLN, they favored the formation and growth of the Social Christian Unity Party (PUSC). Rafael Angel Calderón Fournier's administration (1990 to 1994) in principle embraced structural adjustment, which seriously lowered the short-term economic well-being of most Costa Ricans. By good luck, however, the party escaped having to sign a structural-adjustment agreement while in power, shifting much of the blame for the resulting austerity to the PLN. In power the PUSC subverted austerity policies by diverting public infrastructure and health and education spending into palliative social programs in housing and temporary welfare assistance.[35] In 2004, twin corruption scandals broke in Costa Rica, implicating former PUSC presidents Calderón and Rodríguez and members of their administrations in taking bribes and committing campaign-finance violations. In 2009 Calderón was convicted of embezzlement, a conviction that was later upheld, though his sentence was reduced. Rodriguez, convicted on corruption charges in April 2011, later successfully appealed his conviction. By 2006 the PUSC had all but collapsed from a lack of voter support.[36]

PAC. The PAC arose in 2000 from a schism in the PLN. By emphasizing citizen participation, transparency, and anti-neoliberalism, it capitalized on the growing disenchantment with the status quo. The party reached out to popular organizations and promised to allocate 50 percent of its legislative seats to women, 10 percent more than required by the 1996 quota law.[37] For a new party the PAC did very well; in 2002 its presidential candidate Ottón Solís captured 26 percent of the vote. The PAC also won 14 of 57 seats in the Assembly. By 2006, the PAC had displaced the PUSC as the second party in Costa Rica's duopoly. Arias narrowly defeated Solís, who won nearly 40 percent of vote. The PAC also became the second-largest party in the legislature with 17 seats.

Other Parties. The number of parties in Costa Rica increased from four in the 1953 Assembly election to 27 in 2006, the number proliferating during the 1990s and early 2000s. Meanwhile, older parties of the left shrank and lost representation in the Legislative Assembly. Several small regional parties, some of them of long standing, competed in 2006 legislative elections but none won seats.[38] The Libertarian Movement Party of Costa Rica (Partido Movimiento Libertario de Costa Rica, PML) enjoyed early success as an alternative party to emerge in the wake of growing discontent. The Libertarians won six seats (one more than the PUSC) and 9 percent of the 2006 legislative vote.

Party System Legitimacy. Would this party-system turmoil threaten the legitimacy of Costa Rica's democratic regime? Surveys after 1990 expressed citizens' declining satisfaction with parties and other national institutions and a waning interest in politics. Trust in parties in general declined between the early 1990s and 2002 and remained low thereafter. Among all Central Americans, Costa Ricans reported the lowest support for their parties in a 2008 survey, and the second lowest in 2012.[39] Votes for third parties in 1998 roughly doubled previous levels, then trebled in 2002. Twenty-seven deputies from parties other than the PLN or PUSC were elected in 2006, six more than in 2002.[40]

After splitting, the PLN came back in 2006 to narrowly defeat the PAC (see Appendix, Table A.6), and the PUSC seemed to collapse entirely in the 2006 election. In 2010 the PLN had lived to fight again as first among equals in Costa Rica's party system. The wave of scandals did not end, however, and left most Costa Ricans increasingly weary of politics as usual. More change would ensue in the 2014 election cycle (see below). Costa Rica's political malaise, partly due to the shortcomings of the PUSC and PLN, was beginning to spread into a larger disaffection of its citizens with the constitutional regime and democracy (see Chapter 9).

ECONOMIC POLICY

The political and economic impacts of the neoliberal economic model were palpable in Costa Rica in the short term. Successive administrations experienced tremendous pressure from domestic elites and the international community to curtail public spending and privatize key state-owned enterprises—especially telecommunications—in an effort to forestall a potential fiscal crisis and meet IMF conditionality.[41] Throughout the 1980s real wages and public-investment spending declined in health and education.[42] The effects on the well-being of average Costa Ricans became clear. Between 1990 and 2000 Costa Rica fell from twenty-eighth to forty-eighth in the Index of Human Development.[43] In 2006 Costa Rica ranked fiftieth, two places behind Cuba, and by 2012 ranked sixty-second.[44]

Economic stagnation and neoliberal policies proved a volatile mix. The administrations of presidents Rodríguez and Pacheco in the early 2000s pursued privatization despite legislative and popular opposition. President Rodríguez won legislation allowing foreign investors to provide public services. In 2000 the legislature approved privatization of the Costa Rican Electrical Institute (ICE). Following some of the largest demonstrations in the country's history, the Constitutional Tribunal ruled the measure unconstitutional.[45] Public-sector employees turned increasingly against government policy. In 1999, 15,000 striking teachers protested wages and disinvestment.[46] Strikes by teachers and workers from the energy and telecommunications sectors continued through the Pacheco administration. Adding to public dissatisfaction, extreme poverty increased from 5.1 percent in 2003 to 5.6 percent in 2004, owing partly to a 16 percent increase in food prices.[47] President Pacheco pledged to address poverty during his campaign, but once in office instead deepened spending cuts. His administration was plagued by public protest, legislative stagnation, and internal division. By July 2003 the president's approval rating fell to 10 percent.[48]

The free-trade debate dominated the 2006 election. PLN candidate Oscar Arias, like most candidates, supported CAFTA. Ottón Solís of the PAC equivocated, suggesting renegotiating CAFTA's terms and maintaining a dialogue with civil society. The major candidates offered different proposals to ameliorate poverty and inequality. Arias defeated Solís by the slimmest victory in the country's history (40.5 to 40.3 percent; see Appendix, Table A.6), with voter turnout at a historic low. The PLN also won 25 seats in the legislature, followed by the PAC with 17 (see Appendix, Table A.7). Nearly 40 percent of the Assembly seats went to women, the highest percentage in the region.

The CAFTA brouhaha continued after the 2006 election. The Supreme Electoral Tribunal (Tribunal Supremo Electoral, TSE) recommended submitting CAFTA to a popular referendum. The Assembly concurred, making Costa Rica the only country to approve the measure through a popular vote. Although the treaty's constitutionality was challenged before the referendum, the Supreme Court upheld it.[49] CAFTA's support slipped to only 39 percent in 2007 during the referendum campaign.[50] President Arias and business groups energetically advocated ratification. An incendiary internal government memorandum surfaced less than a month before the vote. It proposed a "campaign of fear" to tie the anti-CAFTA campaign to regional leftist leaders Castro, Chávez, and Ortega and suggested reducing the municipal funds of unsupportive mayors.[51] Despite the resulting scandal, Costa Ricans approved the treaty by 51.6 percent. The subsequent passage of thirteen enabling laws delayed final implementation until January 2009. Costa Rica was the last country to implement CAFTA.

The trade agreement required several policies to offset its costs, including replacing lost tax revenues that could curtail social spending.[52] President Arias promised fiscal reform and to reduce poverty by 4 percent during his tenure. He succeeded on both, assisted by an economic recovery. Costa Rica clearly backed away from the neoliberal economic model by reversing earlier social-spending cuts after 2006.[53]

Over the medium term, foreign investment, economic growth, and mean incomes improved after 2000, leaving contradictory evidence on economic-equity outcomes. The share of Costa Ricans living in poverty declined from 27.8 percent of the population in 1992 to 20.3 percent in 2002 to 17.8 in

2012.[54] However, poorer people simultaneously lost ground on income share. The Gini coefficient measuring income inequality rose from 0.46 in 1996 to 0.50 in 2003. Income inequality then declined to 0.48 in 2008, but again increased to 0.51 in 2009 because of that year's slowdown. The longer-term picture suggests a trend toward greater income inequality.[55]

Costa Rica's economy grew rapidly during the late 1990s due to the plant construction and sales of microchip producer Intel.[56] But in 2000–2003 the economy stagnated when coffee and banana prices fell and Intel's computer chip sales fell. This slump revealed the country's continued reliance on a few key exports, albeit more diverse ones than in previous decades.[57] Economic growth then resumed for several years, marred only by a contraction in the recession year 2009. Growth approached 5 percent in each of 2010, 2011, and 2012. Inflation spiked in 2008 but afterward receded. To manage its mounting deficit from 2002 to 2007 the government cut spending and investment, but then accelerated it from 2008 on. Overall, despite occasional setbacks, the Costa Rican economy grew faster than that of other countries in the region by a wide margin from 1990 to 2012 (Table 2.1 and Appendix, Table A.1). For 1960 to 2012, Costa Rica's GDP per capita increased 185 percent, compared to the regional average rise of 90.

CONTEMPORARY COSTA RICAN POLITICS

The PLN, having won so narrowly in 2006, dominated the 2010 elections. The PLN's Laura Chinchilla, vice president and minister of justice under Oscar Arias, won 47 percent of the vote. The PAC's Ottón Solís took 25 percent and the PML's Otto Guevara of the Libertarian Movement Party 21 percent. The PUSC continued its dramatic decline, winning less than 4 percent of the vote. The PLN captured 24 of 57 seats in the Legislative Assembly. The PAC won 11 seats, followed by the PML with nine, the PUSC with six, and the Accessibility without Exclusion Party (PASE) four. Smaller parties divided the remaining three seats. It was a momentous year for women, as Laura Chinchilla became Costa Rica's first woman president and women won 39 percent of the seats in the Legislative Assembly.

Despite her decisive victory, President Chinchilla's administration began and continued in crisis. She inherited a public deficit of almost $1 billion, a growing public-security problem, and a border dispute with Nicaragua over the San Juan River. The growing presence of Mexican drug cartels and public perceptions of insecurity necessitated a swift response to the country's crime problem. Shortly after entering office, Chinchilla authorized the training of 1,000 new police officers. In February 2011, she unveiled a ten-year crime plan, developed with the assistance of the UNDP, to improve law-enforcement training, institutional coordination, and crime-prevention

programs. Critics attacked the *Política Integral y Sostenible de Seguridad Ciudadana y Promoción de la Paz Social para Costa Rica* (Policy for Integral and
Sustainable Citizen Security and Promotion of Social Peace for Costa Rica,
POLSEPAZ) for offering few specific solutions and for not identifying a
source of funding.[58] By 2012, homicide rates had dropped to 8.9 from 11.5
in 2010. The administration claimed that improvements in policing intelligence and technology decreased the crime rate.[59] That said, homicides rose
again in 2013 because of increased drug trafficking.[60]

Dissatisfaction with President Chinchilla arose early in her administration. In April 2011, the opposition in the Legislative Assembly elected the
PAC's Juan Carlos Mendoza, the body's president, the first time in over
four decades the key position went to someone outside the ruling party.[61]
Corruption scandals bloomed. During Chinchilla's first two years in office,
thirteen cabinet ministers resigned. Particularly troubling was the number
of top administration officials implicated in corruption scandals. In March
2012, three high-ranking officials, including Finance Minister Fernando
Herrero, were accused of undervaluing property to evade taxes; Herrero was
forced to resign. It was also revealed that Herrero and his wife, presidential
consultant Florisabel Rodríguez, had benefited from irregular bidding on a
state-owned oil-refinery project. A related investigation ensnared Vice President Luis Lieberman and Minister of Education Leonardo Garnier, a founding member of a consultancy firm with Herrero and Rodríguez.[62] Although
the attorney general's ethics office found that both men had breached ethics
rules, Chinchilla claimed that they had not acted in bad faith and rejected
the Assembly's calls to dismiss them. Her decision was wildly unpopular—
one poll indicated that 95 percent of those familiar with the case disagreed
with her decision.[63] The scandals and resignations complicated her relationship with the Legislative Assembly, which refused to pass any bills until the
end of July.[64]

Minister of Public Works Francisco Jiménez resigned in May 2012 amid
allegations of corruption on a road project along the San Juan River. Scandal embroiled Chinchilla herself in 2013 when a jet she flew on to Peru and
Venezuela was linked to drug traffickers. This brought the resignations of the
Presidency Vice Minister Mauricio Boraschi, who was also head of the Office
of Intelligence and Security and the anti-drug commissioner, and the Com-
munications Minister, Francisco Chacón, as well as a presidential aide. This
calamitous record undermined public confidence in her administration and
her ability to govern. By July 2013, only 9 percent of Costa Ricans approved
of her performance, the worst presidential approval rating in two decades.[65]
Even former PLN president Oscar Arias was critical of her administration.[66]
The 2012 LAPOP survey revealed that Costa Rican support for the political
system and democracy had declined under Chinchilla.[67]

Despite President Chinchilla's unpopularity, the PLN remained Costa Rica's leading party prior to the 2014 presidential elections.[68] The PLN's presidential nominee Johnny Araya, former mayor of San José and himself implicated in corruption scandals, initially held a strong lead in the field of thirteen candidates, but ongoing corruption within the PLN had taken a toll on dissatisfied voters. Furthermore, his lack of knowledge of the cost of basic goods added to the perception that the party was increasingly out of touch with the average voter. José Villalta of the Frente Amplio enjoyed a late surge in the polls. A relative unknown, Villalta had to fend off comparisons to other leftists in the region and became the focus of Araya's campaign. Election day delivered a surprise. PAC's Luis Guillermo Solís, who had never polled above third place in the race, placed first with 30.6 percent of the vote. Araya followed with 29.7 percent and Villalta with 17.25 percent of the vote. Because no candidate won the 40 percent required to avoid a runoff, Solís and Araya proceeded to a second round of voting scheduled for April 2014.

The PLN also fared poorly in the Legislative Assembly elections, winning only eighteen seats (a loss of six seats), followed by the PAC with thirteen, Frente Amplio with nine, and PUSC with eight. The remaining seats were shared among five small parties. The fractious composition of the legislature ensured that parties would have to work together to pass legislation. Two key provisions of the 2009 electoral code were in effect for the 2014 elections. First, a new quota required that 50 percent of candidates be women. Nevertheless, the number of women elected to the Legislative Assembly actually decreased from 2010.[69] This occurred because the parties positioned women far down the ballot ranking so that mostly men won seats under the proportional representation scheme. Although none of the thirteen presidential candidates were women, the major parties (including PLN, PAC, FA, PUSC) nominated women for vice president. Second, the 2014 elections also marked the first time that Costa Ricans living abroad were able to vote at consulates outside of the country, though fewer than 3,000 of the almost 13,000 voters eligible did so.

In a stunning development in early March 2014, a month before the runoff, PLN candidate Johnny Araya dropped out of the presidential race, assuring the PAC's Solís the presidential victory for the 2014–2018 term. Whether the PAC's 2014 victory constituted yet another seismic change in the party system or a death knell for the PLN would only be known in the next round of elections in 2018.

CONCLUSIONS

During the 1970s, Costa Rica somewhat ameliorated the growing difficulties of working-class victims of rapid economic change and carried this off with low repression. Working-class wages recovered or retained purchasing power.

Policy changes shifted some wealth and income to certain lower-class groups. This combination of low repression and some accommodation of working-class interests, contrasted with high repression and no accommodation in Somoza's Nicaragua, Guatemala, and El Salvador, kept Costa Rica relatively politically stable.

Costa Rica's consolidated democratic regime weathered the 1970s and 1980s intact, but the country nevertheless experienced two major middle-term effects from its shifting role in the international political economy. External structural and political pressures forced Costa Rica to curtail its long-standing social-democratic economic model and embrace neoliberalism. This transformation undermined the traditional platform of the National Liberation Party and eroded its position as the system's dominant party. The newly formed Social Christian Unity Party, more comfortable with neoliberalism, quickly became a formidable competitor. The PUSC seemed to have replaced the PLN as the dominant party, but a series of scandals caused the PUSC's rapid collapse in 2006.

By the early 2000s, Costa Rica's erstwhile social-democratic development model of the 1950s through the 1980s had largely vanished. Under the new development model the state not only opened up the economy to attract investment, it sharply curtailed equality-enhancing economic and human development policies. These programs and their effects had once distinguished Costa Rica from its Central American neighbors and for decades validated the country's exceptionalist myth. The neoliberal economic transformation hurt citizens' well-being for over a decade and affected a previously stable party system. Growing dissatisfaction with the status quo drove a decline of the PLN and rise of the PUSC, followed by the precipitous collapse of the PUSC, the rise of the PAC and Libertarian Movement, and the PLN's partial resurgence. Shrinking margins in the legislature necessitated that the PLN work with minority parties to enact its agenda. The controversy surrounding the CAFTA free-trade agreement displayed continuing tensions between supporters of the neoliberal and social-democratic models. Ultimately two successive National Liberation administrations restored social spending and reduced poverty. Yet despite poverty amelioration and economic recovery, serial scandals during the Chinchilla administration deepened Costa Ricans' national malaise and continued eroding their system support. The PAC's 2014 presidential victory provided another landmark change in the party system.

Recommended Readings and Resources

Booth, John A. 1998. *Costa Rica: Quest for Democracy*. Boulder, CO: Westview Press.

Cortés Ramos, Alberto, Gerardo Hernández Naranjo, and Diego Sánchez-Ancochea. 2013. "Costa Rica." In Diego Sánchez-Ancochea and Salvador Martí i Puig, eds. *Handbook of Central American Governance*. London: Routledge.

Lehoucq, Fabrice E., and Ivan Molina. 2006. *Stuffing the Ballot Box: Fraud, Electoral Reform, and Democratization in Costa Rica.* Cambridge: Cambridge University Press.

Paus, Eva. 2005. *Foreign Investment, Development, and Globalization: Can Costa Rica Become Ireland?* New York: Palgrave Macmillan.

Sandoval-García, Carlos. 2004. *Threatening Others: Nicaraguans and the Formation of National Identities in Costa Rica.* Athens: Ohio University Press.

Seligson, Mitchell A., 2002. "Trouble in Paradise: The Impact of the Erosion of System Support in Costa Rica." *Latin American Research Review* 37 (1):160–185.

Seligson, Mitchell A., and Edward Muller. 1987. "Democracy, Stability, and Economic Crisis: Costa Rica, 1978–1983." *International Studies Quarterly* 31 (September):301–326.

Wilson, Bruce. 1998. *Costa Rica: Politics, Economics and Democracy.* Boulder, CO: Lynne Rienner Publishers.

Yashar, Deborah J. 1997. *Demanding Democracy: Reform and Reaction in Costa Rica and Guatemala, 1870s–1950s.* Stanford, CA.: Stanford University Press.

NOTES

1. On the negative side, critics argue that Costa Rican exceptionalism is often carried to xenophobic and racist extremes, especially vis-à-vis Nicaraguans. This charge is articulated by Costa Rican scholar Carlos Sandoval-García in *Threatening Others: Nicaraguans and the Formation of National Identities in Costa Rica* (Athens: Ohio University Press, 2004), the Spanish edition of which won the 2002 Costa Rican National Monograph Award.

2. Bruce M. Wilson, *Costa Rica: Politics, Economics, and Democracy* (Boulder, CO: Lynne Rienner Publishers, 1998); John A. Booth, *Costa Rica: Quest for Democracy* (Boulder, CO: Westview Press, 1998); William I. Robinson, *Transnational Conflicts: Central America, Social Change, and Globalization* (London: Verso, 2003).

3. John A. Booth, "Representative Constitutional Democracy in Costa Rica: Adaptation to Crisis in the Turbulent 1980s," in Steve Ropp and James Morris, eds., *Central America: Crisis and Adaptation* (Albuquerque: University of New Mexico Press, 1984), Table 5.1. Other material on the evolution of Costa Rica drawn from Mitchell A. Seligson and Miguel Gómez, "Ordinary Elections in Extraordinary Times: The Political Economy of Voting in Costa Rica," in John A. Booth and Mitchell A. Seligson, eds., *Elections and Democracy in Central America* (Chapel Hill: University of North Carolina Press, 1989); John A. Booth, "Costa Rica: The Roots of Democratic Stability," in Larry Diamond, Juan J. Linz, and Seymour Martin Lipset, eds., *Democracy in Developing Countries,* Volume 4: *Latin America* (Boulder, CO: Lynne Rienner Publishers, 1989), pp. 387–422; Lowell Gudmundson, *Costa Rica before Coffee* (Baton Rouge: Louisiana State University Press, 1986); and from interviews by Booth with Costa Rican scholars and political experts during author's visits there in August 1987, January 1988, and December 1990. See also Booth, *Costa Rica: Quest for Democracy,* Ch. 3.

4. See Booth, *Costa Rica: Quest for Democracy*, pp. 40–42; Astrid Fischel, *Consenso y represión: Una interpretación sociopolítica de la educación costarricense* (San José: Editorial Costa Rica, 1987).

5. Booth, *Costa Rica: Quest for Democracy*, p. 42; and Fabrice E. Lehoucq and Ivan Molina, *Stuffing the Ballot Box: Fraud, Electoral Reform, and Democratization in Costa Rica* (Cambridge: Cambridge University Press, 2002), Ch. 1.

6. John A. Booth and Thomas W. Walker, *Understanding Central America*, 3rd ed. (Boulder, CO: Westview Press, 1999), Appendix, Tables A.1 and A.2.

7. See Chapter 2 or, for more detail, John A. Booth, "Socioeconomic and Political Roots of National Revolts in Central America," *Latin American Research Review* 26, No. 1 (1991), pp. 33–74.

8. Booth and Walker, *Understanding Central America*, 3rd ed., Appendix, Table A.6.

9. See also Victor Bulmer-Thomas, *The Political Economy of Central America Since 1920* (New York: Cambridge University Press, 1987), Table 10.7, p. 219; Víctor Hugo Céspedes, Alberto di Mare, and Ronulfo Jiménez, *Costa Rica: La economía en 1985* (San José, Costa Rica: Academia de Centroamérica, 1986), Cuadro 19, p. 71.

10. Booth and Walker, *Understanding Central America*, 3rd ed., Appendix, Table A.7 and see Table A.6.

11. Víctor Hugo Céspedes, *Evolución de la distribución del ingreso en Costa Rica* (San José, Costa Rica: Instituto de Investigación en Ciencias Económicas, Universidad de Costa Rica, 1979), Cuadro 6; and Céspedes et al., *Costa Rica: La economía en 1985,* Cuadro 20, p. 73; David Felix, "Income Distribution and the Quality of Life in Latin America: Patterns, Trends, and Policy Implications," *Latin American Research Review* 18, No. 2 (1983), pp. 3–34.

12. For further data, see John A. Booth, "Representative Constitutional Democracy in Costa Rica: Adaptation to Crisis in the Turbulent 1980s," in S. Ropp and J. Morris, eds., *Central America: Crisis and Adaptation* (Albuquerque: University of New Mexico Press, 1984), p. 171. On the operation and impact of the Costa Rican development model, see John A. Booth, *Costa Rica: Quest for Democracy* (Boulder, CO: Westview Press, 1998), Ch. 3 and 8.

13. Mitchell A. Seligson, *Peasants of Costa Rica and the Development of Agrarian Capitalism* (Madison: University of Wisconsin Press, 1980), pp. 122–170; see also Francisco Barahona Riera, *Reforma agraria y poder político* (San José: Editorial Universidad de Costa Rica, 1980), pp. 221–422; and Donaldo Castillo Rivas, "Modelos de acumulación, agricultura, y agroindustria en Centroamérica," in D. Castillo Rivas, ed., *Centroamérica: Más allá de la crisis* (México City: Ediciones SIAP, 1983), pp. 210–213.

14. Booth and Walker, *Understanding Central America,* 3rd ed., Appendix Table A.8.

15. E. Lederman et al., "Trabajo y empleo," in Chester Zelaya, ed., *Costa Rica contemporánea, Tomo II* (San José: Editorial Costa Rica, 1979); James Backer, *La Iglesia y el sindicalismo en Costa Rica* (San José: Editorial Costa Rica, 1978), pp. 135–207;

Gustavo Blanco and Orlando Navarro, *El solidarismo: Pensamiento y dinámica social de un movimiento obrero patronal* (San José: Editorial Costa Rica, 1984).

16. Rodrigo Fernández Vásquez, "Costa Rica: Interpretación histórica sobre reforma social y acción eclesiástica: 1940–1982," *Estudios Sociales Centroamericanos* 33 (September–December 1982), pp. 221–248.

17. This material is from John A. Booth, "Costa Rica: The Roots of Democratic Stability," in Larry Jay Diamond, Seymour Martin Lipset, and Juan J. Linz, eds. *Democracy in Developing Countries,* Volume 4: *Latin America* (Boulder, CO: Lynne Rienner Publishers, 1989); and Booth, "Representative Constitutional Democracy."

18. Booth and Walker, *Understanding Central America,* 3rd ed., Appendix, Tables A.5 and A.6.

19. "Costa Rica," *Mesoamérica* (April 1990), pp. 11–12; "Costa Rica," *Mesoamérica* (July 1990), pp. 7–8; "Costa Rica," *Mesoamérica* (October 1990), p. 9; "Costa Rica," *Mesoamérica* (November 1990), pp. 9–10; "Costa Rica," *Mesoamérica* (December 1990), p. 11; "Costa Rica," *Mesoamérica* (January 1991), pp. 4–7; "Costa Rica," *Mesoamérica* (February 1991), pp. 4–5; "Costa Rica," *Mesoamérica* (April 1991), pp. 1–2.

20. John A. Booth, "Political Parties in Costa Rica: Sustaining Democratic Stability in a Latin American Context," in Paul Webb and Stephen White, eds., *Political Parties in New Democracies* (Oxford: Oxford University Press, 2007); Mitchell A. Seligson and Edward Muller, "Democracy, Stability, and Economic Crisis: Costa Rica, 1978–1983," *International Studies Quarterly* 31 (September 1987), pp. 301–326; and Booth, "Costa Rican Democracy."

21. Booth, "Representative Constitutional Democracy," pp. 173–176; Booth, "Costa Rican Democracy," pp. 39–40; Seligson, *Peasants,* pp. 105–114; US Department of State, *Country Reports on Human Rights Practices* (Washington, DC: US Government Printing Office, February 2, 1981), pp. 241–244. See also Booth, *Costa Rica: Quest for Democracy,* pp. 114–121.

22. This section draws heavily on Booth, "Political Parties in Costa Rica." Data are drawn from Mary A. Clark, "Nontraditional Export Promotion in Costa Rica: Sustaining Export-Led Growth," *Journal of Interamerican Studies and World Affairs* 37, No. 2 (1995), pp. 181–223; Wilson, *Costa Rica: Politics, Economics, and Democracy,* pp. 113–150; Booth, *Costa Rica: Quest for Democracy,* Ch. 8; and Booth and Walker, *Understanding Central America,* 3rd ed., Appendix, Tables A.1, A.4, and A.5.

23. Robinson, *Transnational Conflicts,* pp. 64–65.

24. Booth, *Costa Rica: Quest for Democracy,* Ch. 8.

25. Ibid.

26. International Institute for Democracy and Electoral Assistance, Voter Turnout: Voter turnout data for Costa Rica, www.idea.int/vt/countryview.cf?id=54#pres, accessed October 1, 2013.

27. Alan Heston, Robert Summers, and Bettina Aten, *Penn World Table Version 6.1* (Philadelphia: Center for International Comparisons at the University of Pennsylvania

94   4: COSTA RICA

[CICUP], October 2002); Inter-American Development Bank, country notes, www
.iadb.org/exr/country/, accessed June 14, 2004.

28. Robinson, *Transnational Conflicts*, Ch. 4.

29. See our Table 2.1 and the World Bank Group, Latin America and the Caribbean, Costa Rica: Social Spending and the Poor, http://web.worldbank.org/WBSITE
/EXTERNAL/COUNTRIES/LACEXT/COSTARICAEXTN/0,,contentMDK
:20252791~pagePK:141137~piPK:141127~theSitePK:295413,00.html, accessed January 6, 2005.

30. This section draws heavily on Booth, "Political Parties in Costa Rica."

31. Kenneth M. Roberts, "Rethinking Economic Alternatives: Left Parties and the
Articulation of Popular Demands in Chile and Peru," and Carlos M. Vilas, "Participation, Inequality, and the Whereabouts of Democracy," both in Douglas A. Chalmers,
Carlos M. Vilas, Katherine Hite, Scott B. Martin, Kerianne Piester, and Monique
Segarra, eds., *The New Politics of Inequality in Latin America: Rethinking Participation
and Representation* (Oxford: Oxford University Press, 1997); and William I. Robinson, *Promoting Polyarchy: Globalization, U.S. Intervention, and Hegemony* (Cambridge: Cambridge University Press, 1996).

32. Regine Steichen, "Cambios en la orientación política-ideológica de los partidos políticos en la década de los '80," and Marcelo J. Prieto, "Cambios en las organi-
zaciones políticas costarricenses," both in José Manuel Villasuso, ed., *El nuevo rostro de
Costa Rica* (Heredia, Costa Rica: Centro de Estudios Democráticos de América Latina,
1992); Wilson, *Costa Rica: Politics, Economics, and Democracy*; and Carlos Sojo, "En
el nombre del padre: Patrimonialismo y democracia en Costa Rica," in Manuel Rojas
Bolaños and Carlos Sojo, *El malestar con la política: Partidos y élites en Costa Rica* (San
José, Costa Rica: Facultad Latinoamericano de Ciencias Sociales, 1995), pp. 84–86.

33. Oscar Alvarez, "Costa Rica," *Boletín Electoral Latinoamericano* 17 (January–
June 1997), p. 60.

34. Booth, "Political Parties in Costa Rica," Tables 2 and 3.

35. Ibid., and Manuel Rojas Bolaños, "Las relaciones partido gobierno," in Manuel Rojas Bolaños and Carlos Sojo, *El malestar con la política: Partidos y élites en Costa
Rica* (San José, Costa Rica: Facultad Latinoamericano de Ciencias Sociales), pp. 36–
50; Booth, *Costa Rica: Quest for Democracy*, Ch. 8; and Wilson, *Costa Rica: Politics,
Economics, and Democracy*, p. 161.

36. Booth, "Political Parties in Costa Rica."

37. Amaru Barahona, "Costa Rican Democracy on the Edge," *Envio* 250 (May
2002).

38. Tribunal Supremo de Elecciones, Costa Rica, "Elecciones 6 de febrero 2006:
Escrutinio definitivo para elección de diputados," http://www.tse.go.cr/escrutinio
_f2006/Diputados/0.htm/, accessed June 17, 2009.

39. The number of effective parties in the legislature increased from 2.82 in 1998 to
3.32 in 2006; see Booth, "Political Parties in Costa Rica," Tables 2, 3, and 5. Poll data
drawn from the 2008 Latin American Public Opinion survey (see Chapter 9 for details).

40. Booth, "Political Parties in Costa Rica."

41. See Robinson, pp. 142–146.

42. Robinson, p. 245.

43. The World Bank Group, Latin America and the Caribbean, Costa Rica: Social Spending and the Poor, http://web.worldbank.org/WBSITE/EXTERNAL /COUNTRIES/LACEXT/COSTARICAEXTN/0,,contentMDK:20252791~pagePK :141137~piPK:141127~theSitePK:295413,00.html, accessed January 6, 2005.

44. Some observers argue that Latin American countries' recent slide in these rankings, despite improvements in income and social indicators, occurs because other nations are rising relatively faster. Source for data: United Nations Development Program, 2007/2008 Human Development Report, Costa Rica, http://hdrstats .undp.org/en/countries/data_sheets/cty_ds_CRI.html;   http://hdrstats.undp.org/en /countries/profiles/CRI.html.

45. "Protests Put Privatization on Hold," *Central America Report* (April 7, 2000), p. 6; "Telecom Privatization Ruled Unconstitutional," *Central America Report* (May 12, 2000), p. 6.

46. *Central America Report* (May 1999), p. 7.

47. "Poverty Increases," *Central America Report* (January 7, 2005).

48. *Central America Report* (September 2003).

49. Latin American Database, "Constitutional Way Cleared for Cafta in Costa Rica; Referendum Is Next," *NotiCen* (July 12, 2007).

50. Latin American Database, "Scandal Topples Costa Rican Vice President, Clouds Outlook as CAFTA Referendum Nears," *NotiCen* (September 27, 2007).

51. Ibid.

52. Matthew Brooks, "Social Agenda Arises Post-Referendum," *Central America Report* (October 19, 2007).

53. Economic Commission for Latin America and the Caribbean, Data Bases and Statistical Publications, Statistics and Indicators, http://estadisticas.cepal .org/cepalstat/WEB_CEPALSTAT/estadisticasIndicadores.asp?idioma=i, accessed November 20, 2013.

54. Economic Commission for Latin America and the Caribbean (ECLAC), Data Bases and Economic Publications, http://estadisticas.cepal.org/cepalstat/WEB _CEPALSTAT/perfilesNacionales.asp?idioma=i, accessed December 6, 2012.

55. The World Bank Group, Latin America and the Caribbean, Costa Rica: Social Spending and the Poor, http://web.worldbank.org/WBSITE/EXTERNAL /COUNTRIES/LACEXT/COSTARICAEXTN/0,,contentMDK:20252791~page PK:141137~piPK:141127~theSitePK:295413,00.html, accessed January 6, 2005. Note that the Gini coefficients cited in this source range from 0 to 100 in the original. We have changed them here to 0 to 1.0 metric for consistency with our tables elsewhere.

56. Ibid.

57. *Central America Report* (November 2000), p. 6, and (June 2001).

58. "Limitado aporte Polsepaz," *La Nación* (February 17, 2011), http://www
.nacion.com/opinion/editorial/Limitado-aporte-Polsepaz_0_1178082231.html;
and Alex Sanchez, "Costa Rica: An Army-less Nation in a Problem-Prone Region,"
Council on Hemispheric Affairs (June 2, 2011), http://www.coha.org/costa-rica-an
-army-less-nation-in-a-problem-prone-region/.

59. "Costa Rica's Judiciary Reports First Drop in Homicide Rate in Six Years;
Minister's Goal is Eliminating Epidemic." *NotiCen* (June 21, 2013).

60. Corey Kane and Zac Dyer, "Drugs Drive Rising Homicide Rates in Costa Rica,"
The Tico Times (August 21, 2013), http://www.ticotimes.net/More-news/News-Briefs
/Drugs-drive-rising-homicide-rates-in-Costa-Rica_Wednesday-August-21-2013.

61. The PLN briefly maneuvered to hold on to the presidency by holding the vote
without a quorum, required by Assembly rules.

62. Alvaro Murillo and Esteban Mata, "Fiscalía investiga a Liberman y a Garnier por tráfico de influencias," *La Nación* (July 6, 2012), http://www.nacion.com
/nacional/politica/Fiscalia-investiga-Liberman-Garnier-influencias_0_1279072125
.html, and "Costa Rica's Finance Minister Resigns over Tax Scandal," *Inside Costa
Rica* (April 3, 2012), http://www.insidecostarica.com/dailynews/2012/april/03
/costarica12040301.htm; http://ladb.unm.edu/noticen/2012/08/23–078719.

63. Esteban Oviedo, "Ministro: la gente opinó sobre una mala percepción," *La
Nación* (August 4, 2012), http://www.nacion.com/archivo/Ministro-gente-opino
-mala-percepcion_0_1284871706.html; http://www.nacion.com/archivo/Presidenta
-absuelve-Liberman-Garnier-archiva_0_1279272178.html.

64. "Fallout from Costa Rican Tax Scandal Ceases After Congress-Government
Tug of War," *NotiCen* (August 23, 2012).

65. Esteban Oviedo, "Laura Chinchilla saca peor nota de los últimos 6 gobier-
nos," *La Nación* (July 8, 2013), http://www.nacion.com/nacional/politica/Chinchilla
-saca-peor-ultimos-gobiernos_0_1352464780.html.

66. "Ex president Oscar Arias critica la gestión de Laura Chinchilla," *Repretel*
(July 6, 2013), http://www.repretel.com/el-expresidente-óscar-arias-critica-la-gestión
-de-laura-chinchilla

67. Ronald Alfaro-Redondo and Mitchell Seligson, "Cultura política de la democracia en Costa Rica, 2012: La erosión de los pilares de estabilidad política," http://
www.vanderbilt.edu/lapop/cr/Costa_Rica_Country_Report_2012_Reduced_W.pdf.

68. Eillyn Jiménez Badilla, "Araya sigue siendo el predilecto," *Diario Extra* (August 5, 2013), http://www.diarioextra.com/Dnew/noticiaDetalle/137814.

69. Álvaro Murillo, "Nueva ley electoral fracasa en llevar más mujeres al Congreso
de Costa Rica," *La Nación* (February 17, 2014), http://www.nacion.com/nacional
/elecciones2014/Nueva-electoral-Congreso-Costa-Rica_0_1397260302.html.

5

NICARAGUA

NICARAGUA HAS ABUNDANT ARABLE LAND, CONSIDERABLE hydroelectric, thermal, wind, and (possibly) fossil energy reserves, and significant timber and mineral resources. It also has access to two oceans and a lake and river system that could make it an ideal site for an interoceanic waterway. Yet Nicaraguans today are the poorest Central Americans and Latin Americans. The paradox arises from the extreme dependency established in the colonial period, institutionalized in the twentieth century, and deepened by war and geopolitics. Despite paroxysms of war, revolution, and counterrevolution, Nicaragua's perennially fractured political and economic elites continue to fail to advance the country's development.

HISTORICAL BACKGROUND

Nineteenth-century Nicaragua was plagued by civil wars and foreign interference. During the first several decades, the Liberal and Conservative elites, based in the cities of León and Granada, respectively, struggled to control the national government. At the same time, Britain and the United States—both interested in building a transoceanic waterway—maneuvered to insert themselves into the power vacuum left by Spain.

At mid-century, foreign interference and the Liberal-Conservative conflict caused a war. In the late 1840s the British and Americans almost fought over a British attempt to seize the mouth of the San Juan River. In the resulting Clayton-Bulwer Treaty (1850), the United States and Britain mutually renounced the right to any unilateral exploitation of the region. However, the California gold rush of the 1850s deepened US interest in Central America as a shortcut between the eastern and western coasts of North America. In 1855 one of two competing transit companies in Nicaragua and Panama became embroiled in Nicaragua's Liberal-Conservative clash. Liberals, seeking advantage in the business dispute, imported a small mercenary army of North Americans commanded by adventurer William Walker to help them defeat the Conservatives. The plan backfired when the flamboyant Tennessean seized power for himself. This left Nicaragua's Liberals so discredited by association with the interloper that the Conservatives ruled virtually unchallenged until 1893.

In the nineteenth century, globalization in the form of spreading coffee cultivation brought profound social and economic changes. Before 1870, intra-elite turmoil and relatively low foreign economic control had permitted Nicaragua to develop an internal market and a surprisingly large free peasantry. One foreign observer stated: "Peonage such as is seen in Mexico and various parts of Spanish America does not exist in Nicaragua. . . . Any citizen whatever can set himself up on a piece of open land . . . to cultivate plantain and corn."[1] This pattern changed radically when growing international demand for coffee brought its widespread cultivation to Nicaragua. Coffee required new lands and cheap labor. By the 1870s the elite began to dispossess peasant and Indian farmers in the northern highlands, using chicanery, self-serving legislation, and violence. The displaced peasants had few options except peonage on coffee plantations. When some of them rebelled in the War of the Comuneros of 1881, the elite-run government crushed the uprising by killing thousands.

Coffee production that displaced peasant smallholdings accelerated under a modernizing Liberal dictator, José Santos Zelaya (1893–1909). Zelaya also built educational and governmental infrastructure (censuses, archives, a more modern army) and defended the interests of Nicaragua and Central America against a burgeoning imperialist urge in the United States. After the United States decided to build a trans-isthmian canal in Panama, Zelaya sought a canal deal with US rivals Germany and Japan. To protect its canal monopoly, in 1909 the United States encouraged Zelaya's Conservative opposition to rebel and then landed marines to protect the rebels. In 1909, Zelaya resigned and in 1910 the Liberals relinquished power to the minority Conservative Party. By 1912, however, the Conservatives performed so badly that a combined Liberal-Conservative rebellion occurred. That revolt was put down when US marines physically occupied Nicaragua.

From most of the period from 1912 to 1933, the United States militarily occupied Nicaragua. US-dominated governments generally followed Washington's dictates, even when clearly contrary to Nicaraguan interests. The Chamorro-Bryan Treaty of 1916, for example, gave the United States rights to build a canal in Nicaragua. The Americans had no intention of constructing such a canal; they simply wanted to block competition for the US-built waterway just completed in Panama. In 1928, another puppet government under US pressure gave Colombia several important Nicaraguan islands, including San Andrés, to mollify Colombian resentment of the US role in taking Panama from Colombia in 1903.

And finally, during the latter part of this period, the United States forced Nicaragua to create a modern constabulary combining army and police—the Nicaraguan National Guard (Guardia Nacional). A movement resisting US occupation sprang up in 1927, led by the charismatic guerrilla-patriot Augusto C. Sandino. US marines could not defeat Sandino's resistance, so the National Guard was significantly enlarged to assist in the struggle. The war was a standoff, and the United States eventually withdrew its troops at the end of 1932. The National Guard then became the vehicle by which its first Nicaraguan commander, Anastasio Somoza García, created and consolidated the Somoza family dictatorship, which subsequently brutalized Nicaragua for over four decades.

As commander of the National Guard, Anastasio Somoza García had Sandino assassinated in 1934 and used the Guard to seize political power in 1936. Thereafter, three Somozas held power from 1936 until 1979. Somoza García was either president or the power behind puppets until his assassination in 1956. His son, Luis Somoza Debayle, ruled directly or through surrogates until 1967. Luis' younger brother, Anastasio Somoza Debayle, was "elected" to the presidency in 1967 and held power from then until 1979. Throughout this period, the Somoza dynasty rested on two primary pillars of support: the United States and the National Guard. A Somoza always commanded the Guard and purposely isolated it from the people. They allowed the Guard to become thoroughly corrupt to ensure its loyalty to the Somozas. A sort of Mafia in uniform, the Guard ran prostitution, gambling, and protection rackets, took bribes, and extorted kickbacks for various legal and illegal activities.

The Somozas secured US support in two ways: personal ingratiation and political subservience. They expertly cultivated Americans. Each was educated in the United States, spoke fluent vernacular English, and knew how to be a "good old boy" among ethnocentric, often homesick North American diplomats and visitors. The Somozas always supported US policy, whether anti-Axis during World War II or anti-Communist thereafter. They allowed Nicaragua to serve as staging grounds for the CIA-organized exile invasions of Guatemala

(1954) and Cuba (1961), participated in the US occupation of the Dominican Republic in 1965, and offered to send Nicaraguan troops to fight in both Korea and Vietnam.

As a result, US support for the Somozas usually remained strong and visible. Especially after the beginning of the Alliance for Progress in 1961, the United States gave Nicaragua many millions in assistance for social and economic projects (despite ample evidence that the Somozas and their accomplices stole much of the aid). US ambassadors were normally unabashedly pro-Somoza. What is more, during the 1960s and 1970s, the dictatorship received far more US military support than other Central American and Latin American countries (see Appendix, Table A.3).

GLOBAL FORCES AND INSURRECTION

Effects of Rapid Economic Growth. Under the direction of the Somozas and the stimulus of the Central American Common Market and Alliance for Progress, Nicaragua underwent rapid industrialization and expansion of commercial export agriculture during the 1960s and early 1970s. Overall economic growth statistics were impressive; per capita gross domestic product (GDP) rose an average of almost 3.9 percent each year from 1962 to 1971, and an average of 2.3 percent annually between 1972 and 1976, by far the fastest increase in the region.[2] This brought other social change: between 1960 and 1980 Nicaragua had Central America's biggest surge in urban population and manufacturing output, and its biggest decline in the agricultural workforce (see Appendix, Tables A.1 and A.2).

Despite impressive growth, government policies prevented the benefits from this new economic activity from reaching poorer Nicaraguans. The regime repressed unions and kept wages—normally set by the regime—low. Consumer prices rose moderately between 1963 and 1972. But after the 1973 Organization of Petroleum Exporting Countries (OPEC) oil embargo, escalating oil prices drove inflation up to almost 11 percent a year from 1973 through 1977. Real wages (corrected for inflation) among ordinary Nicaraguans peaked in 1967 and began a long slide that by the late 1970s ate away a third of their 1967 purchasing power. Workers' share of national income increased during the 1960s but also fell sharply in 1974 and 1975.[3] Wage-earning Nicaraguans suffered a palpable drop in their ability to feed and shelter their families.

Income inequality between rich and poor Nicaraguans had become very great by 1977, when the wealthiest fifth of the people earned 59.9 percent of the national income, while the poorer half was left with only 15.0 percent.[4] The devastating Managua earthquake of December 24, 1972, aggravated this income shift by putting tens of thousands of white- and blue-collar workers out of work.

Nicaragua's middle class experienced a decade of improving living standards during the 1960s followed by a sharp reversal as of 1973. Middle-class employment shrank markedly in the mid-1970s when the earthquake destroyed many small businesses and commercial jobs. Nine thousand manufacturing jobs (about 13 percent of the total) disappeared from 1972 to 1973, as did 15,000 service sector jobs (over 7 percent of the total). New jobs shifted to the lesser-paying construction sector, which nearly doubled in size by 1974, and to the informal sector.[5] The government levied a stiff surtax on those still employed to finance reconstruction, but corrupt officials stole much of its proceeds. The workweek was increased by as much as 25 percent without increasing pay.[6]

During the Central American Common Market (CACM) boom, employment failed to keep up with rapid workforce growth. Underemployment—an inability to find full-time work, or acceptance of agricultural wage labor because of insufficient farmland for family subsistence farming—affected up to five times as many as were unemployed. Unemployment rose from below 4 percent in 1970 to 13 percent by 1978 despite rapid economic growth.[7] Hardest hit were workers the earthquake left jobless and peasants forced off the land by the rapid expansion of agricultural production for export.

In agriculture, concentration of land ownership increased from the 1950s through the 1970s, especially in the fertile and populous Pacific zone. High cotton prices permitted speculating largeholders to squeeze subsistence cultivators off the land and into the oversupplied wage labor market.[8] "The process of agricultural development was a concentrator of both land and income."[9] In the 1950s and 1960s the government gave preferential treatment in trade, credit, and financial policies and material-technical support to agro-industries belonging to the Somozas and their cohorts.

During the 1960s and 1970s, Nicaragua's three major capitalist factions, which centered around the Banco de América, the Banco Nicaragüense, and the Somoza family interests, began to converge.[10] Once separated from each other by regional, clan, and political party differences, these investor factions increasingly prospered and intertwined under the CACM. Following the Managua earthquake, however, the Somoza faction became aggressively greedy, undermining other investor groups. Growing political and labor unrest caused many Nicaraguan capitalists to doubt whether the regime could sustain growth. Anastasio Somoza Debayle's upper-class support began to erode in the mid-1970s.

By both relative and absolute measures, poor and middle-class Nicaraguans lost some of their share of overall national income and wealth, and suffered a sharp drop in their real earning power during the 1970s. Even some wealthy Nicaraguans lost ground in the 1970s. Such losses doubtless created strong economic grievances.

Popular Mobilization. The decline of working-class wages in the late 1960s and early 1970s revitalized the nation's long-suppressed industrial labor movement,[11] which stepped up organization, work stoppages, and strikes in pursuit of wage gains in 1973–1975.[12] The erosion of middle-class living standards also expanded union membership and organization, and brought strikes by teachers and health personnel. Catholic social workers, missionaries, and priests began organizing unions among Pacific-zone peasant wage laborers in the 1960s. As a tool for teaching the gospel, Catholic social promoters also organized hundreds of small Christian base communities (*comunidades eclesiales de base,* CEBs) among urban and rural poor people. CEBs, joined by Protestant-organized groups after the Managua quake, encouraged community self-help activism and demanded better urban services and housing.[13] Peasant unions increasingly pressed for wage gains, especially after 1975.[14]

As the economy deteriorated, especially after 1974, Nicaraguan private-sector pressure organizations grew and more boldly criticized the government. Such private-sector groups as the business leader–dominated Democratic Liberation Union (Unión Democrática de Liberación, UDEL) called for political and economic reform.

New opposition political parties (particularly, the Social Christian Party) became active in Nicaragua in the 1960s and 1970s.[15] New anti-Somoza factions of the old Conservative and Liberal parties developed during the 1970s. Elements from the Conservative Party united with the Social Christian Party and the anti-Somoza Independent Liberal Party in the National Opposition Union (Unión Nacional Opositora, UNO) to contest the 1967 national election. Student opposition to the regime grew rapidly during the 1970s. The Sandinista National Liberation Front (Frente Sandinista de Liberación Nacional, FSLN), the only surviving rebel group of some twenty guerrilla bands that had appeared between 1959 and 1962, greatly expanded its links to and support from university student groups during the 1970s.[16]

Government Repression and Its Effect on Opposition. President Anastasio Somoza Debayle declared a state of siege and escalated repression in late December 1974 after an embarrassing FSLN hostage-taking incident. The National Guard murdered several thousand mostly innocent rural people suspected as subversives or possible FSLN sympathizers during the ensuing three-year reign of terror.[17] During a brief lifting of the state of siege because of Carter administration pressure, public protests against the regime rose rapidly. The government then redoubled repression in urban areas. The National Guard murdered hundreds of youths suspected of pro-Sandinista sympathies. From 1977 on, the intensifying war against the citizenry drove thousands, especially young people, to join the FSLN.

Following the January 1978 assassination of Pedro Joaquín Chamorro, editor of the opposition newspaper *La Prensa,* bourgeois elements redoubled their anti-regime efforts. Key business interests such as the Superior Council of Private Initiative (Consejo Superior de la Iniciativa Privada, COSIP) joined unions and moderate parties to support general strikes and to form the Broad Opposition Front (Frente Amplio Opositor, FAO). Strongly backed by the United States and Nicaragua's Catholic hierarchy, the FAO strove unsuccessfully to negotiate an end to the Somoza regime lest the FSLN overthrow it.[18]

Popular uprisings spread across urban Nicaragua between August and October 1978. On August 23, 1978, a small Sandinista unit seized the National Palace, taking more than 2,000 hostages, including most members of the Chamber of Deputies. They negotiated the release of 60 Sandinistas from prison, a ransom, and safe passage out of the country. Days afterward, opposition leaders called a successful general strike. In September, thousands spontaneously attacked National Guard posts and drove the regime's troops out of several communities. These revolts in Masaya, Rivas, Jinotega, Matagalpa, Estelí, and Managua typically occurred without much FSLN coordination. The National Guard crushed each uprising, slaughtering civilians and damaging property and public services.

The FSLN, split for several years over tactics, eventually realized that popular outrage had rendered its internal debate sterile. The three Sandinista factions quickly reunified in 1979 under the Joint National Directorate (Dirección Nacional Conjunta, DNC) and built a network of wealthy and prominent supporters embodied by the Group of Twelve (Grupo de los Doce). When the FAO-regime negotiations collapsed in early 1979, moderate and even conservative anti-Somocistas turned to the Sandinistas as the last option to defeat the regime. In 1979 the FSLN forged the United People's Movement (Movimiento Pueblo Unido, MPU) and National Patriotic Front (Frente Patriótico Nacional, FPN) coalitions, confederations that united virtually the entire opposition. Under the military leadership of the FSLN, the MPU and FPN were committed to the defeat of the Somoza regime. In May 1979 an FSLN-led provisional government formed in San José, Costa Rica, to formally embody the opposition's revolutionary claim to sovereignty.

By opening its military ranks to all regime opponents and by forging broad alliances, the FSLN won extensive resources for the final offensive against the regime. Its military ranks ballooned from fewer than 500 troops under arms in mid-1978 to between 2,500 and 5,000 by June 1979. The revolutionary coalition in 1979 enjoyed effective control over parts of northern Nicaragua, sanctuary for bases and political operations in Costa Rica, and diplomatic support from France and various Latin American regimes. FSLN agents purchased weapons from dealers in the United States and took delivery at a base camp in Honduras. Cuba, Venezuela, Panama, and Costa Rica assisted arms shipments to the FSLN for the final offensive. Whenever FSLN forces entered a community in combat, many local residents spontaneously fought alongside them or otherwise assisted them, vastly enhancing the guerrillas' strength and capabilities.

The Outcome. The FSLN-led coalition's unity, material resources, popular support, military capacity, and external backing all grew rapidly in late 1978 and 1979. The coalition's revolutionary government in exile in 1979 took advantage of support from Costa Rica, where it enjoyed political sanctuary, popular sympathy, and secure FSLN bases. Within Nicaragua, FSLN troops enjoyed massive voluntary popular support in combat against the National Guard.

The Somoza regime's strength faded in 1978 and 1979 while its opposition grew. Numerous spontaneous popular uprisings against the government took place in late 1978. The regime lost the support of virtually all social classes and interest sectors, save portions of Somoza's Liberal Nationalist Party (Partido Liberal Nacionalista, PLN) and the National Guard. PLN and regime supporters—many corrupt and anxious to escape with their wealth—began leaving Nicaragua. The desertion of Somocistas became a flood after National Guard troops casually murdered ABC reporter Bill Stewart before the network's cameras on June 20, 1979. The tyrant's associates sensed that this horrible deed had stripped away their remaining legitimacy outside Nicaragua.

The Carter administration had announced its opposition to Somoza's continued rule, a big loss for the regime. The United States struck new aid to Nicaragua from the 1979 budget and blocked pending deliveries by some of Somoza's arms suppliers. Although the US government wanted Somoza out, it also tried ineffectually to keep the Sandinistas from power. The Organization of American States and numerous Latin American regimes had openly sided with the opposition by 1979. The National Guard fought tenaciously against the Sandinistas and Nicaraguan people but became encircled and was pushed back toward Managua during the seven-week final offensive. Having looted the national treasury, Somoza ultimately gave up and left Nicaragua for Miami on July 17, 1979. When the Guard collapsed two days later, the Sandinista-led rebel coalition took power. These dramatic events mark the first great regime change we examine in Central America in the 1970s and 1980s: Nicaragua's passage from personalistic military rule to revolution. This shift started processes of transformation and violent resistance in Nicaragua and prompted much change elsewhere in the isthmus (Chapters 6 through 8).

THE REVOLUTION

The revolutionary government faced many problems. The war had killed 50,000 people—almost 2 percent of the populace. (An equivalent loss to the United States today would be nearly 6 million—some 125 times the US death toll in the Vietnam War.) Property losses approached $1.5 billion, and important export and domestic crops went unplanted. The new government inherited

THE TRIUMPH. FSLN militia guard a checkpoint in Northern Nicaragua and jubilant citizens destroy the horse from Anastasio Somoza's statue in Managua, July 1979 (photos by Thomas Walker).

$1.6 billion in international debts from the old regime. To its chagrin, the new government realized that it would have to assume and pay Somoza's debt to remain creditworthy in international financial circles. Grave and long-standing problems of public health, housing, education, and nutrition, all exacerbated by the war, awaited the new regime.

In power, the Sandinista-led revolutionary coalition sought to destroy the Somoza regime and its economic power base, to replace its brutality and inequities with a fairer, more humane, and less corrupt system, and to reactivate the economy. The Sandinistas themselves wanted to move the economy toward socialism in order to improve the lot of the lower classes, to build participatory democracy under their own leadership, and to integrate all Nicaraguans into the national social and political system. Others in the coalition disagreed about much of the revolutionary program and hoped to share power with, or wrest it away from, the FSLN. Such differences over the ends of the revolution quickly established new lines of conflict and shattered the anti-Somocista alliance.

US-Nicaraguan Relations and the Contra War. The Sandinistas feared that the United States might try to reverse the Nicaraguan revolution, as it had other reformist or revolutionary Latin American governments (Guatemala in 1954, Cuba in 1961, the Dominican Republic in 1965, and Chile in 1973). Although the Carter administration had criticized and opposed Somoza, it had worked tenaciously to keep the Sandinistas from power. Even before the FSLN took over, President Carter authorized the CIA to fund segments of the press and labor movement.[19]

The Carter administration offered the new regime a nervous gesture of friendship with diplomatic recognition, emergency relief aid, and the release of suspended loans from prior years' aid packages in 1979, and a new $75 million loan commitment in 1980. In 1979 and 1980 the Sandinistas had fairly good working relations with the United States but warily regarded US links to several thousand National Guardsmen who had escaped to Honduras and the United States. First the Argentine military and then the CIA organized the ex-Somocista forces, which began to conduct terrorist attacks on Nicaragua from their Honduran refuge.[20] In 1981 the incoming Reagan administration began trying to reverse the Nicaraguan revolution and destabilize the Sandinista government. Reagan accused Nicaragua (with little evidence) of trafficking arms to El Salvador's rebels, and cut off the balance of the Carter administration's $75 million loan credits for wheat purchases.

The United States thereafter escalated its harassment, pressure, and aggression against Nicaragua. Military pressure included massive aid to build up the Honduran military, continuous "maneuvers" in Honduras, and intensive espionage from air, sea, and land. The United States worked continuously to isolate Nicaragua diplomatically from its neighbors in Central America. These pressures, sweetened with generous US aid, persuaded both Honduras and Costa Rica to provide sanctuary to anti-Sandinista rebels. The United States blocked a possible peace agreement among Central American nations negotiated by the Contadora group of Latin American conflict-mediating nations (Mexico, Panama, Colombia, and Venezuela). Washington convinced multilateral lending and development agencies to cut off credit to Nicaragua, and on May 7, 1985, embargoed trade with Nicaragua. US propaganda—energetic and inaccurate—denounced the revolutionary government and exalted the Sandinistas' enemies.

The Reagan administration mounted a proxy military-political effort to topple the Sandinistas. In 1981 Reagan gave the CIA $19.8 million to support and augment an exile army of anti-Sandinista counterrevolutionaries known as the Contras. Their nucleus consisted of former National Guard officers and soldiers and political allies of the former dictator. From 1982 on, attacks across the Honduran border occurred almost daily. Contra forces regularly sabotaged bridges and other economic targets and took almost a thousand civilian and military lives within Nicaragua by late 1982.

By 1983 there existed major Contra groups; the most important were the Honduras-based Nicaraguan Democratic Force (Fuerzas Democráticas Nicaragüenses, FDN), the Costa Rica–based Revolutionary Democratic Alliance (Alianza Revolucionaria Democrática, ARDE), and two Miskito Indian groups. A Contra political directorate was organized by the United States to present a palatable public front and facilitate continued funding by Congress. In 1983 the Contras began extensive guerrilla operations within Nicaragua, especially in the rugged northeast and southeast. The CIA added to the destruction by blowing up Nicaraguan oil-storage tanks and pipelines, and mining harbors on both coasts. The CIA also provided the Contras intelligence, funding, and training (including a sabotage manual for Contra soldiers and another for Contra leaders that recommended assassination of pro-Sandinista civilians).[21]

By 1985 the Contras had 15,000 troops but had achieved few successes against the Nicaraguan military. They had, however, established a clear record of economic sabotage and atrocities and had killed 13,000 people. In the mid-1980s, the US Congress reacted to these developments by withdrawing funding for the Contra war and legally restraining US efforts to topple the Sandinistas. The Reagan administration responded with covert efforts to fund and assist the Contras that included operations (some flatly illegal) by the National Security Council's Colonel Oliver North and other agencies. North brokered an illicit arms deal with Iran to provide off-the-books funds for the Contras. The United States also promoted cash gifts to the Contras from private domestic donors, compliant foreign governments, and allegedly even drug smugglers.[22]

When these efforts came to light in October 1986 they became known as the Iran-Contra scandal, which placed further US funding to the Contras in doubt. Reagan then pressed the Contras to intensify their offensive. Supported by a CIA-run military supply operation in 1987, an escalation brought the war to its destructive peak and raised the death toll for the entire war to just under 31,000. Despite more combat operations, the Contras' military successes remained limited. After the Central American Peace Accord was signed in August 1987, the Contras eventually entered negotiations with the Sandinista government (1988), and the war began to wind down. The new Bush administration called for continued US aid to help hold the Contras together. Direct US aid to the Contras by 1989 had totaled over $400 million. In the long run, they would not be formally disarmed and disbanded until mid-1990, months after the Sandinistas lost the externally manipulated election of February 1990.

The Revolutionary Government. What kind of government elicited such antagonism from three US administrations? The FSLN consolidated its political
dominance over the new government by early 1980 but kept other coalition
members on the junta, in the cabinet, and in the Council of State (Consejo de
Estado). Though the FSLN's nine-man DNC held ultimate veto power over
the government and its programs, the Sandinistas created a pluralistic system
that encouraged representatives of the upper-class minority to participate. Upper-class, business, and various political party interests, although in the coalition, could not control policy and therefore became increasingly antagonistic
toward the FSLN. The regime maintained a dialogue with business interests
and with a coalition of opposition parties.[23]

The Sandinistas promoted their own brand of democracy emphasizing
popular participation in making public policy and providing services and programs for the poor. At first scornful of elections because the Somoza regime
had always manipulated them, the revolutionary government in mid-1980
announced its intention to postpone national elections until 1985. Immediately after the rebel victory, however, local elections had taken place all over
Nicaragua. The Sandinistas also promoted grassroots organizations of women,

THE CONTRA WAR.
Peasant children in a feeding
program at a war-refugee,
agricultural, self-defense,
resettlement camp (photo
by Steve Cagan).

workers, peasants, youth, children, and neighborhoods. Through these organizations hundreds of thousands of Nicaraguans debated and voted on issues, worked on local problems, took part in national health and literacy campaigns, petitioned their government, and met with officials of governmental bodies and national organizations. Encouraged by the regime, organized labor grew rapidly. Labor's demands for higher wages, however, soon clashed with government needs for economic austerity and the FSLN desire for dominance within the movement.

The Sandinistas argued all along that the new system must tolerate diversity of political opinion because they had come to power as part of a coalition, because they sought a mixed economy requiring the cooperation of business, and because the international climate required political pluralism to safeguard the revolution. When the junta added new pro-Sandinista groups to the Council of State in 1980, several other party groups cried foul and began voicing open opposition to the government. The climate for political opposition remained open but not completely free. Press coverage and public activities of other parties suffered under the state of emergency decreed in 1982. Pro-regime crowds (*turbas*) sometimes harassed critics of the regime, especially between 1982 and 1984.

The Council of State passed opposition-influenced election and party laws that set elections for president and National Assembly (to replace the junta and Council of State) for November 1984. The government lifted most restrictions on parties and the press for the campaign; it allowed free and uncensored access to government radio and television. A vigorous campaign ensued among seven parties. International election observers and the press[24] concurred that no fraud or intimidation by the FSLN occurred. Observers found the election marred by US pressure that contributed to a conservative coalition's decision not to participate and that prompted one party's presidential candidate's attempt to drop out late in the campaign. Daniel Ortega Saavedra, DNC member and coordinator of the junta, became president with 63 percent of the total vote. Opposition parties divided about one-third of the National Assembly.

The National Assembly immediately became a constituent assembly tasked to write a new constitution. Contrary to US criticism, the constitution drafting was open and democratic. The resulting document provided for the rule of law, protection of human rights, checks and balances, and competitive elections to be held at six-year intervals.[25] The new election system, constitution, and government structures formalized and institutionalized the revolutionary regime. It left the Sandinistas in power, but presiding over a regime that had much in common with other electoral democracies—the government accepted constitutional restraints and could be replaced in an election.

Despite the external attacks and obstruction, the Sandinistas began their revolution successfully. They shaped a new governmental system, reactivated and reshaped much of the war-ravaged economy, and implemented numerous social programs. They provided expanded health services; national vaccination and health education campaigns significantly lowered rates of polio, malaria, and infant mortality. A literacy crusade raised literacy rates from slightly under 50 percent to about 87 percent. Agrarian reform programs promoted increased national self-sufficiency in food production, formed thousands of cooperative farms, and distributed considerable farmland to individuals and cooperatives.[26]

The growing Contra war, however, forced the government to reorganize to defend the revolution and postponed or undermined social and economic programs. By 1987 over half of the national budget went for military expenditures; the armed forces expanded to 60,000 regulars and 100,000 militia. Social reforms; medical, health, and educational programs; and public services suffered. Medical care deteriorated, garbage pickup and water service in Managua were curtailed, schools went without supplies and repairs, buses and taxis lacked parts and repairs. From 1979 through 1983 regular visitors to Nicaragua noticed evident material progress, but after 1984 signs of decay proliferated.

The Sandinistas' human rights performance, though not perfect, was good for a revolutionary regime and superior to that of Somoza and all other Central American governments except Costa Rica.[27] The government moved swiftly to prevent its own supporters and forces from abusing human rights in the chaotic days after seizing power. It established a new Sandinista Police and Sandinista Popular Army and worked to prevent abuses of authority. It humanely treated captured National Guard troops and officials, who were investigated, tried for their crimes, and sentenced. International human rights agencies criticized the unfair procedures of the Special Tribunals used to try the 6,300 former guardsmen, but the special courts dismissed charges against or acquitted 22 percent of the prisoners. Despite the heinous crimes of some, no one was executed. By 1985 more than half of those sentenced had completed their sentences, been pardoned, or been released.[28]

Despite La Prensa's receiving US CIA funding,[29] the regime allowed the opposition daily newspaper to operate for several years without censorship. During that period, however, the government briefly closed the paper several times for publishing false information in violation of the press law. Under the mounting pressure of the Contra war, the revolutionary government in 1982 decreed a state of emergency that suspended many civil guarantees. This implemented prior censorship of news content of all media, including the FSLN's own newspaper Barricada. Before the 1984 election, censorship eased and most civil rights were restored. Deepening war in 1985 and 1986 brought reinstituted rights restrictions. The government closed La Prensa indefinitely in June 1986 for endorsing US aid to the Contras,[30] but permitted it to reopen without prior censorship after the Central American Peace Accord was signed in 1987.

Two areas of human rights proved problematic for the revolutionary government. In 1982 the growing Contra war prompted relocation of 8,000 Miskito Indians from their homes in the war zone along the Río Coco. The poorly handled relocation angered Miskitos. Thousands fled and many joined anti-Sandinista guerrilla groups. "The external conflict created a context in which Miskito demands for self-determination were seen by the Sandinistas as separatist and related to US efforts to overthrow the government by arming indigenous insurgents and by attempting to turn world opinion against the Sandinistas through false accusations of 'genocide.'"[31] Real abuses of Miskito rights worsened tensions in the area,[32] but no credible observers concurred with US genocide charges.[33] By late 1983 the government changed course and began autonomy talks with Atlantic Coast indigenous peoples, aimed at increasing local self-determination. In 1985 it permitted the Miskitos to return to their homes, tensions subsided, and Miskito support for the Contras waned. The autonomy law passed in 1987.

Religious practice remained generally free in Nicaragua under the revolution, but the government became increasingly intolerant of expressions of anti-regime political goals through religious practice or groups. The government admitted many foreign missionaries of various sects and permitted churches to take part in the literacy crusade of 1980 and 1981. Many Catholics and numerous Protestant congregations had provided logistical support to the FSLN during the insurrection and supported the new government. The Catholic Church hierarchy, however, strongly and increasingly opposed Sandinista rule. Church-regime conflict became overt by 1982. Missionaries from certain Protestant sects were denied entry to Nicaragua, and pro-FSLN groups on one occasion occupied properties of one sect before police evicted them.[34]

Government–Catholic Church relations nosedived during and after the trip of Pope John Paul II to Nicaragua in 1983. Each side apparently deliberately provoked the other. Archbishop Miguel Obando y Bravo—long hostile to the Sandinistas—had become the leader of the internal opposition by 1984. Until the end of the Sandinista period, Obando (elevated to cardinal in 1985) and Catholic bishops repeatedly denounced government policy. Despite some efforts to seek dialogue with the Church, the Sandinista government periodically closed Catholic Radio and deported a dozen foreign-born priests active in opposition politics. In 1986, when Bishop Pablo Antonio Vega endorsed US aid for the Contras, the government exiled him.[35] Following the signing of the Central American Peace Accord in 1987, Vega and other priests were permitted to return to Nicaragua.

In summary, assailed by increasing domestic criticism, economic woes, and the Contra war, the revolutionary government's human rights performance deteriorated. Things improved around the 1984 election, but declined again after 1985. Repression of government critics and opponents remained much less violent than in Guatemala and El Salvador but included intimidation, harassment, and illegal detention of opponents, independent union leaders, and human rights workers; press censorship; curtailment of labor union activity; and poor prison conditions. In 1988, however, the human rights climate improved again as the government offered concessions to the opposition and announced national elections for early 1990.[36]

The Economy. Moderate and pragmatic economic policy diverged from models followed by other Marxist-led governments. The revolutionary government accepted the international debt of the Somoza regime and obtained hundreds of millions of dollars in grants and "soft" loans, mostly from Western governments and international organizations. And though it confiscated the properties of the Somozas and their cohorts, it preserved a private sector that accounted for between 50 and 60 percent of GDP. Early on, the economy recovered much of its prewar production. Agrarian reform did not heavily emphasize state farming, but rather responded to peasant demands by forming individual or cooperative smallholdings.[37] Though error-plagued, agrarian policy included credit and pricing policies to encourage production by the largest, export-oriented private farmers. US pressures to curtail Western credit to and trade with Nicaragua forced increasing reliance on the Eastern bloc for credit, other aid, and trade in the mid-1980s.[38]

Nicaraguan capitalists nevertheless felt insecure and reluctant to invest under the revolution. Contributing to their insecurity were the business sector's lack of control of politics, the Sandinista leadership's Marxist philosophy, and the changed economic rules of the game when the government nationalized the import-export sector, a key source of control over the business environment. Moreover, industry suffered from the general decline of the Central American Common Market's import-substitution development model, a worldwide recession, and the US credit and trade embargoes.[39]

The Sandinista government adopted several policies to benefit the majority of poor Nicaraguans: wage increases, food price subsidies, and expanded health, welfare, and education services. As economic austerity pressures grew, however, the newly expanded labor movement was legally prohibited to strike (many strikes were nonetheless tolerated). The government borrowed heavily abroad to cover revenue shortfalls. Security and social welfare spending eventually outran tax and foreign credit resources. To maintain continued critical foreign credit, the government by 1986 began serial currency devaluations and cuts in food subsidies and social programs.

The war, economic mismanagement, austerity measures, withdrawal of Soviet-bloc economic aid, and declining public and private investment drove rapid inflation of consumer prices.[40] Shortages grew rapidly between 1985 and

1989, and popular living standards and services deteriorated. "Urban wages in 1988 had fallen, according to some statistics, to only 10 percent of 1980 levels."[41] Inflation reached 1,200 percent in 1987 and then a mind-boggling 33,602 percent in 1988. Only new and harsher austerity programs in late 1988 and early 1989 brought inflation for 1989 down to 1,690 percent.[42] These policies, however, weakened social services and benefits for ordinary Nicaraguans and left thousands of government employees jobless.

REPLACING THE REVOLUTION

The 1990 Election. By 1989 the US-orchestrated Contra war and economic strangulation inflicted severe economic hardship on Nicaraguans. US policy makers knew that, in any democratic system, when economic conditions get bad voters tend to vote incumbents out of office. Washington also knew that Nicaraguans had wearied of the war's destruction, including 30,865 people who had died by the end of 1989.[43] Thus by the late 1980s internal conditions in Nicaragua had changed so radically that the US strategy toward the 1990 elections differed significantly from 1984.

The United States followed two tracks for Nicaragua's 1990 election. One was to denounce the electoral laws, procedures, and conditions in case the Nicaraguan people might re-elect the FSLN. The groundwork was thus laid to denounce a possible Sandinista victory as fraudulent. The second track was to promote an opposition victory. Washington used millions of covert and overt dollars[44] to weld a united opposition, the National Opposition Union (Unión Nacional Opositora, UNO), out of fourteen disparate and squabbling microparties.[45] It then promoted UNO candidates—in particular, presidential nominee Violeta Barrios de Chamorro. The United States thus "micromanaged the opposition"[46] and applied massive external pressure on the electorate. The Contra war escalated sharply over the year before the election.[47] President Bush called President Ortega "an animal [and] . . . a bull in a china shop,"[48] and received Violeta Chamorro at the White House. The United States promised to end the war and the economic embargo should she win.

UNO scored a clear-cut victory on February 25, 1990; Chamorro won about 55 percent of the valid presidential votes to Daniel Ortega's 41 percent. Of 92 seats in the National Assembly, UNO captured 51, the FSLN won 39, and two independent parties took one apiece. (See Appendix, Tables A.6 and A.7, for selected election results.) On April 25, 1990, Daniel Ortega placed the sash of presidential office on Chamorro's shoulders.

The Chamorro Years, 1990 to 1997. The Chamorro era provides challenges to interpretation.[49] The new administration's economic and social policies were harshly austere. Per capita GDP stagnated from 1990 through 1996, the worst economic performance in Central America, and real wages remained far below

THE END OF AN ERA. Revolutionary president Daniel Ortega places the sash of office on the shoulders of his US-approved successor, Violeta Barrios de Chamorro, on April 25, 1990 (photo courtesy of *Barricada*).

their levels in prior decades (see Appendix, Table A.1).[50] Indeed, the United Nations Development Program's Human Development Index (based on per capita income, education levels, and life expectancy) lowered Nicaragua's rank among nations from 85th in the world when Chamorro took office to 117th by the time she left.[51] But her administration tamed runaway inflation and, after several years, restarted modest economic growth (see Appendix, Table A.1). President Chamorro worked hard to make peace and heal the political wounds of the Nicaraguan family. She viewed reconciliation as essential for successful governance and democratic consolidation.

The Chamorro administration did not introduce economic neoliberalism to Nicaragua. The Sandinistas had already imposed harsh structural reforms in the late 1980s in response to hyperinflation caused mainly by Contra war spending. But the Chamorro administration embraced neoliberalism and intensified its implementation. "The Nicaraguan government signed its first

Contingency Agreement with the IMF in 1991, and then signed a comprehensive Enhanced Structural Adjustment Facility (ESAF) with the Fund in 1994, followed by a second ESAF in 1998."[52] Government properties were privatized, public expenditures cut, budgets balanced, and tariffs lowered. The downsizing of government, cutbacks in social services, privatization of state enterprises, and credit policy that favored export agriculture over peasant production of domestic foodstuffs combined to exacerbate the misery of ordinary Nicaraguans. For example, the US Agency for International Development (USAID), in managing US loans and thus shaping agricultural credit policy, imposed "efficiency criteria" that starved the peasant agricultural sector. "Deprived of credit and other state services and therefore the means to compete in the market, peasants were forced to sell their land."[53] Unemployment, underemployment, drug addiction, crime, homelessness (especially among children), and domestic violence all soared.

Other social programs changed rapidly after the Sandinistas left office. Ideologically conservative administrators reshaped public education. They replaced carefully drafted Sandinista-era textbooks with US-approved and financed generic texts, many of them years out of date. The demobilization of the Contras and most of the national armed forces threw tens of thousands of young men into the economy with little training or experience. The Chamorro administration failed to fulfill promises of land and resettlement benefits for ex-combatants. Sporadically throughout the 1990s rearmed Contras, ex-Sandinista military, and mixed units of both renewed guerrilla activity or took up banditry in rural areas. Organized armed conflict gradually declined, but remnants persisted into the late 1990s.[54]

Despite losing almost 3 percent of its population in the insurrection and Contra wars between 1978 and 1990, Nicaragua overall progressed toward national reconciliation and democratic consolidation in the Chamorro years. Grassroots organizations representing the poor played a significant role. The Rural Worker's Association (Asociación de Trabajadores del Campo, ATC), the National Union of Farmers and Ranchers (Unión Nacional de Agricultores y Ganaderos, UNAG), and mixed groups of ex-combatants helped negotiate the privatization of state farms and some land transfers to former workers and ex-combatants. The National Workers' Front (Frente Nacional de Trabajadores, FNT) did the same in the privatization of urban state-owned properties. When the government was unresponsive, grassroots groups demonstrated and protested to force government respect for their interests.

President Chamorro resisted pressures by the United States and domestic right-wingers to engage in a vengeful "de-Sandinization" program. By allowing Sandinista general Humberto Ortega to remain head of the military, she thus assured that there would be no anti-Sandinista bloodbath. The FSLN accepted the rapid demobilization of the army from 80,000 to 12,000 troops by 1998.

The military's "senior commanders recognized that the only way to guarantee the military's survival was to sever its FSLN ties and accept increased civilian control."[55] In addition, the Chamorro government, FSLN leaders, and a wide spectrum of politicians engaged in frequent bargaining, negotiation, and pact making. This ultimately resulted in a majority consensus in the National Assembly, which allowed promulgation of a new Military Code (1994) that unlinked the armed forces from the FSLN, some revisions of the 1987 constitution (1995), and the passage of a Property Stability Law 209 (1996) that set a framework for dealing with property disputes arising from the revolution. Clean elections held on the Atlantic Coast in 1994 also boded well.

However, many problems arose. President Chamorro's gestures of reconciliation toward the Sandinistas alienated parts of UNO. A nasty dispute over constitutional reforms that strengthened the National Assembly, expanded the Supreme Court, and prevented presidential self-succession paralyzed the government for much of 1994 and 1995.[56] Many ex-UNO party leaders had won positions as mayors in Nicaragua's largest cities. Nurtured with USAID funding destined exclusively for municipalities that had voted the Sandinistas out, these individuals cultivated popular support with public works. Under their leadership, the old Liberal Party—the majority party of Nicaragua until corrupted by the Somozas—resuscitated as various splinter groups and then fused into the Liberal Alliance (Alianza Liberal, AL).

A leading figure of this era was Arnoldo Alemán, a lawyer and farmer who had been a Liberal since the Somoza era. During the revolution he developed a hatred for the Sandinistas because they had nationalized the bank he worked for, seized his agricultural properties, and put him under house arrest while his wife was dying. Elected mayor of Managua in 1990, Alemán governed the city as a neopopulist. US assistance funds underwrote visible public works, patronage, and jobs for supporters. He courted poor constituents and blamed the Sandinistas for Nicaragua's problems. With financial and moral support from Cuban and Nicaraguan exiles in Miami, he and other Liberal mayors built the Liberal Alliance. Alemán won the AL presidential nomination for 1996.

The Sandinistas experienced serious problems during the Chamorro administration. As lame ducks in 1990, the FSLN government passed unseemly laws transferring much state property to top Sandinistas (dubbed *la piñata*). Out of power, the old guard discredited itself further by clinging to leadership when challenged to reform the party in 1994. Factions within the party questioned party leadership and internal democracy, and criticized the party's direction.[57] A schism resulted; the breakaway Sandinista Renovation Movement (Movimiento de Renovación Sandinista, MRS) in 1995 took much of the intellectual and leadership talent out of the FSLN, leaving mainly hard-line supporters of former president Daniel Ortega, now the party's virtual caudillo.[58] Ortega easily won the FSLN presidential nomination.

The 1996 Election and Alemán Administration. For many, the 1996 election left much to be desired. In the highly polarized pre-election atmosphere, the right wing had insisted on a series of last-minute changes in the electoral law and personnel of the Supreme Electoral Council (Consejo Supremo Electoral, CSE). These changes and inadequate funding caused confusion, disorganization, and increased partisanship on electoral boards around the country. Anomalies occurred in voter registration, the campaign, preparation and delivery of materials, operation of polling places, voting, vote tabulation, and vote reporting. Ultimately the CSE threw out the votes from hundreds of precincts.

The Liberal Alliance triumphed by a margin that made the discarded presidential votes immaterial. AL presidential candidate Alemán (51 percent of the vote) beat perennial FSLN candidate Ortega (38 percent). With 86 percent turnout, the Liberals took 42 National Assembly seats, the FSLN 36 seats, and nine minor parties split 15 seats. Ortega and another presidential candidate denounced the Liberal victory as illegitimate, but later the FSLN accepted the outcome.[59]

CONTEMPORARY NICARAGUAN POLITICS

Hating the Sandinistas and having sat out the bargaining that rewrote the rules of the political game in the mid-1990s, Alemán and his AL plurality in the Assembly questioned the Chamorro-era laws on the military, property, and the 1987 constitution. The AL and allies maneuvered to deprive the FSLN of their rightful seats on the executive body of the National Assembly. This prompted a wave of retaliatory general strikes, demonstrations, angry invective, renewed armed insurgency, FSLN boycotts of the National Assembly, constitutional challenges, sporadic attempts at public dialogue, and behind-the-scenes bargaining between the leaders of the two major political forces. Eventually, international and domestic pressure forced a compromise. In late 1997 FSLN-government negotiations resolved the thorny property issue; the Assembly enacted the Law of Urban and Rural Reformed Property after a brief debate. It guaranteed formal land titles for many of the smallholder beneficiaries of untitled property distribution during the 1980s and 1990s, indemnified people who lost property, and required major beneficiaries of *la piñata* to pay for their confiscated houses.[60]

By 1998, and with the settlement of the property issue, a "new normalcy" began to emerge in Nicaragua. The International Monetary Fund renewed support that had been suspended for two years, and a multilateral donors' group of various countries and organizations pledged loans of $1.8 billion over four years to promote macroeconomic stability, the development of agriculture, and governability. A second round of clean (though low-turnout) local elections was held in the Atlantic region. Simultaneously, however, the leaders of the two major parties each suffered personal scandals. Escalating rumors of corruption engulfed Alemán and eventually led to his prosecution and imprisonment. For his part, Ortega's 30-year-old stepdaughter accused him of having sexually abused her for many years.[61] Although Alemán delayed his legal difficulties until after leaving office and Ortega clung to his role as leader of the FSLN, each suffered irreparable damage to his prestige. Nor did Nicaragua's economic and political elite unite under neoliberal globalist leaders as others did in Central America during this era. Robinson identifies two feuding capitalist groups: one modernizing and externally oriented group identified with the Central Bank, globalist think tanks, and US and multilaterally backed financial institutions; the other linked to the old "agro-export oligarchy . . . imbued in the traditional politics of partisan corruption and patronage."[62] Political and economic leadership remained divided and national economic development, stagnant. Late in 1998, hurricane Mitch unleashed widespread flooding, deaths, and infrastructure damage that worsened Nicaragua's already deeply depressed economy and challenged the Alemán administration. Much of the north of the country suffered heavily, with severe damage to areas producing most of the nation's basic grains and coffee. The storm killed over 2,800 people, destroyed or damaged almost 42,000 homes, left 65,000 in shelters, and overall harmed 370,000 people—roughly one Nicaraguan in twelve. Hurricane Mitch's damage to the economy persisted for several years.

In 1999 the caudillos of the FSLN and AL again unexpectedly conspired to their mutual benefit. With both men facing legal problems, Ortega and Alemán forged a broad pact to reform the constitution and electoral law. One provision guaranteed losing presidential candidates and the immediate ex-president seats in the Legislative Assembly, which came with immunity from prosecution for both leaders. The Alemán-Ortega pact also packed the Supreme Court, strengthened both party leaders within their own parties, and rewrote the electoral law to advantage the Liberal Constitutionalist Party (Partido Liberal Constitucionalista, PLC) and FSLN at the expense of all other parties and political movements. Immediate effects included sharp reductions of smaller-party representation in the 2001–2006 Assembly and of the number of parties certified to compete in future elections. Many Sandinistas who viewed the pact as undermining important party principles of democracy and pluralism resigned from the party.[63]

In 2001 the Liberal Alliance nominated Alemán's vice president, businessman Enrique Bolaños Geyer, to run for the presidency against FSLN nominee Daniel Ortega. Ortega led Bolaños in the polls until shortly before the election. However, following the September 11 terrorist attacks in the United States, the Bush administration engaged in a smear campaign against Ortega, labeling him a "terrorist."[64] The notion that the US "war on terror" could spread to Nicaragua under an Ortega administration revived memories of the Contra war. The United States also convinced Conservatives to align with the Liberals to prevent ticket splitting among voters on the right. In the end, Bolaños won 56.3 percent of the vote. The Sandinistas won 38 Assembly seats to the AL's comfortable majority of 51. The Conservative Party, once second to the Liberals, captured only one Assembly seat and almost suffered decertification as a party. Though fallen from their revolutionary era dominance, the Sandinistas had clearly supplanted the Conservatives as the Liberals' opposition in the post-revolutionary political system.

As part of his anti-corruption campaign, President Bolaños worked with the National Assembly to repeal the amnesty law for ex-presidents embodied in the Alemán-Ortega pact. In 2002 the Assembly stripped Alemán of immunity, and he was placed under house arrest on charges of laundering $100 million to party candidates and embezzling $1.3 million for himself. In 2004 Alemán received a twenty-year sentence, but the Supreme Court overturned his conviction in January 2009.[65] Bolaños himself was beset by charges of campaign finance fraud as opponents called for his impeachment. Bolaños secured help from the OAS in fighting what he charged was politically motivated revenge by Alemán's and Ortega's supporters.

Bolaños' prosecution of Alemán divided the PLC, controlled by Alemán supporters. Bolaños quit the party and helped found the Alliance for the Republic (Alianza para la República, APRE), a center-right alternative before the 2004 municipal elections. The FSLN benefited from the divisions among Liberals and won new municipal government seats throughout the country. Most important for the FSLN was the mayoralty of Managua. The beleaguered PLC lost some 100,000 votes while Bolaños' party also performed poorly.[66] Many voters expressed their dissatisfaction or disinterest; abstention exceeded 50 percent.[67]

In November 2004 the National Assembly passed constitutional reforms intended to undermine presidential authority. The reforms would have given the Assembly the power to appoint government ministers, diplomats, and other executive appointees.[68] President Bolaños resisted the reforms, and the resulting impasse between him and the FSLN-PLC faction in the Assembly paralyzed the country.[69] The crisis ended when Bolaños agreed not to challenge the reforms, provided that their implementation was delayed until after the 2006 elections. The FSLN dropped its insistence that Bolaños be removed from office and allowed the Central American Free Trade Agreement (CAFTA) to pass.

The FSLN again nominated Daniel Ortega for president for the 2006 elections. He selected former Contra Jaime Morales as his running mate. The choice of Morales was part of a greater campaign strategy to soften Ortega's image, guided by the theme of "reconciliation." As in 2001, the Sandinistas eschewed their traditional red and black colors in favor of pink and made campaign staples of messages of peace, love, and God. Ortega also secured the support of the Catholic Church by repairing his relationship with Cardinal Miguel Obando y Bravo and supporting a ban on therapeutic abortions just days before the elections.[70] In a campaign of contradictions, Ortega vowed to fight poverty while endorsing market forces and CAFTA.

The opposition included the divided right and the Sandinista Renovation Movement (MRS) of former Sandinistas. Eduardo Montealegre, Alemán's former minister of the presidency and foreign relations, broke from the PLC in 2005 in opposition to Alemán's continued control of the party. Montealegre headed the newly formed Nicaraguan Liberal Alliance (Alianza Liberal Nicaragüense, ALN) ticket in a coalition with the Conservative Party. US ambassador Paul Trivelli all but publically endorsed Montealegre, known for his anti-corruption, anti-pact, pro-market views. Both Liberal campaigns offered a "democratic" alternative for the left. The PLC nominated José Rizo Castellón, Bolaños' former vice president who ran an "anti-Castro candidacy" that highlighted Ortega's ties to Fidel Castro and Hugo Chávez.[71] Herty Lewites, the popular former mayor of Managua, was expelled from the FSLN as a traitor for suggesting that Ortega compete for the nomination in a party primary.[72] Lewites became the MRS presidential candidate but died in July 2006, months before the election, and was replaced by economist Edmundo Jarquín.

US intervention again plagued the campaign; various US sources emitted warnings of consequences should Ortega win. Venezuela weighed in on the other side, sending oil and fertilizer to FSLN municipalities.[73] Ortega prevailed with a scant 38 percent of the votes, 5 percent less than he had won in 2001. Montealegre received 29 percent, Rizo (PLC) 26 percent, and Jarquín (MRS) 6 percent. It was hardly a mandate for Ortega and the FSLN. Daniel Ortega owed victory to the split among Liberals and the electoral law's low threshold of votes (35 percent) required to avoid a runoff.[74] The FSLN and PLC dominated the National Assembly with 38 and 25 seats, respectively. The ALN won 24 seats and the MRS won five. Voter turnout, while down slightly, remained a respectable 70 percent.

President Ortega's social policies took aim at Nicaragua's overwhelming poverty. In 2007, 46 percent of the population lived in poverty; rural poverty was much higher. According to the UNDP, as much as 80 percent of the population lived on less than US$2 per day. During his first year in office, Ortega unveiled free education, health, and literacy programs. The Zero Hunger program gave livestock to program participants. The government established a microcredit program that provided low-interest loans to women. Although popular, the programs were plagued by a lack of resources and, critics suggested, of transparency. Ortega also established neighborhood committees,

Citizens Power Councils (CPCs), to administer local anti-poverty programs.[75] The councils were part of the National Plan for Human Development (Plan Nacional para el Desarrollo Humano, PNDH) and were headed by Ortega's wife, Rosario Murillo. Proponents described the CPCs as expressions of people power, open to participation regardless of political affiliation; 50 percent of *La Prensa* poll respondents said they contributed to citizen participation.[76] Critics said the CPCs undermined civil society and were political tools reminiscent of Sandinista Defense Councils (CDS) of the 1980s.[77] The opposition disliked the CPCs. The PLC, ALN, and MRS voted to nullify the presidential decree that established the committees. Ortega vetoed the measure and the Supreme Court upheld the veto.

The Nicaraguan economy grew slower than the regional average, reaching only 3.7 percent in 2006 and 3.8 percent in 2007. Inflation, unemployment, and underemployment were high and remained persistent problems. Migration and remittances increased dramatically following Hurricane Mitch. The Inter-American Development Bank estimated that remittances from Nicaraguans abroad grew from $345 million in 1999 to nearly $1 billion in 2008. Crime, while significantly lower than in the rest of the region, also increased. There was some relief in the form of debt forgiveness under the Heavily Indebted Poor Countries (HIPC) Initiative and other debt-reduction programs, which reduced the country's external debt to 59 percent of GDP. Ortega courted assistance from a number of sources, some of them clearly at odds with one another. In addition to IMF loans, the social aid programs came from Venezuela through its Alianza Bolivariana para las Américas (Bolivarian Alternative for the Americas, ALBA). Venezuelan oil was particularly important, as Nicaragua depended heavily on petroleum to generate electricity while suffering rolling blackouts and an energy crisis from 2005 to 2007.

The 2008 municipal elections took place against a backdrop of violent protests and reprisals against regime critics. The Supreme Electoral Council (CSE) ruled that the MRS and the Conservative Party had failed to meet CSE threshold requirements for public support in the previous election and were thus ineligible to participate. This narrowed the field and prevented votes from being siphoned away from the larger parties.[78] The CSE also refused to accredit international and independent domestic observers to monitor elections internally.[79] Nicaragua had welcomed election observers for the five previous elections held since 1984. The changing electoral atmosphere paralleled a distinct change in the Nicaraguan electorate, as confidence in political parties, elections, and various institutions declined between 2004 and 2008.[80] Additionally, President Ortega's monitoring and intimidating of civil society organizations curtailed civil society activism.[81]

In November 2008, municipal elections were held for 146 of 152 municipalities. The CSE reported FSLN victories in 105, followed by the PLC with

37 and the AL with four. The FSLN won 13 of 17 departmental capitals, including Managua and León. The opposition immediately protested the FSLN landslide. Allegations of fraud included the annulment of ballots (7 percent of the total cast), intimidation from CPCs at polling stations, limited access for opposition parties at polling stations, undistributed voter identification cards, early poll closures, vote counts in excess of registered voters, and the invalidation of votes.[82] The international observation teams who managed to be present, however, found no evidence of fraud. Managua mayoral candidate Eduardo Montealegre, in coalition with the PLC, claimed to have found fraud, but CSE tallies awarded the office to former boxing champion Alexis Argüello of the FSLN.[83] Leading Sandinista movement figures denounced the alleged fraud, including former culture minister Father Ernesto Cardenal.[84] The United States and European Union responded by freezing aid. Months later, the United States cut $62 million from a $175 million program with the Millennium Challenge Corporation citing concerns over the transparency of the elections.[85]

The 2008 elections and the machinations behind the scenes reinforced the FSLN-PLC pact and the prominence of Ortega and Alemán as party caudillos. The two parties controlled the courts and, by extension, the electoral field. With Alemán's conviction overturned, he announced his intention to run on the PLC ticket in 2011. Ortega sought a way to retain power after his term ended. Nicaragua's constitution prohibited consecutive re-election for the presidency and mayoral contests, and limited presidents to two terms—either of which provision would have negated Ortega's eligibility. After failing to obtain Assembly support to amend the constitution, Ortega turned to the courts. He and over 100 FSLN mayors filed a petition with the Constitutional Chamber of the Supreme Court arguing that the rule did not apply to all elected offices and, thus, was discriminatory. The Constitutional Chamber ruled in their favor in October 2009. The ruling was controversial not merely because it found the provision "inapplicable," but because the three Liberal members of the Chamber were not present for the ruling.[86] The decision was later upheld by the missing Liberal judges and approved by the full Supreme Court of Justice. Ortega's candidacy was approved by the CSE in April 2011.

Another controversy arose in January 2010 when President Ortega faced losing key supporters on the CSE and CSJ when their terms ended. He issued a decree allowing 25 high-ranking officials to retain their posts until successors had been chosen. The National Assembly's failure to reach a compromise on new appointments resulted in a violent episode in April 2010 when FSLN activists blocked opposition lawmakers from entering the National Assembly to prevent them from voting to overturn the decree. After convening their meeting at a Managua hotel, protesters injured three deputies and damaged

THE RETURN OF ORTEGA. President Daniel Ortega in Managua, June 2011 (photo by Christine Wade).

property.[87] The officials remained in office well after their terms expired and into 2014.

Polls revealed Daniel Ortega's popularity to have grown considerably since 2006, which suggested that only a unified opposition could defeat him if he sought re-election. Former president Arnoldo Alemán announced his intention to run on the PLC ticket. Eduardo Montealegre, the 2006 runner-up, refused to run on the same ticket with Alemán and started his own campaign before ultimately supporting 79-year-old radio journalist and station owner Fabio Gadea Mantilla on the PLI-UNE coalition ticket. Montealegre later joined the PLI-UNE ticket as Gadea's vice presidential candidate.

Electoral observation again became controversial in 2011. Most domestic-observer teams were denied accreditation, though some conducted observation nonetheless.[88] Unlike 2008, a number of prominent international observer missions were invited to participate, but so late that some groups felt they could not organize full missions to observe all phases of the election process.[89] Members of the European Union Election Observer Mission (EU EOM), for example, did not arrive in the field until three weeks before election day.

President Ortega resoundingly won re-election with 63 percent of the votes. Gadea captured 31 percent and Alemán only 6 percent. The FSLN won 62 seats in the National Assembly. One additional seat for the outgoing president was transferred by Ortega to his vice president for a total of 63 FSLN seats, enough to guarantee a qualified majority. The PLI won 27 seats and the PLC two. Thirty-six Assembly seats went to women, who now constituted 39 percent of members—33 of them were Sandinistas. International observers reported various irregularities, including issues with getting on the voter rolls, the distribution of voter identity cards, difficulty accessing polling places, and concerns about the CSE's neutrality.[90] The European Union's election observation mission noted "deterioration in the democratic quality of Nicaraguan electoral processes, due to the lack of transparency and neutrality with which they were administered by the Supreme Electoral Council."[91] Though the outcome was not a surprise—months of polling indicated a strong lead for Ortega—Gadea and Alemán denounced the results. Several protesters died and several policemen were injured in post-election violence. The United States expressed disapproval by cutting some $3 billion in bilateral aid.

Whatever the international response to recent Nicaraguan elections, support for President Ortega and the FSLN has grown since 2010. A Mitofsky poll conducted in April 2012 showed Ortega's approval rating was 61 percent, one of the highest in the region. When polled about the state of Nicaraguan democracy under Ortega, 58 percent said it had been strengthened under his administration.[92] Public trust in two of the key institutions involved in the 2011 elections, the CSE and the Supreme Court, increased markedly following the elections. Three-quarters of survey respondents reported seeing no irregularities in the 2011 elections.[93] While these perceptions often depended on party affiliation, there is little doubt that public support for the FSLN has increased dramatically since Ortega's return to office in 2007.

Overall economic performance and the social programs administered by the FSLN likely contributed to Daniel Ortega's rise in public esteem. The economic performance bar is low in the region's poorest country—Nicaragua in 2012 had not yet regained its 1960 level of GDP per capita in constant terms (Appendix, Table A.1). However, after slow economic growth from 1990 through the early 2000s, Nicaragua's GDP growth rate was high most years except 2009. Foreign investment rose, dependence on foreign aid shrank, exports increased, and socioeconomic indicators improved (though much remains to be done in this area). Since returning to office in 2007, Ortega has maintained Nicaragua's agreements with IMF and CAFTA and signed new trade and investment agreements with Panama, Taiwan, Russia, Chile, and ALBA. Nicaragua was twice named by the World Bank's Doing Business Report as the best country in Central America in several investment categories, including investor protection. Additionally, the *Latin Business Chronicle* has consistently ranked Nicaragua highly globalized (in 2011 foreign investment from Canada, Brazil, Korea, Spain, and Mexico nearly doubled to almost $1 billion). Legislation passed since 2007 facilitated much of this investment, winning business-sector praise for President Ortega. In 2013, Nicaragua granted a controversial concession to a Chinese firm to develop a transoceanic canal. One unsettling trend, however, is Nicaragua's increased reliance on remittances, which accounted for part of the economic growth. By 2011, Nicaraguans were sending home more than $1 billion in remittances. Remittances grew 22 percent from 2008 to 2011, the fastest rate of increase in the region.[94]

Nicaragua's economy continued to benefit from its ALBA membership. ALBA continued supplying cheap Venezuelan oil and technological assistance, including generators and a $3.5 billion refinery. Venezuela also provided bilateral aid and short-term, low-interest loans. In 2010, Nicaragua received more than $500 million in oil discounts and aid from Venezuela (equal to 7.6 percent of GDP). Although the FSLN initially opposed CAFTA, the Ortega administration has fully embraced the trade agreement while in power. Exports to the United States grew 71 percent between 2006 and 2011. In 2011 Nicaragua ran a $1 billion trade surplus with the United States. Though trade with Venezuela has increased significantly since 2007, the United States remains the main destination for Nicaraguan exports. Not content to rely on cheap Venezuelan oil, the Ortega administration vigorously pursued renewable energy sources, including wind, solar, and hydroelectric power.

Nicaragua also sought advantage in a long-pending border dispute with Colombia. In 2001 President Alemán filed a petition with the International Court of Justice (ICJ) over the San Andrés islands and waterways it was contesting with Colombia. In 2012 the ICJ ruled to expand Nicaragua's maritime territory at the expense of Colombia.[95] Despite Colombian protests, Nicaragua quickly began exploratory drilling in its new territory. In 2013 Nicaragua filed a complaint with the ICJ over Colombia's continued patrols in the area; Colombia then recalled its ambassador from Managua. Border disputes also eroded deteriorated relations with Costa Rica. A 2009 ICJ ruling on the San Juan River affirmed Nicaragua's sovereignty over the river following the first dispute, but also guaranteed Costa Rica right of use. In October 2012, Nicaragua began dredging the San Juan River, which Costa Rica claimed damaged its wetlands. Rhetoric escalated quickly, with the Chinchilla administration accusing Nicaragua of a military incursion. Months later the ICJ ruled Nicaragua could continue dredging, but that both parties should refrain from sending security forces into the disputed territory.

Venezuelan aid supported the popular social programs that Ortega initiated at the beginning of his term. Three of them together cost US $95 million.[96] Of these, Plan Techo provided roofing materials to low-income families and was the most popular. Other programs supplied low-interest loans and shoes and backpacks to schoolchildren in low-income families to promote increased school attendance. Survey data from 2012 suggested that FSLN sympathizers and middle-class Nicaraguans got more assistance than the rural poor.[97]

Nicaragua controlled crime better than its regional neighbors. The homicide rate, 11 per 100,000 in 2012, was a fraction of those of its northern neighbors.[98] Nicaragua did not suffer the same type of transnational gang problem plaguing other countries, but proved adept at crime prevention by specifically targeting the country's youth. Nicaragua's community-policing model helped hold down crime. Crime rates, including homicides, were much higher in the Atlantic area Autonomous Zones than elsewhere because of drug trafficking and organized crime.[99]

Nicaragua also made limited progress on one of its most enduring crimes—violence against women and girls. Nicaragua has the highest rate of inter-partner violence in Central America. Many victims of sexual violence (including incest) were distressingly young. According to Amnesty International more than two-thirds of the rape victims between 1998 and 2007 were under the age of 17. Between 2002 and 2009, the number of girls aged 10 to14 who gave birth increased 48 percent.[100] In January 2012 the National Assembly passed the Comprehensive Law against Violence Toward Women (Law 779). The law addressed both physical and structural forms of violence and set sentencing guidelines for various violent crimes against women, including femicide.[101] Religious leaders protested the law, saying that it kept families apart and would be abused by women seeking revenge. Opponents of the law challenged it before the Supreme Court, calling it unconstitutional because it prohibited mediation between victim and abuser. In August 2013, Law 799 was upheld, though the National Assembly subsequently reformed it to permit mediation despite protests by women's groups.

The FSLN-dominated National Assembly approved several changes to the municipal elections law. These changes eliminated the re-election ban for mayors, tripled the number of municipal councilors, and provided that half of all candidates for municipal office must be women. A year after Ortega's re-election, the FSLN further solidified its electoral dominance in the November 2012 elections, winning 134 of 153 municipalities. The PLI won 13, followed by Yatama with three, the PLC with two, and the ALN with one. The CSE rejected challenges by the PLC and PLI.[102] Although concerns persisted about the voter registry and the transparency of the CSE, the elections effectively consolidated the FSLN's hegemony.

In late 2013 the FSLN National Assembly delegation introduced some 97 constitutional amendments. The government briefly consulted with some members of the opposition, civil society, and the business community (e.g., COSEP) after unveiling the proposals. Opponents decried the lack of broader and more meaningful consultation. As required, the amendments were approved twice by the Assembly and took effect in February 2014. Among the more controversial amendments were provisions that eliminated term limits and another that allowed government appointees to remain in their posts beyond their terms, each of which codified current practices. Other amendments were intended to solidify the Sandinistas' commitment to participatory democracy on the community level. Some of the amendments, such as redefining the country's borders to include the recent ICJ decision, provisions for the trans-isthmian canal project, and the requirement that women comprise 50 percent of party lists at all levels, had considerable popular support. Still other amendments came under withering criticism for consolidating FSLN power and further eroding democratic practices. These included amendments that allowed active duty military officials to temporarily hold executive branch appointments under extenuating circumstances, another that could force Assembly deputies to vote with their party or lose their seats, and a third implementing a simple plurality standard for victory in presidential elections, eliminating runoff elections.

Elections for regional councils were held in the North and South Atlantic Autonomous Regions (RAAN and RAAS, respectively) in March 2014. The FSLN won almost 52 percent of the votes in the RAAN and 48 percent of votes in the RAAS amid opposition claims of fraud and irregularities.

CONCLUSIONS

Global economic forces, US economic assistance, and cooperation among Central American regimes in response to recessions of the 1940s and 1950s led to the formation of the Central American Common Market. After rapid economic growth in the 1960s and 1970s, internal policies aggravated by the 1972 Managua earthquake and 1973 spike in oil prices worsened living conditions for working-class Nicaraguans. This mobilized many people into the political arena to seek modest reforms. The Somoza regime's brutal repression, however, united opponents, radicalized their demands, and rallied support behind the once-weak FSLN. This rebel coalition marshaled progressively greater resources while those of the regime deteriorated, leading the revolutionaries to power.

The beginning of the Nicaraguan revolution in 1979 proved as important a historical moment for Central American history as the National War of 1857 and the completion of the Panama Canal. However, when the Sandinistas consolidated their domination over the revolution, they catalyzed powerful internal and external political forces that led to drastic actions across the isthmus. The revolutionary government took steps toward democracy with the 1984 election and 1987 constitution. Internal opposition to the FSLN's program continued to develop, and the United States mobilized and financed an armed counterrevolution from abroad. Eventually, the Contra war and related programs of economic strangulation caused such economic deterioration and misery that a majority of the Nicaraguan people voted to replace their revolutionary government with one acceptable to Washington. The April 1990 administration change from Daniel Ortega to Violeta Barrios de Chamorro confirmed Nicaragua's transition to electoral democracy.

Viewed from the vantage point of 2014, Nicaragua presents ample cause for concern. The country's dramatic social and economic deterioration—generated by the 1970s insurrection, capital flight, the Contra war, and externally imposed economic strangulation—worsened under increasingly strict neoliberal "reforms" in the 1990–2006 period. Nicaragua effectively *de-developed* economically and has only begun recuperating since around 2010. Corruption, political polarization, and truly squalid, self-serving deal-making among elites became common features of the political landscape. Nicaraguan democracy suffered as the FSLN and PLC limited political space and then as the Liberal opposition effectively collapsed. Irregularities in the 2008 and 2012 municipal elections and the 2011 national elections damaged the credibility of the FSLN at home and abroad, but by 2014, the FSLN enjoyed nearly complete dominance of all of the country's institutions and the regime appeared to have become semi-democratic.

That being said, Nicaragua fared better than other countries in the region by escaping the region's crime wave. Extrajudicial killings and political assassinations were practically nonexistent. The FSLN's policies benefited the poor and helped redress somewhat their economic decline under prior administrations. Finally, Nicaraguans expressed more satisfaction with their government and greater support for democracy than some other Central Americans despite the controversy surrounding recent elections and the eroding restraints on the ruling party.

Recommended Readings and Resources

Anderson, Leslie E., and Lawrence C. Dodd, 2005. *Learning Democracy: Citizen Engagement and Electoral Choice in Nicaragua, 1990–2001*. Chicago: University of Chicago Press.

Babb, Florence. 2001. *After Revolution: Mapping Gender and Cultural Politics in Neoliberal Nicaragua*. Austin: University of Texas Press.

Baracco, Luciano. 2011. *National Integration and Contested Autonomy: The Caribbean Coast of Nicaragua*. New York: Algora Press.

Booth, John A. 1985. *The End and the Beginning: The Nicaraguan Revolution*, 2nd ed. Boulder, CO: Westview Press.

Charlip, Julie. 2003. *Cultivating Coffee: The Farmers of Carazo, Nicaragua, 1880–1930*. Athens: Ohio University Press.

Close, David. 1999. *Nicaragua: The Chamorro Years*. Boulder, CO: Lynne Rienner Publishers.

———. 2013. "Nicaragua." In Diego Sánchez-Ancochea and Salvador Martí Puig, eds., *Handbook of Central American Governance*. London: Routledge.

Close, David, and Kalowatie Deonandan. 2004. *Undoing Democracy: The Politics of Electoral Caudillismo*. Lanham, MD: Lexington Books.

Colburn, Forrest D. 1986. *Post-Revolutionary Nicaragua: State, Class, and the Dilemmas of Agrarian Policy*. Berkeley: University of California Press.

Gonzalez Rivera, Victoria. 2011. *Before the Revolution: Women's Rights and Right-Wing Politics in Nicaragua, 1821–1979*. University Park: Pennsylvania State University Press.

Kinzer, Stephen, and Merilee S. Grindle. 2007. *Blood of Brothers: Life and War in Nicaragua*. Cambridge, MA: David Rockefeller Center Series on Latin American Studies.

O'Shaughnessy, Laura Nuzzi. 2009. *Nicaragua's Other Revolution: Religious Faith and Political Struggle*. Chapel Hill: University of North Carolina Press Enduring Editions.

Pastor, Robert. 2002. *Not Condemned to Repetition: The United States and Nicaragua*, 2nd ed. Boulder, CO: Westview Press.

Prevost, Gary, and Harry E. Vanden, eds. 1997. *The Undermining of the Sandinista Revolution*. London: Macmillan.

Robinson, William I. 1992. *A Faustian Bargain: US Involvement in the Nicaraguan Elections and American Foreign Policy in the Post–Cold War Era*. Boulder, CO: Westview Press.

Spalding, Rose. 1994. *Capitalists and Revolution in Nicaragua: Opposition and Accommodation, 1979–1993*. Chapel Hill: University of North Carolina Press.

Vanden, Harry, and Gary Prevost. 1993. *Democracy and Socialism in Sandinista Nicaragua*. Boulder, CO: Lynne Rienner Publishers.

Vilas, Carlos. 1989. *State, Class and Ethnicity in Nicaragua*. Boulder, CO: Lynne Rienner Publishers.

Walker, Thomas W. 1982. *Nicaragua in Revolution*. New York: Praeger.

———. 1985. *Nicaragua: The First Five Years*. New York: Praeger.

———. 1987. *Reagan versus the Sandinistas: The Undeclared War on Nicaragua*. Boulder, CO: Westview Press.

———. 1991. *Revolution and Counterrevolution in Nicaragua*. Boulder, CO: Westview Press.

———. 1997. *Nicaragua without Illusions: Regime Transition and Structural Adjustment in the 1990s*. Wilmington, DE: Scholarly Resources.

Walker, Thomas W., and Christine J. Wade. 2011. *Nicaragua: Living in the Shadow of the Eagle*, 5th ed. Boulder, CO: Westview Press.

NOTES

1. Paul Levy, as quoted in Jaime Wheelock Román, *Imperialismo y dictadura: Crisis de una formación social* (México City: Siglo Veintiuno Editores, 1975), p. 29.

2. See John A. Booth and Thomas W. Walker, *Understanding Central America*, 3rd ed. (Boulder, CO: Westview Press, 1999), Appendix, Table A.1.

3. For an extended discussion of this material, see ibid., pp. 69–76, and data in Appendix, Tables A.5, A.6, A.7, and A.8.

4. Centro de Investigaciones y Estudios de la Reforma Agraria (CIERA), *Informe de Nicaragua a la FAO* (Managua: Ministerio de Desarrollo Agropecuario y Reforma Agraria, 1983), pp. 40–41.

5. Mario A. DeFranco and Carlos F. Chamorro, "Nicaragua: Crecimiento industrial y empleo," in Daniel Camacho et al., *El fracaso social de la integración centroamericana* (San José, Costa Rica: Editorial Universitaria Centroamericana, 1979), Cuadro 2.

6. John A. Booth, *The End and the Beginning: The Nicaraguan Revolution*, 2nd ed. (Boulder, CO: Westview Press, 1985), Ch. 5.

7. See Booth and Walker, *Understanding Central America*, 3rd ed., Appendix, Table A.8. Note that computational methods vary from nation to nation, so that cross-national comparisons of unemployment rates should not be made. Trends within nations in the table, however, are usefully disclosed.

8. Donaldo Castillo Rivas, "Modelos de acumulación, agricultura, y agroindustria en Centroamérica," in D. Castillo Rivas, ed., *Centroamérica: Más allá de la crisis* (Mexico City: Ediciones SIAP, 1983), pp. 202–205; Consejo Superior Universitaria Centroamericana (CSUCA), *Estructura Agraria, dinámica de población, y desarrollo capitalista en Centroamérica* (San José, Costa Rica: Editorial Universitaria Centroamericana, 1978), pp. 204–254.

9. CIERA, *Informe de Nicaragua*, p. 41.

10. Jaime Wheelock Román, *Imperialismo y dictadura: Crisis de una formación social* (Mexico City: Siglo Veintiuno Editores, 1975), pp. 141–198; Amaru Barahona PortoCarrero, *Estudio sobre la historia contemporánea de Nicaragua* (San José: Instituto de Investigaciones Sociales, Universidad de Costa Rica, 1977), pp. 33–44.

11. Material from Ricardo E. Chavarría, "The Nicaraguan Insurrection," in Thomas W. Walker, ed., *Nicaragua in Revolution* (New York: Praeger, 1982), pp. 28–29; Booth, *The End and the Beginning*, Ch. 6.

12. George Black, *Triumph of the People: The Sandinista Revolution in Nicaragua* (London: Zed Press, 1981), pp. 70–72; Centro de Información, Documentación y Análisis del Movimiento Obrero Latinoamericano (CIDAMO), "El movimiento obrero," in G. García Márquez et al., *Los Sandinistas* (Bogotá, Colombia: Editorial Oveja Negra, 1979), pp. 171–176.

13. Michael Dodson and Tommie Sue Montgomery, "The Churches in the Nicaraguan Revolution," in Walker, ed., *Nicaragua in Revolution*, pp. 163–174; Laura Nuzzi O'Shaughnessy and Luis H. Serra, *The Church and Revolution in Nicaragua*, Monographs in International Studies, Latin American Series, No. 11 (Athens: Ohio University, 1986).

14. See also T. Walker, "Introduction," in Thomas W. Walker, ed., *Nicaragua: The First Five Years* (New York: Praeger Publishers, 1985), p. 20; López C., Julio et al., *La caída del somocismo y la lucha sandinista en Nicaragua* (San José, Costa Rica: Editorial Universitaria Centroamericano, 1979), pp. 98–112.

15. Thomas W. Walker, *The Christian Democratic Movement in Nicaragua* (Tucson: University of Arizona Press, 1970).

16. Omar Cabezas, *Fire from the Mountain,* trans. Kathleen Weaver (New York: New American Library, 1986).

17. Booth, *The End and the Beginning,* Ch. 8.

18. See ibid., pp. 97–104; López C. et al., *La caída del somocismo,* pp. 71–98.

19. "A Secret War for Nicaragua," *Newsweek,* November 8, 1982, p. 44. See also Peter Kornbluh, "The Covert War," in Thomas W. Walker, ed., *Reagan versus the Sandinistas: The Undeclared War on Nicaragua* (Boulder, CO: Westview Press, 1987), p. 21.

20. Ariel C. Armony, *Argentina, the United States, and the Anticommunist Crusade in Central America, 1977–1984* (Athens: Ohio University Center for International Studies, 1997).

21. Tayacán [the CIA], *Psychological Operations in Guerrilla Warfare: The CIA's Nicaragua Manual* (New York: Vintage Books, 1985).

22. Michael Isikoff, "Drug Cartel Gave Contras $10 Million, Court Told," *Washington Post,* November 26, 1991, pp. A1, A8. For a detailed discussion of other ways in which drug money was used to finance the Contra effort, see Peter Dale Scott and Jonathan Marshall, *Cocaine Politics: Drugs, Armies and the CIA in Central America* (Berkeley: University of California Press, 1991).

23. See also Rose Spalding's *Capitalists and Revolution in Nicaragua: Opposition and Accommodation, 1979–1993* (Chapel Hill: University of North Carolina Press, 1994).

24. E.g., a detailed report by Latin Americanists, *The Electoral Process in Nicaragua: Domestic and International Influences* (Austin, TX: Latin American Studies Association, November 19, 1984); or Booth, *The End and the Beginning,* pp. 215–223.

25. For a balanced treatment of the building of governmental institutions in Sandinista Nicaragua and, in particular, the 1987 constitution, see Andrew A. Reding, "The Evolution of Governmental Institutions," in Thomas W. Walker, ed., *Revolution and Counterrevolution in Nicaragua* (Boulder, CO: Westview Press, 1991), pp. 15–47. For more discussion of the constitution—pro and con—as well as a complete English translation, see Kenneth J. Mijeski, ed., *The Nicaraguan Constitution of 1987: English Translation and Commentary* (Athens: Ohio University Press, 1991).

26. For details, see Walker, ed., *Nicaragua in Revolution,* and *Nicaragua: The First Five Years.*

27. See Michael Linfield, "Human Rights," in Walker, ed., *Revolution and Counterrevolution in Nicaragua,* pp. 275–294.

28. Lawyers Committee for International Human Rights, *Nicaragua: Revolutionary Justice* (New York: April 1985), pp. 33–40.

29. John Spicer Nichols, "La Prensa: The CIA Connection," *Columbia Journalism Review* 28, No. 2 (July–August 1988), pp. 34, 35.

30. *Los Angeles Times,* June 27, 1986, p. 15.

31. Martin Diskin et al., "Peace and Autonomy on the Atlantic Coast of Nicaragua: A Report of the LASA Task Force on Human Rights and Academic Freedom," Part 2, *LASA Forum* 17 (Summer 1986), p. 15.

32. Americas Watch, *On Human Rights in Nicaragua* (New York: May 1982), pp. 58–80.

33. See Martin Diskin et al., "Peace and Autonomy on the Atlantic Coast of Nicaragua: A Report of the LASA Task Force on Human Rights and Academic Freedom," Part 1, *LASA Forum* 17 (Spring 1986), pp. 1–16; and Part 2, pp. 1–16.

34. Americas Watch, *On Human Rights in Nicaragua,* pp. 58–80.

35. See O'Shaughnessy and Serra, *The Church and Revolution in Nicaragua*; *Los Angeles Times,* June 27, 1986, p. 15, and June 30, 1986, p. 7; and *New York Times,* July 5, 1986, p. 2.

36. "Latin Presidents Announce Accord on Contra Bases," *New York Times*, February 15, 1989, pp. 1, 4; *New York Times*, February 16, 1989, pp. 1, 6; "Nicaragua Pins Hopes on Turning Bureaucrats into Farmers," *Dallas Morning News*, February 22, 1989, p. 12A; and Booth's conversations with Mauricio Díaz of the Popular Social Christian Party and Pedro Joaquín Chamorro Barrios, former director of the Nicaraguan Resistance, Montezuma, New Mexico, February 1989.

37. Joseph R. Thome and David Kaimowitz, "Agrarian Reform," in Walker, ed., *Nicaragua: The First Five Years*; and Forrest D. Colburn, *Post-Revolutionary Nicaragua: State, Class, and the Dilemmas of Agrarian Policy* (Berkeley: University of California Press, 1986).

38. See Booth and Walker, *Understanding Central America*, 3rd ed., Appendix, Table A.9.

39. John Weeks, "The Industrial Sector," and Michael E. Conroy, "Economic Legacy and Policies: Performance and Critique," in Walker, ed., *Nicaragua: The First Five Years*; and interviews by Booth with COSEP members in León, August 1985.

40. See Booth and Walker, *Understanding Central America*, 3rd ed., Appendix, Table A.5.

41. Latin American Studies Association (LASA) Commission to Observe the 1990 Nicaraguan Elections, *Electoral Democracy Under International Pressure* (Pittsburgh, PA: LASA, March 15, 1990), p. 19.

42. [United Nations] Comisión Económica para América Latina y el Caribe, "Balance Preliminar de la Economía de América Latina y el Caribe, 1990," *Notas Sobre la Economía y el Desarrollo*, Nos. 500–501 (December 1990), p. 27.

43. This figure is part of eight pages of statistics on the human cost of the war provided to Walker by the Nicaraguan Ministry of the Presidency in January 1990.

44. LASA Commission, *Electoral Democracy,* pp. 24–26.

45. See Eric Weaver and William Barnes, "Opposition Parties and Coalitions," in Walker, ed., *Revolution and Counterrevolution in Nicaragua*, pp. 117–142.

46. An unidentified US official quoted in "Chamorro Takes a Chance," *Time,* May 7, 1990, p. 43. For documentation of the massive US intervention in Nicaragua's

1990 election, see William I. Robinson, *A Faustian Bargain: U.S. Involvement in the Nicaraguan Elections and American Foreign Policy in the Post–Cold War Era* (Boulder, CO: Westview Press, 1992).

47. Coauthor Thomas Walker served as a member of the LASA Commission to Observe the 1990 Nicaraguan Elections. He was specifically assigned to observe and investigate the campaign and election in the war zone of northern Nicaragua in late 1989 and early 1990.

48. As quoted in "Ortega Livens up San José Summit," *Central America Report* 16, No. 43 (November 3, 1989), p. 340.

49. For a systematic and comprehensive examination of this period see Thomas W. Walker, ed. *Nicaragua without Illusions: Regime Transition and Structural Adjustment in the 1990s* (Wilmington, DE: Scholarly Resources, 1997).

50. See also Booth and Walker, *Understanding Central America*, 3rd ed., Appendix, Tables A.1 and A.6.

51. As cited in Nitlápan-Envío Team, "President Alemán: First Moves, First Signals," *Envío* 16, Nos. 187–188 (February–March 1997), pp. 3–4.

52. William I. Robinson, *Transnational Conflicts: Central America, Social Change, and Globalization* (London and New York: Verso, 2003), pp. 78–79.

53. Ibid., p. 79.

54. See, for instance, "Nicaragua: Atlantic Coast Groups Rearm," *Central America Report* 25, No. 22 (June 11, 1998), p. 3.

55. J. Mark Ruhl, "Curbing Central America's Militaries," *Journal of Democracy* 15, No. 3 (July 2004), p. 141.

56. Shelly A. McConnell, "Institutional Development," pp. 45–64, in Walker, ed., *Nicaragua without Illusions*.

57. "William Grigsby: 'Refounding' the Sandinista Movement." *Envío* 225 (April 2000).

58. The authors interviewed various Nicaraguan political leaders during June and July of 1998, including Víctor Hugo Tinoco, FSLN representative in the National Assembly; Dora María Téllez, professor, former minister of health, and leader of the MRS; René Núñez, a top official of the FSLN; Mariano Fiallos, professor and former head of the CSE; Alejandro Bendaña, author and former foreign ministry official in the Ortega administration; Antonio Lacayo, businessman, farmer, and former minister of the presidency in the UNO government; and Dr. Rigoberto Sampson, mayor of León. There was striking uniformity in their assessment of the FSLN's status.

59. On the election see John A. Booth and Patricia Bayer Richard, "The Nicaraguan Elections of October 1996," *Electoral Studies* 16, No. 3 (1997), pp. 386–393; John A. Booth, "Election Observation and Democratic Transition in Nicaragua," in Kevin J. Middlebrook, ed., *Electoral Observation and Democratic Transitions in Latin America* (La Jolla: Center for US-Mexican Studies of the University of California, San Diego, 1998); *Envío* 15 (December–January, 1996–1997); and Thomas W. Walker, Epilogue, in Walker, ed., *Nicaragua without Illusions*, pp. 305–311.

60. Nitlápan-Envío Team, "An Accord Besieged by Discord," *Envío* 16, No. 196 (November 1997), pp. 3–4.

61. On Alemán's scandal, see David Close and Kalowatie Deonandan, eds., *Undoing Democracy: The Politics of Electoral Caudillismo* (Lanham, MD: Lexington Books, 2004); on the scandal involving Ortega, see Juan Ramón Huerta, *El silencio del patriarca* (Managua: Litografía El Renacimiento, 1998); and "Extractos del testimonio desgarrador de Zoliamérica," *Confidencial* 2 (May 24–30, 1998), pp. 1, 9–11.

62. Robinson, *Transnational Conflicts*, p. 83; see also pp. 82–87.

63. Vilma Núñez de Escorcia, "The FSLN Leadership's Disintegration Goes Way Back," *Envío* 222 (January 2000).

64. See, for instance, "No aceptan Ortega," in *La Prensa Libre,* February 28, 2001, and "Garza tajante contra el FSLN," in *El Nuevo Diario,* April 6, 2001.

65. The Court ruled that Aléman's sentence "should be definitively quashed on the grounds that no evidence was found to ratify either the original sentence in December 2002 or the Appeals Court's 2007 decision to uphold it." See Nitlápan-Envío Team, "Abuse as Usual Means Many Accounts to Settle," *Envío* 330 (January 2007).

66. Latin American Database, "Low Turnout in Nicaragua Elections; Big Win for FSLN," *NotiCen* (November 11, 2004.)

67. Ibid.

68. Latin American Database, "Nicaragua's Legislature Looks to Limit Presidential Powers; Aleman Could Rescue Bolanos," *NotiCen* (January 13, 2005).

69. For more on the constitutional crisis see Shelley McConnell, "Can the Inter-American Democratic Charter Work? The 2004–05 Constitutional Crisis in Nicaragua," presented at the International Studies Association meeting, February 28–March 3, 2007; and Council on Hemispheric Affairs, "Nicaragua: A Three-Way Political Ground," COHA Memorandum to the Press, July 20, 2005.

70. Max Blumenthal, "The Kinder, Gentler Daniel Ortega," *The Nation* (January 19, 2007).

71. Latin American Database, "Nicaragua's Far Right Presidential Candidate Running Against the Regional Tide," *NotiCen* (July 27, 2006).

72. Latin American Database, "FSLN Seeks to Stop Another Sandinista Revolution," *NotiCen* (March 10, 2005).

73. Shelley McConnell, "Ortega's Nicaragua," *Current History* (February 2007), pp. 83–88.

74. Ibid.

75. James C. McKinley Jr., "Nicaraguan Councils Stir Fear of Dictatorship," *New York Times*, May 4, 2008.

76. Latin American Database, "Ortega's First 100 Days as Nicaragua's President," *NotiCen* (April 26, 2007).

77. Asier Andres Fernández, "CPCs: A Sandinista Tool?" *Central America Report*, May 23, 2008; James Smith, "CPCs Get Judicial Seal of Approval," *Central America*

Report, December 7, 2007; Asier Andres Fernández, "Dubious Court Rulings at One Year Mark," *Central America Report*, January 25, 2008.

78. Asier Andres Fernández, "Court Dashes Third Party Hopes in Municipal Elections," *Central America Report*, June 27, 2008; Asier Andres Fernández, "A Murky Pact between Liberals and Sandinistas," *Central America Report*, July 18, 2008.

79. See William Booth, "Democracy in Nicaragua in Peril, Ortega Critics Say," *Washington Post*, November 20, 2008, A-12; Roger Burbach, "Et Tu, Daniel? The Sandinista Revolution Betrayed," *NACLA Report on the Americas*, April 6, 2009; "How to Steal an Election," *The Economist* (November 13, 2008).

80. See Chapter 9.

81. Ibid. See also Tina Rosenberg, "The Many Stories of Carlos Fernando Chamorro," *New York Times*, March 22, 2009.

82. See Instituto para el Desarrollo y la Democracia (IPADE), *Elecciones Muncipales 2008/2009* (Masaya, Nicaragua: IPADE, May 2009); Nitlápan-Envío team, "Nicaragua Is the Municipal Elections' Big Loser," *Envío* 328 (November 2008); Kitty Monterrey, "These Elections Were Won by Both Fraud and Theft," *Envío* 329 (December 2008); Ethics and Transparency Civil Group, "Looking at the Ruins of a Defiled Electoral Process," *Envío* 332 (March 2009).

83. Argüello, who had a history of depression and substance abuse, committed suicide on July 1, 2009.

84. Marc Lacey, "Sandinista Fervor Turns Sour for Former Comrades of Nicaragua's President," *New York Times*, November 24, 2008.

85. Matthew Lee, "US Cuts Aid to Nicaragua," *Washington Post*, June 11, 2009.

86. Author interviews in Managua, Nicaragua, June 2011; Supreme Court of Justice, Constitutional Chamber, Exp. No. 602–09, Judgment No. 504; see also http://www.nytimes.com/2009/11/16/world/americas/16nicaragua.html; http://findarticles.com/p/articles/mi_go1655/is_2011_Feb_3/ai_n56893409/?tag=content;col1.

87. *NotiCen*, 2010–05–06.

88. The lack of accreditation meant that these groups did not have access to polling stations or locations where votes were counted.

89. "Carter Center Statement on November 6 Elections in Nicaragua," September 9, 2011, http://www.cartercenter.org/news/pr/nicaragua-090911.html.

90. Organization of American States, OAS Permanent Council Hears Reports by Electoral Missions in Guatemala and Nicaragua" (November 15, 2011), http://www.oas.org/en/media_center/press_release.asp?sCodigo=E-958/11; Unión Europea, "Misión de Observación Electoral Nicaragua 2011: Elecciones Presidenciales, Legislativas y al Parlacen," Declaración preliminar, Managua 8 de Noviembre 2011, http://www.eueom.eu/files/pressreleases/other/moeue-nicaragua-preliminar-08112011_es.pdf.

91. European Union Election Observation Mission, "Nicaragua Final Report: General Elections and Parlecen Elections 2011," p. 3, http://www.eueom.eu/files/dmfile/moeue-nicaragua-final-report-22022012_en.pdf.

92. Arturo Cruz-Sequeria, "Political Reform in Central America: Are Democratic Institutions at Risk?" *Inter-American Dialogue* (July 2013), p. 7, http://thedialogue .org/uploads/Cruz071213publishedversion.pdf.

93. John A. Booth and Mitchell A. Seligson, "Political Culture of Democracy in Nicaragua and in the Americas, 2012: Towards Equality of Opportunity," Latin American Public Opinion Project, Vanderbilt University, 2013, pp. 149, 274.

94. http://www.thedialogue.org/PublicationFiles/IAD8642_Remittance_0424en FINAL.pdf.

95. International Court of Justice, "Territorial Dispute and Maritime Delimitation (Nicaragua v. Colombia) Summary of the Judgment of 19 November, 2012," November 19, 2012, http://www.icj-cij.org/docket/files/124/17180.pdf.

96. Cruz-Sequeria, p. 6, http://thedialogue.org/uploads/Cruz071213published version.pdf.

97. Booth and Seligson, p. 264.

98. Yader Luna, "Disminuyen homicidios," *El Nuevo Diario* (May 30, 2013), http://www.elnuevodiario.com.ni/nacionales/287550-disminuyen-homicidios.

99. Elizabeth Romero, "RAAN urge más atención," *La Prensa* (July 31, 2013), http://www.laprensa.com.ni/2013/07/31/ambito/156812-raan-urge-mas-atención.

100. Ben Witte, "Nicaragua's Femicide Law Slow to Produce Results,"*NotiCen* (May 13, 2013).

101. Maria Teresa Blandón, "Comments on the Integral Laws Against Violence Against Women," *Nicaragua Dispatch* (March 9, 2012), http://www.nicaraguadispatch .com/news/2012/03/comments-on-the-integral-law-against-violence-against -women/2720; Ipas, "Rapporteur) for Women's Rights Visits Nicaragua, Urges Reforms to Address Sexual Violence and Unsafe Abortion" (July 16, 2012), http://www .ipas.org/en/News/2012/July/Rapporteur-for-womens-rights-visits-Nicaragua -urges-reforms-to-address-sexual-violence-an.aspx; Latin American Database, "Cash-Strapped Femicide Law Takes Effect in Nicaragua,"*NotiCen* (July 26, 2012).

102. CINCO, "Elecciones Municipales 2012 en Nicaragua" (November 26, 2012), http://www.cinco.org.ni/noticia/373; Ben Witte, "Sandinistas Dominate Municipal Elections in Nicaragua," *NotiCen* (November 15, 2012), http://ladb.unm .edu/noticen/2012/11/15–078810; Organization of American States, "Statement of the OAS Mission on the Municipal Elections in Nicaragua" (November 5, 2012), http://www.oas.org/en/media_center/press_release.asp?sCodigo=E-399/12.

6

EL SALVADOR

To visitors, El Salvador's most striking characteristic is overpopulation. Foreigners sometimes argue that the tiny country lacks the resources to support its teeming population, but other densely populated countries (the Netherlands, Japan, China) manage to feed their people. El Salvador's real problem, as in the rest of northern Central America, is extreme maldistribution of resources brought about by centuries of external dependence and elite control.[1]

After thirteen years of extreme political violence as insurgents challenged military regimes and their civilian elite allies for power in the 1980s and early 1990s, El Salvador's warring factions agreed to adopt formal civilian democracy. In 1992, the country became more stable—and did so more quickly—than most observers expected. Given the historical record of El Salvador's elites, its government's embrace of very conservative economic policies, and the nation's role in the world economy, the country appeared likely to maintain debilitating socioeconomic inequalities and external dependency indefinitely. Yet by the early twenty-first century El Salvador was more politically peaceful than at any time in the previous century, but it was also far more dangerous.

HISTORICAL BACKGROUND

During most of a century after independence in 1823, a Liberal elite controlled El Salvador. Guatemalan intervention occasionally imposed Conservative rulers, but they were exceptions. Like their regional counterparts, Salvadoran Liberals staunchly advocated free enterprise and economic modernization to link the country to the world economy. They promoted economic and service modernization to build up agricultural exports. The elite regarded the mestizo and indigenous masses both as obstacles to progress and as an essential labor supply.

El Salvador's nineteenth-century economy revolved around the production, extraction, and export of indigo dye. By the mid-nineteenth century, cheaper European chemical dyes sharply cut international demand for the deep blue colorant, forcing El Salvador's elite to turn to coffee production, best cultivated on the higher, volcanic terrain previously disdained by large landowners. The mountain slopes, however, were occupied by mestizo and indigenous communal farmers whose ancestors had been displaced from the valley floors by the Spanish. The powerful would-be coffee growers used their control of the government to appropriate good coffee land.

In 1856, the state mandated that communes plant at least two-thirds of their lands in coffee or have the lands confiscated. This wiped out many communes lacking the considerable capital necessary to buy and plant coffee trees and wait several years for a crop. Those that survived the 1856 law collapsed in the early 1880s when legislation simply outlawed communal holdings. Wealthy coffee farmers bought the newly available land. The government also passed "vagrancy" laws that forced the now-landless peasants to work on the coffee plantations. Outraged by this legalized theft of their land and forced-labor schemes, peasants several times unsuccessfully rebelled in the late nineteenth century. But coffee's promoters prevailed, and the privileged classes brought El Salvador into the twentieth century with one of the most unequal land-distribution systems in Latin America. A coffee-growing elite, thereafter known (inaccurately) as the "fourteen families," controlled most of the country's resources. Coffee cultivation continued expanding into the twentieth century. In 1929, for instance, the socially conscious editor of *La Patria* wrote: "The conquest of territory by the coffee industry is alarming. It . . . is now descending into the valleys displacing maize, rice and beans. It is extended like the conquistador, spreading hunger and misery, reducing former proprietors to the worst conditions—woe to those who sell!"[2]

The situation reached a political breaking point when the Great Depression lowered the demand and prices for Salvadoran exports in the 1930s. Coffee growers attempted to cushion this blow by cutting the already miserable wages of their workers. Meanwhile popular hopes for justice soared during an aberrant period of democratic reform in 1930 to 1931, only to crash when General Maximiliano Hernández Martínez established another reactionary dictatorship. The turmoil and economic travail spawned an ill-coordinated peasant uprising in January 1932. The government and landowners quickly crushed it by massacring over 30,000 peasants (but few actual insurgents). The promoter of the revolt, a charismatic Marxist intellectual, Augustín Farabundo Martí, was captured before the revolt and shot and beheaded in its wake. His memory, like that of Sandino in Nicaragua, would linger decades later.

The five decades following the rise of General Hernández Martínez and the 1932 massacre (known to this day as *la Matanza*—"the Slaughter") forms an epoch in Salvadoran history. Whereas before the Liberal elite had normally ruled through civilian dictators drawn from among themselves, they now entrusted the government to an uninterrupted series of military regimes. Ruling dictatorially, Hernández Martínez protected the coffee elite and initiated modernization projects. Post–World War II demands for reform from labor and middle-class elements and from within the military ended the Hernández Martínez regime in 1944. In 1948 the armed forces restructured the regime by establishing a military-dominated party, the Revolutionary Party of Democratic Unification (Partido Revolucionario de Unificación Democrática, PRUD). The party promoted neither revolution, democracy, nor unity but instead provided the military "an impressive machine of patronage and electoral mobilization."[3] In 1960 the PRUD was replaced by its own clone, the National Conciliation Party (Partido de Conciliación Nacional, PCN).

After 1948 the Salvadoran military, supported by much of the bourgeoisie it defended, ruled essentially on behalf of itself and became increasingly powerful and corrupt. Military rule developed a cycle of "change" that maintained the status quo. Responding to popular unrest and national problems, young military officers who pledged to institute needed reforms would overthrow an increasingly repressive regime. Then conservative army elements backed by the agrarian oligarchy would reassert themselves and drop the recent reforms. This would provoke civil unrest, followed by increased repression, disaffection by another reformist military faction, and a new coup.[4]

One such cycle produced the PRUD between 1944 and 1948, and another brought the PRUD's restructuring itself into the PCN in 1961. In January 1961, just after John F. Kennedy's inauguration in the United States, a conservative coup encouraged by the Eisenhower administration occurred in El Salvador. Although Kennedy recognized the new government, he apparently also employed the Alliance for Progress to pressure the interim junta to implement mild democratic and social reforms.

The US-created Alliance for Progress and the Central American Common Market (CACM) promoted rapid economic growth in El Salvador. The government developed infrastructure while domestic and foreign capitalists invested in manufacturing and commerce. Reformist rhetoric in the mid-1960s sparked popular hopes for change. During this period the Christian Democratic Party (Partido Demócrata Cristiano, PDC) formed. Its popular leader, José Napoleón Duarte, advocated gradual reformism of the sort supported by the Alliance. Duarte twice won the mayoralty of San Salvador.[5]

This tentative process of political transition, aided by rapid economic growth, quickly vanished in the familiar way. The mild reforms and the PDC's progress alarmed the oligarchy. El Salvador's establishment press labeled President Kennedy a "Communist" for promoting agrarian reform. When the PDC's Duarte apparently won the 1972 presidential election, the military answered the oligarchy's call. The regime overthrew the election, installed rightist Colonel Arturo Armando Molina as president, and arrested, tortured, and exiled the defrauded Duarte.

GLOBAL FORCES AND INSURRECTION

Effects of Rapid Economic Growth. The CACM, the Alliance for Progress, and new investment caused rapid economic growth in El Salvador. Gross domestic product (GDP) per capita grew over 2 percent annually between 1962 and 1978. But as in Nicaragua, the benefits of general economic growth were very unevenly distributed. Consumer prices in El Salvador inflated at a mild rate of about 1.5 percent per year from 1963 to 1972. The OPEC oil-price shock, however, drove inflation up to an average of 12.8 percent annually from 1973 through 1979.[6]

Unlike prices, real working-class wages in El Salvador declined after 1973, losing about one-fifth of their real purchasing power by 1980. Salvadorans' median income was already consistently the second lowest in Central America. The reader should bear in mind that, taking into account the maldistribution of income, the disposable annual income of the poorest half of the population probably amounted to no more than a US dollar or two per day. Meanwhile, food and clothing costs were similar to those in the much more prosperous United States. Thus even for those luckily employed throughout the CACM boom, officially fixed wages steadily lost effective purchasing power.

Despite rapid industrialization and productivity growth, the capital-intensive production of consumer goods generated relatively few new jobs for the growing workforce—just the opposite of what CACM and Alliance promoters hoped. Moreover, changes in the agrarian economy pushed hundreds of thousands of peasants off the land, also swelling joblessness. Estimates place unemployment in El Salvador at around 16 percent in 1970. By 1978 the unemployment level—aggravated by oil-price increases and investor fears generated by the insurrection in Nicaragua—reached an estimated 21 percent. After 1980 unemployment rose even faster because of El Salvador's own developing insurrection. Nervous investors closed some plants; disrupted Central American trade forced others to close.[7]

After 1950 much of the best agricultural land was converted to capital-intensive cultivation of export crops (in particular cotton) at the expense of subsistence-farming tenants, squatters, and smallholders. During the 1960s, pressure on the land increased dramatically—the overall number of farms grew by 19 percent while cultivated land shrank by 8 percent. The 1965 agricultural minimum wage law lowered the number of *colonos* and *aparceros* (peasants cultivating for subsistence a plot of land donated by the owner) to one-third of the 1961 level by 1971, and the amount of land so employed to one-fifth of the earlier level.[8]

Thus, in the 1960s a dramatic change in Salvadoran rural class relations greatly increased rural poverty. Rental and ownership of tiny (less than 2.0 hectares) farms increased sharply while the average size of these small plots shrank. Despite an increase in the number of small plots, the number of newly landless peasants more than tripled between 1961 and 1971. Large farms (over 50 hectares) also shrank in number and size as their owners sold part of their holdings for capital to invest elsewhere. Many members of the rural bourgeoisie moved some of their wealth into the fast-expanding industrial sector during the 1960s and 1970s. They invested in modern, capital-intensive industries that generated large profits. Industrial production and industrial worker productivity grew rapidly while real industrial wages and level of employment actually declined.

Wealth continued to concentrate in fewer hands during the 1970s.[9] Workers' share of the burgeoning national income deteriorated while production and investment became more centralized.[10] Major coffee growers invested roughly four times as much in industry as any other Salvadoran group and attracted joint ventures with about 80 percent of the foreign capital invested in the country. Total industrial output more than doubled between 1967 and 1975 while the number of firms producing goods diminished by 10 percent, concentrating wealth and income among the owners of the industrial sector.[11] In Montgomery's words, "The old saying that 'money follows money' was never truer than in El Salvador. . . . These investment patterns not only contributed to an ever-greater concentration of wealth, but confirm that the traditional developmentalist assumption that wealth . . . will 'trickle down' in developing nations is groundless."[12] Orellana agreed: "The majority of Salvadorans, excluded from the benefits of that growth, were prevented from adequately satisfying their basic needs."[13]

Although El Salvador's capitalist elite grew relatively and absolutely wealthier during the mid-1970s, this trend changed abruptly in 1979. The impact of the Sandinista revolution in nearby Nicaragua on El Salvador's economy, combined with the onset of extensive domestic popular mobilization within El Salvador in 1978, sharply reduced Salvadoran investment and economic growth. Falling coffee prices and the breakdown of Central American trade due to the exhaustion of the CACM import-substitution growth model accelerated the recession. El Salvador's rapid GDP growth of the mid-1970s became instead a 3.1 percent *decline* in overall production and a 5.9 percent *drop* in GDP per capita in 1979. This economic contraction became severe and persisted for years. The deep depression harmed the interests of El Salvador's coffee producers and industrialists and caused massive layoffs of their employees.[14]

In summary, the development model followed by the Salvadoran state under the Central American Common Market increased overall production as well as the share of wealth controlled by the national capitalist class. The Salvadoran working classes became not only relatively but absolutely and markedly poorer during the 1970s. The purchasing power of working-class wage earners declined rapidly from 1973 on. Joblessness and underemployment rose steadily during much of the 1970s and accelerated late in the decade. Living standards eroded badly during this period. Most Salvadorans measured this adversity in terms of how much food they could put on the table each day. Their impoverishment provided powerful political grievances to many Salvadorans.

Popular Mobilization. Although the military's PRUD-PCN Party controlled the national government, new opposition parties from across the ideological spectrum appeared during the 1960s.[15] Giving early signs of growing political opposition in 1959–1960 were two new reformist parties: the social democratic National Revolutionary Movement (Movimiento Nacional Revolucionario, MNR) and the Christian Democratic Party (Partido Demócrata Cristiano, PDC). The Democratic Nationalist Union (Unión Democrática Nacionalista, UDN), a leftist coalition, formed in 1967.[16] The PDC and MNR briefly formed a legislative coalition with dissident PCN deputies in the late 1960s. This coalition anticipated a major reform push by the National Opposition Union (Unión Nacional Opositora, UNO), an electoral coalition of the PDC, MNR, and UDN. UNO's presidential candidate, José Napoleón Duarte, apparently won the 1972 election but was denied the office by fraud. UNO reportedly also won the 1977 presidential election, but again lost to electoral fraud.

Myriad organizations from unions to self-help groups to peasant leagues developed during the late 1960s and the 1970s, many promoted by the Church and new political parties. The number of cooperatives grew from 246 to 543 between 1973 and 1980.[17] Labor union membership among blue-collar and middle-class workers rose steadily from the late 1960s, reaching 44,150 in 1970 and 71,000 by 1977. Several unions, especially among public employees, became increasingly militant.[18] The number and frequency of strikes rose dramatically from 1974 on as inflation eroded living standards.

Development programs sponsored by the Catholic Church, PDC, and even the US Agency for International Development (USAID) swelled the number of working-class organizations in El Salvador during the 1960s and early 1970s. Catholic Christian base communities (CEBs) spread widely through urban and rural poor neighborhoods. In the 1970s CEBs increasingly demanded political and economic change on behalf of the poor. Many peasant organizations also developed during this period, in part encouraged by the Molina regime's mid-1970s land reform proposals. Peasant leagues demanded land reform and higher wages. The United Popular Action Front (Frente de Acción Popular Unida, FAPU), a coalition of labor, peasant, and university student organizations, and the Communist Party of El Salvador (Partido Comunista de El Salvador, PCS) formed in 1974. FAPU was the first of several similar coalitions that together would eventually build a very broad opposition network.

Between 1970 and 1979 five Salvadoran guerrilla organizations arose to present an armed challenge to the PCN (see Appendix, Table A.4). Each forged a coalition with unions and other popular organizations after 1974. These five broad-front coalitions greatly enhanced opposition capability and resources, facilitating strikes and mass demonstrations while providing material resources for the armed opposition.

Government Repression and the Opposition. After 1970, successive military regimes responded to swelling popular mobilization with escalating repression.[19] A rightist paramilitary organization directly tied to public security forces formed in the late 1960s, the Nationalist Democratic Organization (Organización Democrática Nacionalista, ORDEN). Its acronym spells the Spanish word for "order." ORDEN recruited tens of thousands of peasants from among former military conscripts. The anti-Communist militia's main objective was to suppress peasant organization. It quickly built a grisly record by attacking and killing striking teachers in 1968 and thereafter murdering organizers of workers, peasants, or political opposition.

President Molina (1972–1977) and his handpicked successor Carlos Humberto Romero (1977–1979), both military officers with close links to the agrarian oligarchy, staunchly opposed political and economic reform. As the first guerrilla actions began to occur and labor and peasant organizations grew after 1973, regular security forces openly escalated repression. In 1974 National Guard and ORDEN forces murdered six peasants and "disappeared" several others affiliated with a Church-PDC peasant league. On July 30, 1975, troops killed at least 37 students protesting the staging of the Miss Universe pageant in San Salvador. Regular government troops in the capital massacred an estimated 200 UNO supporters among protesters of fraud in the 1977 presidential election. From 1975 on, "death squads," a misnomer employed to disguise political terror by regular security forces and ORDEN,[20] became increasingly active. (As we discuss elsewhere, their use in El Salvador is just one example of US-sanctioned death squad activity throughout the Americas beginning in 1969.)[21] Beginning with the public assassination of opposition legislator and labor leader Rafael Aguiñada Carranza in 1974, death squads assassinated and kidnapped dissidents, Catholic social activists, and priests and attacked Church property. Eighteen Catholic clergy and religious personnel, including Archbishop Oscar Arnulfo Romero, were murdered between 1977 and 1982.[22]

Repression in El Salvador reached such heights in the late 1970s that official mortality statistics began to reflect the curve of terror. Following a big increase in labor disputes in 1977–1979, two separate violence indicators shot upward. The government's own annual tally of violent deaths, reported in official statistical abstracts, rose from normal background levels of an average of 864 murders per year for 1965–1966 to 1,837 in 1977, and then skyrocketed to 11,471 violent deaths in 1980.[23] A Catholic human rights agency reported that political murders rose from an average of about 14 per year for 1972–1977, to 1,030 by 1979; 8,024 in 1980; and 13,353 in 1981.[24]

Statistics fail to convey the intensity of governmental assaults on human rights in El Salvador. The following became commonplace: searches of persons and residences on a massive scale; arbitrary, unmotivated, and unappealable arrests by secret police/military agencies; widespread and systematic use of physical and psychological torture; kidnappings; arbitrary and indefinite retention of prisoners (often without charges); use of "confessions" extracted through torture or intimidation; official refusal to provide information about detainees; judicial corruption; abysmal prison conditions; systematic impunity for human rights violators; government antagonism toward humanitarian, human rights, and relief agencies; and intimidation and harassment of prisoners or released prisoners and of their families. Common types of torture by the military and police of El Salvador were the following:

> Lengthy uninterrupted interrogations during which the prisoner is denied food and sleep; electrical shocks; application of highly corrosive acids to the prisoner's body; hanging of prisoners by the feet and hands; hooding prisoners [for long periods]; introduction of objects into the anus; threats of rape; disrespectful fondling and rape; threats of death; simulation of death of the prisoner by removing him from the cell, blindfolded and tied, late at night, and firing shots [toward the prisoner but] into the air; all manner of blows; . . . [and] threats of rape, torture, and murder of loved ones of the prisoner. Among the thousands of murdered detainees, the signs of torture reach uncommon extremes of barbarism: dismemberment [of various types], mutilation of diverse members, removal of breasts and genitals, decapitation . . . and leaving of victims' remains in visible and public places.[25]

After this escalation of government repression in the mid-1970s, four large opposition coalitions formed. Each linked various labor, peasant, and student groups to one of the guerrilla organizations. FAPU formed in 1974, the

Revolutionary Popular Bloc (Bloque Popular Revolucionario, BPR) in 1975, the 28th of February Popular Leagues (Ligas Populares 28 de Febrero, LP-28) in 1978, and the Popular Liberation Movement (Movimiento de Liberación Popular, MLP) in 1979. By allying with each other and with armed rebels, the coalitions' constituent groups committed themselves to revolutionary action. Together they could mobilize hundreds of thousands of supporters to demonstrate or strike, and raise funds and recruit for the guerrillas. Guerrilla groups accumulated large war chests by kidnapping wealthy Salvadorans for ransom. After mid-1979 arms flowed to the guerrillas from private dealers in Costa Rica. Other arms came through Nicaragua for a short period during 1980 and early 1981.[26]

Growing opposition mobilization, the escalation of regime and rebel violence, the incapacity of the Romero government to address national problems, career frustration among certain groups of military officers, and apprehension about the Sandinistas' victory in Nicaragua in July 1979 led to another major regime change in El Salvador. Disgruntled senior officers and reformist younger officials ousted President Romero, a former general, on October 15, 1979. The coup temporarily allied these military factions with opposition social democrats of the MNR, the Christian Democrats (PDC), and some business factions. The Carter administration gambled that the reformist inclinations of the junta's members might stem the revolutionary tide and immediately endorsed the coup and the reformist military regime it established.[27] The coup and new junta thus made palatable the resumption of US arms transfers to El Salvador.

This new regime allowed new civilian players (the MNR, PDC) and ousted some others (especially the PCN's Romero and his allies) and, with US encouragement, proposed socioeconomic reforms. The new junta nevertheless failed to contain rapidly escalating official violence. Rightist elements quickly asserted themselves and expelled some of the reformers in early 1980. This prompted the MNR and most of the Christian Democrats to abandon the junta. However, the support of the United States added a crucial new element to the political game and continued the pressure for socioeconomic reform. The coup thus ushered in a reformist military regime that "signaled the exhaustion of traditional forms of political control and the search for a more viable system of domination. The old power apparatus was severely shaken."[28]

The October 1979 coup briefly raised opposition hopes for major changes, but the restructuring of the junta and rising official violence quickly alienated much of the center and left and changed opposition tactics. Further unification of the opposition came early in 1980: The five guerrilla groups joined to form the Farabundo Martí National Liberation Front (FMLN) to increase their political and military coordination. Opposition forces then forged the Revolutionary Coordinator of the Masses (Coordinadora Revolucionaria de

Masas, CRM) in January 1980 and continued massive strikes, protests, and guerrilla warfare. Several parties and mass coalitions, including the MNR and much of the PDC, then united into the Revolutionary Democratic Front (FDR). The FDR and FMLN soon allied to form the joint political-military opposition organization FMLN-FDR, which coordinated overall opposition revolutionary strategy, fielded some 4,000 troops and 5,000 militia, and controlled several zones of the country.

The FMLN-FDR adopted a platform for a revolutionary government, established governmental structures in their zones of control, and began planning to assume ruling power.[29] In recognition of this powerful challenge to the junta's sovereignty, Mexico and France increased the rebels' legitimacy by recognizing the FMLN-FDR as a belligerent force. FMLN-FDR representatives operated openly in Panama, Nicaragua, Mexico, Colombia, and even the United States.

Outcome of the Challenge to Sovereignty. Momentum favored the Salvadoran opposition in 1979 and 1980. The October coup had momentarily linked the major opposition parties, a reformist military faction, and key middle-sector proponents of democracy in an effort to implement major structural reforms and curtail government violence. When rightist elements pushed moderates from the junta and escalated violence, it blocked the reformist opposition's access to power and its reform attempts. This closed a key, less-violent path to change and convinced much of the moderate center-left to ally with the armed opposition. On January 30, 1980, Guillermo Ungo and other moderates resigned from the junta and cabinet. The rebels had built a cooperative popular base, acquired considerable financing, and mobilized several thousand men and women under arms. When the junta reconstituted itself with more conservative elements of the Christian Democrats and government violence continued, the FDR formed (April 1980), followed by the FMLN (October 1980). By late 1980, guerrilla troops had seized effective control of much of Morazán, La Unión, and Chalatenango provinces, so that "1981 opened with the army badly stretched and the undefeated FMLN poised for a major offensive."[30]

The government found itself in disarray. The first junta, internally divided, had scant support from either mass organizations or the private sector. When the conservative remnant of the Christian Democrats joined the junta in 1980, the major organization representing Salvadoran capital, the National Association of Private Enterprises (Asociación Nacional de Empresas Privadas, ANEP), boycotted the government. Rightist elements within and outside the military made several attempts to overthrow the junta. The poor battlefield performance of the armed forces' 15,000 ill-trained troops throughout 1980 appeared to foretell imminent doom for the regime.

Help for the junta came from the US government, which decided to provide military aid to the failing Salvadoran military. This profoundly altered the balance of forces between the regime and insurgents. Military aid and advice and economic assistance worth $5.9 million sent during the waning days of the Carter administration began rescuing the Salvadoran regime. The incoming Reagan administration then greatly boosted US technical assistance and financing. By 1985, US military aid to El Salvador had reached $533 million. Over the twelve years of the Salvadoran civil war, US aid (military plus civilian) totaled about $6 billion.[31]

The Reagan administration supported the PDC's Duarte, helped contain rightist opposition to the government, and provided aid for programs ranging from agrarian reform to constituent assembly elections.[32] US training, arms, munitions, aircraft, and intelligence held the Salvadoran army together long enough to increase its size and capability so it could effectively fight the FMLN. Unlike Nicaragua, where American aid was withdrawn, US assistance in El Salvador rescued the official armed forces. This prolonged the conflict. "The principal reason for the extended nature of the war was the capacity of the junta to hold its piecemeal military apparatus together . . . to ward off guerrilla offensives [and hold] the population in a state of terror. . . . It could only have achieved this or, indeed, survived for more than a few weeks with the resolute support of the US, which Somoza was, in the last instance, denied."[33]

The Salvadoran government after 1979 depended heavily upon several interacting forces—hard-liners in control of the armed forces, major business interests, extremist anti-Communist ideologues of the sort represented by Roberto D'Aubuisson and his Nationalist Republican Alliance Party (Alianza Republicana Nacionalista, ARENA), and the Carter, Reagan, and first Bush administrations. Indeed, pressure by the United States instituted another regime transformation. These Salvadoran actors agreed to replace the junta with a transitional civilian-led government marked by the advent of constitutional reform and elections. The war still went badly for the military during the early 1980s, but massive US economic, military, and technical assistance held off the FMLN.

The right fiercely opposed most reforms and wished to exclude moderates from the government, but their dependence on US aid undermined their resistance. Throughout most of the 1980s, the United States championed José Napoleón Duarte's faction of the PDC as the only political force that could legitimize the struggle against the armed opposition. Backed by the immense resources of the United States, Duarte was installed in the presidency and the PDC won a majority of the legislative seats in the 1984 presidential and 1985 legislative elections—both of very dubious quality.[34] Thus began a shaky civilian transitional government that would eventually provide the institutional and legal foundation for greater democracy. The short-term goal of the United States in 1984 was to establish new political rules with formal civilian leadership and to broaden the spectrum of participants. This liberalization would provide enough political space to moderates to keep them from aligning with the FMLN. Although detested as a "Communist" by the right and distrusted by the military, Duarte with his US backing was indispensable to both because they needed US aid to avoid defeat. US pressure on the military and right sufficed to protect the Duarte/PDC civil government, but could neither control radical rightist forces nor compel them to permit social reform. In a very real sense, Duarte formally held the office of president without ever really coming to power.

US involvement during the Duarte period thus created an unstable and artificial coalition among incompatible elements. The Duarte government exercised no control over the security forces or the war.[35] The Salvadoran military and the United States blocked Duarte's attempts to negotiate with the FMLN-FDR because both wished to win the war rather than negotiate a settlement. The constitution written in 1982 and 1983 barred agrarian reform programs that might have eased the social pressures contributing to the rebellion. The transitional government could muster no support from the business community or conservative parties for needed economic austerity measures. Duarte's main base of mass support, the PDC's allied labor unions, grew increasingly frustrated and uncooperative in the late 1980s. The inefficacy and growing corruption of the PDC, aggravated by internal divisions, led to the party's defeat by ARENA in the 1988 legislative elections. On March 19, 1989, moderate-appearing ARENA candidate Alfredo Cristiani won the presidential election, with party strongman Roberto D'Aubuisson discreetly in the background.

Presiding over this second administration in El Salvador's civilian transitional government, President Alfredo "Freddy" Cristiani came from a wealthy aristocratic family. A graduate of Georgetown University, fluent in English, and diplomatic by nature, Cristiani was quickly embraced by the US government and media as a worthy ally despite his affiliation with ARENA. Cristiani in action proved more moderate than many had expected. On the positive side, his ARENA credentials helped him with the armed forces and, with the assistance of the Central American Peace Accord and eventual US acquiescence, permitted him to negotiate for peace with the FMLN. Among Cristiani's negatives were failing to improve elections or clean up the nation's corrupt judiciary.[36]

War and Peace. The Salvadoran conflict evolved into a bloody stalemate during the 1980s. The rebels held their own against increasingly powerful and sophisticated military pressure until 1984–1985. FMLN troop levels rose to around 10,000 by 1984. However, US training, aid, and intelligence helped the regime's forces steadily gain ground in the mid-1980s as trans-

149

PRIMERO DE MAYO (MAY DAY) DEMONSTRATION IN EL SALVADOR, 1988.
People with signs representing grassroots organizations; government response (photos by
Steve Cagan).

port, logistics, and tactics improved. By 1986, government troop strength rose to 52,000 from the 1980 level of 15,000. By 1985–1986 the government's advantages began affecting the rebels, whose strength apparently shrank to about 5,000, where it remained into the late 1980s.[37] The rebel troop decline came because of growing government air power that shrank the guerrilla-controlled zones, and evolving FMLN strategy. Civilian casualties in rebel-held zones escalated. In 1988 and 1989 the guerrillas revealed a new capacity to operate effectively in urban areas. When the ARENA-led Congress refused to postpone the March 1989 presidential election in response to an FMLN offer to return to peaceful civic competition, the FMLN tried to disrupt the election by causing widespread power outages and attacks on transportation.

A dispassionate summary of some of the horrors of El Salvador's civil war includes the following: virtually all objective observers attribute at least 80 percent of the country's 70,000 deaths between 1979 and 1992 to the military, the police, and ORDEN.[38] The Reagan administration, worried about retaining US Congressional funding for the Salvadoran government, pressured the country's military, police, and ORDEN to curtail sharply the numbers of deaths and disappearances in 1983 and 1984. Despite such efforts—in themselves revealing how much of the repression emanated directly from the security forces—increasing combat operations kept the casualty rate high into the mid-1980s. The intense violence caused over a sixth of Salvadorans to flee the country. Even for those untouched by personal losses, the war, migration, and capital flight deepened the nation's economic depression and human misery. From 1980 through 1987 the economy slowed by almost 10 percent of its 1980 per capita production level.[39]

The Central American Peace Accord, signed in Esquipulas, Guatemala, in August 1987, raised hopes for a negotiated settlement of the Salvadoran war, but little progress came until the early 1990s. Starting in late 1982, the rebels had pushed for a compromise settlement rather than outright victory. In their opinion, to capture ruling power would have brought the type of US-sponsored surrogate war and economic strangulation they observed inflicted on Nicaragua's Sandinista revolution.[40] Throughout the 1980s, however, the United States and the Salvadoran right opposed a negotiated settlement, pressing instead for outright victory. Accordingly, the Salvadoran government sporadically engaged in negotiations for show but sought no real advance for some time. Indeed, the Esquipulas agreement even triggered an upswing in the number of murders by the "death squads"—security forces.

The year 1989 brought things to a head. That spring the FMLN offered to participate in the upcoming presidential elections if the government would postpone them for six months so democratic safeguards could be put in place. The government, however, pressed on without the FMLN. ARENA candidate

FMLN REBELS. Female guerrillas in northern Morazón Province, 1988 (photo by Steve Cagan).

Alfredo Cristiani, who campaigned on peace and economic recovery, easily defeated Christian Democrat Fidel Chávez Mena. President Cristiani immediately began implementing neoliberal reforms, starting with the banking and financial sectors.

Frustrated by the refusal to delay the elections, the rebels escalated military operations in outlying areas to demonstrate their strength and convince the government to negotiate seriously. When this also failed, the FMLN in late 1989 mounted a major and prolonged military offensive in the capital city, San Salvador. The military responded by murdering many noncombatants it viewed as sympathetic to the rebels. Most shocking were the murders of six prominent Jesuit priest-intellectuals, their housekeeper, and her daughter on the campus of the Central American University on November 16, 1989. High-ranking officers, including the chief of staff of the army and the head of the air force, authorized this atrocity by a unit of the US-trained Atlacatl Battalion.[41] The guilty generals all went free, but two years later a colonel and lieutenant who had acted under their orders became the very first Salvadoran officers convicted of human rights violations in the war's twelve-year history.

The guerrilla offensive of late 1989, the embarrassment of the Jesuit massacre and other atrocities, and the end of the Cold War apparently convinced the United States to opt for a negotiated settlement in El Salvador. As a Rand Corporation specialist who wrote a report on El Salvador under contract to the US Department of Defense put it, "the security concerns that impelled the policy have all but evaporated along with the East-West contest. . . . 'Winning' in El Salvador no longer matters much. A negotiated solution, or even 'losing' would no longer carry the same ominous significance."[42] President George H. W. Bush decided to embrace the peace process. This cleared the way for a marathon and ultimately successful effort to bring the warring parties together by outgoing United Nations secretary-general Javier Pérez de Cuellar. Toward the end, US diplomats such as UN ambassador Thomas Pickering and assistant secretary of state Bernard Aronson pushed the Salvadoran government to make concessions. Finally, even ARENA founder Roberto D'Aubuisson—in a last public gesture before dying of cancer—endorsed the peace proposal.

GOVERNMENT AND POLITICS SINCE THE PEACE ACCORD

The 1992 peace agreement changed Salvadoran politics by establishing a civilian democracy that allowed participation by groups across a broad ideological spectrum. Under UN supervision, the government drastically reduced the size of the army and progressed in depoliticizing the services, retiring and reassigning senior officers, and reforming military education. The military abolished its infamous US-trained rapid-deployment forces as well as the Treasury Police and National Guard.[43] The government dismantled the National Police and created a new National Civil Police (Policía Nacional Civil, PNC). Under civilian authority, the PNC drew personnel from both the FMLN and government ranks.[44] A truth commission investigated the civil war. In March 1993 it attributed 95 percent of the human rights abuses committed after 1980 to the armed forces and "death squads." Five days later, the Legislative Assembly passed a general amnesty law ensuring that there would be no legal recourse, either criminal or civil, for crimes committed during the war.[45]

The FMLN demobilized its forces by early 1993 and engaged openly in electoral politics. In 1994 the "election of the century" marked the first truly democratic vote in El Salvador's history. Parties from across the political spectrum vied for seats in the legislature, mayoralties, and the presidency. The FMLN joined a center-left coalition with Democratic Convergence (Convergencia Democrática, CD) in the presidential election. While CD candidate Rubén Zamora managed to force a runoff, ARENA's Armando Calderón Sol easily prevailed in the second round of voting. ARENA also won 39 Legislative Assembly seats, nearly double those won by the FMLN (Appendix, Tables A.6 and A.7).

President Calderón Sol intensified neoliberal reforms by privatizing the telecommunications and energy sectors and reducing tariffs. Economic growth

COMING TO A HEAD IN NOVEMBER 1989. The rebel offensive in San Salvador (photo by Arturo Robles, courtesy of CRIES, Managua). A scene from the aftermath of the murder of Jesuit intellectuals at the Central American University by a unit of the US-trained Atlacatl Battalion (photo by Laurel Whitney, reprinted from *Envio* with the permission of the Central American University, Managua).

buoyed the Salvadoran economy during the early 1990s, but declined later in the decade. This produced tensions between the industrialists and agrarian elites within ARENA.[46] Additionally, the neoliberal model had done little to address poverty, unemployment, or the growing crime problem. Discontent with neoliberal policies helped the FMLN make significant gains in the 1997 legislative and municipal elections. Although ARENA won the most seats, its share declined from 39 to 28. The FMLN won six new seats for a total of 27.[47] The FMLN alone or in coalition also won 54 mayorships, including San Salvador. The tensions within ARENA also aided the right-wing PCN, which increased its representation in the legislature to 11 seats in 1997, up from four in 1994. The Christian Democrats posted significant losses, dropping from 18 to ten seats.

Its electoral successes bolstered the FSLN's repositioning as a party, but considerable internal debate occurred over its direction. One faction, the *renovadores,* favored modernizing the party and compromising with the neoliberals. The *ortodoxo* faction believed that the FMLN's potency at the ballot box indicated the party should reject the neoliberal model. Following a long, heated convention, the FMLN nominated former guerrilla and renovador

Facundo Guardado as its presidential candidate for 1999. ARENA's Francisco Flores easily defeated Guardado 52 to 29 percent in the presidential election. This sizable loss split the FMLN; two groups vied for control of the party. Guardado blamed the ortodoxos for the loss, whereas they blamed his abandonment of the socialist platform. Guardado resigned as the party's general coordinator, and the ortodoxos took over the party.[48]

Like the two previous ARENA governments, the Flores administration committed itself to implementing the neoliberal model. Privatization hit a snag in 1999 when plans to privatize health-care sector services resulted in a five-month strike by health-care workers. Flores' unwillingness to negotiate with the workers played poorly during the campaign. According to one poll, only 37 percent rated Flores as doing a good job, and a majority said that the economy and crime had worsened during the first year of his administration.[49]

The FMLN again benefited from the growing unpopularity of ARENA's policies and became El Salvador's largest party with the 2000 municipal and legislative elections. The FMLN gained 4 seats in the Legislative Assembly and won 77 (10 in coalition races) mayoralties. FMLN coalition candidate and San Salvador mayor Hector Silva soundly defeated ARENA candidate and businessman Luis Cardenal for mayor of San Salvador. ARENA's losses in the 2000 elections brought a major reshuffling of ARENA's executive committee, including the resignation of its director, former president Cristiani. The PCN continued to take advantage of ARENA's losses, gaining three seats in the legislature and 15 mayoralties. Many Salvadorans, however, chose not to vote. As evidence of the decreasing confidence in Salvadoran politics, voter turnout in 2000 fell to 38 percent from 45 percent in 1997.[50]

ARENA's poor showing in the election and El Salvador's economic malaise did not derail Flores' commitment to the neoliberal model. In a highly controversial move, Flores enacted the dollarization of the economy in January 2001. Two major earthquakes in January and February 2001 compounded the effects of El Salvador's economic slowdown. When hospitals and other services were easily overwhelmed, the quakes helped expose the neglect of social services under the neoliberal program. The issue of privatizing certain health services arose again prior to the 2003 municipal and legislative elections. Health-care workers again struck throughout the campaign. When San Salvador mayor Hector Silva intervened to mediate the conflict, the FMLN became furious and accused him of violating party procedure. The FMLN maintained its 31 seats in the Legislative Assembly while ARENA lost two seats in the legislative elections. Additionally, the FMLN retained its mayorship in San Salvador despite losing its popular two-time incumbent Hector Silva.

President Flores' tenure saw two prolonged health-care workers' strikes, economic stagnation, and growing trouble with gangs. By the end of the Flores administration, the Salvadoran economy depended heavily on remittances from

Salvadorans abroad. Combined with the FMLN's momentum from the 2003 elections, it appeared that ARENA could lose the 2004 presidential elections. To toughen its image prior to the 2004 presidential election, the Flores government pushed for harsh anti-gang measures. Known as *mano dura* (effectively an "iron fist"), the legislation, which criminalized gang membership, attracted criticism by domestic and international human rights advocates.

Gangs and remittances brought changes in Salvadoran society. During the war Salvadoran emigration, primarily to the United States, had increased dramatically.[51] But emigration did not end with the war. By 2004 an estimated 1.5 million Salvadorans lived in the United States,[52] most searching for work and security. Emigrants were overwhelmingly young, and about half were women.[53] Remittances increased from $858 million in 1992 to $2.5 billion in 2004. The influx of remittances provided a much-needed source of income to recipient families. Some analysts expressed concern that increasing emigration was contributing to the deterioration of the family, which left young Salvadorans vulnerable to the growing gang culture.[54] The US repatriation of gang members to El Salvador beginning in the mid-1990s fueled the rise in postwar violence.[55] These factors, along with high youth unemployment and socioeconomic marginalization, accelerated the growth of gangs in the country. The politicization of both issues increasingly dominated electoral campaigns.

Controlled by the ortodoxos, the FMLN again failed to turn its legislative and municipal electoral success into a presidential win in 2004. The FSLN's selection of former commander and Communist Party leader Shafick Handal as its presidential nominee drew criticism both at home and abroad. The United States expressed strong misgivings over a possible FMLN victory because Handal had vowed to withdraw Salvadoran troops from Iraq and adamantly opposed the Central American Free Trade Agreement (CAFTA). Former US ambassador Rose Likins and other State Department officials predicted worsened US-Salvadoran relations under a Handal administration.[56] ARENA's candidate, former sportscaster Antonio "Tony" Saca, exploited this potential rupture by emphasizing the country's dependence on remittances, which exceeded $2.5 billion annually. Several US congressmen also suggested that an FMLN victory should result in a review or termination of temporary protected status (TPS) for Salvadorans living in the United States and a reconsideration of remittance policies.[57]

The 2004 presidential elections were the most polarized in a decade. ARENA frequently invoked Cold War imagery and rhetoric, lambasting Handal as a terrorist bent on turning El Salvador into another Cuba. Handal's unpopularity and US interference in the elections eventually thwarted an FMLN victory. ARENA's Saca easily won by a margin of 57 percent to 36 percent. Former San Salvador mayor Hector Silva ran on the United Democratic Center (Centro Democrático Unido, CDU) coalition ticket with the Christian

Democrats, but the CDU-PDC failed to win even 5 percent of the vote. Surprisingly, the outcome of the election had little effect on the ortodoxos' control of the FMLN and Handal remained head of the party. For its part, Saca's resounding victory bolstered ARENA. Despite three successive, lackluster administrations, ARENA managed to win the election with a virtually unknown candidate.

President Saca's administration sought to distinguish itself from prior ARENA administrations by creating programs to alleviate poverty while continuing neoliberal policies. The Common Health Fund (Fondo Solidario para la Salud, FOSALUD) and Solidarity Network (Red Solidaria) targeted some of the poorest municipalities in the country. But years of economic stagnation, a regressive tax system, and growing public debt severely constrained the president's ability to fund these programs. By the end of Saca's term, the general perception was that poverty had actually increased. Ironically, the most effective tool for reducing poverty and inequality was remittances from Salvadorans abroad, which in 2008 exceeded $3.8 billion. Remittances offset El Salvador's trade imbalance and represented the single greatest source of foreign exchange. By 2006 remittances equaled almost 20 percent of GDP, exceeding exports and foreign investment combined. Approximately one-quarter of Salvadoran households received remittances.[58] Not only had they increased Salvadorans' purchasing power, but they significantly reduced poverty and inequality.[59]

President Saca strengthened the *mano dura* policies of the Flores administration as the crime wave continued unabated. When the Supreme Court declared the original law unconstitutional in April 2004, Saca proposed an enhanced *"super mano dura"* to replace it only months after entering office.[60] The new policy led to the arrests of some 11,000 alleged gang members in a single year.[61] These arrests, however, did nothing to reduce the country's crime wave; homicides actually *increased* under the policy. The violence was costly in terms of lives taken, infringed human rights, and economic activity lost. A 2005 UNDP study estimated that violence cost El Salvador nearly 12 percent of its GDP.[62] Crime also provided authorities with a handy excuse to crack down on popular protest. In October 2006, the Salvadoran government approved the Special Anti-Terrorism Law (*Ley Especial contra Actos de Terrorismo*), which criminalized common means of protest, such as demonstrations, marches, occupying buildings, and street blockades.

Crime again stood front and center in the 2006 legislative and municipal elections. The FMLN emphasized rising insecurity and failed *mano dura* policies, whereas ARENA repeatedly suggested that the FMLN and gangs were in cahoots.[63] Although some speculated that Shafik Handal's death a little more than a month before the elections might help the FMLN, the results were mixed.[64] The FMLN won 32 legislative seats, but lost 14 mayorships, including five of seven departmental capitals. Additionally, the FMLN almost lost the mayoralty of San Salvador, a post it had held since 1997. The FMLN's Violeta Menjívar narrowly defeated ARENA candidate Rodrigo Samayoa by 44 votes. In contrast, while ARENA lost San Salvador, its fortunes in the legislative and municipal elections improved for the first time in nearly a decade. The party gained seven legislative deputies and increased its control of municipal governments from 111 to 147.

In 2007 the government conducted its first census since 1992. It counted only 5.7 million citizens, significantly lower than the previous 7.1 million estimate.[65] Possible reasons for the gross overestimation included increased out-migration, declining birthrates, and errors in the 1992 census.[66] The consequences of this adjustment meant that some of El Salvador's indicators, such as per capita income, improved while others worsened. Already the most violent country in the hemisphere, El Salvador saw its homicide rate adjusted upward from 55 per 100,000 to 67 per 100,000.

The 2009 elections represented a major crossroad for Salvadoran democracy. ARENA had governed for twenty years despite widespread dissatisfaction with the direction of the country. Additionally, the 2009 elections were the first time since 1994 that elections for every office in the country would be held concurrently. Without explanation, the electoral tribunal instead set the municipal and legislative elections two months before presidential elections (all were traditionally held the same day). The FMLN increased its share of Assembly seats to 35 from 32 and also gained a few municipalities, but it lost San Salvador, which it had held since 1997. Although ARENA lost two seats in the Assembly (down to 32), its alliance with the PCN nevertheless salvaged a working majority in the legislature. Additionally, winning the capital city emboldened ARENA in advance of the presidential elections.

After bitter infighting within ARENA, President Saca's preferred choice for the party's presidential nominee prevailed—Rodrigo Avila, former director of the national police, vice-minister of security, and deputy in the Legislative Assembly. The FMLN selected popular journalist Mauricio Funes in an attempt to rebrand itself. Considered a moderate, Funes deflected the charges of radicalism that had plagued Guardado and Handal. The selection of former FPL leader Salvador Sánchez Cerén as his running mate, however, evoked suggestions that the hard-liners within the FMLN would ultimately rule.[67]

ARENA's campaign again invoked Cold War rhetoric and attempted to tie the FMLN to Hugo Chávez, Fidel Castro, and even Colombia's leftist guerrillas.[68] They suggested relations with the United States would suffer should the FMLN win, thus threatening remittance flows. Addressing the American Enterprise Institute, Salvadoran foreign minister Marisol Argueta claimed an FMLN victory would endanger US security interests. Although numerous members of the US Congress pledged neutrality, Congressman Dana Rohrabacher renewed his threats from 2004. He called the FMLN

FUNES WINS. Newspaper vendor in San Salvador, March 2009 (photo by Christine Wade).

a "pro-terrorist party" and "an ally of Al-Qaeda and Iran." He claimed the FMLN leadership trafficked arms to Colombia's rebels and called for lifting temporary protected status for Salvadorans in the United States, a threat to remittances, should the FMLN win.[69] Unlike the Bush administration in 2004, the Obama administration issued a statement of neutrality and pledged to work with the winning candidate.

The FMLN's Funes proclaimed himself the candidate of change.[70] His slogan, "This time is different," referred not only to his candidacy but to the possibility of victory. Funes energetically distanced himself from previous FMLN platforms. He pledged to retain dollarization and stay within CAFTA, abandoning two of the FMLN's key previous issues. Funes led by a significant margin in early polls. Shortly after the municipal and legislative elections, the PCN, the PDC, and other parties withdrew their presidential candidates and threw their support to ARENA, which narrowed the gap in the polls before the elections. On election day, 5,000 election observers fanned out throughout the country. Although there were some minor incidents, no evidence of systematic fraud was reported. Funes won the election, 51.3 to 48.7 percent. Ironically, voter turnout declined 5 percent from 2004, to 61 percent—perhaps due to the separate elections.

The importance of this change in ruling parties cannot be underestimated, and it affected many things. Within ARENA, former president Cristiani returned to the helm of ARENA's directorate whereas former president Saca was expelled from the party. Saca and a number of ARENA defectors then founded a new party, the Grand Alliance for National Unity (Gran Alianza por la Unidad Nacional, GANA). GANA formed a working coalition with the FMLN in the Assembly. Signaling his intention to govern from the center, President Funes appointed a cabinet including many centrists, including popular San Salvador ex-mayor and former presidential candidate Hector Silva, along with a few FMLN ortodoxos.

The new government's most pressing problem was the ongoing crime wave. Shortly after entering office, Funes deployed the military into high-crime neighborhoods, continuing the militarization of public security by his predecessors. A new anti-gang law in was passed in September 2010, which criminalized gang membership and established prison sentences of up to six years for members and ten years for leaders. These early steps had little effect.[71] In 2011, the homicide rate was 70 per 100,000 and showed little sign of abating. In a controversial move, Funes appointed former general David Munguía Payés as minister of justice and public security in November 2011 and former General Francisco Salinas as director of the National Civilian Police in January 2012. Critics argued the appointments violated both the letter and spirit of the peace accords, which separated the military from the civilian police.[72] Funes' PNC inspector general, Zaira Navas, resigned in January 2012 over concerns that the military was gaining too much influence in the police.

In a stunning development in March 2012, leaders of the warring MS-13 and 18th Street gangs announced a truce. The truce was purportedly initiated and mediated by El Salvador's chief army and police chaplain, Monsignor Fabio Colindres, and former FMLN guerrilla and legislator Raúl Mijango. Gang leaders issued orders to stop the killings in exchange for being transferred from maximum-security to medium-security prisons, conjugal visits, and cell phone use. The truce included reintegration and vocational training, as well as the establishment of "peace zones," or violence-free municipalities. The truce produced some results, sharply reducing homicides to 42 per 100,000. Public opinion on the truce nevertheless remained decidedly skeptical. Almost 90 percent of those surveyed in a 2012 poll distrusted it, and over 65 percent felt that it had done little to reduce crime.[73] Serious questions arose about the government's involvement in the truce. Although the Funes administration repeatedly tried to distance itself, it ultimately emerged that brokering the deal was part of a larger strategy pursued by Justice Minister Munguía Payés with the government's full knowledge.[74] Some also questioned the effectiveness of the truce. Although homicides were reduced, disappearances seemed to increase.[75] The deal's sustainability was challenged in May 2013 when the Constitutional Chamber of the Supreme Court ruled Munguía Payés' and Salinas' appointments unconstitutional because they violated the law against military serving in civilian security positions. Their removal increased concerns about the fragility of the truce, which appeared to be collapsing by the end of 2013 as homicides increased.[76] In addition to El Salvador's youth gang problem, drug traffickers and organized crime were also contributing to the violence.

In 2009, President Funes announced the *Ciudad Mujer* (City for Women) project. Coordinated by the first lady, the program established centers in numerous departments to provide women with a range of social services, including health care for women and children, domestic violence counseling, and financial counseling.[77] The Legislative Assembly made further strides toward gender equality by passing the 2011 Law of Equality, Equity, and the Eradication of Violence against Women. Among other things, the law guaranteed equal access to education and equal pay, and established "femicide" as a crime. Generalized violence against women remained high, but the gang truce dramatically reduced femicides.[78] Violence and discrimination against women in El Salvador nevertheless remained a serious problem. Although some laws clearly attempted to address the problem, others were contributing to it. For example, in 2006 El Salvador enacted one of the world's strictest abortion bans. It provided for no exceptions, including risk to the life of the mother. It also criminalized abortions and imposed jail sentences for the woman, provider, and any accomplices.[79] Not only did the ban increase dangerous "back alley" abortions, but women seeking medical attention for miscarriages have been prosecuted. In 2011, 49 women were convicted of murder or abortion under the law. Several women who reported to hospital emergency rooms with miscarriages were subsequently arrested and convicted of suspected abortions.[80] Some women received up to 30 years in prison, and some have died in prison after being denied medical care following miscarriages and due process.[81] In 2013, the story of a young woman named "Beatriz" captured international attention. Suffering from lupus and kidney failure, she petitioned the Supreme Court to grant her an exception to the abortion ban to save her life and because the fetus showed life-threatening anomalies.[82] The Court ultimately issued a vague ruling that permitted her to have a cesarean delivery rather than an abortion. The baby was born without a brain and died within hours of delivery.

The Funes administration faced two constitutional crises. In June 2011 the Assembly passed and Funes signed Decree 743, which required unanimity from all members of the Constitutional Chamber of the Supreme Court to declare a law unconstitutional. Critics argued the law weakened the judiciary and would effectively prevent the Court from challenging the constitutionality of legislation, including the Amnesty Law. The FMLN and a number of civil society organizations announced their opposition to Decree 743.[83] Following massive public protests the Assembly repealed it in July. The second crisis also stemmed from a power struggle between the legislative and judicial branches.

Following the 2012 elections but before the new Assembly had been seated, the outgoing 2009–2012 Assembly appointed new justices to the Supreme Court. The Constitutional Court overruled these appointments, and as well retroactively overturned those the Assembly had made in 2006, on grounds of unconstitutionality because each session is only permitted one round of appointments.[84] The FMLN and GANA, who had joined to make the appointments, challenged the Court's decision before the Central American Court of Justice, which ruled in favor of the Assembly. The dispute's settlement, ultimately mediated by President Funes, allowed the Constitutional Chamber judges elected in 2009 to retain their positions and allowed the re-election of the 2006 and 2012 Supreme Court judges.[85]

El Salvador's 2012 legislative and municipal elections could be read as a referendum on the Funes administration. High crime, a stagnant economy (growth languished at only about 1.4 percent in 2010 and 2011), and an unpopular decree were fresh on voters' minds as they headed to the polls. ARENA won 33 Assembly seats; the FMLN followed with 31 seats, down four from the 2009 elections. ARENA interpreted the results as a major triumph; FMLN spokesmen rationalized that things could have been worse. Former president Saca's new GANA party won 11 seats, establishing itself as the largest of the smaller parties in El Salvador's legislature, followed by the National Conciliation (CN) with seven, and the Party of Hope (PES) and the Democratic Change Party (PDC) with one seat each. ARENA also won the most mayorships with 116; the FMLN captured 95 (10 in coalition races), followed by the CN with 26, GANA with 18, the PES with four, and the PDC with three. In addition to losing four seats in the legislature, the FMLN lost several long-held mayorships and failed to recapture San Salvador. But the 2012 elections also held significance because of changes in the election system. Not only was the traditional party ballot replaced with a new one that listed individual candidates, but for the first time independent candidates were allowed to run.

Funes broke with past administrations on human rights, particularly violations committed during the civil war. He was the first president to apologize for or even acknowledge government abuses during the war. On January 17, 2012, during twentieth anniversary ceremonies to commemorate the peace accords, President Funes apologized for the 1981 massacre at El Mozote and named those responsible.[86] In December 2012, the Inter-American Commission for Human Rights ruled that the amnesty law violated international law, did not cover crimes committed during the war, and ordered the government to investigate the 1981 El Mozote massacre.[87] Months later the Human Rights Institute of the Central American University challenged the Amnesty Law in the Supreme Court, and the attorney general's office agreed to open investigations into the El Mozote case in September 2013.

The possibility of criminal prosecutions and of overturning the Amnesty Law unsettled some. Tutela Legal, the Archbishop's Human Rights and Legal Aid Office, established by Archbishop Romero in 1977, closed without warning; the fate of the office's records remained unclear at the time of this writing. The office had documented more than 50,000 cases of human rights abuses during and since the war. Shortly after Tutela Legal's closing, armed gunmen ransacked files and set fire to the offices of Pro Búsqueda, an organization that searches for children who disappeared during the war. The incident occurred just days after adult children represented by the organization testified before the Supreme Court about their parents' murders.[88]

Despite the many challenges he faced, Funes maintained significant public support throughout his presidency. At least some of his approval came from his handling of the 2012 constitutional crisis.[89] Funes' approval rating rose to 86 percent in one 2013 poll, and 68 percent of ARENA supporters approved of his performance.[90] The 2014 presidential elections would determine whether the FMLN would remain in power, or bring back ARENA or perhaps even a former president. Throughout Funes' presidency, some FSLN factions sought to distance themselves from him as too centrist. In a clear sign that the party intended to shift back toward the left, the FMLN selected Funes' vice president and education minister, Salvador Sanchez Cerén, to head its presidential ticket, with Santa Tecla mayor Oscar Ortiz as his running mate. Both had been guerrillas in the FPL, although they represented different FMLN tendencies. ARENA selected San Salvador major Norman Quijano as its candidate. Former President Saca ran on the UNIDAD ticket, a coalition of GANA, PES, and the CN. Saca's candidacy aroused controversy. El Salvador's constitution allows for a second, non-consecutive term, and Saca became the first former president to seek re-election. His candidacy threatened to undercut ARENA's vote and potentially cost it a first-round election victory. Several claims were filed arguing that his candidacy was unconstitutional, citing fraud, the timeliness of his candidacy, and conflict of interest. Meanwhile, corruption allegations dogged the ARENA and UNIDAD candidates. Quijano was under investigation for the misuse of funds. During the campaign, the public learned that Saca's personal wealth had grown from $600,000 in 2003 to $10.5 million by the time he left office in 2009.[91] The revelation came just weeks after the attorney general ordered arrests of seven Flores administration officials. Flores himself, campaign manager for Quijano, came under investigation for the misuse of donations from Taiwan.

The campaigns focused on the economy and violence. Sanchez Cerén pledged to continue social programs, deepen socioeconomic reforms, and remain supportive of the gang truce. Quijano, adamantly opposed to the truce, advocated resuming the failed law-and-order strategy of prior ARENA governments. Saca said he would continue many of the FMLN's social programs, such as Ciudad Mujer, opposed the truce, and pledged to promote employment and the agricultural sector. All three campaigned in US cities with significant Salvadoran populations because, for the first time, Salvadorans living abroad would be allowed to vote in elections.[92] This change enfranchised the approximately 1.8 million Salvadorans living in the United States, but few were expected to vote.[93]

Saca's candidacy virtually guaranteed a second round of voting. That said, a first-round victory only narrowly eluded the FMLN's Sanchez Cerén, who won 48.9 percent of the vote. ARENA's Quijano won 38 percent and Saca 11 percent of the vote. Only 1,909 Salvadorans used the vote abroad option. Sanchez Cerén and Quijano proceeded to a runoff election in March 2014. Despite some polls giving Sanchez Cerén as much as an 18-percentage point lead, the election was astonishingly close. Preliminary results on election night revealed that Sanchez Cerén held a razor-thin 6,600 vote advantage over Quijano. Turnout actually *increased* in the second round, a rarity in runoffs. Quijano's final count in the runoff rose by some 440,000 over the first round, and Sanchez Cerén picked up approximately 180,000 new votes. The number of voters abroad inched up to 2,334, with over 60 percent favoring the FMLN in both rounds. Although it is likely that many of Saca's first-round supporters voted for ARENA rather than the FMLN as some anticipated, ARENA's runoff campaign also relentlessly promoted fears El Salvador would succumb to turmoil like that under way in Venezuela should the FMLN win. The campaign invigorated the conservative base and drew out voters who had stayed home during the first round. The final tally revealed 1,495,815 votes for the FMLN and 1,489,451 for ARENA, giving the FMLN a margin of victory of about 6,300 votes. At 50.11 to 49.89 percent, it was the closest presidential election in Salvadoran history. Quijano and ARENA attributed their loss to fraud, though international observers praised the elections as free and fair. Quijano and ARENA demanded a full vote-by-vote recount of the ballots (the electoral code only reviews tallies, or *actas*, not individual ballots), petitioned for the nullification of the election, and told a crowd of supporters on election night that the armed forces were watching and would enforce democracy—a comment he later said was misinterpreted. In 2014, the country seemed as polarized as it had been in decades past.

CONCLUSIONS

Following the peace accords, El Salvador changed markedly. Foreign assistance smoothed transition to civilian democracy, encouraged the formation of hundreds of civil society organizations, and trained former combatants for new occupations. The peace process brought a restructuring of the armed forces, dismantling of state security organizations, and creation of a new civilian police force. The FMLN contested elections and won seats in the legislature, mayorships, and city councils, and in 2009 finally won the presidency. ARENA accepted the FMLN victory and peacefully transferred power to the FMLN on June 1, 2009, an important step in the consolidation of democracy in El Salvador. But the turmoil over the 2014 election signaled an increasing polarization among political parties, and ARENA's rhetoric on the campaign trail and following the elections provided cause for concern.

Despite decades of doubt about FMLN rule, the Funes administration demonstrated that a center-left government offered nothing to fear. Indeed, President Funes consistently maintained one of the highest levels of popular support for any president in the Americas—a feat unmatched by any of his predecessors. Although his administration was no stranger to controversy, he also demonstrated a willingness to tackle difficult issues. Perhaps most important, his administration sought to clarify the historical record, demonstrated respect for the rule of law, and finally began to address the impunity of prior administrations.

That said, serious problems remained. Criminal violence and corruption still threatened to undermine El Salvador's institutions. Mexican drug cartels exercised growing influence in the country. There were also troubling signs that some would resist attempts to reconcile crimes committed during the war. El Salvador's economy performed second best in the region from 1960 to 2012 and since 1990. But part of the 54 percent GDP per capita growth since 1990 came from rising remittances. These fell sharply during the most recent global economic crisis and only recovered to prerecession levels in 2012. Low economic growth, public and external debt, and persistent poverty posed serious challenges to the country's recovery. How and whether the incoming Ceren administration would successfully address these problems remained to be seen.

RECOMMENDED READINGS AND RESOURCES

Almeida, Paul D. 2008. *Waves of Protest: Popular Struggle in El Salvador, 1925–2005.* Minneapolis: University of Minnesota Press.

Anderson, Thomas. 1971. *Matanza: El Salvador's Communist Revolt of 1932.* Lincoln: University of Nebraska Press.

Baloyra, Enrique. 1982. *El Salvador in Transition.* Chapel Hill: University of North Carolina Press.

Boyce, James K., ed. 1996. *Economic Policy for Building Peace: The Lesson of El Salvador.* Boulder, CO: Lynne Rienner Publishers.

Byrne, Hugh. 1996. *El Salvador's Civil War: A Study in Revolution.* Boulder, CO: Lynne Rienner Publishers.

Clements, Charles. 1984. *Witness to War: An American Doctor in El Salvador.* New York: Bantam Books.

Dunkerley, James. 1982. *The Long War: Dictatorship and Revolution in El Salvador.* London: Verso.

Hume, Mo. 2013. "El Salvador." In Diego Sánchez-Ancochea and Salvador Martí i Puig, eds. *Handbook of Central American Governance.* London: Routledge.

Ladutke, Larry. 2004. *Freedom of Expression in El Salvador: The Struggle for Human Rights and Democracy.* Jefferson, NC: MacFarland.

Lindo Fuentes, Hector. 1990. *Weak Foundations: The Economy of El Salvador in the Nineteenth Century.* Berkeley: University of California Press.

McClintock, Cynthia. 1998. *Revolutionary Movements in Latin America: El Salvador's FMLN and Peru's Shining Path.* Washington, DC: US Institute of Peace.

Montgomery, Tommie Sue. 1995. *Revolution in El Salvador: Origins and Evolution.* Boulder, CO: Westview Press.

Moodie, Ellen. 2010. *El Salvador in the Aftermath of War.* Philadelphia: University of Pennsylvania Press.

Pelupessy, Wim. 1997. *The Limits of Economic Reform in El Salvador.* New York: St. Martin's.

Popkin, Margaret. 2000. *Peace Without Justice. Obstacles to Building Rule of Law in El Salvador.* University Park: Pennsylvania State University Press.

Spence, Jack. 2004. *War and Peace in Central America: Comparing Transitions Toward Democracy and Social Equity in Guatemala, El Salvador and Nicaragua.* Boston: Hemisphere Initiatives.

Stanley, William. 1996. *The Protection Racket State: Elite Politics, Military Extortion, and Civil War in El Salvador.* Philadelphia: Temple University Press.

Williams, Philip J., and Knut Walter. 1997. *Militarization and Demilitarization in El Salvador's Transition to Democracy.* Pittsburgh, PA: University of Pittsburgh Press.

Wood, Elisabeth Jean. 2003. *Insurgent Collective Action and Civil War in El Salvador.* New York: Cambridge University Press.

NOTES

1. See Tommie Sue Montgomery, *Revolution in El Salvador: Origins and Evolution* (Boulder, CO: Westview Press, 1982); and Enrique Baloyra, *El Salvador in Transition* (Chapel Hill: University of North Carolina Press, 1982).

2. As quoted in Montgomery, *Revolution in El Salvador*, p. 46.

3. Baloyra, *El Salvador in Transition*, p. 35.

4. Tommie Sue Montgomery, "El Salvador: The Roots of Revolution," in Steve C. Ropp and James A. Morris, eds., *Central America: Crisis and Adaptation* (Albuquerque: University of New Mexico Press, 1984), p. 78.

5. See Stephen Webre, *José Napoleón Duarte and the Christian Democratic Party in Salvadorean Politics: 1960–1972* (Baton Rouge: Louisiana State University Press, 1979).

6. For a more detailed discussion and data on the CACM growth boom in El Salvador, see John A. Booth and Thomas W. Walker, *Understanding Central America*, 3rd ed. (Boulder, Colo.: Westview Press, 1999), Ch. 7 and Appendix.

7. See ibid., Appendix, Table A.8; Hugo Molina, "Las bases económicas del desarrollo industrial y la absorción de fuerza de trabajo en El Salvador," in Daniel Camacho et al., *El fracaso social de la integración centroamericana* (San José, Costa Rica: Editorial Universitaria Centroamericana, 1979), pp. 245–254; Phillip L. Russell, *El Salvador in Crisis* (Austin, TX: Colorado River Press, 1984), pp. 76–78; Victor Antonio Orellana, *El Salvador: Crisis and Structural Change*, Occasional Paper Series No. 13 (Miami: Latin American and Caribbean Center, Florida International University, 1985), pp. 5–9; and Victor Bulmer-Thomas, *The Political Economy of Central America since 1920* (Cambridge: Cambridge University Press, 1987), pp. 175–229.

8. Dirección General de Estadística y Censos (DGEC–El Salvador), *Anuario Estadístico, 1981, Tomos III–V* (San Salvador, El Salvador: Ministerio de Economía, 1983), Cuadros 311-01, 311-02; Bulmer-Thomas, *Political Economy of Central America*, pp. 201–207.

9. See especially Montgomery, *Revolution in El Salvador*; Donaldo Castillo Rivas, "Modelos de acumulación, agricultura, y agroindustria en Centroamérica," in D. Castillo Rivas, ed., *Centroamérica: Más allá de la crisis* (México City: Ediciones SIAP, 1983), pp. 204–207; and James Dunkerley, *The Long War: Dictatorship and Revolution in El Salvador* (London: Junction Books, 1982), pp. 87–118.

10. Orellana, *El Salvador: Crisis*, pp. 5–10; Molina, "Las bases económicas," pp. 245–254.

11. Orellana, *El Salvador: Crisis*, pp. 5–7.

12. Montgomery, *Revolution in El Salvador*, pp. 94–95.

13. Orellana, *El Salvador: Crisis*, pp. 6–7.

14. Booth and Walker, *Understanding Central America*, 3rd ed., Tables 1.1, Appendix, A.6.

15. From Montgomery, *Revolution in El Salvador*; Dunkerley, *The Long War*, pp. 90–102; Jorge Cáceres Prendes, "Radicalización política y pastoral en El Salvador: 1969–1979," *Estudios Sociales Centroamericanos* 33 (September–December 1982), pp. 97–111.

16. Russell, *El Salvador in Crisis*, pp. 71–78; Tomás Guerra, *El Salvador en la hora de su liberación* (San José, Costa Rica: n.p., 1980), pp. 103–108; Baloyra, *El Salvador in Transition*, pp. 43–52.

17. DGEC–El Salvador, *Anuario Estadístico, 1981,* Tomos III–V.

18. Rafael Menjívar, *Formación y lucha del proletariado industrial salvadoreño* (San José, Costa Rica: Editorial Universitaria Centroamericano, 1982), pp. 115–162; Russell, *El Salvador in Crisis*, p. 71.

19. See Michael McClintock, *The American Connection*, Volume 1: *State Terror and Popular Resistance in El Salvador* (London: Zed Books, 1985), pp. 156–209, for

details on the rise of repression in El Salvador; see also Inforpress Centroamericano, *Central America Report*, January 20, 1984, p. 23.

20. McClintock, *The American Connection*, pp. 174–177.

21. Even in 2004, recourse to death squads—this time in quelling insurgents in Iraq—was reportedly still being advocated by certain US officials who were veterans of the 1980s anti-Communist crusade in Central America. See Michael Hirsh and John Barry, "The Salvador Option: The Pentagon May Put Special-Forces Led Assassination and Kidnapping Teams in Iraq," *Newsweek*, January 8, 2005, http://www.msnbc.com /id/680692/site/newsweek.

22. Tommie Sue Montgomery, "El Salvador: The Roots of Revolution," in Ropp and Morris, eds., *Central America: Crisis and Adaptation*, pp. 86–90.

23. Taken from DGEC–El Salvador, *Anuario Estadístico,* for years 1965, 1966, 1968, 1969, 1971, 1977, 1980, and 1981; the figure reported is the total number of "homicides" plus other, unexplained violent deaths.

24. Based on data reported in Baloyra, *El Salvador in Transition*, p. 190; and Richard Alan White, *The Morass: United States Intervention in Central America* (New York: Harper and Row, 1984), p. 44; and Inforpress Centroamericano, *Central America Report*, January 20, 1984, p. 23.

25. Comisión de Derechos Humanos de El Salvador (CDHES), *Primer Congreso de Derechos Humanos en El Salvador* (San Salvador, El Salvador: CDHES, November 1984), pp. 30–31, authors' translation.

26. It is unclear whether the Sandinistas were aware that arms were coming through their territory. When confronted with that charge by US ambassador Lawrence Pezzullo, Daniel Ortega of the Nicaraguan junta promised to stop the flow if the United States would indicate where it was originating. He was quickly told the flow was stopped, and the US Department of State then certified that it had stopped. Though no credible evidence of any significant subsequent arms flow from Nicaragua was ever presented, the Reagan and Bush administrations would repeat the charge over and over until it became accepted as fact by the US media.

27. Philip J. Williams and Knut Walter, *Militarization and Demilitarization in El Salvador's Transition to Democracy* (Pittsburgh, PA: University of Pittsburgh Press, 1997), pp. 100–113.

28. Ibid., p. 113.

29. Montgomery, *Revolution in El Salvador*, pp. 140–157.

30. Dunkerley, *The Long War*, p. 175.

31. Benjamin C. Schwarz, *American Counterinsurgency Doctrine and El Salvador: The Frustration of Reform and the Illusion of Nation Building* (Santa Monica, CA: Rand Corporation, 1991), p. v.

32. Baloyra, El *Salvador in Transition*; José Z. García, "El Salvador: Recent Elections in Historical Perspective," in John A. Booth and Mitchell A. Seligson, eds., *Elections and Democracy in Central America* (Chapel Hill: University of North Carolina Press, 1989), pp. 60–89.

33. Dunkerley, *The Long War*, p. 163.

34. For discussions of problems with the US-backed elections in El Salvador in 1982, 1984, and 1985, see Terry Karl, "Imposing Consent: Electoralism vs. Democratization in El Salvador," in P. Drake and E. Silva, eds., *Elections and Democratization in Latin America* (La Jolla, CA: Center for Iberian and Latin American Studies–Center for US-Mexican Studies, University of California, San Diego, 1986), p. 21; Edward S. Herman and Frank Brodhead, *Demonstration Elections* (Boston: South End Press, 1984), pp. 93–152; and García, "El Salvador: Recent Elections," pp. 60–89.

35. See, for instance, Karl, "Imposing Consent," pp. 18–34; and Clifford Krauss, "El Salvador Army Gains on the Guerrillas," *Wall Street Journal*, July 30, 1986, p. 20.

36. On elections see Enrique A. Baloyra, "Elections, Civil War, and Transition in El Salvador, 1982–1994: A Preliminary Evaluation," in Mitchell A. Seligson and John A. Booth, eds., *Elections and Democracy in Central America, Revisited* (Chapel Hill: University of North Carolina Press, 1995). On the military and peace negotiations, see Williams and Walter, *Militarization and Demilitarization,* Chs. 6 and 7; and Ricardo Córdova Macías, "El proceso de diálogo-negociación y las perspectivas de paz," in *El Salvador: Guerra, política, y paz, 1979–1989* (San Salvador, El Salvador: CINAS-CRIES, 1988), pp. 195–219; and Ricardo Córdova Macías, *El Salvador: Las negociaciones de paz y los retos de la postguerra* (San Salvador, El Salvador: Instituto de Estudios Latinoamericanos, 1989).

37. Karl, "Imposing Consent."

38. Comisión de la Verdad, *De la locura a la esperanza: La guerra de doce años en El Salvador.* Informe de la Comisión, published in *Estudios Centroamericanos* (San Salvador, El Salvador) no. 158 (March 1993); Booth and Walker, *Understanding Central America*, 3rd ed., Appendix, Table A.11.

39. Booth and Walker, *Understanding Central America*, 3rd ed., Appendix, Table A.1.

40. Points made in two lengthy interviews with three official FMLN spokespersons conducted by members of the Central American Task Force of the United Presbyterian Church's Council on Church and Society in Managua in November 1992. Coauthor Walker, a member of that task force, was present for the interviews.

41. Written statement of Representative Joe Moakley, chairman of the Speaker's Task Force on El Salvador, November 18, 1991; see also the account in Comisión de la Verdad, *De la locura a la esperanza.*

42. Schwarz, *American Counterinsurgency Doctrine*, pp. v, vi.

43. See Williams and Walter, *Militarization and Demilitarization*, pp. 151–182.

44. For a discussion of police reform see Jack Spence, *War and Peace in Central America: Comparing Transitions Toward Democracy and Social Equity in Guatemala, El Salvador and Nicaragua* (Boston: Hemisphere Initiatives, November 2004), pp. 59–62.

45. For a detailed discussion of the reforms under Cristiani and Calderón Sol see Jack Spence, David Dye, Mike Lanchin, and Geoff Thale, *Chapultepec: Five Years Later* (Boston: Hemisphere Initiatives, January 16, 1997. See Margaret Popkin, *Peace*

Without Justice. Obstacles to Building Rule of Law in El Salvador (University Park: Pennsylvania State University Press, 2000).

46. Growth averaged 6 percent annually between 1990 and 1995, but dropped to 3.0 percent from 1996 to 2000; Oscar Melhado, *El Salvador: Retos económicos de fin de siglo* (San Salvador, El Salvador: UCA Editores, 1997).

47. José Miguel Cruz, "Por qué no votan los Salvadoreños?" *Estudios Centroamericanos*, Nos. 595–596 (May–June 1998), www.uca.edu.sv/publica/eca/595art2.html, accessed August 14, 2009.

48. Guardado and several others were expelled from the FMLN in 2001.

49. Instituto Universitario de Opinión Pública (IUDOP), *Evaluación del primer año del gobierno de Francisco Flores* (San Salvador, El Salvador: Universidad Centroamericana José Simeon Cañas, 2000).

50. Tribunal Supremo Electoral de El Salvador.

51. See Cecilia Menjívar, *Fragmented Ties: Salvadoran Immigration Networks in America* (Berkeley: University of California Press, 2000); Carlos Cordova, *The Salvadoran Americans* (Westport, CT: Greenwood Press, 2005).

52. According to the 2000 US Census, there were 817,336 Salvadorans in the United States.

53. See United Nations Development Program, *Informe sobre desarrollo humano, El Salvador 2005: Una mirada al nuevo nosotros, El impacto de las migraciones* (San Salvador, El Salvador: UNDP, 2005).

54. Coauthor Wade interviews in San Salvador, El Salvador, October–November 2006.

55. Many Salvadoran youth became involved in the gang culture in the United States and brought it back to El Salvador when they were deported. The country's most notorious gangs, Mara Salvatrucha (MS-13) and the 18th Street Gang, were founded in Los Angeles. See Washington Office on Latin America (WOLA), *Youth Gangs in Central America; Issues in Human Rights, Effective Policing and Prevention* (Washington, DC: WOLA, 2006); Ana Arana, "How the Youth Gangs Took Central America." *Foreign Affairs* 84, 3 (2005), pp. 98–110.

56. "Embajadora E.U.A. advierte contra FMLN," *La Prensa Gráfica*, June 4, 2003; "Peligraría la inversión americana; Entrevista: Rose M. Likins," *La Prensa Gráfica*, June 4, 2003; "Diferencias con FMLN: Noriega pide tomar la mejor decisión," *El Diario de Hoy*, February 7, 2004.

57. In place since the 1980s, TPS is a concession by the United States of an exceptional right of many Salvadoran citizens to remain within the United States (there are hundreds of thousands of them) and to work. Its maintenance would guarantee continuation of the remittance flow from US-based Salvadorans to their families, a mainstay of the Salvadoran national economy. "Disturbing Statement out of El Salvador," *Congressional Record*, March 17, 2004, pp. E394–E395; "El Salvador," *Congressional Record*, March 17, 2004, p. E402; "Election in El Salvador," *Congressional Record*, March 17, 2004, p. E389.

58. Christine Wade, "El Salvador: Contradictions of Neoliberalism and Building Sustainable Peace, *International Journal of Peace Studies* 13, No. 4 (August–Winter 2008), 24.

59. The Gini coefficient, a measure of inequality of income, for those who receive remittances is 0.44, as opposed to 0.52 for non-recipients. The Gini coefficient ranges from 0 (no inequality or perfect equality) to 1.0 (complete inequality); ibid., 25.

60. "No Place to Hide: Gang, State and Clandestine Violence in El Salvador," International Human Rights Clinic, Human Rights Program, Harvard Law School, February 2007, http://www.law.harvard.edu/programs/hrp/documents/Final ElSalvadorReport(3-6-07).pdf.

61. USAID, "Central America and Mexico Gang Assessment, Annex1: El Salvador Profile." April 2006, http://www.usaid.gov/locations/latin_america_caribbean /democracy/els_profile.pdf.

62. United Nations Development Program, "*¿Cuánto cuesta la violencia en El Salvador?*" San Salvadore: UNDP El Salvador (2005).

63. William Grigsby, "The 2006 Elections: A Contradictory Outcome," *Envío* 297 (April 2006), accessed at http://www.Envío.org.ni/articulo/3252.

64. Shafik Handal died on January 24, 2006, after suffering a heart attack at the Comalapa Airport in El Salvador. He was returning from the inauguration of Evo Morales in Bolivia.

65. Salvadoran officials estimated that the population was actually about 5.9 million, accounting for omissions and lack of registries. See Edith Portillo, "Somos un millón menos . . . y un poco más violentos," *El Faro*, July 9, 2007, http://www.elfaro .net/secciones/Noticias/20070709/noticias6_20070709.asp.

66. Ibid.

67. Joaquín Villalobos, "¿Quién gobernaría, Funes o el FMLN?" *El Diario de Hoy*, December 30, 2008, http://www.elsalvador.com/mwedh/nota/nota_opinion.asp ?idCat=6350&idArt=3182935.

68. Many of the negative television and radio ads that appeared were sponsored by a group called *Fuerza Solidaria*. The organization was founded by Venezuelan Alejandro Peña Esclusa, who is a vocal opponent of Hugo Chávez.

69. Representative Dana Rohrabacher, "Extension of Remarks, El Salvador Election," March 11, 2009, http://rohrabacher.house.gov/UploadedFiles/elsalvador _extension_of_remarks.PDF.

70. So much so that the Obama administration had to request that he stop using his image in the campaign.

71. In fact, gangs responded to the passage of the Anti-Gang Law by burning a passenger bus in Mejicanos, killing 17 people.

72. "WOLA Expresses Concern About Naming of New Justice and Security Minister in El Salvador," Washington Office on Latin America, November 22, 2011, http://www.wola.org/news/wola_expresa_profunda_preocupacion_por_el _nombramiento_del_nuevo_ministro_de_justicia_y_segurid.

73. IUDOP, "Los salvadoreños y salvadoreñas evalúan la situación del país a finales de 2012," *Boletín de prensa Año*, 27 No. 4, December 12, 2012, http://www .uca.edu.sv/publica/iudop/archivos/boletin4_2012.pdf.

74. Oscar Martinez, "Making a Deal with Murderers," *New York Times*, October 5, 2013, http://www.nytimes.com/2013/10/06/opinion/sunday/making-a-deal -with-murderers.html?pagewanted=1&_r=3&hp.

75. Jessel Santos, "Hallazgos de osamentas aumentaron 81% en 2013," *La Prensa Gráfica*, March 8, 2013, http://www.laprensagrafica.com/hallazgos-de-osamentas -aumentaron-81-en-2013; and Daniel Valencia Caravantes, "Los desparacidos que no importan," *El Faro*, January 21, 2031, http://www.salanegra.elfaro.net/es /201301/cronicas/10773/?st-full_text=0.

76. Nelson Rauda Zablah, "Perdomo: Pandillas están en guerra," *La Prensa Gráfica*, November 21, 2013, http://www.laprensagrafica.com/2013/11/21/perdomo-pandillas -estan-en-guerra; and Geoff Thale, "Public Security in El Salvador: Civilan Leadership and the Challenges Ahead," Washington Office on Latin America, May 21, 2013, http://www.wola.org/commentary/public_security_in_el_salvador_civilian_leadership _and_the_challenges_ahead.

77. "In El Salvador, Women's Rights Come to the Forefront," May 28, 2013, http://www.worldbank.org/en/news/feature/2013/05/28/derechos-de-la-mujer -pasan-a-primer-plano; and "Cuidad Mujer: City of Hope for Salvadoran Women," June 6, 2011, http://www.iadb.org/en/news/webstories/2011–06–06/ciudad-mujer -hope-for-salvadoran-women,9369.html.

78. Ben Witte, "Femicide Numbers Fall in El Salvador, *NotiCen* (August 22, 2013).

79. Jack Hitt, "Pro-Life Nation," *New York Times*, April 9, 2006, http://www. nytimes.com/2006/04/09/magazine/09abortion.html?pagewanted=all&_r=0.

80. Tim Rogers, "El Salvador High Court Upholds Abortion Ban as 'Beatriz' Challenges Law," *Christian Science Monitor*, May 30, 2012, http://www .csmonitor.com/World/Americas/2013/0530/El-Salvador-high-court-upholds -abortion-ban-as-Beatriz-challenges-law; and Luisa Cabal, "El Salvador Abortion Controversy Shows Lack of Progress on Cairo Agenda," *The Guardian*, July 5, 2013, http://www.theguardian.com/global-development/poverty-matters/2013/jul/05 /el-salvador-abortion-womens-rights.

81. "Center for Reproductive Rights Files Case Revealing the Horrifying Reality of El Salvador's Abortion Ban," Center for Reproductive Rights, March 21, 2012, http://reproductiverights.org/en/press-room/center-for-reproductive-rights-files -case-revealing-the-horrifying-reality-of-el-salvador.

82. Rogers, "El Salvador High Court Upholds Abortion Ban as 'Beatriz' Challenges Law," *Christian Science Monitor*, May 30, 2012, at http://www.csmonitor .com/World/Americas/2013/0530/El-Salvador-high-court-upholds-abortion-ban-as -Beatriz-challenges-law.

83. Gabriela D. Acosta, "Funes' Broken Promises," Council on Hemispheric Affairs, June 24, 2011, http://www.coha.org/funes-broken-promises/http://www.coha.org/funes-broken-promises/; and Washington Office on Latin America, "El Salvador: Troubling Attacks on the Independence of the Judiciary," June 29, 2011, http://www.wola.org/commentary/el_salvador_troubling_attacks_on_the_independence_of_the_judiciary.

84. Geoff Thale, "Tensions Rise Between El Salvador's National Assembly and the Supreme Court: Understanding (and Misunderstanding) the Salvadoran Constitutional Crisis," Washington Office on Latin America, July 18, 2012, http://www.wola.org/commentary/tensions_rise_between_el_salvador_s_national_assembly_and_the_supreme_court_understanding.

85. Transparencia Activa, "Partidos políticos llegan a acuerdo en Casa Presidencial que pone fin a conflicto sobre Corte Suprema de Justicia," August 19, 2012, http://www.transparenciaactiva.gob.sv/partidos-politicos-llegan-a-acuerdo-en-casa-presidencial-que-pone-fin-a-conflicto-sobre-corte-suprema-de-justicia/.

86. Ben Witte, "El Salvador President Funes Irks Armed Forces with Emotional El Mozote Apology," *NotiCen* (July 4, 2012).

87. Elisabeth Malkin, "El Salvador: Court Orders Investigation of 1981 Massacre," *New York Times*, December 10, 2012, http://www.nytimes.com/2012/12/11/world/americas/el-salvador-court-orders-investigation-of-1981-massacre.html?_r=1&.

88. Lynette Wilson, "El Salvador: Human Rights, Justice Organizations Weary in Face of Attacks," *Episcopal News Service*, November 18, 2013, http://episcopaldigitalnetwork.com/ens/2013/11/18/el-salvador-human-rights-justice-organizations-weary-in-face-of-attacks/.

89. "Funes eleva popularidad tras papel de mediador en crisis," El Mundo, July 29, 2012, http://elmundo.com.sv/funes-eleva-popularidad-tras-papel-de-mediador-en-crisis.

90. "Funes Wins Stratspheric Approval Rating," *Latin News*, http://www.latinnews.com/component/k2/item/6198-el-salvador-funes-wins-stratospheric-approval-rating.html; and "76% de los salvadoreños aprueba la imagen de Funes," *La Pagina*, May 16, 2013, http://www.lapagina.com.sv/nacionales/81719/2013/05/15/76-de-los-salvadorenos-aprueba-la-imagen-de-Funes.

91. Gabriel Labrador, "Ganancias de las empresas de Saca se multiplicaron hasta por 16 cuando fue president," *El Faro* November 19, 2013, http://www.elfaro.net/es/201311/noticias/13936/.

92. "Asamblea aprueba voto en el exterior," *Contra Punto*, January 24, 2013, http://www.contrapunto.com.sv/gobierno/asamblea-aprueba-voto-en-el-exterior.

93. Martin Austermuhke, "Thousands of Miles from Home, Salvadoran Candidates Woo Local Voters," WAMU Radio, September 13, 2013, http://wamu.org/programs/metro_connection/13/09/13/salvadoran_politicians_woo_voters_in_dc_thousands_of_miles_from_home.

7

GUATEMALA

GUATEMALA'S LONG, VIOLENT PASSAGE FROM MILITARY AUTHORITARIAN rule to electoral democracy differed from Nicaragua's but resembled El Salvador's, though rapid economic change and repression drove turmoil and regime change in all three. In Guatemala, as in El Salvador, rebels and power holders fought a protracted civil war marked by three regime changes, the last of which established a democracy, curtailed military power, and permitted former rebels into the political arena. Unlike El Salvador, Guatemala's military governments had largely kept rebels at bay without much visible involvement by the United States.

HISTORICAL BACKGROUND

Although Guatemala stands apart from the rest of modern Central America in its large, only partly integrated indigenous population, it shares historical legacies with nineteenth-century Nicaragua and El Salvador. In each, consolidation of Liberal control followed early Liberal-Conservative conflict. The Liberals' "reforms" produced profound socioeconomic realignments and shaped contemporary social and political problems.

The Liberals took control of Guatemala in 1871 and with minor exceptions held power until the 1940s. Liberal dictator-president Justo Rufino Bárrios (1873–1885) modernized by building roads, railways, a national army, and a more competent national bureaucracy. He promoted the new crop, coffee, and encouraged foreign investment. Barrios opened Church and indigenous communal lands to cultivation by large landowners (*lati-fundistas*). By 1900 coffee accounted for 85 percent of Guatemala's exports. Landownership concentrated increasingly in the hands of latifundist coffee growers, who also dominated Guatemalan economics and politics. Forced from their land, indigenous Guatemalans fell prey to debt peonage and "vagrancy" laws, enacted and enforced by the coffee grower–dominated government, which coerced them to labor on coffee plantations.

In the late nineteenth century, the construction of a railroad to the Atlantic coast created the banana industry. Early in the twentieth century, the US-based United Fruit Company (UFCO), formerly mainly a shipper/exporter, squeezed out Guatemalan banana growers. UFCO eventually owned key public utilities and vast landholdings. The Liberal development program continued in the twentieth century. In politics, Manuel Estrada Cabrera's brutal dictatorship (1898–1920) inspired Nobel laureate Miguel Angel Asturias' chilling novel of state terror, *El Señor Presidente.* Big coffee plantations, many foreign-owned, expanded at the expense of small subsistence farmers.

The world economic crisis of 1929 slashed Guatemala's exports. Worker unrest grew. President Jorge Ubico assumed dictatorial powers in 1931 and violently suppressed unions, Communists, and other political activists while centralizing power in the national government. Ubico continued promoting government and infrastructure development (banks, railways, highways, telephones, the telegraph, and electrical utilities). Although originally an admirer of European Fascists Mussolini and Franco, Ubico seized the opportunity provided by World War II to confiscate over $150 million in German-owned properties, mainly coffee plantations. He amended vagrancy laws to require the indigenous Indians to work a certain number of days per year for the state, effectively converting the government into Guatemala's major labor contractor.

Labor unrest, middle-class democratization pressures, and a loss of US support caused Ubico to resign in 1944. Student- and labor-backed military reformers called for elections for later that year. Educator and former exile Juan José Arévalo Bermejo, who called himself a "spiritual socialist," won the presidency. During his five-year term, Arévalo began numerous reforms, instituting social security, a labor code, professionalization of the military, rural education, public health promotion, and cooperatives. Arévalo vigorously encouraged union and peasant organization and open elections. His economic policies, described as an "explicit attempt to create a modern capitalist society,"[1] did not address the extreme maldistribution of land—a legacy of the "liberal" reforms—that underlay the country's social problems.

In 1950 Guatemalans elected a young army officer, Jacobo Arbenz Guzmán, to succeed Arévalo. Arbenz sought to deepen social reforms despite growing conservative and US opposition. In 1951 he legalized the Communist Party, called the Guatemalan Labor Party (Partido Guatemalteco del Trabajo, PGT). The PGT began actively organizing labor and promoting agrarian reform. Over five hundred peasant unions and three hundred peasant leagues formed under the Arbenz government.[2] The 1952 Agrarian Reform Law began the confiscation and redistribution of farmland to 100,000 peasants.

Arbenz's reforms and the growth of peasant and worker organizations threatened the rural labor supply system by shifting economic power toward workers and peasants and away from latifundists and employers. These threatened interests took action when Arbenz nationalized land belonging to United Fruit, offering compensation to the company at its previously declared tax value. This, of course, troubled several high Eisenhower administration officials with ties to UFCO. The nationalization, the presence of some Communists in the government, and Guatemala's purchase of light arms from Czechoslovakia prompted the United States to label the Arbenz government Communist. In 1953 the United States undertook to destabilize Arbenz's administration with financial sanctions, diplomatic pressure in the Organization of American States, and Central Intelligence Agency (CIA) disinformation and covert actions. The CIA engineered a conspiracy with a rightist army faction. In June 1954 the tiny, CIA-supported National Liberation Army, led by Colonel Carlos Castillo Armas, invaded Guatemala. The armed forces refused to defend the government, and President Arbenz had to resign.[3]

Colonel Castillo Armas, head of the National Liberation Movement (Movimiento de Liberación Nacional, MLN), assumed the presidency with US and Catholic Church backing. With ferocious anti-Communist propaganda, the counterrevolution dismantled the labor and peasant movements, killed and jailed thousands, repressed political parties, revoked the Agrarian Reform Law, and returned confiscated lands to their former owners. Castillo's regime suppressed working- and middle-class and pro-revolutionary organizations and pursued "a continuing . . . promotion of upper-sector interests."[4] Military and business sectors gained influence within the government. Foreign policy aligned closely with the United States, and US and multilateral aid programs promoted economic growth by financing extensive infrastructure development.

The MLN became a political party during the late 1950s, drawing together coffee-plantation owners, municipal politicians and bureaucrats, owners of midsized farms, and certain military elements united in anti-Communism and in their hostility toward the 1944–1954 revolution. Confusion followed Castillo's assassination in 1957, and the army imposed General Miguel Ydígoras Fuentes as president. The Ydígoras government endorsed Guatemala's participation in the Central American Common Market (CACM), permitted CIA-backed anti-Castro Cuban forces to train in Guatemala for the Bay of Pigs invasion of 1961, and continued police terror against supporters of the revolution and labor and peasant leaders.

Continued violence and corruption in the Ydígoras government prompted an abortive coup by reformist army officers in 1960. Escaped coup plotters then formed the nucleus of the first of several rebel groups. The leaders of the Revolutionary Armed Forces (Fuerzas Armadas Revolucionarias, FAR) and the 13th of November Revolutionary Movement (Movimiento Revolucionario del 13 de Noviembre, MR-13) eventually adopted a Marxist-Leninist ideology and guerrilla-war strategy patterned after Fidel Castro's in Cuba. US military aid to Guatemala increased rapidly, but early military operations against the guerrillas proved ineffective. Military dissatisfaction and a desire to block the next election culminated in Colonel Enrique Peralta Azurdia's overthrow of Ydígoras in 1963, and rapid expansion of counterinsurgency operations.

In 1965 the military decided to return the government nominally to civilians, and the 1966 election campaign was generally free and open.[5] The Revolutionary Party (Partido Revolucionario, PR) candidate, Julio César Méndez Montenegro, who denounced the twelve-year counterrevolution, won the presidency. After Méndez took office, however, counterinsurgency accelerated and military control of politics deepened despite the civilian president. The army's 1968 Zacapa campaign, heavily US-backed and US-trained, killed an estimated ten thousand civilians, dealt the guerrillas a severe blow, and earned its commander, Colonel Carlos Arana Osorio, the sobriquet of "the Butcher of Zacapa."

One decade of reform/revolution followed by another of counterrevolution left Guatemalan society deeply polarized. Some rightists feared the 1966 election would end the counterrevolution and took drastic action. Several right-wing "death squads" formed and commenced terrorizing persons vaguely associated with the left and reformist politics. Regular national security forces (army and police), peasant irregulars armed by the government in areas of insurgency, and right-wing terrorist groups permitted and encouraged by the regime conducted a terror campaign against the political opposition (although many victims were apolitical) and effectively intimidated, demobilized, and disarticulated much of it.

In these circumstances the 1970 presidential election—though conducted cleanly by the Méndez government—resulted in victory for Colonel Carlos Arana Osorio, the nominee of both the MLN and the military's own Institutional Democratic Party (Partido Institucional Democrático, PID). With US aid at its historic peak during his administration, Arana consolidated the military's power and deepened its corruption. An aggressive economic-modernization program created huge public-sector enterprises and projects (some under army control) to increase the financial autonomy of the armed forces and the graft available to top officers. Terror against unions, political parties, and suspected critics of the regime escalated anew.

GLOBAL FORCES AND CONFLICT

The political situation of the late 1960s, with a counterinsurgency-oriented military regime confronting an ongoing insurgency, seemingly offered scant prospect for economic growth. Much of the violence, however, occurred in Guatemala's indigenous highlands or lowland jungles and away from urban areas. This allowed parts of Guatemala—even during the conflict—to experience rapid economic growth driven by Central American Common Market and Alliance for Progress policies.

Income. Under the economic guidance of the military-business partnership, Guatemala experienced rapid economic growth, as in Nicaragua and El Salvador. Per capita gross domestic product (GDP) rose an average of 3 percent annually from 1962 through 1971, and 2.6 percent from 1972 through 1980. During the CACM boom, per capita GDP in constant 1986 dollars rose 70 percent, the second-highest growth rate in Central America.[6]

As in Nicaragua and El Salvador, Guatemalan economic growth did not increase the income of the poor. The average annual change in the consumer price index, which was only 0.7 percent from 1963 through 1972, rose to 12.3 percent per annum for 1973–1979. Real wages badly lagged inflation. Working-class wages peaked in 1967 then declined throughout the 1970s. In 1979 the purchasing power of real working-class wages had declined by one-fourth of 1967 levels.[7] Income distribution became markedly less equal during the CACM boom. Between 1970 and 1984 income concentrated increasingly in the hands of the wealthiest fifth of the people, whose national income share rose from 46.5 to 56.8 percent between 1970 and 1984. The income share of Guatemala's poorest fifth shrank from 6.8 to 4.8 percent for the same years. That of the middle three-fifths of income earners also shrank, from 46.7 percent in 1970 to 38.4 percent in 1984.[8]

Employment. Official unemployment statistics for Guatemala indicate a steady growth of unemployment even during the fastest CACM-induced GDP growth. Official unemployment rates rose from 4.8 percent in 1970 to 5.5 percent in 1980 and then to 10.0 percent by 1984. Estimated *under*employment rates rose steadily from 24.5 percent in 1973 to 43.4 percent in 1984.[9]

Wealth. Guatemalan data on wealth distribution are scarce, but some studies permit inferences.[10] Land has long been unequally distributed. The agrarian census of 1950 reported that farms smaller than 5 *manzanas* (roughly 3.5 hectares) made up 75.1 percent of the farms but only occupied 9.0 percent of the cultivated land. The 1.7 percent of farms larger than 64 manzanas (45

hectares) made up 50.3 percent of the cultivated land.[11] The 1979 agricultural census revealed that landownership inequality in Guatemala had become
the greatest in Central America. Rapid rural population growth shrank the
amount of arable land per capita from 1.71 hectares/capita in 1950 to less
than 0.79 by 1980.[12]

In the late 1970s, indigenous agrarian unemployment began rising while
wages deteriorated. Ladinos (mestizos) were reportedly appropriating com-
munally and privately held land in the indigenous highlands. Concentration
of landownership caused highland people to relocate to cities or public lands
newly opened in Petén and Izábal. However, military officers and politicians
amassed much land in those departments by driving many smallholders off
their new plots in the region.[13] In 1976 a great earthquake devastated the
western highlands and further worsened the poverty of tens of thousands of
indigenous peasants.

Worker productivity in manufacturing grew steadily from the 1950s
through the 1970s, but real wages and the working- and middle-class shares
of national income declined sharply during the 1970s. The main beneficiaries
of increasing productivity were foreign and national investors.[14] During the
same period, the ownership of the means of industrial production became
more concentrated among fewer large firms. Private-sector pressure-group
organization became more extensive and sophisticated.[15] In some industries
modernization of production and growing ownership concentration displaced
many workers.

Guatemala's upper classes prospered during the 1970s because of the industrialization boom and relatively high coffee prices, but conditions deteriorated under an economic output that declined from 1981 through 1985.
Causes of this recession included declining commodity prices, political unrest
elsewhere in Central America, and capital flight. Guatemala's general recession
(as distinct from deteriorating real working-class wages) lagged four years behind a similar one in Nicaragua and two years behind El Salvador's. It eroded
the economic position of Guatemalan economic elites sufficiently that some
criticized the economic management of successive military presidents and reconsidered their commitment to the regime.

Popular Mobilization. Reformists under Guatemala's democratic governments of 1944 to 1954 suffered badly after the 1954 coup. The MLN government's and military's demobilization campaign decimated the ranks of
reformist politicians, unionists, and indigenous people who had supported the
Arévalo and Arbenz governments. Marxist guerrilla opposition to the regime
first appeared in 1962, but was set back greatly by heavy general repression
and an intense counterinsurgency campaign in the late 1960s.[16]

Popular mobilization rekindled during the 1970s as real wages and income
distribution worsened. Mobilization in Guatemala, however, lagged behind

that in Nicaragua and El Salvador because of heavier repression and its ethnic divisions.[17] Increased unionization and industrial strikes during the government of General Eugenio Kjell Laugerud García (1974 to 1978) followed a decline in manufacturing wages in the early 1970s. Laugerud momentarily relaxed repression of unions in 1978, and a wave of strikes ensued. The 1976 earthquake's devastation of lower-class housing mobilized slum dwellers into two confederations. These civil society groups pressed for housing assistance and in 1978 organized a transport boycott protesting increased bus fares. The FAR resurfaced and two new, indigenous-based guerrilla organizations—the Guerrilla Army of the Poor (Ejército Guerrillero de los Pobres, EGP) and the Organization of the People in Arms (Organización del Pueblo en Armas, ORPA)—also appeared. All grew rapidly and began overt military activity in the late 1970s.

During the 1960s and 1970s the Christian Democratic Party (Partido Demócrata Cristiano de Guatemala, PDCG) promoted hundreds of agrarian cooperatives and a labor union movement to build a constituency and organizational base. As in El Salvador and Nicaragua, Christian base communities (CEBs) appeared throughout much of poor rural and urban Guatemala during the early 1970s. CEBs organized community and labor groups among Guatemala's long quiescent indigenous populace. Despite military rule and repression, civil society and opposition parties multiplied. The PDCG and other centrist and leftist parties including the Democratic Socialist Party (Partido Socialista Demócrata, PSD) and the United Front of the Revolution (Frente Unido de la Revolución, FUR) called for new policies and ran for office. Citizens organized, but also lost confidence in elections because the military regime fraudulently manipulated several presidential elections. Abstention among registered voters rose from 44 percent in 1966 to 64 percent in the 1978 national election.[18]

State Response and Opposition. During the post-1954 counterrevolution, Guatemalan rulers intensely repressed union activists, students, peasant groups, indigenous peoples, opposition parties, and other dissidents. Somewhat relaxed during the early 1960s, repression of the same groups escalated sharply from 1966 on. In that year both private and public security-force death squad terrorism began consistently taking dozens of lives a month. The army's 1968–1970 counterinsurgency campaign decimated the Revolutionary Armed Forces (FAR) and the Edgar Ibarra Guerrilla Front (Frente Guerrillera Edgar Ibarra, FGEI) guerrilla movements.

In the political turmoil of the 1978 election, all parties again nominated military officers as presidential candidates. Soon after General Lucas García took office, government forces brutally crushed Guatemala City bus fare protests. As opposition parties grew in 1978 and 1979, security-force death squads assassinated dozens of national and local leaders of the Democratic Socialist and Christian Democratic parties and of the reformist FUR. Hundreds of union leaders, university faculty, and student leaders also disappeared or were assassinated during the Lucas government.

Campesino organizations led by the Peasant Unity Committee (Comité de Unidad Campesina, CUC) stepped up organizing. The CUC staged a major strike against sugar planters in 1980. In 1978 and 1979 the regrouped FAR and ORPA began military activity in the western highlands. Soon afterward the Guerrilla Army of the Poor (EGP), also with strong indigenous support, resumed combat against the regime in the highlands. Estimates placed the number of guerrilla troops at around 4,000 by 1982; the rebels' popular support was widespread. Counterinsurgency escalated and included massacres of indigenous villagers to discourage support for the guerrillas.

From 1960 on, the US embassy tracked Guatemalan political murders, most committed by government security forces and rightist death squads.[19] The average political murder rate, mainly in urban areas, rose from about 30 per month in 1971 to 75 per month in 1979 and then soared to nearly 303 per month by 1982.[20] Some experts believe that army counterinsurgency operations in rural areas killed even many more than did the urban violence. Despite such massive human rights violations, Guatemala continued to receive new economic assistance from the United States that totaled over $60 million from 1979 through 1981.[21] Guatemala's truth commission, the Historical Clarification Commission, later referred to the period from 1978 to 1985 as the "most violent and bloody period of the confrontation." Deaths likely totaled 200,000.[22]

The armed forces, the backbone of the Lucas regime, faced three critical problems in 1982. First was the extensive indigenous support for the guerrillas in the western highlands and growing rural unrest elsewhere. Second, the economy slowed in 1979–1980, then contracted sharply in 1981–1982. Third, the Lucas government began to lose allies. When news leaked that President Lucas had perpetrated another election fraud in 1982, younger army officers overthrew him and installed General Efraín Ríos Montt as president. This coup began a gradual process of regime changes that took 14 years to complete.

The coup leaders pursued a dual strategy of increasing repression to crush the rebels and demobilize growing opposition while also slowly reforming the political rules of the game with elections and eventual civilian rule under military tutelage. In the first phase, President Ríos Montt abolished the old rules by annulling the electoral law and 1965 constitution, dissolved Congress, suppressed political parties, and imposed a state of siege. Pursuing a political reform agenda largely obscured by the regime's de facto nature, a Council of State decreed a new electoral law and called July 1984 elections for an assembly to draft a new constitution.

On the military agenda, repression escalated with a new rural counterinsurgency campaign in indigenous zones. Ríos Montt's press secretary Francisco Bianchi justified the campaign: "The guerrillas won over many Indian collaborators. Therefore, the Indians were subversives, right? And how do you fight subversion? Clearly, you had to kill Indians because they were collaborating with subversion. And then they would say, 'You're massacring innocent people.' But they weren't innocent. They had sold out to subversion."[23] The army massacred numerous whole villages and committed other atrocities against suspected guerrilla sympathizers. The army forced the relocation and concentration of indigenous people, many pressed into work on modern, army-owned farms producing vegetables to export to the United States. The military formed army-controlled, mandatory "civil self-defense patrols" involving virtually all of the adult rural males. Estimates of the rural counterinsurgency's toll range up to 150,000 dead between 1982 and 1985. US embassy statistics often overlooked such massacres because embassy staff could not easily verify the incidents.[24] The war displaced at least 500,000 persons, mostly indigenous, internally or abroad.[25] Robinson contends that the war's dislocation of the rural indigenous population contributed to the development of a new supply of cheap labor to support Guatemala's embrace of the neoliberal economic model.[26]

Unable to detect meaningful political reform under Ríos Montt, centrist political activists hunkered down or fled, while the leftist opposition worked toward coalitions to enhance their power and resource base.[27] The Democratic Front Against Repression (Frente Democrático Contra la Represión, FDCR) appeared in 1979, made of numerous unions, the PSD, and the FUR. Two years later, several of the FDCR's more radical elements—including the peasant federation CUC—split with the FDCR and formed the January 13th Popular Front (Frente Popular 13 de Enero, FP-13). In 1982 the FP-13 and the FDCR endorsed yet another coalition, the Guatemalan Committee of Patriotic Unity (Comité Guatemalteco de Unidad Patriótica, CGUP). Guerrilla groups united into the Guatemalan National Revolutionary Union (Unidad Revolucionaria Nacional Guatemalteca, URNG) in 1982; their revolutionary manifesto challenged the regime's sovereignty.

The URNG's drive for a broader coalition bogged down, possibly a victim of the regime's efforts to reestablish civilian rule. Labor unions remained reluctant to form political links that might jeopardize their legal status—even with legal political parties.[28] The government curtailed rightist terrorism in urban areas after 1982 while intensifying rural counterinsurgency. When President Ríos Montt's increasingly erratic public behavior embarrassed the military reformists, they replaced him with General Oscar Humberto Mejía Victores in August 1983. Political reforms advanced: the electoral registry was reformed and voter registration redone. The constituent assembly, elected in 1984, produced a new constitution that took effect in May 1985. President Mejía immediately called for elections, and the regime allowed some long-suppressed political forces of the center and left to resurface.

Elections for president, Congress, and municipalities took place in late 1985. Although military pressure excluded leftist parties, centrist parties participated. Despite its backdrop of three decades of brutal demobilization, this election itself was generally free from terrorism against opposition parties. The Christian Democrats, led by Vinicio Cerezo Arévalo, won the presidency and a majority of the Congress in clean elections in late 1985.[29] Party spokesmen affirmed that they participated in the 1984 and 1985 elections and the constituent assembly because they believed the military seriously intended to reduce its role in governing.[30] This opening to civilian politicians in the mid-1980s dissuaded some opposition parties from allying with the revolutionary left.

The 1985 election brought Guatemala's second critical regime change in the lengthy military-managed liberalization. It established a civilian transitional regime with new electoral rules and institutions and admitted a broader spectrum of political actors into the arena. Powerful economic sectors that once supported military rule, reeling from a half decade of miserable economic performance, embraced the prospect of a government and economy managed by elected civilians. Citizens showed their hopes for an end to Guatemala's long political nightmare by voting. Compared to prior elections, Guatemalans voted at much higher rates—78 percent in 1984 and 69 percent in 1985. Turnout increased most in urban areas where violence had diminished and political freedom increased.

THE CIVILIAN TRANSITIONAL REGIME
AND THE CIVIL WAR

The civilian transitional regime confronted critical, interconnected needs. The first was to end the civil war, but President Cerezo and his successors held limited influence over the armed forces or the rebels. Second was to consolidate civilian rule and progress toward democracy. To accomplish this, any settlement would have to pacify the rebels and curtail the military's great power in national life. Constituencies that supported the war needed to be persuaded to accept civilian constitutional rule. Third, Guatemala needed economic recovery, but the economy remained desultory. Progress on each front was halting. During the Cerezo administration, however, globally oriented capitalists, intent on modernizing the economy by reducing the power of the traditional agro-export elite, coalesced around several economic organizations and think tanks actively encouraged by a US Agency for International Development (USAID) program of Private Enterprise Development.

"The emerging New Right groupings began to explore the development of the transnational project in Guatemala and to gain an instrumental hold over the state in policy development. . . . At the behest of this emerging private sector bloc, the government approved a series of liberalization and deregulation measures."[31]

President Cerezo actively embraced the August 1987 Central American Peace Accord, which provided a draft blueprint for political reconciliation, dialogue, and formal democratization. Cerezo's effort to end the civil war, however, stagnated because the military and rebels failed to cooperate fully. Cease-fire talks with the URNG in Madrid fell apart. Dialogue between the government and other national political and economic forces was limited. Indeed, the guerrilla war intensified in late 1987 as the URNG and the army sought to improve their positions.[32]

The balance of resources between the warring parties began shifting gradually in the government's favor. Although economic and military assistance from the United States remained a tiny fraction of that received by El Salvador (see Appendix, Table A.3), the military's and government's institutional capabilities remained fairly high. Political reform isolated the rebels from a broader coalition while the army's rural counterinsurgency program increasingly denied them access to their indigenous supporters. Economic performance improved after 1987. Moreover, the military's retreat from executive power, the election of a new government, and some progress on the abysmal human rights situation—enactment of habeas corpus and other protections of individual rights embodied in *amparo* laws; [33] a human rights ombudsman; and judicial reforms—increased the government's domestic and external legitimacy.

Despite a promising beginning, the Cerezo administration performed poorly in many areas. Business groups, opposition parties, and labor broadly criticized Cerezo and the Christian Democratic Party for corruption, indecision, policy errors, economic problems, failure to address the needs of the poor, and lack of progress on human rights. Social mobilization increased. External human rights monitors and the government's own human rights ombudsman denounced continuing army and police abuses against labor activists, union members, homeless street children, students, human rights advocates, religious workers, political party leaders, and foreigners.[34]

Peace talks commenced in Oslo, Norway, but too late to benefit Cerezo and the PDCG. Before negotiations commenced, the URNG changed its goal from military victory to winning a negotiated settlement. In the early 1990s, several factors reinforced that decision, including the difficulty of fighting while cut off from its indigenous base and potential moderate allies, the Soviet bloc's collapse, and the electoral defeat of Nicaragua's Sandinistas. The army's new willingness to negotiate reflected its eroding support among the bourgeoisie, increasing criticism of military human rights violations, and the continuing attrition of the war. The negotiations progressed little during Cerezo's term.

Cerezo's dismal record handicapped the Christian Democratic Party in the 1990 election. Parties of the old right (landed oligarchy and military) such as the MLN and PID declined. In their place new parties appeared, several representing transnationally oriented economic elites who had been gaining rapidly in influence. These included the Union of the National Center (Unión del Centro Nacional, UCN), the Solidarity Action Movement (Movimiento de Acción Solidaria, MAS), and the National Advancement Party (Partido del Avance Nacional, PAN). The 1990 vote was relatively free and clean despite the left's exclusion. Barely half of Guatemala's dispirited voters turned out for the two rounds of 1990 elections (a major decline from 1985). Voters rejected the discredited PDCG, so the presidential runoff occurred between two new-right conservatives, newspaper publisher Jorge Carpio Nicolle of PAN and engineer Jorge Serrano Elías of MAS. Serrano, a Protestant with a populist flair who promised to push the peace negotiations, won.[35]

President Serrano, a former minister in Ríos Montt's cabinet, appointed numerous military officials to his government. He addressed himself to human rights violations with unexpected vigor by detaining and prosecuting military officials, and energetically pursued peace negotiations. However, when the economy slumped further in 1991, Serrano imposed a package of tough structural adjustment measures informed by the transnational capitalist sector and its think tanks.[36] Adversely affected popular groups protested widely, and the security forces replied with a typical barrage of human rights abuses.

Serrano plunged the civilian transitional regime into crisis on May 25, 1993, when (apparently supported by part of the military) he attempted an *autogolpe* ("self-coup"). He illegally dissolved the Supreme Court and Congress, censored the press, restricted civil liberties, and sought to rule by decree. Citizens, civil society organizations, and governmental institutions energetically protested the "Serranazo." The United States, the Organization of American States, and other external actors quickly warned Guatemalan political actors, military included, that the international financial institutions so essential to Guatemala's economic recovery would be very unhappy about a deviation from constitutional practice.[37]

Combined internal and external pressure undermined the Serranazo and kept the civilian transitional regime on track. The Court of Constitutionality (Corte de Constitucionalidad, CC), backed by an institutionalist military faction, removed Serrano from office under provisions of the 1985 constitution. Congress elected Ramiro de León Carpio, the human rights ombudsman, to finish out the presidential term. President de León, unaffiliated with a political party but backed by a broad array of civil organizations, pushed through Congress several constitutional reforms that were ratified by popular referendum in January 1994. This initiated the election of a new Congress in August 1994 to serve out the rest of the term.[38]

Peace negotiations gained momentum in 1994 under the mediation of the United Nations (UN).[39] A January "Framework Accord" established a timetable and provided for an Asamblea de la Sociedad Civil (Assembly of Civil Society, ASC) made up of most political parties and a diverse array of nongovernmental organizations, including women's and indigenous groups, to advise negotiators. Progress came steadily thereafter. In March 1994 negotiators signed a critical human rights accord establishing a UN human rights monitoring mission that commenced its work in November. There followed agreements on refugee resettlement and a historical clarification commission to study the long-term violence (June 1994) and an accord on indigenous rights (March 1995).[40]

As negotiations continued into 1995, another national election took place. Guatemala City mayor Alvaro Arzú of the National Advancement Party (PAN) announced his candidacy, as did Efraín Ríos Montt of the right-wing populist Republican Front of Guatemala (Frente Republicano de Guatemala, FRG). Ríos' candidacy prompted a legal battle because the constitution barred participants in prior de facto regimes from becoming president. The election tribunal ruled against the former dictator. A sign of the left's growing confidence in its ability to participate in the system came when several leftist groups coalesced into a new party, the New Guatemala Democratic Front (Frente Democrático Nueva Guatemala, FDNG) to contest the election. The URNG suspended military actions during the final weeks of the campaign. In the November 1995 general election the FDNG took 6 of 80 seats in Congress, the PAN 43, and the FRG 21. Turnout increased over the 1990 election. The FDNG and various indigenous civic committees won several mayoral races. Arzú, a businessman active in the new transnationally oriented coalition, narrowly won the presidency in a January 1996 runoff.[41] (See Appendix, Tables A.6 and A.7, for selected presidential and legislative election results.)

Alvaro Arzú took office under worsening political portents,[42] but moved decisively toward peace by shaking up the army high command and police, meeting with rebel leaders, and embracing negotiations. There followed an indefinite cease-fire between the URNG and the army in March 1996, an accord on socioeconomic and agrarian issues (May 1996), and another on civil-military relations to increase civilian control of the armed forces, limit military authority to external defense, and replace the violent and corrupt national police (September 1996).

THE PEACE ACCORDS AND
CONTEMPORARY GUATEMALAN POLITICS

On December 29, 1996, the government and the URNG signed the Final Peace Accord in Guatemala City, ending 36 years of civil war.[43] This agreement on new political rules embraced the previously negotiated accords and established an electoral democratic regime. The military came under increased civilian authority and found their responsibilities curtailed. Police reforms began. URNG rebels, many groups of the left, the new FDNG, and indigenous peoples—previously repressed or otherwise excluded—gained access to the political system as legal players. The URNG agreed to demobilize its forces and participate within the constitutional framework. A broad array of civil society organizations, including those representing the bourgeoisie (heretofore ambivalent about the peace process and new democratization), embraced the new regime. Guatemala's political party system would continue to be unstable for subsequent decades; there were 19 presidential nominees in 1995 and ten or more through 2011.

Arzú's economic program of neoliberal reforms (privatization of electricity and telecommunications, budget cuts, fiscal reforms, trade and foreign exchange liberalization, and reduction of regulation) appeared destined to promote new economic growth but at the cost of worsening the nation's highly unequal distribution of income and increased poverty.[44] There remained potential for violent forces antagonistic to the democratic project and needed socioeconomic reforms to undermine the new regime. Nothing more clearly revealed the challenges of the consolidation of civilian democracy in Guatemala than the murder of Auxiliary Archbishop Juan Gerardi Conedera on April 26, 1998. Two days after the Catholic Church's Human Rights Office issued a report on civil war political violence to Guatemala's Historical Clarification Commission, Bishop Gerardi—one of its authors—was bludgeoned to death. A death squad long connected to the presidential guard later claimed credit for the murder and began intimidating other Catholic human rights workers.[45] The investigation eventually blamed two army captains and a sergeant and a priest for Gerardi's murder. In June 2001, Colonel Disrael Lima Estrada, Captain Lima Oliva, Sergeant Jose Villanueva, and Father Mario Orantes were convicted in his death.[46] Although an appeals court overturned the verdicts the following year, Guatemala's Supreme Court ultimately upheld their convictions and sentences.[47]

In 1999 the Historical Clarification Commission's (Comisión para el Esclarecimiento Histórico, CEH) report, *Guatemala: Memory of Silence*, found that over 200,000 persons had died in the war and roughly 1.5 million were displaced. The report attributed 93 percent of the war's acts of violence—most intense from 1978 to 1984—to the army and state security forces (Civil

Patrols).[48] It described the killings as genocidal because 83 percent of the victims were indigenous, and the attacks on the indigenous population were part of a deliberate strategy to rid the rebels of support.[49] The report attributed 626 massacres of Mayan communities to the state[50] and found that US military assistance to Guatemala "had significant bearing on human rights violations during the armed conflict."[51] Shortly after the unveiling of the report, US president Bill Clinton publicly apologized for the US role in supporting Guatemala's state security forces during the war.[52]

President Arzú downplayed the report's findings and recommendations on preservation of memory, victim compensation, national reconciliation, and strengthening democracy and human rights. Arzú also openly rejected the commission's recommendations to create a commission to investigate and purge army officers for acts of violence, stating that the military had already investigated itself and "purified" its forces. The peace accords received another setback in 1999 when, with a 56 percent majority, voters defeated a referendum on constitutional reforms (including judicial and military reform), required to implement some provisions of the accords.

Growing social violence and socioeconomic woes were the main issues of the 1999 elections. The FRG nominated Alfonso Portillo after the party's leader, retired general Efraín Ríos Montt, was ruled ineligible to run for office due to his role in the 1982 coup. After failing to win a majority in the first round of voting, Portillo easily defeated the PAN candidate, Guatemala City mayor Oscar Berger, in a runoff. The FRG also dominated the Congress with 63 of 113 seats and elected Ríos Montt as the body's president.[53] The leftist New Nation Alliance (Alianza Nueva Nación, ANN), which included the URNG, did better than expected, winning 13 percent of the vote.

Considered a populist by some, President Portillo fared little better than Arzú in addressing Guatemala's persistent socioeconomic problems. Initiatives to reduce poverty, such as increasing the minimum wage, kept Portillo at odds with the Guatemalan business community throughout his term. In 2002 Portillo established the National Compensation Program to compensate war victims. The $400 million program also included possible payments to some 400,000 former members of the militias known as Patrullas de Autodefensa Civil (PAC), many of whom had been forcibly recruited during the war. Although later ruled unconstitutional, the payments issue highlighted continuing tensions within society.[54]

The few advances of the Portillo government were tempered by its failures to combat Guatemala's crime wave, including continuing attacks on human rights workers, and to promote further implementation of the peace accords. Rather than reduce and reform the role of the military in Guatemalan society, Portillo and Ríos Montt ousted reformist military officers appointed by President Arzú and replaced them with ones more likely to sympathize with the FRG administration. "Contrary to the regional trend, the corrupt FRG government also significantly increased the military's budget and duties," giving command of the military to "an unsavory trio of discredited former army officers allegedly associated with past human rights abuses and organized crime."[55] Portillo's government became notorious for high levels of corruption.[56] In 2003 the US government decertified Guatemala for failing to contain the narcotics trade in the country.[57] Under Portillo, Guatemala captured a mere fraction of previous cocaine tonnage seizures, despite evidence that transshipments actually increased.[58] In addition, the US Drug Enforcement Administration (DEA) estimated that Guatemala's corrupt Department of Anti-Narcotic Operations stole more than twice the amount reported seized in 2002.[59]

The 2003 presidential campaign season was tumultuous. In May 2003, the FRG nominated Ríos Montt as its presidential candidate. Attempting to register as a candidate, he was again refused because of his role in the 1982 coup. The Supreme Electoral Tribunal (Tribunal Supremo Electoral, TSE) agreed, and denied his two appeals. His request for an injunction was denied by the Supreme Court of Justice (Corte Supremo de Justicia, CSJ). He then appealed to the Court of Constitutionality (Corte de Constitucionalidad, CC), which granted the injunction and authorized his candidacy. When the CSJ suspended voter registration in protest, Ríos Montt arranged a violent protest by thousands of demonstrators demand his registration.[60] The protests drew widespread criticisms of Ríos Montt's actions, including from the US State Department. The CC ordered the TSE to instate his candidacy. Although he ran a distant third, Ríos Montt won nearly 20 percent of the vote,[61] forcing a runoff between National Unity of Hope (Unidad Nacional de la Esperanza, UNE) candidate Alvaro Colom and Great National Alliance (Gran Alianza Nacional, GANA) candidate Oscar Berger. With voter turnout less than 50 percent, Berger defeated Colom in the second round 52.8 percent to 47.2 percent. GANA also won 49 congressional seats, with the FRG winning 41, the UNE 30, and the PAN 17.[62]

President Berger, who had campaigned on job creation and renewed support for the peace accords, swiftly appointed indigenous rights activist and Nobel Peace laureate Rigoberta Menchú to oversee the implementation of the peace accords, and noted human rights attorney Frank La Rue to head the president's human rights office.[63] Speaking at a ceremony on the fifth anniversary of the truth commission, Berger apologized for the war and pledged to compensate victims.[64] The Supreme Court rulings in the Myrna Mack and Bishop Gerardi trials also helped to refocus attention on the peace accords and human rights. Additionally, Berger replaced problematical senior military commanders and pledged to reduce the size of the military by 35 percent and its budget (fixed at 0.33 percent of GDP).[65]

As in other Central American countries, violence surged in Guatemala after the end of the civil war. In the first six months of 2004, nearly 2,000 people were murdered. Berger responded to the crime wave by firing both the interior minister and the chief of police.[66] In a somewhat more controversial move, Berger then ordered 1,600 soldiers to join the police in combating crime.[67] One horrific trend was the murders of more than 1,183 young women between January 2002 and June 2004.[68] Many of these women were raped and tortured before they were murdered; some were decapitated or burned beyond recognition. Although government and media sources attributed many of these killings to gangs, few were investigated.[69] In an effort to curb gang activity, Berger signed an agreement with the governments of El Salvador, Honduras, and Nicaragua that would allow warrants issued in one country to be shared with all signatories. Gang members responded by decapitating a man and pinning a note to his body warning Berger against anti-gang laws.

Some crime could be attributed to youth gangs, but much came from organized crime syndicates and clandestine security organizations.[70] In fact, homicide statistics revealed that regions with the highest levels of homicide were not those with the highest level of gang activity.[71] A UNDP study found violent homicide negatively correlated with poverty and indigenous municipalities.[72] Murder victims routinely included human rights activists, unionists, journalists, and protestors, presumably because they threatened business, political, or bureaucratic interests. Many murder victims bore evidence of torture, especially younger victims. Death squads appeared within the Interior Ministry and National Police, many of whose members were reportedly Protestant evangelicals who claimed a "mission" to rid Guatemala of such "evil" undesirables as gang members, prostitutes, and homosexuals through so-called social cleansing (*saneamiento social*).[73] The roots of post-conflict violence in Guatemala increasingly linked back to the war. Clandestine security organizations created during the war had never been fully dismantled.[74] They morphed into organized crime networks that infiltrated the military, police, other state agencies, and political parties. This insured they would operate with impunity in crimes including drug trafficking, extortion, and money laundering.

In February 2007 three Salvadoran representatives to the Central American Parliament (PARLACEN) were murdered and their car torched in Guatemala.[75] Authorities quickly arrested four Guatemalan policemen, including the head of the organized-crime unit, as suspects. But the captive officers were found dead, their throats slit, in their maximum security cells at El Boquerón prison before they could be interrogated by the US FBI, which had been invited to assist with the inquiry. Further investigation initially pointed toward a former UNE congressman and former Jutiapa mayor, Manuel Castillo Medrano, who was apprehended in August 2007. It was later determined that disgraced Salvadoran politician Carlos Roberto Silva

had ordered the murders through Castillo. Silva, on trial in El Salvador for
money laundering and corruption, allegedly ordered the killings to avenge
ARENA for lifting his immunity from prosecution.[76]

The case highlighted how deeply criminal networks had infiltrated Guatemala's security apparatus. In response to the killings, the minister of the
interior and the national police chief were forced to resign, and 1,900 police
officers were fired.[77] The PARLACEN killings also helped advance Berger's
fight against impunity for rights violations. In 2006 the Berger government
and the United Nations agreed to establish the International Commission
against Impunity in Guatemala (Comisión Internacional contra la Impunidad
en Guatemala, CICIG).[78] Approved by Congress in 2007, largely in response
to the PARLACEN murders, CICIG began its original two-year mandate in
2008, later extended three times through 2015. The primary responsibilities
of CICIG were to "investigate and dismantle violent criminal networks," assist
in prosecutions, and recommend policies. CICIG could also file complaints
against civil servants who interfere with its mandate.[79] CICIG participated
in the prosecution of 20 high-profile cases through October 2013, including
corruption, impunity, smuggling, narco-trafficking, extrajudicial killings, and
abuse of authority.[80] One of CICIG's most notable cases was that of former
president Alfonso Portillo. Charged with embezzling more than $15 million
while in office, Portillo fled to Mexico in February 2004 after being stripped
of his immunity from prosecution. Mexico in 2006 approved Portillo's extra-
dition to Guatemala, but he did not return for another two years. Though
eventually acquitted in Guatemala in 2011, Portillo was extradited to the
United States in May 2013 to face charges of money laundering in a New
York court.[81] He pled guilty and received a six year prison sentence.

THE ECONOMY

Guatemala's overt political violence obscures the ubiquitous hardships caused
by dependent development and poverty. As the National Statistical Institute
(Instituto Nacional de Estadística, INE) reported in its Survey on Living Standards 2006, more than half of the Guatemalan population lived below the
poverty line, 13 percent in extreme poverty (see Table 2.1). Poverty was much
worse in rural areas in the country's north and west. In Petén, for example,
extreme poverty reached 40 percent. The poverty rate for indigenous populations was 56 percent compared to 44 percent among Ladinos.[82] Guatemala
was also the most unequal country in the region with a 2007 Gini coefficient
of 55. The wealthiest 20 percent of the country's people owned two-thirds of
its wealth, whereas the poorest 20 percent received just 3 percent (see Tables
1.1 and 2.1).

Guatemalan poverty statistics would be much worse if not for the remittances from citizens working abroad. Guatemala has become increasingly dependent on remittances,[83] which increased dramatically between 2002 and 2008. Remittances totaled almost $600 million in 2002 and increased greatly, to $4.3 billion, in 2008. The remittance flow contracted in 2009 and 2010 because of the world recession, falling from above 12 percent of GDP to 9.5 percent in 2011, despite a recovery to $4.5 billion that year.[84] Remittances had risen to $5.4 billion in 2013. Without this critical stream of income to many Guatemalan families, some estimate that poverty could increase by 5 percent.

Poverty and inequality increasingly pitted business-elite interests against those of the poor majority. Social protest erupted in 2005 over controversial government policies, such as mining and the Central American Free Trade Agreement (CAFTA). Small-scale agricultural producers, unions, and others feared CAFTA's provisions removing trade barriers and opening markets to foreign goods, firms, and capital. There were numerous anti-CAFTA demonstrations in which activists demanded that the issue be decided by referendum.[85] In the end, business interests prevailed, as the measure was approved in Guatemala's Congress by a vote of 126 to 12; most opposing votes came from the URNG members. Even after CAFTA's ratification, protests continued. The army fired on CAFTA protesters in Huehuetenango, killing one and injuring others.[86]

CONTEMPORARY POLITICS

The 2007 election season was the most violent in the country's short democratic history. The fluid party system offered up 14 presidential candidates, and 15 parties competed for seats in Congress. Even at the local level, politics remained Guatemala's blood sport. More than 50 congressmen, candidates, and activists were killed in pre-election violence.[87] About one-quarter of the victims were from the UNE party, including a congressman's 14-year-old daughter. UNE candidate Alvaro Colom narrowly won the first round of voting to face Otto Pérez Molina of the Patriot Party (Partido Patriota, PP) in a runoff. Pérez Molina, a retired general, participated in counterinsurgency during the civil war. Rigoberta Menchú headed the ticket of the new Encounter for Guatemala (Encuentro por Guatemala, EG) but won only 3 percent of the first-round vote. Former president Alvaro Arzú was re-elected for a third term as mayor of Guatemala City. In the congressional elections UNE won 52 two seats, PP won 29, the Grand National Alliance (Gran Alianza Nacional, GANA) won 37, and the FRG won 14. Voter turnout was 60 percent, the highest since the end of the war.

In the runoff campaign, Colom claimed a Pérez Molina victory would represent a return to the country's brutal civil war. Colom, a candidate twice before, pledged to increase social investment and to fight impunity and corruption. Pérez Molina, whose campaign symbol was a fist, argued Guatemala needed more order and vowed to use the military to restore it.[88] Each man charged the other with having organized crime and drug cartel links (a claim that had plagued the UNE in recent years). Colom defeated Pérez Molina in the second round, 53 percent to 47 percent, with runoff turnout falling to 53 percent.

Colom's first year in office was mired in controversy and rising violence. The crime wave escalated; homicides increased 9 percent to 6,292. Public bus drivers became targets for extortion—in 2008 criminals murdered 175 bus drivers, attendants, and company owners.[89] Frustrated with poor official response to rampant crime, Guatemalan mobs lynched numerous suspected criminals as well as municipal and police officials.[90] From 2002 to 2004 femicides (murders of women because they are women) increased 57 percent, more than twice the rate of murders of men.[91] In 2007, 722 femicides were reported, almost 10 percent of all reported homicides that year. Only a fraction of these crimes resulted in convictions.

In 2008 the Congress approved the Law Against Femicides and Other Forms of Violence Against Women, unanimously supported by all 19 congresswomen.[92] The law criminalized all forms of violence against women whether economic, sexual, psychological, or physical.[93] The Congress also passed the Arms and Ammunitions Act, which banned arms trafficking, required a psychological test for a gun license, and limited to three the number of weapons an individual might own. The United Nations estimated that there were 1.5 million illegal arms in Guatemala.

President Colom also especially emphasized human rights. He ordered declassification of military archives accidentally discovered in a munitions depot in July 2005.[94] The army refused to obey the order as unconstitutional, but the Constitutional Court disagreed and granted a petition from the Human Rights Ombudsman for the production of the documents. Colom also significantly increased reparations payments made by the Berger administration. By May 2009, the administration had delivered almost 10,500 reparations checks to survivors. Colom, whose uncle was murdered by death squads, also sent letters to victims' families asking for forgiveness for the state's offenses.[95]

Rumors of coup conspiracies swirled around Colom during his first year in office. When hidden listening devices and video cameras were discovered in the presidential offices and residence in September 2008, Colom fired the attorney general. Soon after, the 2009 murder of prominent attorney Rodrigo Rosenberg threatened to destabilize Colom's government. In a bizarre videotape recorded before the lawyer's death, Rosenberg blamed Colom for his demise. He denounced an alleged drug-related conspiracy among the directors of the Rural Development Bank and referenced certain anti-poverty programs run by Colom's wife.[96] Opponents and supporters of Colom filled the streets in the days following the video's release. Observers speculated the sensational affair constituted an attempt to force Colom out of office.[97] Colom requested that CICIG and the FBI investigate the murder. The investigation ultimately revealed Rosenberg orchestrated his own death in a deliberate attempt to implicate Colom, whom he blamed for the murder of his married lover.[98]

In 2009 the Inter-American Court on Human Rights ruled that Guatemala's 1996 amnesty law did not bar the prosecution of crimes against humanity. Shortly thereafter, prosecutors issued warrants for Kaibil soldiers accused of participating in the massacre. In 2010, President Colom appointed Claudia Paz y Paz as Guatemala's new attorney general. Shortly after entering office she implemented a new evaluation system for prosecutors that caused the retirement of almost 80 percent of prosecutors.[99] In addition to prosecuting drug cartels and organized crime, Paz y Paz also oversaw the prosecution of former president Portillo for corruption. But it was the prosecution of crimes committed during the war that drew international attention. In 2011 warrants were issued for both former dictator Oscar Mejía Victores and former head of the armed forces Hector Mario López Fuentes, though both were ruled too ill to stand trial. By 2011 Guatemalan courts had tried and convicted several lower-ranking participants (civil defense patrol members and army officers) in civil war atrocities.[100]

Despite some progress on prosecuting criminals, Guatemala remained a haven for drug traffickers and organized crime.[101] Mexico's Sinaloa Cartel and the Zetas operated with relative impunity, particularly in the north. In December 2010, the Colom administration declared a state of siege in Alta Verapaz where the Zetas preyed upon the local population. Months later, Colom declared a state of siege in Petén following the massacre of dozens of workers and children at the Los Cocos ranch.[102] Troubling but not surprising evidence surfaced that the very members of the military that had been tasked with fighting the traffickers were also colluding with them.[103] In addition to the Mexican cartels, dozens of other traffickers operated in the country. In July 2011 Argentine folk singer Facundo Cabral was murdered in Guatemala City in an ambush targeting Nicaraguan music promoter Henry Fariña. Costa Rican drug traffickers operating in Guatemala had allegedly targeted Fariña, who survived the attack.[104]

The 2011 elections again saw high levels of campaign violence, high levels of spending, and high levels of voter malaise.[105] More than three dozen activists, mostly candidates for local offices, were killed before the September elections.[106] Despite ten candidates for the presidency (Appendix, Table A.6), some felt that the elections merely reaffirmed elite interests. Allegations accused several candidates of ties to drug traffickers.[107] The PP again nominated Otto Pérez Molina, former general and director of army intelligence. Pérez Molina, the early leader in polls, campaigned on the mano dura policies that had failed elsewhere. First Lady Sandra Torres divorced President Alvaro Colom months before the election in hopes of circumventing a constitutional ban against allowing relatives to run for president. The Constitutional Court ultimately disqualified her; it ruled her last-minute divorce was fraudulent and did not lift her ineligibility.[108] The ruling left UNE without a presidential candidate. Pérez Molina's primary challenger then became Manuel Baldizón of the Renewed Democratic Liberation Party (LIDER). A wealthy businessman, Baldizón had served in Congress as a member of PAN before joining UNE in 2006. He and other UNE defectors then formed LIDER in 2008. His running mate was the ex-wife of former president Vinicio Cerezo. Both candidates promised to get tough on crime. Baldizón's style and rhetoric took the more populist tone, emphasizing social programs, suggesting public executions, and even promising to get Guatemala's soccer team to the World Cup.

Pérez Molina failed to win a majority in the first round of voting, winning 36 percent to Baldizón's 23 percent. Physicist Dr. Eduardo Suger of Compromiso, Renovación y Orden (CREO) placed third with 16 percent. The Patriotic Party performed very well in the congressional elections, gaining 25 seats more than the 2007 elections (35 percent of total seats). UNE won 48, down three from 2007 (30 percent of total seats). LIDER captured 9 percent of the vote, or 14 seats, as did the National Union of Change (UCN) (see Appendix, Table A.7). Smaller parties divided the remaining 26 seats. Although his military past—including allegations of participation in genocide—troubled some, many Guatemalans perceived Pérez Molina's background in military and intelligence as an asset for combatting crime.[109] He won the November runoff, 53.7 to 46.3 percent. He became the first president with a military background since 1986. His vice president, Roxana Baldetti, became the first woman to occupy that office.

In 2013 former president General Efraín Ríos Montt stood trial before a Guatemalan court on charges of genocide and crimes against humanity in the 1982 Dos Erres massacre, the murder of 1,771 Ixil people, and the rapes of nearly 1,500 women and girls. His intelligence chief, José Mauricio Rodríguez Sánchez, also stood trial.[110] The pretrial hearings and trial were contentious. The defense filed more than 100 legal challenges to delay the proceedings and undermine confidence in the judicial system. Ríos Montt's supporters mounted a sometimes menacing campaign against the trial.[111] On May 10, 2013, Ríos Montt was convicted of genocide and crimes against humanity and sentenced to 80 years in prison. It marked the first time in history a former head of any state had been convicted of genocide in a national court. Ten days later, the Constitutional Court cited procedural errors and partially annulled the verdict, and ordered the original trial to resume at a certain point when Ríos Montt's attorney had been expelled from court. Testimony from the original trial would stand, but closing arguments would now be given before a new tribunal. The trial was pushed back to January 2015, allegedly because the court docket was full.[112] It remained uncertain at this writing whether Ríos Montt's trial would actually resume, because he would be 88 by then. Another uncertainty was whether President Pérez Molina would face trial for crimes he allegedly committed during the war once his immunity from prosecution expired upon leaving office.[113] The Constitutional Court's removal of Attorney General Paz y Paz several months before the end of her official term raised doubts about institutional commitments to justice and human rights. Soon after, the Congress passed a resolution denying that the genocide occurred

The homicide rate declined significantly between 2009 and 2012, from 46 per 100,000 to 34 per 100,000. Though virtually unchanged in 2013, homicides remained well below the rates of neighboring Honduras and El Salvador.[114] Guatemala nevertheless remained the most violent country in the region for women, with the third-highest femicide rate in the world.[115] Murders of women declined 9 percent between 2011 and 2012, but appeared to increase slightly in 2013. Despite improving murder rates, many Guatemalans did not view Pérez Molina positively. Although his May 2013 approval rating was 58 percent, 70 percent viewed his administration as the same or worse than the previous administration.[116] Guatemalans remained concerned about unemployment and the economy. Social programs implemented by his administration, such as *Hambre Cero* (Zero Hunger), accomplished little to reduce food insecurity. More than half of Guatemalans still lived below the poverty line, and chronic malnutrition among children was endemic. Corruption, which plagued previous administrations, remained a serious problem.[117] Concerns grew about infringement of basic rights as repression of journalists and trade unions increased.[118] The use of the military to combat crime, a trend throughout the region, also posed a threat to human rights. In October 2012, seven indigenous people were killed and dozens injured during a protest over an electricity rate hike in Totonicapán. One army colonel and eight soldiers were ordered to stand trial in the massacre.[119]

Indigenous Guatemalans. Mayan indigenous peoples constitute more than half of the population.[120] The nation's history has been profoundly shaped by the minority Ladino population's efforts to dominate the indigenous population and control their labor, movement, and political behavior. More than four-fifths of the dead from the civil war were indigenous, and most of the violence and massacres took place in predominantly indigenous areas. Civil war terror disrupted indigenous communities, and many migrated abroad or to the cities. Their communities and leaders have thus mobilized very cautiously. The Historical Clarification Commission (CEH) viewed the treatment

of Guatemala's Mayan people as so central to the problem of returning Guatemala to peace that it encouraged the government especially to promote their
political participation, incorporate indigenous professionals in the public sector, teach the public tolerance, and provide reparations for the injuries done
during the violence. Voters in 1999, however, rejected several constitutional
reforms required to implement the accords.

How different are the political behavior and attitudes of Guatemala's Ladino and indigenous populations? As in 1995 and 2008 surveys,[121] Guatemala's indigenous citizens in 2012 were significantly poorer and less educated
than Ladinos. In 2012, 80 percent of Guatemala's indigenous people lived in
poverty, and nearly 60 percent of indigenous children suffered from chronic
malnutrition. Poor access to schools in rural communities and too few bilin-
gual instructors posed impediments to young indigenous Guatemalans, particularly at the primary-school level.[122] The 1995 survey revealed few other
differences between the indigenous and Ladino populations. By 2012, however, the picture had changed considerably. Indigenous persons still remained
badly underrepresented in public offices (only ten won seats in Congress in
the 2011 elections, and only one served in Pérez Molina's cabinet).

Surveys in 2012 revealed no significant difference between indigenous and
Ladino Guatemalans on diffuse political system support and agreement that
"one should support the political system." Indigenous Guatemalans expressed
greater confidence that the political system "protects basic rights" and greater
pride in the system. No significant differences appeared in left-right ideological orientation or democratic attitudes. (Survey results from 2004 and 2008
had shown the indigenous supported democratic norms less than did Ladinos,
so this new parity of democratic values is notable.) In political participation,
indigenous respondents reported contacting officials more than did Ladinos,
and resorted much more to civil society activism, but evinced no difference
in voting or party and campaign activism. Overall, this picture suggests that,
despite their economic disadvantages, indigenous Guatemalans have become
more integrated into the system—more supportive of it and as politically active or more so than Ladinos. One difference stands out—despite protesting
less than Ladinos, indigenous people supported confrontation and rebellion
more. Greater willingness to consider confrontation or rebellion is not surprising, given Guatemala's history of victimizing its indigenous people. On balance, the indigenous populace displays considerable social capital and robust
political engagement.[123]

CONCLUSIONS

The year 2014 marked the sixtieth anniversary of the US coup that ended Guatemala's democratic revolution. The ensuing 36-year civil war left some 200,000

dead, and many more missing and displaced. The 1996 peace accords and formal democratization notwithstanding, turmoil of many kinds continued to plague Guatemala, and democratic consolidation remained elusive. Although the creation of the anti-impunity agency CICIG and legislative reforms passed during the Colom administration signaled some positive changes, much remained to be done to stabilize the political system, curtail social violence, and improve the lot of the very numerous poor. Likewise, though important elements of the 1996 peace accords have not yet been implemented, and there seems little likelihood that they ever will be, prosecutions of crimes committed during the civil war give some hope for some measure of justice for Guatemalans. Little has been done to address the rights of Guatemala's indigenous population, and marginalization and systemic racism persist. The indigenous community, however, is politically more active and organized than Ladinos.

Just as the Guatemalan legal system was reckoning with the country's past of rampant official abuses, voters were embracing politicians who promised to get tough on crime. The election of Otto Pérez Molina in 2011 revealed an electorate more concerned about rising crime than past abuses. Although there was some notable success in reducing Guatemala's homicide rate by 2012, drug traffickers and organized crime networks undermined public security and the economy, and deepened already severe corruption. "Social cleansing" and clandestine security organizations underscored the impunity and corruption that characterized the Guatemalan state. In sum, Guatemala remained a violent society that still had far to travel before winning a meaningful peace.

RECOMMENDED READINGS AND RESOURCES

Adams, Richard N. 1970. *Crucifixion by Power: Essays on Guatemalan National Social Structure, 1944–1966.* Austin: University of Texas Press.

Anderson, Thomas P. 1982. *Politics in Central America: Guatemala, El Salvador, Honduras, and Nicaragua.* New York: Praeger.

Burrell, Jennifer. 2013. *Maya After War: Conflict, Power and Politics in Guatemala.* Austin: University of Texas Press.

Carliner, David, Joseph Eldridge, Margaret Roggensack, and Bonnie Teneriello. 1988. *Political Transition and the Rule of Law in Guatemala.* Washington, DC: International Human Rights Law Group, Washington Office on Latin America.

Chase-Dunn, Christopher, Susanne Jonas, and Nelson Amaro. 2001. *Globalization on the Ground: Postbellum Guatemalan Democracy and Development.* Lanham, MD: Rowman and Littlefield.

Garrard-Burnett, Virginia. 2011. *Terror in the Land of the Holy Spirit: Guatemala Under General Efraín Ríos Montt, 1982–1983.* New York: Oxford University Press.

Gleijeses, Piero. 1991. *Shattered Hope: The Guatemalan Revolution and the United States, 1944–1954.* Princeton, NJ: Princeton University Press.

Goldman, Francisco. 2007. *The Art of Political Murder.* New York: Grove Press.

González, Pablo. 2013. "Guatemala." In Diego Sánchez-Ancochea and Salvador Martí i Puig, eds. *Handbook of Central American Governance.* London: Routledge.

Grandin, Greg. 2000. *The Blood of Guatemala: A History of Race and Nation.* Durham, NC: Duke University Press.

Historical Clarification Commission. 1999. *Guatemala: Memory of Silence.* Guatemala City; http://shr.aaas.org/guatemala/ceh/report/english/toc.html.

Immerman, Richard H. 1982. *The CIA in Guatemala: The Foreign Policy of Intervention.* Austin: University of Texas Press.

Jonas, Susanne. 1991. *The Battle for Guatemala: Rebels, Death Squads, and US Power.* Boulder, CO: Westview Press.

———. 2000. *Of Centaurs and Doves: Guatemala's Peace Process.* Boulder, CO: Westview Press.

Little, Walter E., and Timothy J. Smith, eds. 2009. *Mayas in Postwar Guatemala: Harvest of Violence Revisited.* Tuscaloosa: University of Alabama Press.

McAllister, Carlota, and Diane Nelson, eds. 2013. *War by Other Means: Aftermath in Post-Genocide Guatemala.* Durham, NC: Duke University Press.

Menchú, Rigoberta. 1984. *I, Rigoberta Menchú: An Indian Woman in Guatemala.* London: Verso.

Nelson, Diane M. 2009. *Reckoning: The Ends of War in Guatemala.* Durham, NC: Duke University Press.

Sanford, Victoria. 2003. *Buried Secrets: Truth and Human Rights in Guatemala.* New York: Palgrave Macmillan.

Schirmer, Jennifer. 1999. *The Guatemalan Military Project: A Violence Called Democracy.* Philadelphia: University of Pennsylvania Press.

Schlesinger, Stephen, and Stephen Kinzer. 2005. *Bitter Fruit: The Story of the American Coup in Guatemala.* Cambridge, MA: David Rockefeller Center for Latin American Studies.

Short, Nicola. 2007. *The International Politics of Post-Conflict Reconstruction in Guatemala.* New York: Palgrave Macmillan.

Stanley, William. 2013. *Enabling Peace in Guatemala: The Story of MINUGUA.* Boulder, CO: Lynne Rienner Publishers.

Stoll, David. 1999. *Rigoberta Menchú and the Story of All Poor Guatemalans.* Boulder, CO: Westview Press.

Weld, Kristen. 2014. *Paper Cadavers: The Archives of Dictatorship in Guatemala.* Durham, NC: Duke University Press.

Notes

1. George Black et al., *Garrison Guatemala* (New York: Monthly Review Press, 1984), p. 13.

2. Jerry L. Weaver, "Guatemala: The Politics of a Frustrated Revolution," in Howard J. Wiarda and Harvey F. Kline, eds., *Latin American Politics and Develop-*

ment (Boston: Houghton Mifflin, 1979), p. 337; Piero Gleijeses, *Shattered Hope: The Guatemalan Revolution and the United States, 1944–1954* (Princeton, NJ: Princeton University Press, 1991).

3. Richard H. Immerman, *The CIA in Guatemala: The Foreign Policy of Intervention* (Austin: University of Texas Press, 1982), Ch. 2–7; see also Gleijeses, *Shattered Hope*.

4. Richard Newbold Adams, *Crucifixion by Power: Essays on Guatemalan National Social Structure, 1944–1966* (Austin: University of Texas Press, 1970), p. 195.

5. See John Sloan, "The Electoral Game in Guatemala," Ph.D. dissertation, University of Texas at Austin, 1968.

6. See Appendix, Tables A.1 and A.2, in John A. Booth and Thomas W. Walker, *Understanding Central America*, 3rd ed. (Boulder, CO: Westview Press, 1999).

7. Ibid., Appendix, Tables A.5 and A.6.

8. Inforpress Centroamericana, *Guatemala: Elections 1985* (Guatemala City: n.p., 1985), p. 19.

9. Booth and Walker, *Understanding Central America*, 3rd ed., Appendix, Table A.8.

10. Ibid.; Thomas P. Anderson, *Politics in Central America: Guatemala, El Salvador, Honduras, and Nicaragua* (New York: Praeger, 1982), pp. 19–62; "Guatemala," *Mesoamérica*, May 1982; Consejo Superior Universitaria Centroamericana (CSUCA), *Estructura agrária, dinámica de población, y desarrollo capitalista en Centroamérica* (San José, Costa Rica: Editorial Universitaria Centroamericana, 1978), pp. 77–132; Technical Commission of the Great National Dialogue, *Economic and Social Policy Recommendations to the Head of State* (Guatemala City: Technical Commission of the Great National Dialogue, 1985); Lars Schoultz, "Guatemala: Social Change and Political Conflict," in Martin Diskin, ed., *Trouble in Our Backyard* (New York: Pantheon, 1983), pp. 178–183; Brockett, *Land, Power, and Poverty*, pp. 99–123; and Susanne Jonas, *The Battle for Guatemala: Rebels, Death Squads, and US Power* (Boulder, CO: Westview Press, 2000), Ch. 5.

11. Julio Castellano Cambranes, "Origins of the Crisis of the Established Order in Guatemala," in Steve C. Ropp and James A. Morris, eds., *Central America: Crisis and Adaptation* (Albuquerque: University of New Mexico Press, 1984).

12. Mitchell A. Seligson et al., *Land and Labor in Guatemala: An Assessment* (Washington, DC: Agency for International Development, Development Associates, 1982), pp. 1–18.

13. Black et al., *Garrison Guatemala*, pp. 34–37; Schoultz, "Guatemala," p. 181; Seligson et al., *Land and Labor*.

14. Gustavo A. Noyola, "Integración centroamericana y absorción de mano de obra: Guatemala," in Daniel Camacho, Mario A. de Franco, and Carlos F. Chamorro, *El fracaso social del la integración centroamericana: Capital, tecnología, empleo* (San José, Costa Rica: Educa, 1979).

15. Adams, *Crucifixion by Power*; Black et al., *Garrison Guatemala*, pp. 48–51.

16. John A. Booth, "A Guatemalan Nightmare: Levels of Political Violence, 1966–1972," *Journal of Interamerican Studies and World Affairs* 22 (May 1980), pp. 195–225.

17. Gabriel Aguilera Peralta, et al., *Dialéctica del terror en Guatemala* (San José, Costa Rica: Editorial Universitaria Centroamericana, 1981); Americas Watch, *Human Rights in Guatemala: No Neutrals Allowed* (New York, 1982), and *Little Hope: Human Rights in Guatemala, January 1984–1985* (New York, 1985); John A. Booth et al., *The 1985 Guatemalan Elections: Will the Military Relinquish Power?* (Washington, DC: International Human Rights Law Group, Washington Office on Latin America, 1985); see also Gordon L. Bowen, "The Origins and Development of State Terrorism," in Donald E. Schulz and Douglas H. Graham, eds., *Revolution and Counterrevolution in Central America and the Caribbean* (Boulder, CO: Westview Press, 1984); and "Guatemala," *Mesoamérica,* July–August 1982, pp. 2–4; Jonas, *The Battle for Guatemala,* Ch. 5–7; Brockett, *Land, Power, and Poverty,* pp. 112–119; Black et al., *Garrison Guatemala,* pp. 61–107; Anderson, *Politics,* pp. 19–60; Inforpress Centroamericana, *Guatemala: Elections 1985,* pp. 8–11; Jonathan Fried et al., *Guatemala in Rebellion: Unfinished History* (New York: Grove, 1983), pp. 151–316.

18. Héctor Rosado Granados, *Guatemala 1984: Elecciones para Asamblea Nacional Constituyente* (San José, Costa Rica: Instituto Centroamericano de Derechos Humanos-Centro de Asesoría y Promoción Electoral, 1985), p. 41; "Guatemala," *Mesoamérica,* March 1982, pp. 2–4; Margaret E. Roggensack and John A. Booth, *Report of the International Human Rights Law Group and the Washington Office on Latin America Advance Election Observer Mission to Guatemala* (Washington, DC: International Human Rights Law Group–Washington Office on Latin America, 1985), Appendix B; Robert Trudeau, "Guatemalan Elections: The Illusion of Democracy," paper presented to the National Conference on Guatemala, Washington, DC, June 15, 1984.

19. Data for selected periods drawn from US Embassy–Guatemala reports from 1966 through 1984, reported in Booth, "A Guatemalan Nightmare," and US Department of State, *Country Report on Human Rights Practices* (Washington, DC: US Government Printing Office, February 2, 1981), p. 441; later data came from Inforpress Centroamericana, *Central America Report,* February 1, 1985, p. 31; November 22, 1985, p. 357; and January 21, 1988, p. 12.

20. For 1982 and after, see US Embassy–Guatemala, "A Statistical Comparison of Violence (1982–1985)," Guatemala City, xerox, 1985. Recent investigations have confirmed the extent of the violence; see for instance, Francisco Mauricio Martínez, "Guatemala, Never More: 55,000 Human Rights Violations," and "URNG Committed 44 Massacres," both from *La Prensa Libre* (Guatemala City), April 14, 1998, translated into English in *Human Rights News Clips,* Foundation for Human Rights in Guatemala, http://www._fhrg.org/042098.htm//G, accessed July 13, 1998, pp. 1–3.

21. Lars Schoultz, "Guatemala: Social Change and Political Conflict," in Diskin, ed., *Trouble in Our Backyard,* pp. 188–189.

22. Historical Clarification Commission (CEH), *Guatemala: Memory of Silence* (Guatemala City, 1999), Ch. 1, section 27.

23. Quoted by Allan Nairn in "Guatemala Can't Take 2 Roads," *New York Times*, July 20, 1982, p. 23A. Material on the reformist military regime drawn in part from US Department of State, *Background Notes: Guatemala*, Bureau of Inter-American Affairs, March 1998, http://www.state.gov/www/background_notes /guatemala_0398_bgn.html, pp. 3–4.

24. Booth's conversation with US Embassy personnel, Guatemala City, September 1985; see also Roggensack and Booth, *Report*.

25. Material based on Booth's field observations in Guatemala in 1985 and on Americas Watch, *Human Rights in Guatemala* and *Little Hope*; Booth et al., *The 1985 Guatemalan Elections*; Inforpress Centroamericana, *Guatemala: Elections 1985*; British Parliamentary Human Rights Group, "Bitter and Cruel . . . ": Report of a Mission to Guatemala by the British Parliamentary Human Rights Group (London: House of Commons, 1985); and Black et al., *Garrison Guatemala*, pp. 61–113. Much of the volume (55,000 deaths) and responsibility (80 percent military, 20 percent URNG) for human rights abuses in this period alleged in early reports has been confirmed and fleshed out in a preliminary report to a national truth commission compiled by the human rights office of the Archdiocese of Guatemala; see Martínez, "Guatemala, Never More," and "URNG Committed."

26. William I. Robinson, *Transnational Conflicts: Central America, Social Change, and Globalization* (London: Verso, 2003), pp. 106–108.

27. Black et al., *Garrison Guatemala*, pp. 107–109.

28. Interviews with Guatemalan labor sources, September–October 1985 and April–May 1987, Guatemala City; see Booth et al., *The 1985 Guatemalan Elections*, pp. 39–40, and David Carliner et al., *Political Transition and the Rule of Law in Guatemala* (Washington, DC: International Human Rights Law Group, Washington Office on Latin America, January 1988), pp. 7–8. For confirmation see also Jonas, *The Battle for Guatemala*.

29. Booth et al., *The 1985 Guatemalan Elections*.

30. Interviews with spokesmen for various parties, September–October 1985, Guatemala.

31. Robinson, *Transnational Conflicts*, quote, pp. 111–112, and see pp. 110–113.

32. See Latin American Studies Association (LASA), *Extraordinary Opportunities . . . and New Risks: Final Report of the LASA Commission on Compliance with the Central America Peace Accord* (Pittsburgh, PA: LASA, 1988), pp. 15–20; Booth's interviews with various Guatemalan political figures and expert observers, September 1988; "Año de tumulto en Guatemala," *Excelsior* (Mexico City), December 30, 1988, p. 4A; *Christian Science Monitor*, February 14, 1989, p. 3.

33. US Department of State, *Background Notes: Guatemala*, Bureau of Inter-American Affairs, March 1998. http://www.state.gov/www/backqround_notes/guatemala_0398 _bgn.html. *Amparo* and *habeas corpus* are court orders for the government to cease violating constitutional rights, helpful in protecting citizens from wrongful detention and other abuses of power.

34. Killed were US citizens Diana Ortiz, a nun, and businessman Michael Devine, and Salvadoran Social Democratic Party leader Héctor Oqueli. On counterinsurgency and indigenous, see Washington Office on Latin America, *Who Pays the Price? The Cost of War in the Guatemalan Highlands* (Washington, DC, April 1988). See also Carliner et al., *Political Transition;* LASA, *Extraordinary Opportunities . . . and New Risks*, pp. 15–20; "Guatemala," *Mesoamérica*, April 1990, pp. 4–5; "Guatemala," *Mesoamérica*, May 1990, p. 6; "Guatemala," *Mesoamérica*, June 1990, pp. 4–5; "Guatemala," *Mesoamérica*, July 1990, p. 2; "Guatemala," *Mesoamérica*, August 1990, pp. 5–6; "Guatemala," *Mesoamérica*, October 1990, pp. 2–3; "Guatemala," *Mesoamérica*, November 1990, pp. 2–3; "Guatemala," *Mesoamérica*, January 1991, pp. 1–2; "Four Guatemalan Troops Charged in Killings," *Boston Globe,* September 30, 1990, pp. 1–2; and "Amnesty International Reports Guatemalan Police and Private Sector Forces Torture and Murder Street Children," *Excelsior* (Mexico City), November 10, 1990, p. 2A.

35. Robinson, *Transnational Conflicts*, p. 112.

36. Ibid., p. 113; "Guatemala," *Mesoamérica,* April 1991, pp. 3–4; "Guatemala," *Mesoamérica,* May 1991, pp. 10–11; "Guatemala," *Mesoamérica*, June 1991, pp. 4–5; "Guatemala," *Mesoamérica,* August 1991, pp. 11–12; "Guatemala," *Mesoamérica,* September 1991, pp. 1–2; Katherine Ellison, "Celebrity of Guatemalan Rights Activists Could Save His Life," *Miami Herald*, November 22, 1990, p. 20B; "Guatemalan Troops Said to Kill 11 Protesting Raid," *New York Times*, December 3, 1990, p. 8A; "Government Accuses Death Squads of Wave of Killings, Denies Connections to Armed Forces," *Excelsior,* August 5, 1991, p. 2A; Haroldo Shetemul, "National Blackout in Guatemala: Police Chief Assassinated," *Excelsior*, August 6, 1991, p. 2A; "Attacks on Journalists Condemned by President Serrano Elias," *Excelsior*, September 1, 1991, p. 2A.

37. Susanne Jonas, "Electoral Problems and the Democratic Prospect in Guatemala," and John A. Booth, "Introduction: Elections and Democracy in Central America: A Framework for Analysis," both in Mitchell A. Seligson and John A. Booth, eds., *Elections and Democracy in Central America, Revisited* (Chapel Hill: University of North Carolina Press, 1995), pp. 35–36, p. 1.

38. Susanne Jonas, "The Democratization of Guatemala through the Peace Process," in Christopher Chase-Dunn, Susanne Jonas, and Nelson Amaro, eds., *Globalization on the Ground: Postbellum Guatemalan Democracy and Development* (Lanham, MD: Rowman and Littlefield, 2001); and US Department of State, *Background Notes: Guatemala*, pp. 4–5.

39. This section is drawn mainly from Susanne Jonas, *Of Centaurs and Doves: Guatemala's Peace Process* (Boulder, CO: Westview Press, 2000), and Jonas' "The Democratization of Guatemala."

40. The indigenous rights accord, a landmark in this country profoundly marked by anti-indigenous racism, stated that Guatemala is a multiethnic, multicultural, and multilingual society and provided for education reform and indigenous representation in governmental structures; see Kay B. Warren, "Pan-Mayanism and Multiculturalism

in Guatemala," a paper presented at the Symposium on Development and Democratization in Guatemala: Proactive Responses to Globalization, Universidad del Valle, Guatemala City, March 18, 1998, pp. 1–5.

41. Ibid., pp. 4–5; and US Department of State, *Guatemala: Background Notes,* p. 5; "Mayans Win Local Representation," *Cerigua* (Peace Net), *Weekly Briefs,* No. 3, January 18, 1996; Tim Johnson, "Maya Mayor Triumphs over Entrenched Racism," *Miami Herald,* January 15, 1996, p. 1A; Robinson, *Transnational Conflicts,* p. 112.

42. "FDNG Activists Assassinated," *Cerigua* (Peace Net) *Weekly Briefs,* No. 2, January 11, 1996; "Human Rights Violations Continue to Rise," *Cerigua* (Peace Net) *Weekly Briefs,* No. 5, February 1, 1996; Michael Riley, "Refugees Outside Looking In," *Christian Science Monitor,* January 10, 1996, p. 5; Larry Rohter, "Specter in Guatemala: Iron-Fisted General Looms Large Again," *New York Times,* January 10, 1996, p. 4A; "Arzú Greeted by Strikes and Protests," *Central America Report* (Guatemala City), January 19, 1996, p. 3.

43. Jonas, *Of Centaurs and Doves*; US Department of State, *Background Notes: Guatemala,* pp. 10–11; J. Mark Ruhl, "Curbing Central America's Militaries," *Journal of Democracy* 15, No. 3 (July 2004).

44. See Chapter 1, Table 1.1, and Chapter 2, Table 2.2. See also US Department of State, *Background Notes: Guatemala*, pp. 5–8; Jonas, *Of Centaurs and Doves*; "Uncertain Future: Social Watch Evaluates Guatemala," *Cerigua Weekly Briefs,* June 4, 1998; "President Accused of 'Killing the Media,'" *Central America Report,* March 26, 1998, p. 1; Celina Zubieta, "Victims of Death Squads or Gang Warfare?" InterPress Service (Peace Net), March 31, 1998; Mike Lanchin, "Death Squad Claims Responsibility for Bishop's Death," *National Catholic Reporter,* May 22, 1998, p. 2; Francisco Mauricio Martínez, "Progress Towards Peace Evaluated," *La Prensa Libre,* www.prensalibre.com, December 28, 1998.

45. "CEH Pressured to Denounce Genocide," *Central America Report,* May 21, 1998, p. 5; Lanchin, "Death Squad Claims," p. 12.

46. The three military officers received sentences of thirty years, and Father Orantes, who had been Gerardi's cook, received a twenty-year sentence for assisting in the crime.

47. Another closely watched trial was that of Colonel Juan Valencia Osorio for the murder of anthropologist Myrna Mack in 1990. Convicted by a trial court in 2002, his conviction was also overturned by the Fourth Appeals Court. In January 2004 the Guatemalan Supreme Court reinstated the conviction and sentence, making his the first conviction of a high-ranking officer for human rights abuses.

48. CEH, *Guatemala,* Ch. 2, section 82.

49. See Victoria Sanford, *Buried Secrets: Truth and Human Rights in Guatemala* (New York: Palgrave Macmillan, 2003), for a complete discussion of this issue.

50. CEH, *Guatemala,* Ch. 2, section 86.

51. Ibid. Ch. 1, section 13.

52. Charles Babington, "Clinton: Support for Guatemala Was Wrong," *Washington Post,* March 11, 1999.

53. The PAN won thirty-seven seats.

54. The Berger administration planned to continue the policy of payments to ex-PAC members, but the payments were deemed unconstitutional by the Constitutional Court in 2004. The Court ruled that Portillo did not have the power to authorize the payments. See Latin American Database, "PAC Holds Guatemala's Feet to Fire; They Want Their Money," *NotiCen*, July 1, 2004.

55. Ruhl, "Curbing Central America's Militaries," p. 144; see pp. 144–146.

56. In early 2004 Guatemala's Constitutional Court stripped ex-president Portillo and his vice president Francisco Reyes Lopez of their immunity, which they enjoyed as members of the Central American Parliament. Portillo immediately fled to Mexico, whereas Reyes Lopez was arrested months later on corruption charges. See "Accused in Corruption Case, Ex-President Leaves Country," *Miami Herald*, February 20, 2004; "Guatemala Former Vice President Arrested for Graft," Reuters, July 28, 2004.

57. Decertification as a cooperating nation would mean the loss of some US aid.

58. According to the DEA, cocaine seizures fell from 9.2 and 10.05 metric tons in 1998 and 1999 to 1.4, 4.1, and 2.8 metric tons in subsequent years. US Drug Enforcement Administration, *Drug Intelligence Brief, Country Brief: Guatemala*, www.dea.gov/pubs/intel/03002/03002.htm, April 2003.

59. Ibid., p. 5.

60. The paid protesters were apparently bused in from the countryside accompanied by hooded guards. One reporter died of a heart attack while covering the story.

61. URNG candidate Rodrigo Asturias won less than 3 percent of the vote.

62. The remaining eighteen seats were split among six parties.

63. Berger also offered Colom a position in his administration, which Colom rejected.

64. "Guatemalan President Apologizes for Civil War," *U.N. Wire*, February 27, 2004, www.unwire.org/UNWire/20040227/449_13525.asp.

65. Latin American Database, "Guatemala: Government Backs Away from Truth Commission Recommendations," *NotiCen*, April 15, 1999.

66. Frank Jack Daniel, "Guatemala Calls in Troops to Fight Crime Wave," Reuters, July 26, 2004.

67. The 1996 Guatemalan Peace Accords forbid the use of the military for policing duties.

68. Jo Tuckman, "Land Where Women Are Killers' Prey," *The Observer*, June 6, 2004, www.guardian.co.uk/gender/story/0%2C11812%2C1232430%2C00.html; and Marion Lloyd, "Guatemala Activists Seek Justice As Women Die," *Boston Globe*, June 14, 2004, www.boston.com/news/world/latinamerica/articles/2004/06/14/guatemala_activists_seek_justice_as_women_die/?rss_id=Boston.com+/+News.

69. See the United Nations Economic and Social Council, "Integration of the Human Rights of Women and the Gender Perspective: Preliminary Note on the Mission to El Salvador and Guatemala," submitted by Special Rapporteur on Violence Against Women, Yakin Erturk, United Nations document number E/CN.4/2004/66/Add.2.

70. Washington Office on Latin America (WOLA), *The Captive State: Organized Crime and Human Rights in Latin America* (Washington, DC: WOLA, October 2007).

71. Washington Office on Latin America (WOLA), *Transnational Youth Gangs in Central America, Mexico and the United States* (Washington, DC: WOLA, 2007).

72. United Nations Development Program Guatemala, *Informe Estadístico de la Violencia en Guatemala* (Guatemala: Programa de Seguridad Cuidadana y Prevención de la Violencia del PNUD Guatemala, December 2007), http://www.pnud.org.gt/data /publicacion/Informe%20Estad%C3%ADstico%20de%20la%20Violencia%20en %20Guatemala%20final.pdf.

73. James Mckinley Jr., "In Guatemala, Officers' Killings Echo Dirty War," *New York Times*, March 5, 2007; "Congressman's Murder: Rogue Death Squads Run Amok," *Central America Report*, March 9, 2009.

74. WOLA, *The Captive State,* pp. 7–8.

75. Eduardo D'Aubuisson was the son of ARENA founder and death squad leader Roberto D'Aubuisson.

76. "Fiscal guatemalteco acusa a Silva Pereira de asesinato de diputados," *El Faro*, February 23, 2009, http://www.elfaro.net/secciones/Noticias/20090223/noticias4 _20090223.asp.

77. United Nations, *Promotion and Protection of All Human Rights, Civil, Political, Economic, Social and Cultural Rights, Including the Right to Development,* Report of the Special Rapporteur on Extrajudicial, Summary or Arbitrary Executions, Philip Alston, Addendum, Follow-up to Country Recommendations–Guatemala (May 2009), http://www2.ohchr.org/english/bodies/hrcouncil/docs/11session/A. HRC.11.2.Add.7.pdf.

78. The CICIG was actually the second attempt to create an international body to investigate impunity for criminal behavior, especially by public officials. The first such agency had been declared unconstitutional in 2004.

79. International Commission Against Impunity in Guatemala (CICIG), "One Year Later," September 2008, http://huwu.org/Depts/dpa/docs/CICIG1reportEn.pdf.

80. A record of CICIG's convictions is available at http://www.cicig.org/uploads /documents/2013/SENT-20131018–01-EN.pdf.

81. Bob Van Voris and Patricia Hurtado, "Ex-Guatemala President Portillo Enters Not Guilty Plea," Bloomberg News, May 28, 2013, http://www.bloomberg.com /news/2013–05–28/ex-guatemalan-president-portillo-enters-not-guilty-plea.html.

82. Latin American Database, "Hardly a Dent in Guatemalan Poverty," *NotiCen,* October 4, 2007.

83. Unlike their Salvadoran and Nicaraguan neighbors, Guatemalans are not eligible for temporary protected status under US immigration law. This means that they are subject to deportation from the United States if apprehended, making them and the vital income stream they send to Guatemala very vulnerable.

84. World Bank, Migration and Remittances Database, http://search.worldbank .org/data?qterm=migration+and+remittances+2013&language=EN&format=; and World

Bank, Annual Remittances Data (updated as of October 2013), http://econ.worldbank
.org/WBSITE/EXTERNAL/EXTDEC/EXTDECPROSPECTS/0,,contentMDK
:22759429~pagePK:64165401~piPK:64165026~theSitePK:476883,00.html
#Remittances, both accessed November 23, 2013.

85. Latin American Database, "Guatemala's Congress Ratifies, and the Masses
Reject, CAFTA," *NotiCen*, March 17, 2005.

86. Xuan-Trang Ho, "Return to the Bad Old Days? Guatemala and CAFTA,"
Counterpunch, March 31, 2005, http://www.counterpunch.org/ho03312005.html,
accessed June 11, 2009.

87. Marc Lacey, "Drug Gangs Use Violence to Sway Guatemala Vote," *New York
Times*, August 4, 2007; Luis Solano, "Political Violence Takes a New Twist," *Central
America Report,* October 19, 2007.

88. Manuel Roig-Franzia, "Choosing a Future from Tainted Pasts," *New York Times*,
November 4, 2007.

89. Robert Lummack, "Growing Bloodshed Rocks Guatemala," *NACLA*, December 15, 2008.

90. "Report Highlights Widespread Societal Violence," *Central America Report,*
March 6, 2009.

91. Ginger Thompson, "Guatemala Bleeds in Vise of Gangs and Vengeance," *New
York Times*, January 1, 2006.

92. Louise Reynolds, "Congress Approves Law Against Femicide," *Central America Report*, April 18, 2008.

93. Accessed at http://www2.ohchr.org/english/bodies/hrcouncil/docs/11session
/A.HRC.11.2.Add.7.pdf.

94. Anne-Marie O'Connor, "The Emerging Secrets of Guatemala's Disappeared,"
Washington Post, April 11, 2009.

95. Anne-Marie O'Connor, "Payments and Apologies for Victims of Guatemala's
Civil War," *Washington Post*, May 6, 2009.

96. Marc Lacey, "Guatemalan Leaders Under Pall in Lawyer's Killing," *New York
Times*, May 22, 2009; "Rosenberg Case Divides Political Spectrum," *Central America
Report,* May 29, 2009.

97. "Killing of Prominent Lawyer: A Plot to Oust Alvaro Colom?" *Central America Report,* May 15, 2009; "The Rosenberg Case: A State Orchestrated Murder or a
Coup Plot?" *Central America Report*, May 22, 2009.

98. David Grann, "A Murder Foretold," *The New Yorker*, April 4, 2011, http://
www.newyorker.com/reporting/2011/04/04/110404fa_fact_grann.

99. Louisa Reynolds, "The Woman Who Reduced Impunity of Guatemala,"
Inter Press Service, November 5, 2013, http://www.ipsnews.net/2013/11/the-woman
-who-reduced-impunity-in-guatemala/.

100. See, for example, BBC News, "Guatemala Dos Erres Massacre Soldier
Given 6,060 Years," March 13, 2012, http://www.bbc.co.uk/news/world-latin-america
-17349774, accessed December 4, 2012.

101. For an analysis of the origins and transformation of organized crime in Guatemala, see Julie Lopez, "Guatemala's Crossroads: The Democratization of Violence and Second Chances," Woodrow Wilson International Center for Scholars, Working Paper Series of Organized Crime in Central America, December 2010. http://www.wilsoncenter.org/sites/default/files/Lopez.Guatemala.pdf.

102. Hannah Stone, "Guatemala Imposes State of Siege in Wake of Massacre," May 17, 2011, http://www.insightcrime.org/news-analysis/guatemala-imposes-state-of-siege-in-wake-of-massacre.

103. James Bargent, "US Report Shows Zetas Corruption of Guatemala's Special Forces," November 8, 2013, http://www.insightcrime.org/news-briefs/us-report-shows-zetas-corruption-of-guatemalas-special-forces.

104. Farina himself was convicted of drug trafficking and money laundering in Nicaragua in 2012 and sentenced to thirty years in prison.

105. Mike Allison, "Most Guatemalans Unhappy with Options in This Weekend's Presidential Election," *Christian Science Monitor*, September 9, 2011.

106. Louisa Reynolds, "Otto Pérez Molina Leads the Polls Ahead of Guatemala's Presidential Election," *NotiCen*, September 1, 2011, https://ladb.unm.edu/noticen/2011/09/01-078289.

107. Chris Arsenault, "Narco Elite vs Oligarchy: Guatemala Votes," *Al Jazeera*, September 11, 2011, http://www.aljazeera.com/indepth/features/2011/09/20119111843 55644496.html.

108. "Registro de Ciudadanos niega inscripción a Torres, por fraude de ley," *Prensa Libre*, June 30, 2011, http://www.prensalibre.com/decision_libre_-_actualidad /RC-niega-inscripcion-Torres-fraude_0_508749142.html.

109. Damien Cave, "Desperate Guatemalans Embrace an 'Iron Fist,'" *New York Times*, September 9, 2011, http://www.nytimes.com/2011/09/10/world/americas /10guatemala.html?pagewanted=1&_r=2&ref=Americas.

110. He was acquitted of all charges.

111. Mike Allison, "Guatemala: Ríos Montt Genocide Trial Ends in Historic Verdict," *Al Jazeera*, May 15, 2013, http://www.aljazeera.com/indepth/opinion/2013 /05/201351591259267287.html.

112. "Guatemala Ríos Montt Genocide Trial to Resume in 2015," *BBC News*, November 6, 2013, http://www.bbc.co.uk/news/world-latin-america-24833642.

113. Mica Rosenberg and Mike McDonald, "New Guatemala Leader Faces Questions About Past," Reuters, November 10, 2011, http://www.reuters.com/article /2011/11/10/us-guatemala-perez-idUSTRE7A93OP20111110.

114. For a discussion of the 2013 increase in homicides, see Eylssa Pachico, "Explaining the Jump in Guatemala's Murder Rate," May 9, 2012, http://www.insightcrime.org/news-analysis/explaining-the-jump-in-guatemala-murder-rate.

115. Geoffery Ramsey, "Guatemala on Course for 10 percent Drop in Femicides," October, 30, 2012, http://www.insightcrime.org/news-briefs/femicides-guatemala -10-drop.

116. "Aprobación de gestión presidencial de Otto Pérez baja 20 por ciento," *El Periodico*, May 23, 2013, http://elperiodico.com.gt/es/20130523/pais/228683/.

117. Louisa Reynolds, "Administration of Guatemalan President Otto Pérez Molina Scores Badly in Recent Poll," *NotiCen*, August 2, 2013.

118. Anna-Claire Bevan, "Guatemala: The Worst Place in the World to Be a Trade Unionist," August 26, 2013, http://www.ticotimes.net/More-news/News-Briefs/Guatemala-The-worst-place-in-the-world-to-be-a-trade-unionist_Monday-August-26–2013.

119. Louisa Reynolds, "Guatemalan Army Colonel, Eight Soldiers Will Stand Trial for Totonicapán Massacre," *NotiCen*, February 14, 2013, https://ladb.unm.edu/noticen/2013/02/14–078895.

120. Estimates for the indigenous population in Guatemala vary. The UNDP estimated that the indigenous population was 66 percent in 2003. See United Nations Development Program, *Human Development Report 2004: Cultural Liberty in Today's Diverse World* (New York: United Nations Development Program, 2004), http://hdr.undp.org/en/media/hdr04_complete.pdf. This conforms to other estimates in the scholarly literature, including Jonas, *Of Centaurs and Doves*. However, other estimates are much lower. One estimate places the total indigenous population at 40 percent. Central Intelligence Agency, "Guatemala: People," *The World Factbook*, https://www.cia.gov/library/publications/the-world-factbook/geos/GT.html, accessed June 19, 2009. We also estimated the current indigenous population based on the Latin American Public Opinion Project Survey of 2008 for Guatemala. When asked to classify themselves by ethnic group, 42 percent of adult Guatemalans identified themselves as indigenous. Chapter 9 contains technical details for the survey and more details on the specific items referred to in this analysis.

121. John A. Booth, "Global Forces and Regime Change: Guatemala in the Central American Context," *Journal of Interamerican Studies and World Affairs* 42, No. 4 (Winter 2000), pp. 59–87, Table 5.

122. "Education System Accused of Racism," *Central America Report*, January 5, 2007.

123. John A. Booth and Patricia Bayer Richard, *Political Culture and Public Opinion in Latin America* (Washington, DC: Congressional Quarterly Press, 2014), Ch. 7.

8

HONDURAS

HONDURAS SUFFERED FROM THE CENTRAL AMERICAN COMMON Market (CACM) growth boom and the political and economic turmoil of the 1980s and 1990s. Governed by the armed forces well into the 1980s, Honduras shared many regime characteristics with pre-insurrection El Salvador, Guatemala, and Nicaragua. Honduras nevertheless mostly escaped the violent upheaval that plagued its authoritarian neighbors. Indeed, Honduras owed its relative stability to a strategy similar to that followed in Costa Rica. The government made policy that somewhat mitigated eroding popular living standards, and either avoided or ameliorated brutal political repression. Meanwhile, external pressures converted the nation's economic policies to harmonize with the neoliberal rules of the international economic game, and groups sympathetic to these pressures rose to prominence in the political system. After nearly three decades of civilian rule, a constitutional crisis and coup d'état derailed Honduras' democratic regime in June 2009. Despite return to civilian rule, the coup continued reverberating for several years.

HISTORICAL BACKGROUND

Honduras is an unusual and paradoxical country. By a geological quirk, its soil lacks the rich volcanic material prevalent throughout the region's other countries. Geographically isolated, with broken terrain and poor transportation facilities, Honduras developed no significant export economy in the nineteenth century and instead relied on subsistence production. Although ordinary Hondurans were poorer than their Nicaraguan, Salvadoran, or Guatemalan counterparts, Honduran history reveals little mass rebellion or guerrilla warfare. Until the 1970s, the country remained comparatively calm. Honduran party and military elites—often under pressure from such foreign actors as the United States—and not the masses, have intermittently roiled Honduran political waters.

Several factors contributed to this relative stability in the face of mass poverty. Honduras never really developed so coherent or privileged an elite class as did Nicaragua, El Salvador, or Guatemala. Of course, there have always been rich Hondurans, but their wealth remained regionally based. Unlike the rest of Central America, coffee became a significant export crop for Honduras only after World War II. Thus it did not drive wealth redistribution or greatly shape social classes there. Foreigners, rather than Hondurans, developed commercial banana production at the turn of the twentieth century. The banana industry developed along the sparsely populated northern coast and displaced few peasants or indigenous communities. Indeed, though generally poor in quality, land was nearly always plentiful. Poor peasants could usually find free or cheap land to farm. Virtually no land shortage developed until the mid-twentieth century, when foreign market demands and urban population growth led wealthier Hondurans to begin concentrating landownership.

These economic developments had other ramifications.[1] First, absent an angry, dispossessed, and exploited rural working class, the army remained weak well into the twentieth century. Second, the banana industry shaped labor relations differently than in neighboring nations. Because banana companies were foreign-owned, Honduran governments were not very keen to suppress banana workers' wages. Indeed, rising wages meant more basic consumption, helping Honduran entrepreneurs. Moreover, because banana production was less labor-intensive than coffee production, companies could pay higher wages without becoming less competitive. Strikes were frequent, but Honduran governments felt less inclined to forcibly suppress workers. Thus banana companies made wage concessions more easily in Honduras than in other countries or other crops. Thus, although labor unions only became legal in 1954, they had freely operated informally for decades. Over the long haul, Honduras developed a larger and politically more potent organized workforce than other Central American countries.

In another contrast with neighboring nations, the Liberal-Conservative debate began later in Honduras. In the nineteenth century, a succession of non-ideological caudillos simply succeeded each other by force. Party development began under President Marco Aurelio Soto (1876–1883). True to the

Liberal practice of the era, he began modernizing, built a service infrastructure and state apparatus, and attracted foreign investors. By the twentieth century the Honduran Liberal Party (Partido Liberal de Honduras, PLH) had consolidated and dominated politics until the 1930s. The conservative National Party (Partido Nacional, PN) was born in 1923, but only captured power when the PLH split in the 1932 election. National Party caudillo Tiburcio Carías Andino was elected in 1932 and held the presidency until 1949—giving Honduras its longest period of political stability.

After Carías retired, Liberal-National conflict intensified. The Liberal Party's electoral strength recovered as the labor movement grew in the early 1950s. PN efforts to deny the Liberals power prompted the army in 1956 to seize power to end the dispute; there followed a year of military rule. When the military relinquished power, PLH candidate Ramón Villeda Morales swept the 1957 election. Villeda's government signed the CACM accords and passed several modernizing social policies, including social security, labor, and agrarian reform laws. Despite such legislative symbols of progress, Honduras remained the poorest country in Central America.

From the mid-twentieth century onward, Honduras' problems and patterns more resembled those elsewhere in Central America. As noted earlier, land hunger intensified during this period. This was partly due to larger landholders appropriating peasant-occupied lands as they sought to take advantage of increased internal and external commodity markets. Another important cause was a sudden rise in population growth rates due to improved public health conditions and practices developed during World War II. Rapidly increasing demand for land in the 1950s and 1960s led to greater tension between classes and to growing peasant mobilization.

Another convergence between Honduras and other countries was the militarization of its political system. With the advent of the Cold War, labor unrest in the banana plantations was labeled "Communist agitation." Seeking to contain "Communism," the United States "concluded several agreements to train and equip the loosely organized armed forces of Honduras. From the early 1950s through 1979 more than 1,000 Honduran personnel received US training."[2] Although during this period there was virtually no guerrilla opposition to the Honduran government, much of the US training emphasized counterinsurgency and "national security." Between 1973 and 1980 US aid (especially military) to Honduras rose sharply compared to earlier periods (Appendix, Table A.3).

The increasing factionalism and conflict within and between the Liberal and National parties left power and leadership vacuums. This and the military's growing strength drew the armed forces deeper into politics. Even though civilian caudillos had run the country for the first half of the twentieth century, after the 1956 coup the armed forces for four decades ruled the nation directly or powerfully influenced civilian rulers from just offstage.

The Honduran military behaved somewhat better, although not well, compared to its counterparts in neighboring states until the 1980s. It served more as an arbiter between other political groups than as an agent of a ruling class. It tolerated labor, peasant, and political party organizations, and allowed Catholic clergy to carry the "social gospel" to the poor and to build grassroots organizations. And especially after the birth of the Alliance for Progress and CACM, there was much talk of basic socioeconomic reforms, some directly promoted by military governments.

In 1963 Air Force colonel Oswaldo López Arellano overthrew Villeda Morales and assumed power in coalition with National Party figures. The regime began to repress labor and peasant activism and to enlarge and strengthen the armed forces. Conservative economic policies, disadvantageous trade relations built into the CACM, and the 1969 war with El Salvador led to growing public unrest as López's presidency ended. The failure of the successor National-Liberal coalition to manage growing national turmoil prompted López Arellano, now a wealthy general, to seize power again. This time, supported by labor, peasant groups, and other progressive elements, he implemented several populist programs, including an agrarian reform.

Military participation in rule changed character in the late 1970s. Embarrassed by a bribery scandal, López in 1975 transferred power to Colonel Juan Alberto Melgar Castro, the first of two military dictators who abandoned López's populist reforms and curtailed civilian participation in national administration. Colonel Policarpio Paz García overthrew Melgar in 1978. Despite the rapid leadership changes, the military continued promoting economic development but de-emphasized social programs. Although the Melgar and Paz regimes largely ignored social justice, they remained relatively respectful of basic human rights and permitted certain civil and political liberties. There were no death squads, no systematized tortures, and no rash of disappearances. The press remained relatively free and boisterously critical of the military governments.

Despite their developmentalist goals, the armed forces proved inept. By the late 1970s corruption scandals, deepening economic difficulties, the fall of the Somoza regime in Nicaragua, and pressures from spurned civilian politicians created powerful incentives for the military to abandon power. Although the Carter administration never severed military assistance to Honduras, it pressured General Paz to relinquish power. Yielding to these pressures, the military in 1980 called elections for a constituent assembly to rewrite the constitution. In November 1981, presidential elections were held.

Liberal Roberto Suazo Córdova won a clear majority and became president in January 1982. The Liberal victory surprised many who believed the armed forces would interfere in favor of its erstwhile PN allies. Colonel Gustavo Alvarez Martínez became head of the armed forces. The Reagan administration put heavy pressure on Honduras to assist US efforts against the Nicaragua's Sandinistas and El Salvador's guerrillas operating in Honduras. A US military spokesman neatly summarized the US appraisal of the situation: "Honduras is the keystone to our policy down there."[3] Suazo and Alvarez accepted US troops on continuous "maneuvers," the construction and expansion of military bases and facilities, and even US training of Salvadoran troops within Honduras. Honduras provided sanctuary and overt cooperation to the Contra army the United States was developing to attack Nicaragua's Sandinista government. Honduras thus became the active ally of the US military strategy for Nicaragua and El Salvador.[4] Wags described the country as an aircraft carrier—the "USS *Honduras*." In exchange, Honduras received hundreds of millions of dollars in US assistance—especially military aid (Appendix, Table A.3).

This US military assistance rapidly expanded the armed forces' size and power. This permitted Alvarez to overshadow and intimidate the civilian president and Congress. Relations with Nicaragua deteriorated. By 1984 Contra forces in Honduras began to rival in number the Honduran military and severely disrupted order along the Nicaraguan border. By 1983 Honduras developed death squads of public security forces and Nicaraguan exile elements. Political disappearances and murders became increasingly commonplace. As repression grew and domestic political tensions rose, several small leftist guerrilla groups appeared and began operations—a novelty in Honduras. Though weak and fragmented, the Honduran guerrilla movement grew in the 1980s. In the next section we will explain why such problems—similar to those in Nicaragua, El Salvador, and Guatemala—did not push Honduras into civil war.

WEATHERING GLOBAL FORCES

The Honduran economy in the late 1970s lagged well behind those of the other four CACM nations, which had industrialized more. Much of its new investment went into agriculture. Honduras' agricultural sector remained the largest in the isthmus; its workforce share only declined from 70 percent to 63 percent of the workforce between 1960 and 1980. Even though the manufacturing workforce more than doubled (from 6 to 13 percent) between 1950 and 1983, the Honduran industrial sector remained the region's smallest.[5]

Despite its lagging development, Honduras did experience sustained overall economic growth of almost 1.5 percent per year of GDP per capita between 1962 and 1971. As a consumer rather than exporter of manufactured consumer goods, Honduras developed trade imbalances with other CACM nations, especially neighboring rival El Salvador. These imbalances and resulting economic difficulties worsened after the 1969 war with El Salvador. Economic growth slowed to only 0.4 percent from 1972 through 1979. Overall, per capita gross domestic product (GDP) in Honduras rose from $1,700 in 1960 to $2,280 by 1980. Thereafter, however, the economy stagnated—per capita GDP in constant dollars even declined slightly to $2,224 in 1990 and to $2,049 in 2000.[6]

Income. Our theory about the onset of rebellion in Central America argues that severe declines in real working-class wages and living conditions play an important role in mobilizing many people into labor, political, and protest organizations and activities.[7] Because many urban and rural wage earners in Central American societies live on earnings that give them little or no margin of safety, a drop in their real earnings (wages corrected for inflation) can have catastrophic effects on their ability to survive. A rapid erosion of life chances can provide a powerful motive to join political or labor groups seeking redress of such problems.

Honduran wage workers lost ground relative to other income earners in the mid-1970s, but then recovered much of their purchasing power by 1978–1979. Wages fluctuated somewhat but experienced no sustained declines like those occurring in Guatemala, El Salvador, and Nicaragua at the same time. Honduran working-class wages fell in 1974 and 1975, recovered in 1976, fell again in 1977, and then rose to above 1973 levels again in 1978 and 1979. Real working-class wages in Honduras declined again in 1981, recovered in 1982, but then declined every year afterward into the early 1990s, sparking considerable labor unrest in the 1990s. In sum, working-class earnings and living standards declined in Honduras during the mid-1970s, but less severely than those in neighboring countries.[8]

Income Distribution. Another way to examine economic class disparity in Honduras involves shifts in the distribution of income among classes. One measure of changing income inequality during the 1970s is the share of national income paid out as employee compensation. A decrease in overall employee compensation would indicate a relative shift of income away from salaried and wage-earning workers and toward investors and entrepreneurs. Between 1970 and 1975, the employee compensation share of Honduran income fluctuated somewhat, but overall tended to increase. Honduran employee compensation improved markedly in the early 1970s.[9] Overall, it appears that wages and salaries in Honduras continued to rise until the early 1980s.

In summary, Honduras during the 1970s and 1980s presented a clear contrast to Nicaragua, El Salvador, and Guatemala in both relative and absolute income trends. Throughout this period, Hondurans' wages fluctuated sharply downward on occasion, but then recovered within a year or two. As shown in Chapters 5, 6, and 7, however, in the other three countries during the same period, real and relative income for working-class citizens suffered sustained and severe declines.

Wealth. Honduras also did not undergo the marked increases in wealth inequality observed in Nicaragua, El Salvador, and Guatemala during the 1970s. Although Honduras was a member of the CACM and experienced the rapid energy-driven consumer price increases of the mid-1970s, data reveal that these factors affected wealth distribution in Honduras (and Costa Rica) less than in the rest of the isthmus.

The least industrialized nation in the CACM, Honduras underwent the least dramatic changes in socioeconomic structure in the first two decades of the Common Market. During the 1970s, Honduras experienced smaller and slower wealth and income inequality increases than in Guatemala, El Salvador, and Nicaragua.[10] As noted above, working-class wages tended to recover from inflation in the late 1970s, and income distribution did not sharply disfavor wage and salary earners. Honduran governments vigorously encouraged export agriculture in the 1960s and 1970s, and colonizable agricultural land continued to be available until the late 1970s. Both factors helped to prevent a rapid growth of rural unemployment. Peasant organization and mobilization during the 1960s and 1970s led the government to undertake an ambitious agrarian reform program.[11] From 1975 to 1979 it distributed some 171,480 hectares to roughly 10 percent of Honduran landless and land-poor campesino families.[12] The reform distributed only about one-fourth of its goal and was criticized as insufficient and co-optative, but nevertheless constituted a major transfer of wealth toward campesinos. After 1980, peasant organizations, facilitated by the 1970s reform legislation, invaded much additional land in what amounted to an informal or quasi-legal redistribution program.[13] Efforts by the government of Rafael Leonidas Callejas to scale back land transfers sharply in 1991 provoked violent clashes between peasants and the government. The government quickly restored the program.

Popular Mobilization. In Honduras,[14] popular mobilization generally increased during the 1960s and 1970s.[15] The already large union movement expanded. The greatest growth came among peasant wage workers and landless peasants organized into land occupation movements by several federations. The Catholic Church promoted some rural mobilization in the 1960s but generally retreated from it in the 1970s. The Liberal Party remained out of power during military rule from 1963 through 1981. The National Party collaborated with the first López Arellano regime in the 1960s but was frozen out afterward. Two new, small, centrist parties developed during the 1970s: the Christian Democratic Party of Honduras (Partido Demócrata Cristiano de Honduras, PDCH) and the Innovation and Unity Party (Partido de Inovación y Unidad, PINU). When elections resumed in 1979, however, neither PINU nor the Christian Democrats had taken much support from the Liberal or National parties.

Private-sector organizations also multiplied and exerted more policy demands upon the state during the 1960s and 1970s. Although its relative underdevelopment had heretofore left Honduras without a unified bourgeoisie or dominant upper-class sector, economic elites became much more active in politics during the 1980s. Robinson argues that, spurred by USAID encouragement and by a decade of heavy US military and diplomatic presence in the country, bourgeois groups linked to the emergent transnational economy formed and began to influence the main national parties and the military. In the process, "clusters came together, penetrated, and largely captured both [Liberal and National] parties by the 1990s, but without the coherence" between business and political organizations in El Salvador or Guatemala.[16]

Several small leftist guerrilla groups appeared in Honduras during the 1970s and early 1980s (see Appendix, Table A.4).[17] In 1960 a pro-Castro splinter from the Honduran Communist Party (Partido Comunista de Honduras, PCH) formed the Morazán Front for the Liberation of Honduras (Frente Morazanista para la Liberación de Honduras, FMLH), a guerrilla group sporadically active in the 1960s and early 1970s. In 1979 the FMLH reappeared. In 1978, the PCH spun off more dissidents, who formed the Popular Movement for Liberation (Movimiento Popular de Liberación, MPL), known as the Chichoneros. The MPL's most spectacular action was taking 80 San Pedro Sula business leaders hostage in 1982. The Lorenzo Zelaya Popular Revolutionary Forces (Fuerzas Populares Revolucionarias "Lorenzo Zelaya," FPR), founded by a pro-Chinese faction of the PCH, appeared in 1981 and conducted various acts of urban political violence. The Revolutionary Party of Central American Workers of Honduras (Partido Revolucionario de Trabajadores Centroamericanos de Honduras, PRTCH), the Honduran branch of a regional revolutionary group, was founded in 1977. In 1983 the guerrilla groups formed the National Directorate of Unity (Dirección Nacional de Unidad, DNU) to coordinate their activities on the revolutionary left. Despite the rise of armed opposition, insurgent violence in Honduras remained low compared to neighboring nations.

One new guerrilla group, the Army of Patriotic Resistance (Ejército de Resistencia Patriótica, ERP-27), appeared in Honduras in 1989. However, reconciliation efforts and a government amnesty program for political prisoners and exiles brought the release of more than 300 persons from jail in 1991. Several exiled guerrilla leaders from four different groups also returned to Honduras from exile, and four Chichoneros abandoned armed struggle and formed a new political party.[18]

Overall, then, the levels of popular and elite mobilization of various sorts increased in Honduras during the 1970s and continued into the 1980s. Indeed, protest and violence against regime policies developed to include incipient guerrilla struggle by various leftist factions.

Government Response to Popular Mobilization. Honduras' military authoritarian regime of the 1960s and 1970s included elements with developmentalist and populist orientations. It revealed less intention to control all aspects of national life than the military regimes of El Salvador and Guatemala. The second military government of General Oswaldo López Arellano (1971–1975) accommodated burgeoning campesino mobilization and developed a populist agrarian reform program. A conservative military faction led by Colonel Juan Alberto Melgar Castro deposed López for the second time in 1975. Labor repression then increased, marked by a massacre of 14 protesters at Los Horcones in 1975. Yet in an astounding departure from what would have happened in neighboring nations, the government then used civilian courts to prosecute, convict, and imprison army officers implicated in the massacre.[19]

Violent regime repression of opponents (illegal detentions, disappearances, and murders) rose significantly in Honduras in the early 1980s, but remained moderate by Central American standards.[20] For instance in 1982, a year when Guatemala and El Salvador each had over 10,000 political disappearances and murders, Honduran human rights activists reported a total of only 40 assassinations and "permanent disappearances."[21] Political parties, unions, peasant leagues, and a free press operated openly and likely helped restrain human rights violations by vigorously denouncing government abuses of authority.[22]

Honduran security forces took numerous measures to curtail armed opposition, including forming rural militias called Civil Defense Committees (Comités de Defensa Civil, CDCs) in several areas, and stepped up counterinsurgency efforts. Right-wing elements, apparently involving some Nicaraguan exiles benefiting from military complicity, began to kidnap, torture, and murder suspected subversives and government critics in the early 1980s. By 1982, "extra-judicial action [had become] standard operating procedure for the Honduran armed forces in dealing with violent opposition. The methods include[d] disappearances, torture, use of clandestine detention centers, and . . . execution of prisoners."[23]

One key aspect of the Honduran case was the process by which the armed forces returned formal power to civilians. Despite the growing strength of the military during the 1960s and 1970s, the Honduran armed forces never controlled the state apparatus so extensively as did the militaries of neighboring countries. Moreover, as the punishment of military officials for the Los Horcones massacre revealed, the Honduran military never fully exempted itself from accountability to the law and constitution.

In a clear indication of how leaders' choices can divert a nation from catastrophe, the military-authoritarian regime headed by then-president General Policarpio Paz García voluntarily undertook political reform rather than choosing the massive repression practiced by the rulers of Honduras' three immediate neighbors. Popular unrest had grown in the mid- and late 1970s, and its repression by the army and military-dominated police, the Public Security Forces (Fuerzas de Seguridad Pública, FUSEP), brought increasing pressure for reforms from the Carter administration. The military government's corruption became an increasing embarrassment, and the military's traditional National Party allies became disaffected from the regime. Finally, developments elsewhere in the isthmus in 1979 troubled the military leadership: Nicaraguan revolutionaries ousted the repressive despot Somoza, destroyed his National Guard, and began a revolution. Popular mobilization and growing violence in El Salvador portended similar problems there.

Rather than risk civil war, revolution, or destruction of the military, General Paz and the senior military officers' council decided to return power to civilians, ushering in a brief reformist military regime. General Paz called an election for a constituent assembly in 1980. The Liberal Party, long mistrusted by the armed forces, captured a near majority of the constituent assembly. With Paz holding the provisional presidency to maintain military ascendancy, the Liberals drafted a new constitution, which set elections for a civilian government for 1981.

Confounding the expectations of many, the armed forces permitted both traditional parties (including the Liberals' social-democratic left) and the two new groups (PINU and the Christian Democrats) to take part in a generally free 1981 election. And again contrary to expectations, the military did not rig the 1981 elections on behalf of its longtime PN allies. Liberal candidate Roberto Suazo Córdova won a clear majority in a clean election, and General Paz relinquished the presidency in early 1982.[24]

So began the civilian transitional democratic regime in Honduras, engineered by the armed forces to prevent civil war and further institutional damage to the military itself. For over a decade the military would remain powerful in the transitional civilian regime, resistant to civilian control and feared by civilian politicians. Military power largely escaped civilian control until the mid-1990s, blocking transition to full formal democracy. Indeed, during the 1980s, the Honduran military's power and resources actually increased despite having relinquished formal power. US military assistance to Honduras during the 1980s ballooned from $3.1 million per year for 1977–1980 to $41.5 million annually for 1981–1984 and eventually hit $57.7 million per year for 1985–1988 (Appendix, Table A.3). The United States provided this military aid (and copious economic assistance) in exchange for the Honduran military's help with US efforts to contain revolutionary movements in neighboring El Salvador and Nicaragua. In trade for effectively ceding control over much of southern Honduras to the Nicaraguan Contras, cooperation with the US-advised Salvadoran armed forces against the FMLN, and a heavy US military presence, the Honduran military waxed rich in US-built bases and

US equipment and training. Human rights abuses by the army and FUSEP increased during the mid-1980s.

The prospects for civilian rule appeared to dim in the early 1980s. US military assistance expanded the power of the armed forces and permitted General Alvarez to overshadow and intimidate the civilian president and Congress.[25] Opposition violence and repression rose under Alvarez's leadership of the military. But in 1984 senior armed forces officers unexpectedly ousted Alvarez from his command for deepening Honduras' role in the US-Nicaragua imbroglio, allowing Salvadoran troops to train in Honduras, and disregarding the military's tradition of corporate decision making.

In another poor augury for democratic prospects, in 1985 President Suazo himself precipitated a constitutional crisis by seeking to retain power. The armed forces, labor movement, and United States applied counter-pressure and blocked Suazo's efforts to amend the constitution.

The military's adherence to constitutional rule helped save the trappings of civilian democracy in 1985, but the civilian transition remained wobbly. The 1986 election brought José Azcona Hoyos, the leading Liberal candidate, to the presidency. Azcona represented a new modernization-oriented agro-industrial and manufacturing faction of the Liberal Party, the Popular Liberal Alliance (Alianza Liberal Popular, ALIPO). During Azcona's term protests grew over Honduran support for the US-backed Contras. Other obstacles to effective civilian rule were the military's power, elites' uneven commitment to democracy, and continued human rights violations by the military and FUSEP. Economic troubles accumulated: expected cutbacks in US assistance, a sharp contraction in GDP per capita (1989–1991), rapid consumer price increases, and declining real wages.[26]

When the Liberals lost a clean election in 1990, President Azcona peacefully passed power to Rafael Callejas of the National Party. Callejas led a reformist faction of urban businessmen and economic technocrats and represented the neoliberal wing of the National Party. The economy had suffered considerable capital flight, but had been buoyed up by heavy US aid. This allowed Honduras to avoid the full neoliberal structural adjustment imposed on the rest of the region. But when the end of the Sandinista revolution in Nicaragua augured reduced US aid to Honduras, pressures mounted to embrace neoliberalism. Callejas agreed in March 1990 to the first of three major structural adjustment programs negotiated with the IMF, USAID, and other international lenders. Two more structural adjustment packages promoting economic austerity, free markets, nontraditional exports, tourism, free-trade zones, and assembly plant manufacturing *(maquiladoras)* followed over two successive administrations.[27]

The peaceful transfer of power from incumbents to a victorious opponent in 1990 was a step toward democracy, but prospects for full transition to a civilian democratic regime remained in question. The Contras left Honduras in 1990 and 1991 following the 1990 Nicaraguan election and peace accord, and afterward anger about them subsided. A 1991 amnesty law allowed members of armed insurgent groups to abandon violent opposition; some eventually rejoined legal politics. This effectively dismantled the tiny revolutionary left. The Callejas administration's embrace of neoliberal reforms attracted new foreign capital and dozens of assembly plants. Callejas' austerity measures and devaluation of the lempira (the Honduran currency), however, spawned hardship, labor unrest, and popular protest. Security forces often harshly repressed such mobilization, but the military and government exercised continuing restraint. In late 1990 the military high command chose a new commander who curtailed and punished abusive military behavior and reconciled with guerrilla, peasant, and labor leaders. Human rights abuses were investigated and some perpetrators punished.[28]

The opposition Liberals won Honduras' 1993 presidential and congressional elections. President Carlos Roberto Reina, a human rights leader, campaigned on a promise to curtail military power and corruption. Again an incumbent government relinquished power to a victorious opponent, another step toward democratic consolidation. However, the military commander, General Luis Discua, immediately showed displeasure with Reina's proposals to end the draft, cut the military budget, and transfer the police agency FUSEP to civilian control. Despite military objections, Reina and Congress passed and ratified the constitutional reform transferring FUSEP to civilian control. In a sad irony, as in El Salvador and Guatemala, the police reform process led to a crime wave. Congress revised the draft law and allowed the military draft to lapse and reduced force levels. Civilians curtailing military power signaled a critical political game rule change and effectively reduced the military's political role. We believe these changes marked 1996 as the year of Honduras' transition to civilian democracy.[29]

Reina's successor, Liberal Carlos Roberto Flores Facussé, took office in January 1998 after yet another clean election. (See Appendix, Tables A.6 and A.7, for data on presidential elections and the distribution of legislative seats.) Despite campaign rhetoric critical of IMF policies, Flores' economic plan proposed to strengthen the neoliberal model through the expansion of the *maquila* industry, increasing tourism, and expansion of the agro-export sector.

The neoliberal reforms exacerbated decades of environmental degradation, including deforestation and soil erosion, as many migrated to the cities seeking work.[30] In October 1998 Hurricane Mitch struck Honduras; it killed 11,000 people and left 2 million homeless.[31] Many victims were migrants who had settled in crowded neighborhoods washed away from the hillsides surrounding Tegucigalpa. The hurricane caused nearly US$4 billion in losses, and devastated the agricultural and shrimping sectors. The World Bank's Heavily Indebted Poor Countries (HIPC) initiative allowed Honduras to suspend payments on its US$4.4 billion debt, which had consumed 46 percent of its annual budget. Creditors canceled US$900 million of Honduras' debt.

This restructuring of Honduras' debt and the extension of additional loans required the Flores administration to pursue structural adjustment policies while pledging to reduce poverty. After selling the airports, political resistance stymied Flores' effort to privatize telecommunications. The IMF froze Honduras' loans and demanded an acceleration of privatization and poverty reduction programs. These requisites contradicted each other because neoliberalism reduced state resources just as poverty and unemployment grew sharply after Hurricane Mitch.

Oddly, the hurricane disaster helped consolidate civilian rule in Honduras. The military responded incompetently to Mitch, undermining its stature. Moreover, the military's power eroded with President Flores' constitutional amendments that subjected the military to direct control of the civilian president for the first time since 1957. Some army officers plotted to overthrow Flores, but the coup never occurred. Flores then demonstrated his authority over a divided military when in 1999 he dismissed its uniformed commander and most of the army's top echelon. It would be more than a decade before the armed forces would again interfere in governance.[32]

Human rights and indigenous organizations denounced the human rights abuses of the 1980s and 1990s with increasing energy. The government began investigating past rights abuses by the military. A civilian judge seized military intelligence and counterintelligence services' files that implicated numerous high-ranking officers. Evidence of serious ongoing human rights problems nevertheless persisted, including renewed activity by death squads and the assassination in February 1998 of Ernesto Sandoval, a leader of the country's principal human rights organization, the Human Rights Committee of Honduras (Comité de Derechos Humanos de Honduras, CODEH).[33]

Two Liberal administrations managed the early transition to democracy but failed to address mounting socioeconomic problems. After controversy regarding his eligibility, the former central bank president, Ricardo Maduro of the National Party, won the 2001 presidential elections. The PN captured only 61 of 128 seats, the first time in two decades the governing party did not control Congress. A later coalition with the Christian Democrats gave the PN legislative edge over the Liberals, with 55 seats. Maduro pledged to crack down on crime and corruption. He acted quickly to reduce government perks by selling off hundreds of government luxury vehicles. Initial attempts failed to limit immunity for crimes and human rights abuses and reduce the number of elected officials.

Crime. Honduras' prolonged crime wave was a major theme of the 2001 elections. In 2000, the murder rates in Tegucigalpa and San Pedro Sula were

51 and 95 per 100,000, respectively, making Honduras one of the most violent countries in the hemisphere.[34] Much of the crime originated with the
gangs that had proliferated over the previous decade. Gang violence hurt business as firms and factories relocated to avoid becoming victim to a rash of
kidnappings of foreign businessmen. It was estimated that nearly 500 gangs
(*maras*) had more than 100,000 members, including the infamous Mara
Salvatrucha and Mara 18. President Maduro, whose son died in a bungled
kidnapping, continued his predecessors' militarization of the police force. Op-
eración Guerra Contra la Delincuencia sent 10,000 officers into the streets
and appointed a military official as the head of security.[35] Maduro's hard line,
including a mandatory twelve-year sentence for gang membership, spawned
retaliation. In December 2004 gang members opened fire on a public bus in
San Pedro Sula. They killed 28 people and left a note at the scene claiming the
act was to protest a possible reimposition of the death penalty.

Another aspect of the crime wave was the extrajudicial killings of Honduran youth, primarily street children presumed to be involved in gang activity. Between 1998 and 2002 more than 1,500 youths were murdered, mostly
young males.[36] Human rights organizations, such as Amnesty International
and Casa Alianza, ascribed some of these deaths to "social cleansing" by state
and private security forces. One United Nations report sharply criticized the
impunity surrounding these murders and cited a failure to investigate and
prosecute the crimes.[37] Mounting criticism of its human rights performance
forced the government to commission its own report, which implicated police
and security forces in a small percentage of the killings. Evidence of social
cleansing by security forces extended into prisons, which held many suspected
gang members incarcerated under *mano dura* ("iron fist") policies. Several
prison massacres, including fires at an El Porvenir prison in May 2003 and at
a prison in San Pedro Sula in 2004, killed more than 100 gang members and
suggested deliberate efforts by authorities to exterminate *mara* inmates.[38]

CONTEMPORARY HONDURAN POLITICS

President Maduro's economic plan intensified social unrest. After contentious
negotiations with the IMF, the technocratic administration pledged to reinvig-
orate the privatization of government-owned firms. Meeting the demands of
the international financial community while simultaneously reducing poverty
and fighting violent crime proved to work at cross-purposes. Maduro tried to
reduce the number of elected officials and other bureaucrats, but resisted a
reduction in public employment. Civil society mobilized increasingly against
privatizing state-owned utilities and government services. In 2003, 25,000
people protested government plans for civil-service reform and the privatization of water systems.[39]

Crime and the economy dominated the 2005 elections. Congress president and National Party candidate Porfirio "Pepe" Lobo Sosa ran on a pro-business, tough-on-crime platform and vowed to reinstate capital punishment. Liberal Party candidate José Manuel Zelaya Rosales also pledged to crack down on crime and double the police force, but also to create gang-rehabilitation programs. His "citizen power" campaign promised decentralization and transparency while emphasizing his "rural roots."[40] Zelaya won by less than 4 percent, the closest margin in Honduran history and with turnout at only 46 percent.[41] The Liberal Party also won 62 of 128 seats in Congress (see Appendix, Tables A.6 and A.7). Because of an electoral reform, Hondurans for the first time voted directly for candidates instead of party lists.

As many as 200 protests marked President Zelaya's first year in office.[42] His relationship with the media was so poor that he mandated that all private television stations broadcast ten two-hour segments on government programs initiated during his administration.[43] This drew comparisons to populist Venezuelan president Hugo Chávez, to whom Zelaya grew increasingly close. Zelaya's policies spanned the ideological spectrum and alienated him from the opposition, social sectors, his own party, the media, and the United States. His seemingly contradictory embrace of neoliberal projects and populist rhetoric led him to support ratification of the US-backed Central American Free Trade Agreement (CAFTA) in 2006, and membership in the Bolivarian Alternative for the Americas (Alianza Bolivariana para las Américas, ALBA) in 2008, which worked to counter US-backed policies.[44] His ties to Venezuela's Chávez and Bolivia's president Evo Morales drew broad criticism and cost him support from within his own Liberal Party. In September 2008, Zelaya delayed the accreditation of the new US ambassador in solidarity with Bolivia's decision to expel its US ambassador.

The Heavily Indebted Poor Countries (HIPC) initiative of the International Monetary Fund relieved Honduras of US$3.7 billion in foreign debt in 2008, much of the benefit coming during the Zelaya administration.[45] Although the economy grew steadily during Zelaya's term, rising inflation undercut the benefits for many.[46] The cost of the basic food basket increased from $213 at the beginning of Zelaya's term to $252 by October 2007, a large increase for the impoverished population.[47] Rising costs led Zelaya to instate a price freeze on basic goods in late 2007, and in 2008 Honduras joined the PetroCaribe Agreement, established by Venezuela in 2005 to supply oil to members at on preferential terms. In December 2008, Zelaya further alienated business elites and his own party by raising the minimum wage 60 percent.

Rising prices reinforced the country's growing dependence on remittances while out-migration rose steeply in the early 2000s. Hurricane Mitch had deepened reliance on the cash Hondurans abroad sent home to their families. In 2000 remittances totaled about $400 million (6 percent of GDP). They rose to

$860 million (12 percent of GDP) by 2003,[48] and to $2.7 billion in 2008 (20 percent of GDP). One report estimated remittances from Hondurans abroad reduced the number of families living in extreme poverty by 20.5 percent.[49]

The government's inability to reduce crime eroded the public's security and public life. In 2006 the homicide rate was 46.2 per 100,000, up slightly from 45.9 in 2004. Ineffective *mano dura* policies were supplemented by short-term joint operations among police, armed forces, and private security forces. This privatization of security, however, brought new rights abuse problems because private security forces were generally unregulated and they greatly outnumbered state police forces.[50] The administration's tactics failed to adjust as gang violence declined while international organized crime increased.[51] By 2009 Honduras' Caribbean coast had become a major transshipment location for drug trafficking, and organized crime infiltrated government itself. One former security minister estimated that 30 percent of police officers had ties to organized crime, and over half of Police Investigative Unit officers belonged to Mexican narcotics cartels.[52] These problems provided the backdrop for the November 2008 presidential primary elections. Once again, the candidates pledged to address poverty and crime. The National Party's Pepe Lobo again secured his party's nomination. The Liberal Party's former vice president Elvin Ernesto Santos Ordóñez defeated the National Congress' president Roberto Micheletti, a fierce opponent of President Zelaya.[53]

The Coup and Its Aftermath. In March 2009 President Zelaya announced his plan for a June 28, 2009, consultative referendum (*encuesta*, essentially a poll) calling for a constituent assembly to rewrite the Honduran constitution He argued that the constitution should reflect changes in Honduran society, and invoked the 2006 Citizen Participation Law to justify the consultation with citizens. If approved in the intended June 28 vote, a later, formal referendum would have been submitted to voters during the 2009 elections on whether to convene a constitutional assembly. Opponents viewed the proposed poll as similar to measures in Venezuela and Bolivia—ultimately intended to extend the president's tenure in office—despite Zelaya's never mentioning presidential term limits.[54] Congress then challenged the constitutionality of the poll. Days before the scheduled vote, Congress passed a law prohibiting referenda within a period of six months prior to an election in an ex post facto effort to block the poll.[55] An administrative court ruled the poll to be illegal and enjoined it. The Supreme Court sustained that ruling and declared the proposed June 28 poll illegal.[56] The head of the Honduran armed forces, General Romeo Vásquez, then refused the military's assistance to conduct the poll, and the Supreme Electoral Tribunal ordered confiscation of all ballot boxes intended for the poll.

Hemmed in by legislation, court rulings, and military and administrative actions, President Zelaya then summarily fired armed forces head General

Vásquez, which the constitution clearly allows (Article 280). The Supreme Court quickly overturned General Vásquez's dismissal and ordered his reinstatement.[57] Zelaya and several hundred supporters then escalated the conflict by retrieving the election materials from the military storage facility where they had been held for the June 28 poll. The Honduran constitution makes no provision for the impeachment and removal of a president, even for illegal or unconstitutional actions. With no orderly constitutional process for adjudicating charges of presidential malfeasance, Honduras was virtually assured a national political crisis should a president act unconstitutionally or illegally, as the Honduran Supreme Court ruled in the case of the poll.

The rapidly developing crisis became a coup d'état on June 28, 2009, when the armed forces exceeded their Supreme Court order to arrest President Zelaya and instead removed him from his residence at gunpoint during the night and flew him to Costa Rica. The expulsion of the president from Honduras manifestly violated the constitution's Article 102 that "no Honduran may be expatriated." Indeed, several mid-ranking military officers later protested Zelaya's expulsion as unconstitutional.[58] The armed forces then compounded its illegalities by presenting the National Congress with a forged letter of resignation purportedly from Zelaya. Congress then embraced the coup by accepting the "resignation" by voice vote and immediately swearing in its presiding officer, Roberto Micheletti, a rival and critic of the deposed leader, as president.

The de facto government suspended civil liberties and initiated a curfew after protesters demanded Zelaya's return and reinstatement. There were also public demonstrations in support of the coup. The international community condemned the coup, and the Organization of American States (OAS) suspended Honduras after the de facto government refused to reinstate President Zelaya. The European Union withheld more than $90 million in aid, and the United States cut $33 million in military and economic assistance. Costa Rican president and Nobel peace laureate Oscar Arias agreed to mediate the conflict in hopes of securing Zelaya's return to office to complete his term. Micheletti and others maintained their action was constitutional, casting it as saving democracy from a would-be demagogue. The de facto government quickly hired Washington lobbyists and public-relations specialists to press its cause with US policy makers and the international media. Though some policy makers proclaimed the crisis ended, negotiations in San Jose, Costa Rica, failed to forge a solution to restore constitutional government.[59] One important outcome of the San Jose Accords, however, was the establishment of a Truth and Reconciliation Commission charged with investigating the coup. Micheletti and his backers in the business elite and government resisted all efforts to reinstate Zelaya for the final months of his term.[60] The period following the coup was characterized by extensive violation of civil liberties, random curfews, and the brutal police suppression of protestors and political opponents. Journalists, human rights workers, and civil society organizations reported harassment and threats; some were killed. The Interamerican Commission on Human Rights found evidence of serious human rights violations and widespread impunity following the coup.[61]

In this environment in November 2009 Hondurans went to the polls to elect their next president from among five candidates.[62] The PN's Porfirio Lobo won with 56.6 percent of the vote. The PL's Elvin Santos Lozano, Zelaya's vice president, won 38 percent, and three minor parties won about 2 percent each. The PN also won the most seats in Congress, 71, followed by the PL with 45. The 12 remaining seats were divided among three small parties. Not surprisingly, voter turnout remained low at 49 percent. Following his inauguration in January 2010, Lobo faced significant challenges: the country was deeply divided, many countries refused to recognize his government, the economy was in dire shape, and criminals had used the power vacuum to escalate their activities.

Venezuelan president Hugo Chávez and Colombian president Juan Manuel Santos sponsored talks in April 2011 in hopes of resolving the crisis. In May, Lobo and Zelaya signed the Cartagena Accords, which allowed Manuel Zelaya to return to Honduras without fear of prosecution and provided recognition of his new National Popular Resistance Front (Frente Nacional de Resistencia Popular, FRNP). The agreement affirmed the right of citizens to modify the constitution through referenda, the chief issue that had precipitated the coup. The OAS readmitted Honduras in June 2011. The following month the Truth and Reconciliation Commission released its report on the coup. It found that the removal of Zelaya from office constituted an illegal coup, and that the interim government under Micheletti was illegal. That said, the commission claimed that Zelaya's push for a referendum was partially to blame for the crisis. Thus, the commission attributed responsibility for the coup to all parties. The commission also blamed the military for at least a dozen deaths in the aftermath of the coup. Despite this, no one has been charged in relation to the coup, and it is unlikely that anyone ever will be. A Supreme Court ruling against the prosecution of six generals charged with exiling Zelaya ended the only attempt at prosecuting the coup makers.

As if Honduras' political crisis were insufficient woe, drug traffickers, organized crime, and transnational gangs increased their activity. The 2011 homicide rate was 92 per 100,000, and although it declined slightly to 86 per 100,000 in 2012 and 83 per 100,000 in 2013, it remained the highest in the world. Most murders were never investigated, nor murderers sent to trial. The Lobo administration approached the growing crime problem by increasingly militarizing Honduras' thoroughly corrupt police forces. President Lobo in May 2012 appointed a controversial new police chief, Juan Carlos

Bonilla, who had allegedly been involved with a police death squad. Bonilla, also known as *El Tigre* (The Tiger), initiated a widespread purge of the notoriously corrupt police force shortly after assuming his post.[63] The United States attempted to skirt human rights concerns and maintain assistance by directing police aid to officers below Bonilla. Bonilla, who was removed from the post in December 2013, claimed no officers functioned beyond his control.[64]

In December 2012, the Honduran Congress precipitated a major constitutional crisis by voting to remove four of five Supreme Court justices in response to rulings on recent legislation. The first rejected law, passed in May 2012, was the Special Police Purge Law, which required officers to undergo tests, including a polygraph examination, to establish their suitability for their jobs. The Constitutional division of the Supreme Court rejected the law on several counts, including the absence of an appeal process. An angry President Lobo accused the justices of taking the side of criminals, which provoked a response from the Court emphasizing judicial independence. Days later, Congress removed the four justices. An outcry ensued over the removal, which many characterized as illegal.[65] The justices appealed their firings to a special court, which voted 13–2 not to admit their appeal.[66]

By early 2013, Honduras seemed on the brink of disaster. The budget deficit and foreign debt made it impossible to even pay bills.[67] Teachers were on strike because they had received no pay in months; pay to soldiers and other government workers was sporadic, and even surveillance cameras were shut off.[68] Remittances, which declined after the 2009 coup, had yet to return to their pre-coup levels, thus further hamstringing the economy. With a compliant Supreme Court, Congress passed several new laws, including an amended police "purification" law and another establishing Employment and Economic Development Zones (Zonas de Empleo y Desarrollo Económico, ZEDE), commonly referred to as the Model Cities law that had also been struck down by the previous Court.[69] Congress further enacted a law empowering itself to remove any elected official and to bar citizens from challenging the constitutionality of laws.[70] Overwhelmed by crime and stymied by the slow pace of police purges, the Honduran government increasingly relied on the military to address the country's devastating security problem.[71] In 2013, Congress authorized the creation of a new security organization, the Military Police of Public Order (PMOP) and combined the ministries of defense and security. This action raised concerns about the continued militarization of Honduran society.[72]

Hondurans returned to the polls in 2013 to elect a new government. The campaign season was contentious—new political forces appeared and campaign violence flared. One effect of the 2009 coup was a proliferation of political parties and a split among the Liberals. Eight parties competed, including the traditionally dominant National and Liberal parties. Juan Orlando Hernández, the president of Congress, won a hotly contested party primary to become the National Party nominee. The Liberals selected Mauricio Villeda, son of former president Ramón Villeda Morales (1957–1963). Two new parties broadened the field. Vying for disgruntled Liberals' votes was former president Manuel Zelaya's new party, the Liberty and Refoundation Party (Partido Libertad y Refundación, LIBRE). Xiomara Castro, Zelaya's wife, was its presidential candidate. The Anti-Corruption Party (PAC), selected sportscaster Salvador Nasralla as its candidate. Security and corruption were the predominant issues of the campaign. Hernández emphasized his support for the role of the military in fighting crime. Castro campaigned on the need for a constituent assembly to rewrite the constitution, the issue that caused her husband's ouster. Indeed, the 2009 coup was never far from the campaign trail, as Zelaya was a routine presence in Castro's campaign. The murders of numerous party activists and candidates provided a grim reminder of the country's not-so-distant past. Most victims came from LIBRE, including two killed the morning of the election.

Although the elections were deemed relatively "free and fair" by the European Union and OAS election observer missions, other observers reported harassment by immigration officials and difficulty entering polling stations.[73] The military's presence throughout the country was notable. At one point the military surrounded the station of Radio Globo, which had come under attack during the post-coup environment. Election observers noted a wide variety of irregularities throughout the day, ranging from problems with voter lists, to vote buying, to errors in the transmissions of vote counts from the tables to the Supreme Electoral Tribunal's (TSE) offices. Equally troubling was the rush to declare a winner and pronounce the elections clean. Both Hernández and Castro, the frontrunners going into election day, proclaimed victory with only a quarter of the vote counted. Premature calls of congratulation from world leaders came in for Hernández, including from Nicaragua's President Ortega, days before official results were announced. The TSE was slow to announce official results, which exacerbated suspicions and accelerated denunciations of fraud. Castro and the LIBRE party officially contested the results and, after a failed recount effort, demanded that the elections be annulled.[74]

Official results gave the National Party's Hernández 36.8 percent, followed by LIBRE's Castro with 28.8 percent. Villeda (PLH) won 20 percent of the vote and Nasralla (PAC) 14 percent. In congressional elections, the PN won 47 seats, followed by LIBRE's 39 and the Liberal Party's 26. The Anticorruption Party captured 13, and PINU, PUD, and Christian Democrats one seat each. Although Castro's claims of fraud garnered the most attention, the election results told another very important story: the long-standing duopoly of the National and Liberal parties had fractured. LIBRE had won enough votes to constitute a "second force" in Honduran politics.[75] With only 38 percent of the deputies in Congress, the National Party and its new president would have to woo the cooperation of at least 18 members of other parties to enact laws. The passage of constitutional reforms would require the PN to secure the collaboration of at least 39 deputies from other parties to reach the required two-thirds majority (86 votes).[76]

CONCLUSIONS

During the 1970s Honduras at least partly ameliorated the growing inequalities affecting working-class victims of rapid economic change while employing only moderate repression. We emphasize that the Honduran armed forces exercised only *comparative* restraint. The Honduran military's 1,000 victims during the 1980s and 1990s paled in comparison to the combined toll of over 300,000 lives taken by the security forces of Somoza's Nicaragua, and military regimes in El Salvador and Guatemala during the 1970s and 1980s. Modest socioeconomic reforms, combined with some restraint in repression and accommodative political reforms, saved Honduras from the abyss of internecine violence that beset three of its neighbors, and enabled the country to maintain relative political stability. The military's transfer of nominal control of executive and legislative power to a constitutional regime in 1981 began a process of political reform that eventually led to electoral democracy.

As in other Central American nations, Honduras adopted neoliberal economic policies by 2000. This undermined the state-led programs that had been critical to political stability. Neoliberalism thus restricted Honduras' ability to respond to the profound socioeconomic crises plaguing the country. As poverty, inequality, and unemployment increased, more and more Hondurans migrated to the United States to seek work. Their remittances provided a valuable, albeit temporary, infusion of capital into the country. Crime proliferated, breeding insecurity in an already vulnerable population. The "iron fist" policies of two administrations failed to reduce crime, in part because they misunderstood the changing nature of crime in the country. The street-gang threat was increasingly displaced by organized crime related to drug trafficking, which had quickly infiltrated and threatened to undermine Honduras' fragile institutions.

Having avoided civil war, Honduras seemed to progress toward formal democracy for two decades, but the progress proved temporary. Institutional and economic performance remained poor enough that in 2008 Hondurans reported the lowest satisfaction with their institutions, democracy, and economic performance in Central America. The 2009 coup that toppled Zelaya—the first post–Cold War coup in the region—demonstrated how popular dissatisfaction could embolden elites to take antidemocratic actions. The breakdown of law and order that followed the coup brought more crime, poverty, and inequality. In 2012, as in 2008, Honduras had the lowest average satisfaction with their institutions and the economy and the lowest democratic norms in all of Latin America.[77] At this writing, as much as 70 percent of the Honduran population remained in poverty, nearly 40 percent of those in extreme poverty.

Honduran elite behavior during the constitutional crisis and coup of 2009 and continuing under the Lobo administration reflected weak commitment to democratic norms and constitutional rule. Combined with popular mobilization and support on both sides of the conflict, these attitudes and events made manifest Honduras' failure to consolidate democracy. The outcome of the November 2013 election had left the National Party victorious and the rest of the country bitterly divided. In a presidential contest with eight candidates, it was almost inevitable that the winner would receive well less than half of the vote. But a situation in which more people voted against the president than voted for him was hardly what Honduras needed to move forward. One notable outcome of the elections was the emergence of new political forces to disrupt the long-standing domination of the traditional ruling parties. Some interparty cooperation would now be required to pass legislation. Whether and how Honduran political elites could do that remained to be seen.

Recommended Readings and Resources

Acker, Alison. 1989. *Honduras: The Making of a Banana Republic*. Boston: South End Press.

Anderson, Thomas P. 1982. *Politics in Central America: Guatemala, El Salvador, Honduras, and Nicaragua*. New York: Praeger.

Argueta, Jose R. 2008. *The Dynamics of Electoral Accountability in Two-Party Systems: The Case of Honduras*. Verlag/Jahr: VDM Verlag Dr. Müller.

Benjamin, Medea. 1989. *Don't Be Afraid, Gringo: A Honduran Woman Speaks from the Heart: The Story of Elvia Alvarado*. New York: Harper Perennial.

Euraque, Darío. 1996. *Reinterpreting the Banana Republic: Region and State in Honduras, 1870–1972*. Chapel Hill: University of North Carolina Press.

Morris, James A. 1984a. *Honduras: Caudillo Politics and Military Rulers*. Boulder, CO: Westview Press.

———. 1984b. "Honduras: The Burden of Survival in Central America." In Steve C. Ropp and James A. Morris, eds. *Central America: Crisis and Adaptation*. Albuquerque: University of New Mexico Press.

Nazario, Sonia. 2007. *Enrique's Journey*. New York: Random House.

Reichman, Daniel. 2011. *The Broken Village: Coffee, Migration, and Globalization in Honduras*. Ithaca, NY: Cornell University Press.

Rosenberg, Mark, and Phillip Shephard. 1986. *Honduras Confronts Its Future*. Boulder, CO: Lynne Rienner Publishers.

Rudolph, James D. 1984. *Honduras: A Country Study*. American University Foreign Area Studies series. Washington, DC: US Government Printing Office.

Ruhl, J. Mark. 2004. "Curbing Central America's Militaries." *Journal of Democracy* 15 (3):137–151.

Schulz, Donald E. and Deborah Sundloff Schulz. 1994. *The United States, Honduras, and the Crisis in Central America*. Boulder, CO: Westview Press.

Taylor-Robinson, Michelle M. 2013. "Honduras." In Diego Sánchez-Ancochea and Salvador Martí i Puig, eds. *Handbook of Central American Governance*. London: Routledge.

Tucker, Catherine. 2008. *Changing Forests: Collective Action, Common Property, and Coffee in Honduras*. New York: Springer.

NOTES

1. See James A. Morris, "Honduras: The Burden of Survival in Central America," in Steve C. Ropp and James A. Morris, eds., *Central America: Crisis and Adaptation* (Albuquerque: University of New Mexico Press, 1984), pp. 189–223; James A. Morris, *Honduras: Caudillo Politics and Military Rulers* (Boulder, CO: Westview Press, 1984); and Darío Euraque, *Reinterpreting the Banana Republic: Region and State in Honduras, 1870–1972* (Chapel Hill: University of North Carolina Press, 1996).

2. James A. Morris, "Honduras: A Unique Case," in Howard J. Wiarda and Harvey F. Kline, eds., *Latin American Politics and Development* (Boston: Houghton Mifflin, 1979), p. 349.

3. As quoted in "Commentary: The Region," *Mesoamérica*, September 1982, p. 1.

4. See Eva Gold, "Military Encirclement," in Thomas W. Walker, ed., *Reagan Versus the Sandinistas: The Undeclared War on Nicaragua* (Boulder, CO: Westview Press, 1987), pp. 39–56.

5. Data from John A. Booth and Thomas W. Walker, *Understanding Central America*, 3rd ed. (Boulder, CO: Westview Press, 1993), Appendix, Tables A.1 and A.2.

6. Alan Heston, Robert Summers, and Bettina Aten, *Penn World Table Version 6.1*, Center for International Comparisons at the University of Pennsylvania (CICUP), October 2002.

7. This theory is explained in detail in Chapter 2 of this volume.

8. Booth and Walker, *Understanding Central America*, 3rd ed., Appendix, Table A.6; see also Victor Bulmer-Thomas, *The Political Economy of Central America Since 1920* (New York: Cambridge University Press, 1987), Table 10.7, p. 219.

9. Booth and Walker, *Understanding Central America*, 3rd ed., Appendix, Table A.7.

10. Thomas P. Anderson, *Politics in Central America: Guatemala, El Salvador, Honduras, and Nicaragua* (New York: Praeger, 1982), pp. 109–147.

11. Discussion of Honduras drawn from Victor Meza, *Honduras: La evolución de la crisis* (Tegucigalpa: Editorial Universitaria, 1980); Victor Meza, *Historia del movimiento obrero hondureño* (Tegucigalpa: Editorial Guaymuras, 1980), pp. 123–167;

Anderson, *Politics*, pp. 109–121; Mario Posas, *El movimiento hondureño* (Tegucigalpa, Honduras: Editorial Guaymuras, 1981); James A. Morris, "Government and Politics," in James D. Rudolph, ed., *Honduras: A Country Study*, American University Foreign Area Studies series (Washington, DC: US Government Printing Office, 1984), pp. 168–193; Rosa María Pochet Coronado, "El reformismo estatal y la iglesia en Honduras 1949–1982," *Estudios Sociales Centroamericanos* 33 (September–December 1982), pp. 155–188; and J. Mark Ruhl, "Agrarian Structure and Political Stability in Honduras," *Journal of Interamerican Studies and World Affairs* 26 (February 1984), pp. 33–68.

12. Castillo Rivas, "Modelos," pp. 199–201; Posas, *El movimiento campesino hondureño*, pp. 34–42.

13. Author Booth's conversation with Lucas Aguilera, member of the executive committee of the Union Nacional Campesina, Tegucigalpa, and members of the Unión Maraíta cooperative farm, Departamento Francisco Morazán, August 21, 1985.

14. Discussion of Honduras based on Meza, *Historia del movimiento obrero hondureño*, pp. 123–167, and Meza, *Honduras: La evolución*, pp. 14–41; Anderson, *Politics*, pp. 109–121; Posas, *El movimiento campesino*.

15. Morris, "Government and Politics," in Rudolph, ed., *Honduras: A Country Study*, pp. 168–193; Rosa María Pochet Coronado, "El reformismo estatal y la iglesia en Honduras 1949–1982," *Estudios Sociales Centroamericanos* 33 (September–December 1982), pp. 155–188.

16. William I. Robinson, *Transnational Conflicts: Central America, Social Change, and Globalization* (London: Verso, 2003), p. 128.

17. Steve C. Ropp, "National Security," in Rudolph, ed., *Honduras: A Country Study*, pp. 391–396.

18. "Honduras," *Mesoamérica*, April 1990, p. 9; "Honduras," *Mesoamérica*, February 1991, pp. 10–11; "Honduras," *Mesoamérica*, May 1991, p. 12; "Honduras," *Mesoamérica*, June 1991, p. 2; *Excelsior*, January 13, 1991, p. 2A.

19. Richard L. Millett, "Historical Setting," in Rudolph, ed., *Honduras: A Country Study*, p. 47.

20. *Washington Report on the Hemisphere*, October 28, 1987, pp. 1, 60.

21. Ramón Custodio, "The Human Rights Crisis in Honduras," in Mark Rosenberg and Phillip Shepherd, eds., *Honduras Confronts Its Future* (Boulder, CO: Lynne Rienner Publishers, 1986), pp. 69–71.

22. US Department of State, *Country Reports on Human Rights*, p. 46; Morris, "Government and Politics," in Rudolph, ed., *Honduras: A Country Study*, pp. 192–193, and Morris, "Honduras: The Burden of Survival in Central America," in Ropp and Morris, eds., *Central America*, pp. 217–219; Charles W. Anderson, *Politics and Economic Change in Latin America: The Governing of Restless Nations* (New York: Van Nostrand Reinhold, 1967), pp. 116–132.

23. Americas Watch, *Review of the Department of State's Country Reports on Human Rights Practices for 1982: An Assessment* (New York, February 1983), p. 55. The discrepancy between this figure and the number of 40 cited earlier probably stems

from a combination of two factors: different reporting agencies are involved, and they are reporting on somewhat different phenomena. The two figures may not, in fact, be incongruent.

24. Morris, "Honduras: The Burden of Survival in Central America," in Ropp and Morris, eds., *Central America*, pp. 201–204.

25. Donald E. Schulz and Deborah Sundloff Schulz, *The United States, Honduras, and the Crisis in Central America* (Boulder, CO: Westview Press, 1994).

26. Economic data from Booth and Walker, *Understanding Central America*, 3rd ed., Appendix, Tables A.1, A.4, A.5, and A.6. See also Mark Rosenberg, "Can Democracy Survive the Democrats? From Transition to Consolidation in Honduras," in John A. Booth and Mitchell A. Seligson, eds., *Elections and Democracy in Central America* (Chapel Hill: University of North Carolina Press, 1989); Latin American Studies Association (LASA), *Extraordinary Opportunities . . . and New Risks: Final Report of the LASA Commission on Compliance with the Central American Peace Accord* (Pittsburgh, PA: LASA, 1988), pp. 20–26.

27. Robinson, *Transnational Conflicts*, p. 129.

28. "Honduras," *Mesoamérica*, April 1990, pp. 8–9; "Honduras," *Mesoamérica*, January 1991, pp. 9–10; "Honduras," *Mesoamérica*, February 1991, p. 10; "Honduras," *Mesoamérica*, May 1991, p. 12; "Honduras," *Mesoamérica*, June 1991, p. 2; "Honduras," *Mesoamérica*, September 1991, pp. 8–9; *Excelsior*, December 12, 1990, p. 2A; *Miami Herald*, December 15, 1990, p. 24A; *Miami Herald*, December 2, 1990, p. 22A; Robinson, *Transnational Conflicts*, p. 129.

29. J. Mark Ruhl, "Honduras: Militarism and Democratization in Troubled Waters," paper presented at the 21st Congress of the Latin American Studies Association, Chicago, September 25, 1998.

30. Jeff Boyer and Aaron Pell, "Mitch in Honduras: A Disaster Waiting to Happen," *NACLA Report on the Americas*, September–October 1999, pp. 36–43.

31. Latin American Database, "Hurricane Mitch Recovery Moving Slowly After One Year," *NotiCen*, November 4, 1999.

32. J. Mark Ruhl, "Curbing Central America's Militaries," *Journal of Democracy* 15, No. 3 (July 2004), p. 143.

33. Edward Orlebar, "Honduran President Faces Battle with His Own Military," *Los Angeles Times*, December 18, 1993, p. 2A; "Demilitarization Runs into Problems," *Central America Report*, November 21, 1996, p. 1; "Transfer of Police from Military to Civil Power Ratified," *Central America Report*, January 10, 1997, p. 6; "Honduras," *Mesoamérica*, June 6, 1997, p. 4; Thelma Mejía, "Vice President Implicated in Disappearances," *Interpress Service/Spanish* (PeaceNet), January 23, 1998; "Military Files Confiscated," *Central America Report*, February 12, 1998, p. 3; "New Government Seeks to Broaden Support," *Central America Report*, January 29, 1998, p. 7; Thelma Mejía, "Extra-Judicial Executions on the Rise," *Interpress Service/Spanish* (PeaceNet), February 4, 1998; "Death Squads Assassinate Human Rights Leader," *Interpress Service/Spanish* (PeaceNet), February 11, 1998; Thelma Mejía, "The Army Wants You!"

InterPress Service/Spanish (PeaceNet), January 21, 1997; "Honduran Death Squads Active Again, Report Says," *Houston Chronicle*, January 15, 1998, p. 19A.

34. Latin American Database, "Honduras: Security Minister Guatama Fonseca Under Fire as Crime Rates Soar," *NotiCen*, June 14, 2001.

35. Ismael Moreno, S. J., "A New President and Cracks in the Two-Party Structure," *Envío* (January–February 2002), pp. 37–43.

36. Latin American Database, "Honduras: President Ricardo Maduro Promises Action on Killings of Children," *NotiCen*, October 10, 2002.

37. United Nations Report of the Special Rapporteur, *Civil and Political Rights, Including the Question of Disappearances and Summary Executions* (New York: United Nations Economic and Social Council Commission on Human Rights, 2003).

38. Tom Weiner, "Cover-Up Found in Honduras Prison Killings," *New York Times*, May 20, 2003; Freddy Cuevas, "Fire in Honduran Prison Kills 103: Anti-Gang Laws Blamed for Overcrowding in Old Facilities," *Washington Post*, May 18, 2004.

39. Ismael Moreno, S.J., "The March on Tegucigalpa: 'It's Our Water,'" *Envío* 266 (September 2003), pp. 46–51.

40. Latin American Database, "Honduras Primaries Yield Polar Opposites for President in 2006," *NotiCen*, February 24, 2005.

41. Official results were not available until a month after the elections.

42. "Rocky First Year for Zelaya," *Central American Report*, February 16, 2007.

43. Latin American Database, "Honduras' President Takes On Media Moguls for Access to the People." *NotiCen*, June 28, 2007.

44. Other members of ALBA include Venezuela, Nicaragua, Bolivia, and Cuba.

45. International Development Association and International Monetary Fund, *Heavily Indebted Poor Countries (HIPC) Initiative and Multilateral Debt Relief Initiative (MDRI)—Status of Implementation*, International Monetary Fund, September 12, 2008, Table 4, http://www.imf.org/external/np/pp/eng/2008/091208.pdf, accessed June 13, 2009.

46. In an effort to attract investment to Choluteca, which had been devastated by Hurricane Mitch, the government, developers, and labor unions agreed to keep wages below the minimum for five to ten years in order to guarantee a profit for developers. See Pamela Constable, "Hondurans Ride Winds of Change Blown In by Mitch," *New York Times*, July 1, 2007.

47. Latin American Database, "Honduras Takes Action to Relieve Economic Pressure Points," *NotiCen*, November 29, 2007.

48. Latin American Economic System (SELA), "Migration and Remittances in Latin America and the Caribbean: Intra-Regional Flows and Macroeconomic Determinants" (Caracas, Venezuela: SELA, 2005), http://www.sela.org/public_html/aa2k5/ING/consejo/Di9.pdf; Inter-American Development Bank, "International remittances in Honduras" (Centro de Estudios Monetarios Latinoamericanos, 2008), http://www.cemla-remesas.org/informes/report-honduras.pdf.

49. State of the Nation: Region Program, "Informe Estado de la Región," *Program State of the Nation, Costa Rica* (November 2008), p. 262, http://www.estadonacion .or.cr/estadoregion2008/regional2008/capitulosPDF/Cap06.pdf.

50. Thelma Mejía, "Honduras: A Violent Death Every Two Hours," October 30, 2006, http://ipsnews.net/news.asp?idnews=35275; Thelma Mejía, "In Tegucigalpa, the Iron Fist Fails," *NACLA Report on the Americas*, July–August 2007, pp. 26–29.

51. Matthew Brooke, "President Zelaya Says Government Is Powerless to Stop Violence," *Central America Report*, February 29, 2008.

52. Ismael Moreno, "Insecurity, Criminality, Hidden Powers and Visible Roots," *Envío* 312 (July 2007).

53. Santos had to resign his post in order to run for president. His chief party rival Michiletti tried to prevent him from running in the primaries by literally locking the doors of the legislature. See "Elvin Santos on the Rise," *Central America Report*, January 30, 2009.

54. This accusation was problematic, since even if both the June 28, 2009, referendum and a possible November 2009 formal referendum each resulted in a vote for a constituent assembly, the body could not have convened or proposed a new constitution until well after Zelaya's successor would be elected (November 2009) and his term ended (January 2010). On the other hand, the Honduran constitution explicitly forbids any revision of the term of the president, so that any person or body that might have eventually proposed or discussed extending the president's term would ipso facto necessarily violate the constitution.

55. "Sin condiciones para romper Constitución," *La Prensa*, March 14, 2009, http://www.laprensahn.com/Pa%C3%ADs/Ediciones/2009/03/15/Noticias/Sin -condiciones-para-romper-Constitucion; "Artículos pétreos no pueden reformarse ni con plebiscito ni referendo," *La Prensa*, May 26, 2009, http://www.laprensahn .com/Ediciones/2009/05/26/Noticias/Articulos-petreos-no-pueden-reformarse -ni-con-plebiscito-ni-referendo.

56. The Supreme Court documents related to Zelaya's removal were available online at the Honduran Supreme Court official Web site, http://www.poderjudicial .gob.hn/NR/rdonlyres/87E2BFFC-AF4D-44EA-BFC5-D93730D8D81C/2413 /ExpedienteJudicial1.pdf, accessed August 17, 2009.

57. The constitutionality of this situation was quite complicated: Article 280 of the Honduran constitution gives the president authority to "appoint and remove" the head of the armed forces. The Supreme Court, however, later ruled that General Vásquez's removal was unconstitutional and reinstated him. A provision in support of General Vásquez's restitution is Article 323, which states that no civilian or military functionary of the government is obliged to carry out an illegal order. Congress had hastily legislated a law blocking such a poll, and an administrative court and the Supreme Court had ruled that to conduct President Zelaya's proposed referendum was illegal. These references to the constitution are drawn from the *Constitución de*

1982 con reformas hasta 2005 (Political Constitution of 1982 through 2005 reforms), http://pdba.georgetown.edu/Constitutions/Honduras/hond05.html, accessed August 16, 2009.

58. Ibid. The military also arrested and deported President Zelaya's foreign minister, Patricia Rodas; see Toni Solo, "Honduras: A Defining Moment—The West Discredited, ALBA Vindicated," *Scoop*, http://www.scoop.co.nz/stories/HL0907/S00079.htm, accessed July 7, 2009.

59. For more on the coup see Geoff Thale, "Behind the Honduran Coup," *Foreign Policy in Focus*, July 1, 2009, http://www.fpif.org/fpiftxt/6225; Larry Birns, "Caudillismo in Action: Looking Back on Honduras' Plight," Council on Hemispheric Affairs, July 7, 2009, http://www.coha.org/2009/07/caudillismo-in-action-looking-back-on-honduras; Secretary of State Hillary Rodham Clinton, "Breakthrough in Honduras," *U.S. Department of State*, October 30, 2009%E2%80%99-plight/.

60. Tyler Bridges, "Honduras' Interim Leader: Manuel Zelaya Must Face Charges," *Miami Herald*, August 18, 2009, http://www.miamiherald.com/news/americas/story/1190592.html.

61. Inter-American Commission on Human Rights, *Honduras: Human Rights and the Coup D'état*, Organization of American States, OEA/Ser.L/V/II. Doc. 55, December 30, 2009.

62. It is also worth noting that the Carter Center, EU, and OAS all canceled their observer missions for the 2009 elections.

63. "Vicepresidente del Congress, 40 por ciento de la Policía está infiltrada por el crimen," *Proceso*, July 19, 2011, http://proceso.hn/2011/07/19/Termómetro/Vicepresidente.del.Congreso/40028.html; Frances Robles, "Honduras Becomes Murder Capital of the World," *Miami Herald*, January 23, 2012, http://www.miamiherald.com/2012/01/23/2603338_p3/honduras-becomes-murder-capital.html; and Edward Fox, "Dynamics of Honduran Police Corruption Narrow Chance for Reform," *InsightCrime*, January 31, 2012, http://www.insightcrime.org/news-analysis/dynamics-of-honduran-police-corruption-narrow-chance-for-reform.

64. Miriam Wells, "We Will Support Honduran Police But Ignore Their Director: US," *InsightCrime*, March 29, 2013, http://www.insightcrime.org/news-briefs/support-honduran-police-but-ignore-director-us; and Miriam Wells, "Honduran Police Chief Interview Reveals US Dilemma," *InsightCrime*, November 5, 2013, http://www.insightcrime.org/news-briefs/honduras-police-chief-interview-reveals-us-aid-dilemma.

65. Chapter XII of the Honduran Constitution of 1982, Article 309, provides judges may be removed (by implication by Congress which appoints them) only for due cause as specified in law; Constitution of Honduras (English translation), accessed December 1, 2013, http://www.constitutionnet.org/files/Honduras%20Constitution.pdf.

66. "Pleno especial rechaza recursos a favor de magistrados destituidos," *El Heraldo*, February 6, 2013, http://www.elheraldo.hn/Secciones-Principales/Pais/Pleno-rechaza-amparo-de-exmagistrados.

67. "Lobo dejará una economía desastrosa, según economistas," *La Prensa*, January 23, 2013, http://www.laprensa.hn/csp/mediapool/sites/LaPrensa/Honduras /Apertura/story.csp?cid=328201&sid=267&fid=98.

68. "Honduran Government in Chaos, Can't Pay Its Bills, Neglects Basic Services," *Washington Post*, January 24, 2013, http://www.washingtonpost.com/business /honduran-government-in-chaos-cant-pay-its-bills-neglects-basic-services/2013/01 /24/1a5950de-6686-11e2-889b-f23c246aa446_print.html.

69. The "Model Cities" law allows for the creation of private cities that function outside of the control of the Honduran Constitution and raises serious questions about sovereignty.

70. 'Congreso de Honduras aprobó medida que permite destituir presidentes," *Telesur*, January 23, 2013, http://www.telesurtv.net/articulos/2013/01/23/congreso-de -honduras-aprobo-medida-que-permite-destituir-presidentes-4837.html.

71. "Congreso crea 1,000 nuevas plazas en FF AA," *El Heraldo*, June 11, 2013, http://www.elheraldo.hn/content/view/full/154713?utm_source=feedburner&utm _medium=feed&utm_campaign=Feed:+elheraldo_pais+(El+Heraldo+-+Pa%C3 %ADs)&utm_content=Google+Reader.

72. Dana Frank, "In Honduras Military Takes Over with US Blessing," *Miami Herald*, September 11, 2013, http://www.miamiherald.com/2013/09/10/3618867/in -honduras-military-takes-over.html.

73. http://www.eueom.eu/files/pressreleases/english/preliminary-statement-eueom -honduras-2013_eng.pdf.pdf; http://www.hondurassolidarity.org/report1/; http:// america.aljazeera.com/opinions/2013/11/honduras-presidentialelectionfraud intimidation.html; http://upsidedownworld.org/main/honduras-archives-46/4584 -the-results-of-the-elections-in-honduras-were-changed-says-european-union-observer-

74. http://www.nytimes.com/2013/11/26/world/americas/honduras-presidential -race.html?_r=2&pagewanted=all&.

75. "Libre, segunda fuerza parlamentaria de Honduras," *Confidencial*, December 4, 2013, http://www.confidencial.com.ni/articulo/15155/libre-segunda-fuerza -parlamentaria-de-honduras.

76. Impeaching the president would require a three-quarters (96-vote) majority.

77. Americas Barometer 2012 Survey, Latin American Public Opinion Project; authors' analysis.

9

POLITICAL PARTICIPATION, POLITICAL ATTITUDES, AND DEMOCRACY

CLASSICAL DEMOCRATIC THEORY DEFINES DEMOCRACY AS CITIZEN participation in the rule of a society. Political participation includes behaviors ranging from voting and partisan activity to community activism, contacting public officials, civil-society engagement, and protest. Participation in public life conveys citizens' demands to government, and thus helps constrain the expectations and actions of officials and elites. Theorists argue that a society is more democratic when more citizens take part in politics, when their political activities are more varied, and when they affect more arenas of civic life.[1] This chapter employs data from recent public-opinion surveys to explore political engagement among Central Americans.

Participation, however, only tells part of the story about Central Americans and democracy. We need to know to what extent the five nations have begun to consolidate their democratic regimes. *Democratic consolidation*, defined as the institutionalization of democratic expectations and rules within a polity, rests partly on the attitudes and norms of citizens.[2] The more consolidated democracies become, the more their citizens share democratic attitudes, reject authoritarian norms and military rule, and believe their governments are legitimate. We will examine these attitudes among Central Americans.

Another part of democratic consolidation is that political elites must embrace democratic rules of the game, a process not complete in the region.

Domestic and external political contexts shape citizens' beliefs and behaviors. All five countries in Central America became civilian democratic regimes by the 1990s, but many factors other than formal regime type have influenced citizen political engagement and attitudes. Despite their common elements, Central American political histories vary widely, as do levels of political and social violence, crime, corruption, and economic environments. In some undemocratic countries citizens nevertheless adopted democratic norms through contact with more democratic societies as their citizens traveled and worked abroad, through media exposure, or because such norms helped them resist repression.[3] The behavior of regimes and of their international sponsors affects citizen participation and attitudes and thus shapes prospects for democratic consolidation.[4] At the individual level, citizens' educational and economic resources diverge, as do their experiences with official corruption and crime, and these affect their political behavior and their support for government.[5] This chapter, therefore, examines how such factors affect political attitudes as we explore the prospects for democratic consolidation.

CITIZEN PARTICIPATION

We begin with a comparative examination of political participation in 2012 (Table 9.1).[6] To explore the stability or variability of political behavior and attitudes in Central America, we also compare some of these findings with those from previous editions of *Understanding Central America*.

Ninety-two percent of voting-age Central Americans reported being registered in 2012 (Table 9.1), comparing favorably to the United States, where 71 percent of eligible voters registered in 2012.[7] At the high end, 96 percent of Costa Ricans reported being registered in 2012, a 3 percent decline from 2004. In contrast to Costa Rica's recent registration decline, two countries reported increases. Guatemalans reported registering at 87 percent in 2012, an increase of 11 percent over 2004. El Salvador implemented election system reforms in the early 2000s, including the introduction of a universal identification card. Registration rose there to 97 percent in 2012, a gain of 17 percent over 1991. The lower reported registration rates elsewhere likely occurred because other countries made less conscientious efforts at registering all eligible citizens, or because of changing registration rules and procedures (Nicaragua). Compared to results from a similar survey from 2008, Table 9.1 reveals a 2 percent increase in the region over 2008.[8]

A statistical technique known as multiple regression analysis allows us to weigh the simultaneous, independent contribution of several other variables to one of interest. Employed here it reveals that, other factors held

TABLE 9.1 Political Participation, Central American Nations

Type of Political Participation	Costa Rica	El Salvador	Guatemala	Honduras	Nicaragua	Regional Means
VOTING BEHAVIOR						
Registered to vote (%)	96	97	87	93	89	92
Voted in last presidential election (%)	67	68	79	51	80	69
CAMPAIGNING AND PARTISAN ACTIVISM						
Attended political party meetings (%)	2	14	9	12	23	12
Attempted to persuade someone how to vote (%)	29	22	35	28	20	27
Worked for a political campaign or candidate (%)	11	8	8	6	11	9
COMMUNAL ACTIVISM						
Attended community improvement group (%)[a]	9	11	28	16	22	17
Worked with others to solve community problem (%)	21	30	41	37	29	32
CIVIL SOCIETY ACTIVISM						
Church-related group (%)	44	64	73	66	54	60
School-related group (%)	14	29	35	28	45	30
Business-professional group (%)	4	5	8	8	8	7
Mean group activism (%)[b]	21	26	39	34	36	32
CONTACTING PUBLIC OFFICIALS						
Local official (%)	8	22	23	10	18	16
Legislative deputy (%)	4	7	5	7	7	6
PROTEST PARTICIPATION						
Protested or demonstrated within last year	5	4	7	6	8	6

[a]Percentages are for reporting attendance at meetings of each group "once or twice a month" or more frequently, which indicates an intermediate or higher level of involvement.
[b]Average of all three types of groups listed above (church, school, and business-professional) for at least the intermediate- level of involvement ("from time to time").
SOURCE: 2012 AmericasBarometer surveys by the Latin American Public Opinion Project, Vanderbilt University, http://www.LapopSurveys.org.

constant, in 2012 older, better educated, wealthier, and female Central Americans registered to vote more than others. Age had the biggest influence on being registered to vote, although registration tapered off among the very elderly.[9]

We measured voting, another key form of participation, as reported voting in the most recent presidential election. Our respondents reported a region-wide average turnout of 69 percent (unchanged from 2008). The lowest was among Hondurans at 51 percent (Table 9.1). These turnout rates exceed the actual turnout rates reported by national election officials by a regional average of 5 percent[10] because some voters reported to interviewers having voted when they did not. (Overreporting of voting is common in survey research, usually attributed to a desire to comply with desirable social norms.)

Central Americans are active voters when compared to US citizens, whose turnout in recent presidential elections has ranged between 47 (in 2000) and 57 percent (2004 and 2008).[11] We surmise that so many Central Americans vote because of the region's experience with dictatorship, political violence, and fraudulently manipulated elections. Having free elections very probably provides a refreshing opportunity after decades of violence. Central America's intimate political arenas compared to the United States may also encourage voting. With other influences held constant, in the 2012 survey older citizens voted at higher rates than younger ones, but voting declined among those older than 65. More educated and better off citizens voted more. Those supportive of the political system and citizens evaluating government economic management positively reported higher voter turnout.[12]

Comparing 2012 data to those from 2004 revealed a downward trend. In 2012, the regional average reported voting in the last presidential election was 4 percent lower than in 2004, with larger decline occurring in Honduras, Costa Rica, and El Salvador (down 22, 7, and 6 percent, respectively). The plunge in Honduras undoubtedly reflects voter alienation following the 2009 coup. Guatemalans and Nicaraguans reported respective increases of 14 and 5 percent.

Two sources provide data over a longer term. We compare both actual turnout rates as calculated from election results, and survey respondents (urban voters only). This reveals two distinct trends in voter turnout.[13] For 2012, reported urban voter turnout for the most recent presidential election was 24 percent less in Costa Rica than it had been in the early 1990s and 37 percent less in Honduras. The contrast between the cases is striking. Alienated voters in the region's most successful democracy, Costa Rica, have turned out less and less over recent decades. Hondurans, in turn, experienced Central America's first post-democratization coup only months before the 2009 election referenced by the survey. Nearly half of Hondurans failed to vote in 2009. Official nationwide turnout records from each country largely confirm these urban survey results. Between the early 1990s and 2010, Costa Rica registered a 23 percent turnout decline in presidential elections. Honduras' turnout eroded from 78 to 53 percent between 1985 and 2009. Nicaragua's turnout declined 6 percent from 1990 to 2011.[14]

On the improvement side, urban turnout in El Salvador (from surveys) rose from 56 to 70 percent between the early 1990s and 2012, while the change in Guatemala was upward from 71 to 80 percent. Again, official national records of the percentage of the voting-age population that cast ballots in presidential elections showed large gains in these two countries after their civil wars ended. Turnout in El Salvador rose 29 percent from 1994 to 2009. In Guatemala the change was 37 percent between 1995 and 2011. Both countries improved their election administration systems during this period, and their civil conflicts receded further into memory.

Partisan activity, another way of participating in the national arena, requires more time and effort than voting. Our surveys asked respondents how often they attended meetings of political parties; Table 9.1 reveals a regional mean of 12 percent. The lowest party attendance reported was in Costa Rica, at 2 percent. Costa Rica's two major parties adopted primary elections in the late 1980s, reducing the use of local party meetings and "retail" party politics. The National Liberation Party (PLN) and Social Christian Unity Party (PUSC) also experienced major corruption scandals in the late 1990s and 2000s, with sharp electoral reversals for each.[15] At the high end, 23 percent of Nicaraguans reported attending party meetings, up 3 percent from 2004 and 2008. After Daniel Ortega became president again in 2007, his government heavily promoted party and local government participation at the local level.

In Honduras, compared to 2008 and following the 2009 coup, party meeting activity in 2012 declined 7 percent (to 12 percent). Elsewhere party meeting participation ranged from 9 to 14 percent. Guatemala and El Salvador experienced violent repression of certain parties' members and political candidates during their civil wars. Salvadorans have since become more active than Guatemalans in party activities.[16]

Other factors held constant, men and older citizens (tapering off after 65), reported more political party participation in 2012. Evaluative attitudes also shaped party activism: those with higher approval of government economic management, better views of national economic performance, and higher system support were more active in party meetings.[17]

Campaign involvement is the third type of political participation linked to elections. The survey asked people whether they had ever attempted to persuade someone how to vote, or worked for a political campaign or candidate (Table 9.1). The regional average for campaign participation declined from 12 percent in 2008 to 9 percent in 2012, with the only increase observed in

Nicaragua (from six to 11 percent). For attempting to persuade others how to vote, the regional average dropped 10 percent from 2008 to 2012. Hondurans had previously reported the most such efforts, but their efforts fell from 59 to 28 percent between 2008 and 2012. For the same period Costa Ricans reported a 15-point decline (to 29 percent) in vote persuasion efforts. Guatemala was the only country with an increase, rising 8 points to 35 percent in 2012.

When considered together, the observed regional decreases in attendance at party functions, electioneering, and vote persuading since 2008 suggest that by 2012 election campaigns had lost vibrancy compared to the early 2000s. This may have happened because the novelty of such activity being safe wore off in some countries, because citizens held political parties in low esteem, and because in Costa Rica, El Salvador, and Honduras trust in elections had declined.[18]

Other factors held constant, in 2012 males, the better educated, and older citizens (albeit eroding among the elderly) were more likely to be party- and campaign-active. Citizens with higher evaluations of national economic performance, government economic management, and institutions in general reported higher party and campaign activism.[19]

Outside the electoral arena, communal activism—collective self-help or community-improvement work—has a rich history in Central America. Citizens work together to address local problems that government often ignores. Communal activism persisted even through the conflict and repression of the 1980s and early 1990s, possibly because such cooperative activity among neighbors did not appear to challenge authoritarian regimes.[20] Respondents to our 2004 survey reported a regionwide average of one person in five at least occasionally attending a community-improvement group meeting, but by 2012 fewer than one in six reported doing so (Table 9.1). Working with others to solve a community problem remained the same regionwide in 2012 as in 2004.

A review of data from 2004 and 2008 reveals that communal activism had declined in 2012 in Costa Rica and El Salvador, but increased substantially in Guatemala and Nicaragua between 2004 and 2012. Both the Liberal and Sandinista governments in power from 2004 to 2012 promoted community problem-solving organizations. In Honduras, these communal activities dropped sharply in 2008 but recovered substantially in 2012. One possible explanation for the transitory collapse in communal activism in Honduras was a crime wave that one survey reported had frightened people to stay home for safety.[21]

Another aspect of citizens' collaboration is participation in civil society (formal organizations), which provides collective ways to promote their interests. Table 9.1 presents data on the percentage of citizens attending meetings at least "from time to time" in church-related, school-related, and business and professional organizations. In 2012, 73 percent of Guatemalans and about two-thirds of Nicaraguans reported such involvement in church-related groups.[22] At least 44 percent of respondents elsewhere took part in church-related organizations. In Costa Rica, with its well-established education system, participation in school-related groups was below half the participation rates of other countries. Between 28 and 45 percent of other Central Americans reported intermediate attendance at school-related groups. Fewer than one in fifteen respondents regionwide reported business or professional group activity. Guatemalans, Hondurans, and Nicaraguans were more active in this arena than in others.

Over time, our summary measure of mean group involvement for the whole region declined by 3 percent between 2004 and 2012. Close inspection reveals that civil-society activism actually remained unchanged in El Salvador and Guatemala, but decreased 5 to 7 percent in Costa Rica, Honduras, and Nicaragua. In very sharp contrast, Honduras experienced a large decline from 2004's average group activism level of 41 percent to 24 percent in 2012. A 2008 drop in civil society activity occurred in Honduras that resembled that for communal activity noted above; it only partly recovered by 2012. Again, we believe the cause is fear of the crime wave then in progress. Crime was thus suppressing Honduran citizens' common pursuit of their interests. This, we believe, constituted a significant limitation on Honduran democracy.

Other factors held constant, Central Americans in 2012 who were more active in organizations tended to be women, older (with some falloff among the elderly), wealthier, and residents of smaller communities. People with confidence in the political system also took part more in groups.[23]

Citizens typically contact public officials to demand services, benefits, or government attention to problems. Sixteen percent of Central Americans reported having contacted a local public official (Table 9.1) during the year prior to the 2012 survey, a three-point increase above 2008. Guatemalans, Salvadorans, and Nicaraguans contacted local officials more, Costa Ricans and Hondurans considerably less. Only 6 percent reported having contacted a national legislative deputy in the year prior to the 2012 survey, with little variation regionwide.[24]

Overall and holding other factors constant, the most important individual traits contributing to contacting public officials were being older (with a decline among the elderly) and a small-town or rural resident. Citizens viewing positively the nation's economic performance and the government's economic performance contact officials more.[25]

Protest provides an important tool for communicating to government. An average of one in 16 Central Americans reported protesting or demonstrating in the year before the 2012 survey (down from one in 11 in 2008). Nicaraguans (8 percent) were most likely to have done so, followed by Guatemalans at 7 percent. Salvadorans at 5 percent remained the least protest-engaged (Table 9.1), as they were in 2008 and 2004 (Figure 9.1). The biggest change in protest levels came in Honduras, where 2008's level of 18 percent dropped to only 6 percent in 2012. Protest participation varies substantially across time, responding to local political conditions, as Figure 9.1 reveals. Protest generally subsided from 2004 to 2012, but in Honduras it rose sharply in 2008 before the 2009 coup and declined significantly after the coup as the government cracked down on protests.

Nicaragua experienced high levels of protest activity in the post-revolutionary 1990s and 2000s as working-class groups, unions, and organizations linked to the FSLN challenged many of the austerity and privatization plans of recent governments. Nicaragua's 8 percent protest rate for 2012 (Table 9.1) declined from 2004 and 2008 levels, possibly because the Sandinistas had recaptured power in the 2006 election and their supporters and organizations felt less called to protest than when they were in opposition. Costa Rica's 5 percent protest rate for 2012 was down from previous years. Although protest squares poorly with Costa Rica's placid image, the country nevertheless has a lively record of protest.[26]

Other factors held constant, protesters were more educated, urban dwelling, and male. Protesters came from across the age spectrum. Only one evaluation norm mattered—those who felt the government was managing the economy well were more likely to have protested.[27] Although this may seem anomalous at first glance, citizens may protest or demonstrate in favor of incumbents or their programs. Indeed, given the ease of access to the media and organizations for a president, it can be easier for an officeholder to rally demonstrations of support than for regime critics.

To sum up, in 2012 survey data Central Americans engaged their political systems through high voter registration and turnout. They campaigned, tried to persuade others how to vote, attended party meetings, contacted officials, and protested. There were some distinctive national patterns. Despite their record of declining voter turnout, Costa Ricans actively persuaded other voters and worked for political campaigns, but reported very low attendance at party meetings because primary elections undercut citizens' direct engagement with parties. Guatemalans were the most active Central Americans in community improvement and civil society, followed by Nicaraguans, whose engagement had increased by 2012. Salvadorans were the least active in civil society in 2008, replaced in this position by 2012 by Costa Ricans.

Comparing which country ranked first or second in each category of participation in Table 9.1 allows us to make rough overall comparisons of citizen activism. Overall, Guatemalans were the most engaged citizens; they especially stood out in the civil society arenas of community improvement and group engagement. Nicaraguans took second place in their reported participation, having risen considerably over prior surveys. Costa Ricans were by far the least active citizens in 2012 and excelled only in campaign participation. There is irony in Costa Ricans, citizens of the region's oldest democracy, being the least engaged while citizens of every other country were more politically active. But these findings make some sense upon consideration that an older democracy is more settled and its citizens probably more complacent with it. In contrast, residents of the newer democracies are still flexing their muscles as citizens and working together to advance their interests. Overall, to the extent that democracy involves participation in politics, one may conclude that Central America was democratic in 2004 and remained so in 2012, but the intensity and modalities of citizen engagement kept evolving.

Among the individual traits affecting participation across the region, our regression analyses found age, education, and residence in smaller communities predicted higher participation in 2012. Men were more active in protesting, campaigning, and party activity. Females exceeded men in civil society activism. Household wealth modestly elevated only voting and civil society activism. Party and campaign activism, protesting, and contacting officials occur fairly evenly among economic strata in the region.

Evaluations moved several types of participation. Positive views of government economic management increased voting, party and campaign activity, contacting, and (curiously) protest behaviors. General system support encouraged voting, party/campaign work, and civil society activism. Positive views of the national economy elevated campaign and party activism, but reduced contacting. In 2008 we found that positive evaluations of local government, the president, and national economic performance encouraged greater participation. Most interesting, however, was that the most-satisfied and the least-satisfied citizens were the most politically active in various participation modes, while those in the middle on these attitudes were less engaged. Democracy in Central America was thus allowing those at both ends of the legitimacy spectrums to engage the system at high levels.[28] This is good news for democratic consolidation because frustrated citizens in these democracies were not dropping out or rebelling. Rather, just as those who approved of the system engaged it at higher levels, those who were most critical of it also engaged.

CITIZEN ATTITUDES

Latin American political culture once had strong authoritarian components: deference to authority, preference for strong leaders, intolerance of regime critics, and antidemocratic norms.[29] Central American countries shared these cultural traits, which were reinforced by the protracted authoritarian rule. In recent years these old patterns have changed substantially across Latin America. Researchers reported higher democratic norms than anticipated among Nicaraguans—equal in fact to those of Costa Ricans—during the late 1980s despite Nicaragua's limited prior experience with democracy.[30] The emergence of formal democracy in four of five countries and questions about Central Americans' commitment to democracy call us to assess the balance between authoritarian and democratic norms.

To evaluate political attitudes we begin with a question from the 2012 AmericasBarometer question about whether respondents agree/disagree that their country needs "a strong leader who does not need to be elected or worry about elections." As Table 9.2 reveals, in 2012, 20 percent of Central Americans (up 4 percent from 2008) agreed with this viewpoint, inimical to democracy and probably dangerous to it if widely held. Nicaraguans (at 11 percent) expressed the least agreement, and Hondurans (at 43 percent) the most. Except for Nicaragua, preference for a strong, unelected leader rose everywhere between 2008 and 2014. Guatemalans increased agreement 10 percent and Hondurans 14 percent.

Other factors held equal, preference for unelected strongman rule was greater among younger, less educated, poorer, and urban residents. It was considerably lower among strong system supporters, but higher among those satisfied with government economic performance. Voters and contactors of officials supported strongman rule less, but party/campaign activists supported it more.[31]

TABLE 9.2 Political Attitudes, Central American Nations

Attitudes	Costa Rica	El Salvador	Guatemala	Honduras	Nicaragua	Regional Means
Authoritarianism						
Percentage agreeing "we need a strong leader who does not need to be elected."						
2008	17	16	19	39	12	20
2012	20	18	29	43	11	24
Support for a military coup d'état						
Index of support for a military coup under certain circumstances – high or excessive unemployment, crime, or corruption (range 0 = low support . . . 100 = high support)						
2008	N.A.[a]	43	39	51	42	44
2012	28	43	38	35	34	36

Democratic norms

Index of support for general political participation rights[b] (range 0 = low support . . .
100 = high support)

2008	78	74	68	62	83	73
2012	75	65	60	51	81	66

Index of tolerance for political participation rights for regime critics[c] (range 0 = low
support . . . 100 = high support)

2008	57	54	44	47	50	51
2012	53	44	47	37	56	47

Index of support for civil disobedience and confrontational political methods[d]
(range 0 = low support . . . 100 = high support)

2008	13	19	14	24	16	17
2012	19	23	30	25	22	24

Index of support for rebellion or violent overthrow of an elected government[e]
(range 0 = low support . . . 00 = high support)

2008	10	19	12	23	17	16
2012	11	16	23	19	15	17

System support

of general or diffuse support for the political system[f] (range 0 = low support . . .
100 = high support)

2008	72	62	58	53	60	61
2012	56	57	52	41	61	53

Index of specific support for national political institutions[g] (range 0 = low support . . .
100 = high support)

2008	52	46	45	40	41	45
2012	46	52	45	36	52	46

Index of evaluation of national economic performance[h] (range 0 = low support . . .
100 = high support)

2008	48	29	34	34	27	34
2012	46	35	39	37	49	41

[a]Data not available for Costa Rica for 2008. In 2004 Costa Ricans fell at about the regional mean on giving hypothetical justification for coups "under certain circumstances" at 48 percent.
[b]This index incorporates approval of three behaviors: taking part in a legal demonstration, participating in a group working to solve communal problems, and campaigning for a candidate for office or political party.
[c]This index incorporates support for four possible behaviors by critics of the political system: voting, carrying out peaceful demonstrations, running for public office, and giving a speech on television.
[d]This index incorporates approval of three behaviors: taking part in street blockades, invading private property, and taking over factories, offices, or buildings.
[e]This index registers the level of approval of "taking part in group that wishes to overthrow an elected government by violent means."
[f]This index incorporates general or diffuse support for the national political system, its protection of basic rights, pride in the system, and a sense of obligation to support the political system.
[g]This index incorporates citizen support/approval for nine different specific institutions (elections office, legislature, "the government," political parties, supreme court, municipal government, elections, president, and justice system).
[h]This index incorporates four items on citizen evaluation of the performance of the national economic system and their own personal economic situations: "How is the country's economy?" "How is your own personal economic situation?" "Has the country's economic situation improved during the last year?" "Has your own personal economic situation improved during the last year?"
SOURCE: 2008 and 2012 AmericasBarometer surveys by the Latin American Public Opinion Project, Vanderbilt University, http://www.LapopSurveys.org/.

Our surveys asked whether a military coup might be justified if unemployment, crime, or corruption were very high. Thirty-nine percent of the respondents regionwide agreed, down 5 percent from 2008. Costa Ricans embraced a hypothetical coup the least (28 percent), while Salvadorans supported it the most (43 percent). Hondurans' support declined from 51 to 35 percent from before to after the coup there in 2009. We believe the negative political and economic effects of the coup and resulting sanctions caused Hondurans to change their thinking. Although these values might seem worryingly high, they have declined substantially since 2004.

Coup justifiers tended to be females, younger, and less educated. They also had negative evaluations of economic performance, felt insecure in their neighborhoods, and were more often victimized by acts of official corruption (i.e., being solicited for a bribe).[32] In sum, perceived insecurity from crime, corruption, and disappointment with the economy's performance generated potential popular support for antidemocratic adventurism by elites.

When asked what specific hypothetical problems might justify a military takeover of their governments, Central Americans in 2012 cited "high levels of crime" (57 percent), "a lot of corruption" (50 percent), and high unemployment (22 percent). These findings reveal that, regionwide, Central Americans' commitment to civilian rule remains partly contingent on the performance of their regimes. Threats to personal and economic security and problems of public corruption deeply trouble many. Should crime, corruption, or unemployment become sufficiently severe, armed forces or other plotters against the constitutional order might find forbearance for a coup d'état that claimed to rectify such problems.

Table 9.2 reports the national means for an index of agreement with fundamental participation rights for citizens of a democracy. On a scale of zero to 100 (from the least supportive to the most), the citizens of all five countries averaged in the positive end of the scale, with a clear national bias in favor of general democratic participation rights. The regional mean declined three scale points between 2008 and 2012. Nicaraguans and Costa Ricans scored the highest (81 and 75 points, respectively). Hondurans scored the lowest in 2012 at 51 points, just above the scale midpoint and 11 scale points lower than in 2008. In sum, then, most Central Americans retained their support for general participation rights as of 2012, but we note with concern the declines in support for participation rights among Hondurans, Salvadorans, and Guatemalans.

Other factors held equal, in 2012 people with more education and from larger communities supported basic participation rights more. Strong supporters of basic participation rights were more likely to have expressed high diffuse support, evaluated the economy negatively, voted, contacted officials, and protested. Citizens who saw poor economic performance expressed more support for basic participation rights.[33]

Another measure of democratic values, also a zero to 100 scale, shows less tolerance among Central Americans for participation rights for regime critics (those "who speak badly of our form of government") than for participation rights in general. This index measures citizens' belief in one of democracy's more challenging precepts, that of allowing regime critics to take part in politics and try to convince others of their positions. Table 9.2 shows that political tolerance declined four scale points between 2008 and 2012, averaging three points below the scale midpoint. Costa Ricans and Nicaraguans were the more tolerant Central Americans, with scores of 53 and 57, respectively. Tolerance among Hondurans declined ten points from 2008 to only 36 in 2012, well below the scale midpoint. In positive contrast, tolerance scale scores rose significantly in Nicaragua and Guatemala between 2008 and 2012.

Other factors held constant, men and the more educated were more likely to support participation rights for dissenters. Those with higher diffuse support, who voted, contacted officials, protested, had not experienced bribe solicitations, and who engaged more in civil society were more politically tolerant.[34]

Another aspect of citizens' attitudes involves their embrace of protest, civil disobedience, and even political violence. Evaluating citizen reaction to these methods is tricky. On the one hand, protest and even political confrontation may be necessary to create, nurture, or maintain democracy. Indeed, Thomas Jefferson argued that popular unrest was essential to democracy.[35] On the other hand, within formal democracies, confrontational political tactics tend to be unpopular, and if used to extremes may threaten a democratic system. Bearing in mind these complexities, we see that on a zero to 100 scale the regionwide average was 24, indicating a strong shared bias against such techniques. However support for them increased seven points over 2008. Guatemalans most favored confrontational tactics (30 points), up substantially from 2008. Costa Ricans liked them least at 19 (an increase of 6 points over 2008).

When we compared support for confrontational political methods between the 1990s survey and the 2004 survey (urban samples only), we found an increase everywhere but Honduras.[36] As repression diminished with the end of two civil wars and the development and operation of formal democracy more broadly, Central Americans became more supportive of confrontational tactics. Interestingly, the trend also applied for Costa Ricans, who had enjoyed stable democracy for several decades. Because Costa Ricans also increased their approval of protest and confrontation, we surmise that some of the increase stems from reaction to unpopular neoliberal economic reforms. Pressured by foreign lending institutions and governments, debt-strapped regional governments in the 1980s and 1990s cut public services and government employment and privatized public-sector enterprises. Protests provided those affected a tool to influence public policy.

Other factors held equal, Central Americans favoring confrontational tactics tended to be younger and less educated than those who opposed them. Supporters of confrontation were politically active; they protested more but also contacted public officials and engaged in party/campaign work. They were less active in civil society than other citizens. These patterns confirm previous evidence that protest provides a preferred political tool for those with modest resources.[37] Lacking the resources availed by age, education, and organization that could provide influence over policy makers, such disadvantaged citizens may view protest as useful to promote their interests. Other factors contributing to greater support for confrontational political tactics included feeling insecure in one's own neighborhood and having experienced political corruption. Citizens who positively evaluated the economic management of the government also tended to support confrontational tactics. As for protest participation, this correlation is not anomalous; citizens may favor demonstration of support for incumbents or their programs.

In sum, in 2012 most Central Americans disapproved of confrontational political tactics. Yet one respondent in 16 reported taking part in a protest. A minority of Central Americans not only approved of taking political advocacy to the streets, some actually protested, whether legally and peacefully or via more confrontational means. When asked specifically which types of actions they supported, Central Americans disapproved most of occupying buildings and invading property, which create inconvenience or disrupt the lives of others; they disapproved less of blocking streets.

Going beyond support for confrontational tactics, we also asked respondents how much they would approve of someone taking part in a "group wishing to violently overthrow an elected government," an act inimical to democracy itself. Approval of armed rebellion was lower than for confrontation with a mean for the region of 17 out of 100 (Table 9.2), and essentially unchanged from 2004 and 2008. The lowest hypothetical support for rebellion in 2012 was in Costa Rica (11 points), and the highest in Guatemala (23 points). Support for armed rebellion in El Salvador and Nicaragua had declined modestly from 2008. In Honduras, 2012 support for rebellion dropped four scale points from 2008 in the wake of the coup of 2009.

We interpret the expressed willingness of some to support armed rebellion as openness to resisting even an elected government that abuses rights or fails in its fundamental obligations to the citizenry. Thus we see that, despite the horrors of insurrection and war that widely afflicted Central America from the 1970s into the 1990s, some of the region's citizens still reserve the right to challenge and rebel against a bad (even if elected) regime. Other factors held constant, younger and less educated citizens were more likely to support rebellion against an elected government. Voters were less likely to endorse rebellion, while protesters, communal self-help activists, and those who felt unsafe in their neighborhoods were more favorable.[38]

These findings about support for politically confrontational methods and rebellion raise another important issue—how much did Central Americans in 2012 actually support their governments? The changes reported in Table 9.2 on two measures of the legitimacy of the political system—general support for the national system, and support for specific national institutions. There we see that the regional mean on the general system-support index was 53 out of 100—that is, in the positive end of the scale but down eight points from 2008. There was a 16-point decline in Costa Rica and another of 12 points in Honduras in the wake of a three-point improvement regionwide from 2004 to 2008. Nicaraguans at 61 recorded the highest diffuse support, displacing Costa Rica as the leader on this attitude. Diffuse support fell several points each in Guatemala and El Salvador.

Probing further we find that Central Americans in 2012 expressed even lower average satisfaction with a set of nine specific institutions than they did with their systems in general, a gap that also existed in 2008 and 2004. Institutional support also changed notably between 2008 and 2012 by country. Table 9.2 shows that the regional mean on specific institutional support was only 46, below the scale's midpoint. Average institutional approval scores for Salvadorans and Nicaraguans were just above the scale midpoint, whereas other Central Americans registered below it. Nicaraguans increased their approval by 11 points and Salvadorans by six points. Costa Ricans' institutional evaluation—previously the highest in the region—declined six points, and Hondurans' fell by four points.

Which institutions inspired more and less support in 2012? Pooling responses from all five countries, the two most trusted institutions were the armed forces and municipal governments, each of which scored above the midpoint on an approval scale.[39] Trust for the national police had ranked third among institutions across the isthmus in 2008 but slid to next to last by 2012. We suspect continuing revelations about police involvement in drug smuggling to lie behind low evaluations—worst in Guatemala and Honduras. The two least-approved institutions in most countries were political parties and legislatures—we surmise this is because they generate noisy issue conflict. Honduras' and Costa Rica's legislatures were the region's least approved in 2012, tainted by scandal and the Honduran 2009 coup. The relatively high evaluations of national militaries across the region surprises somewhat, given these institutions' nasty track records during past authoritarian episodes. The militaries, however, did return to their barracks and accept some reforms and downsizing after the civil wars. Moreover, armed forces provided relief and helped restore order following natural disasters in several countries. We believe that, as of 2012, the region's militaries had earned some popular respect for staying out of politics and attending to security rather than politics. Of course, the glaring exception to this is Honduras, whose armed forces participated in the coup of 2009 and in 2012 earned the lowest citizen confidence level of any military in the region.

Overall, low and eroding institutional support scores reveal disappointment among Central Americans with the institutional quality of their democracies. Perhaps the most troubling evaluations appear in Costa Rica, the region's oldest democracy. Years of scandal involving major parties and successive governments seem to have disgusted Costa Ricans with many of their institutions. Although most shocking for Costa Rica, to anyone worried about democratic consolidation these low and eroding institutional support levels in several countries raise concerns. We believe it unlikely citizens will rebel, but fear that antidemocratic elites might take such citizen views as justifications to act in ways that harm democracy.

The final legitimacy norm is citizens' evaluations of the economy, shown to be the most influential type of legitimacy in shaping political participation. Table 9.2 demonstrates that Central Americans in 2012 evaluated their economies poorly (41 out of 100), an increase of seven points above 2008. The highest economic performance evaluations were 46 in the richest nation, Costa Rica, and 49 in much poorer Nicaragua. The economic growth data in Table 1.1 reveal clearly that in economic performance over time all the other countries lagged far behind Costa Rica, both in current GDP per capita and in long-term growth. We are not at all surprised that Costa Ricans (while still not even quite at the scale midpoint) were the second-most satisfied given their overall position and recent high growth rates (Chapter 4). In contrast, however low their national output per capita, Nicaraguans reacted favorably to its recent improvement (Chapter 5).

FACTORS SHAPING ATTITUDES AND PARTICIPATION

We have shown that in 2012 Central Americans were active in their political systems in diverse ways—behaving democratically—but that their attitudes demonstrated some ambivalence. On the one hand, most people reported strong democratic norms and repudiated authoritarian leadership. On the other, one person in six reported being willing to approve others seeking to overthrow elected regimes. Over one-third believed a military coup could be justified given sufficient corruption, crime, or inflation. While support for authoritarian rule had increased and political tolerance decreased somewhat between 2004 and 2012, hypothetical support for coups went down substantially, providing us with mixed signals. Basic democratic norms declined between 2008 and 2012, however, while support for rebellion remained low. A slight majority of citizens in all five countries expressed diffuse support for their political systems in 2012. Only in El Salvador and Nicaragua did the evaluations of specific institutions' performances fall even slightly in the approving end of the scale.

These national averages reveal Central Americans' modest diffuse support of their national political systems and modest dissatisfaction with their performance of specific institutions. Most telling, while Costa Ricans still averaged in the positive end of the diffuse support scale, their support for specific institutions dropped several points into the disapproving end of the scale. Costa Ricans expressed less and less support for political institutions from the 1980s to 2012.[40] This raises the question of what might account for such indifferent and declining support. What factors may contribute to low system support?

We suspect that several factors shape support for regimes, including Central American countries' differing historical backgrounds, records of repression, and economic activity. On the one hand, dramatic differences in democracy levels and political repression have declined as old civil wars and dictatorships faded farther into the past and the political systems remained on a formally democratic track (see Figures 2.1 and 2.2). Nevertheless, sharp national differences persist in economic and political performance within the region. We also expect that individuals' resources and their experiences and beliefs affect regime support.

Table 9.3 summarizes some of the possible influences on Central Americans' evaluations of their regimes. We assumed that the better a country's citizens evaluate aspects its performance, the higher would be its broad or diffuse political support scores. Contextual measures vary widely. First, real GDP per capita in constant terms in 2012—a measure of relative economic development—ranged from $5,725 for Costa Rica to $1,353 for Nicaragua. Costa Rican GDP per capita was $2,700 more than the next closest country (El Salvador) and four times higher than Nicaragua's. Second and third in Table 9.3 are a democracy score for 2012 and a measure of political terror and violence (PTS) for 2010–2011. Costa Rica outperformed the other four nations in the isthmus on both measures. In both measures the other four nations are more similar to each other than to Costa Rica. A fourth index is a ten-point scale compiled by *The Economist*'s intelligence unit's experts. It measures how well governments functioned as of 2008 and combines many items that assess the competence, stability, independence, constitutionality, and institutional strength of each government. *The Economist*'s governmental-function score ranged from a high of 8.2 for Costa Rica to a low of 4.4 in Honduras.

Personal experiences that might lower political support include being victims of crime and political corruption. If the state cannot reasonably protect citizens from criminals or if public officials regularly demand bribes, citizens thus victimized may withdraw their support from their regime. Table 9.3 shows that from 11 to 25 percent of Central Americans reported experiencing political corruption in the year before the 2012 survey. When asked how bad they perceived corruption in government to be (not bad = 0 to 100 = extremely bad), Central Americans gave their governments marks averaging between 62 and 77.[41] Between 13 and 21 percent of respondents reported having been a victim of a criminal act in the year prior to the survey. When asked how insecure they felt (on a 0 to 100 scale), respondents' answers ranged from more secure averages of 32 and 33 (Honduras and Nicaragua respectively) to the least secure mean of 44 in El Salvador.[42]

Presidents in many countries symbolize the entire government to the populace. We expected opinions of presidential performance to affect evaluations of the political system. Presidential approval is volatile, especially in comparison to more stable and longer orientations like democratic norms or intermediately diffuse support for the system. It has been found to affect many attitudes about government, and so must be considered in the model.[43] Interviewers in the 2012 survey asked respondents, "How would you rate the job performance of President (incumbent)?" Table 9.3 displays considerable variation across the region. Nicaraguans were the most positive, giving President Daniel Ortega a score of 67 out of 100, compared to Hondurans' 45 points for President Porfirio Lobo. Nicaraguans had improved their evaluation of President Ortega by 24 points over his 2008 evaluation.

Finally, we expected citizens' perception of the climate of civil liberties—in effect, of their freedom to take part in politics—to shape their evaluation of the political system. Table 9.3 reveals that, on a scale of zero (low) to 100 (high), Central Americans ranged broadly on this question in 2012. With a mean of 56 (a 15-point increase over 2008), Nicaraguans had the most favorable sense of their civil liberties climate. Honduras—where a crime wave had

TABLE 9.3 Possible Sources of Low Legitimacy Norms
Among Central Americans

	Costa Rica	El Salvador	Guatemala	Honduras	Nicaragua
Political-Economic Context					
Gross domestic product per capita 2012 (in constant 2005 U.S. $)[a]	5,725	3,023	2,322	1,575	1,353
Combined Democracy Score 2012[b]	10.0	8.3	7.4	6.2	6.8
Political Terror Scale 2010–2011[c]	1.5	3.0	2.8	2.8	2.5
Functioning of Government Index[d]	8.2	5.7	6.1	4.4	6.8

TABLE 9.3 *(continued)*

Personal Experience[e]

Percent of the Population Experiencing Political Corruption (been solicited for a bribe by an official within past year).	21	11	24	25	11
Percent of the Population Victimized by Crime (within past year).	17	17	21	19	13

Perceptions of the Political System[e]

Perceived Government Corruption Levels (scale 0 = none... 100 = extremely high)	74	66	69	77	62
Perceived Level of Personal Insecurity (scale 0 = none... 100 = extremely high)	36	44	38	32	33
Perception of Presidential Performance: "How would you rate the job performance of ___ (current president)? (scale 0 = none... 100 = extremely high)	49	62	56	45	67
Perceived Protection of Human Rights by Government (scale 0 = none... 100 = extremely high)	50	48	45	38	56

[a]Authors' estimate from the Economic Commission for Latin America (see Table 1.1 for source).
[b]Authors' combined democracy index, mean for 20; scale 0 = no democracy . . . 10 = high democracy (see Figure 2.1 for sources).
[c]Political Terror Scale Score, mean for 2010–2011; scale 1 = low violence . . . 5 = high violence (see Figure 2.2 for sources).
[d]Functioning of Government scale measures presence or absence of several characteristics of the political system by the EIU's experts, including freely elected policy makers; legislative supremacy; effective checks and balances; governmental freedom from undue military influence; government free from undue foreign control; government freedom from undue influence by special economic or religious groups; presence of accountability mechanisms between elections; extent of government authority over national territory; governmental transparency; prevalence of corruption, competency of the civil service; and several attitudes if available from recent World Values Surveys. (Source: Economist Intelligence Unit (EIU), The Economist Intelligence Unit's Index of Democracy 2008, accessed June 6, 2009; http://graphics.eiu.com/PDF/Democracy%20Index%202008.pdf.
[e]Source for all public opinion data: AmericasBarometer2012 Survey; www.LapopSurveys.org.

caused citizens to curtail activity outside their homes for the sake of personal safety, and where government repression limited protest activity and threatened the political opposition—had a mean of only 38. Costa Ricans averaged 50 in 2012 (a 12-point decline from 2008), reflective of a general pattern of discontent there.

How do these performance factors affect support for Central American political systems? Turning first to citizens' evaluations of their economies' performances, we anticipated that actual system performance (GDP per capita, democracy, government effectiveness, violence levels; see Table 9.3) and a person's own economic well-being and resources would considerably affect this attitude. Other things held equal, a multiple regression analysis revealed that evaluation of economic performance was higher among those with more income, but lower among older Central Americans (the latter significantly poorer than younger fellow citizens).[44] People who felt unsafe in their neighborhoods evaluated economic performance negatively. Positive views of the incumbent president and the rights performance of the system increased respondents' approval of the economy. Neither a combined measure of overall political-economic system performance[45] nor GDP per capita in 2012 contributed to higher economic-performance evaluations.[46]

We then analyzed factors shaping diffuse (broad general) support for Central American political systems similarly, including evaluation of economic performance as a predictor. The multiple regression analysis found that, other factors held equal, the overall political-economic context measure had a strong positive impact on diffuse support, as did evaluation of presidential performance. A positive evaluation of the economy increased diffuse support for the political system. Being a corruption victim lowered diffuse support, as did living in larger cities. Interestingly, sex, education, and family living standard mattered little for diffuse support, a result similar to those we found in the 2008 survey. The absence of demographic influences shows broad general system support to be widely shared throughout Central American publics rather than concentrated in one class or segment of the population.[47]

Analysis of a measure of specific support for nine national institutions (e.g., political parties, the legislature, the Supreme Court) using 2012 data revealed positive influences for the overall political-economic context variable and evaluation of presidential performance, and evaluation of the national economy.[48] Low family standard of living, being a victim of corruption or crime, fearing for one's personal safety, and living in a large community all lowered support for specific national institutions, a result similar to our findings for 2008. Indeed, it is commonsensical that Central Americans would negatively evaluate public institutions that cannot control crime or corruption. Sex, age, and education made no difference in specific institutional support.

In summary, legitimacy, the evaluation of government performance by citizens, varied in Central America in 2012 in predictable and rational ways based on people's perceptions of whether their lives were safe and free, how the government behaved and what it delivered, and on measurable system-level economic and political performance characteristics. Demographic factors exerted little influence on either diffuse or specific institutional support, while crime and corruption experiences and beliefs, and one's evaluation of political actors and the economy influenced both.

Given Honduras' 2009 coup and resulting unrest, it is important to review that case. In 2008 Hondurans expressed the greatest support among Central Americans for an unelected, strongman leader (39 percent), the greatest support for a hypothetical military coup, and the highest support for confrontational political tactics and for rebellion against an elected government. They expressed the lowest support among Central Americans for general participation rights, tolerance for participation by regime critics, and diffuse and specific institutional support for their political system, as well as the lowest evaluation of national economic performance. Their preference for strongman rule in 2008 had increased since 2004 as their institutional-support levels had declined. These patterns suggested a population whose support for democracy was unconsolidated and deteriorating. To the extent that Honduran political elites were aware of these attitudes, they likely felt little popular pressure to comply with democratic norms and constitutionality.

What were Hondurans' views three years after the coup? Hondurans had apparently learned some lessons. In 2012 they had retreated 16 points from 2008 on their mean support for a hypothetical military coup and four points on their support for rebellion against an elected government. However, other possible lessons learned by Hondurans appeared problematic. In 2012 they expressed the most support for strongman rule (up four points over 2008), and the lowest support in the region for general and critics' participation rights (down ten points each), diffuse political support (down eight points), and specific institutional support (down four points). Thus the coup appears to have undermined support for coups and rebellion, but it also further undermined Hondurans' already tenuous commitment to democratic values.

What might these legitimacy levels mean for potential political stability? In a recent book, Booth and Seligson isolated Central Americans who expressed (1) low levels of institutional support (i.e., below the scales' midpoints), (2) low evaluations of economic performance, and (3) low commitment to basic democratic principles. They reasoned that "triply dissatisfied" citizens—those who combined all three traits—could not be relied upon to support democracy and its institutions, that they might be vulnerable to appeals by antidemocratic elites, and, indeed, that their presence in large numbers might encourage antidemocratic demagogues. They reported that in 2004 Hondurans (12 percent) and Guatemalans (15 percent) were much more likely to be low on all three attitudes than other Central Americans.[49]

We replicated their analysis in 2008 and discovered significant increases—18 percent of Guatemalans and 30 percent of Hondurans (a year before the coup) expressed such triple dissatisfaction. Replicating the analysis again for 2012 we found that 45 percent of Hondurans and 22 percent of Guatemalans were triply dissatisfied. For Guatemala that was a slight increase in triple dissatisfaction from 2008. In Honduras, however, the percentage of triply dissatisfied citizens had almost tripled since 2004. These data again suggested that Honduras remained ripe for political instability in 2012 and that, if anything, the coup had worsened the situation.

Another case worth considering is Costa Rica, where triple dissatisfaction—low commitment to democracy combined with below-midpoint economic-performance evaluations and institutional support—had risen from 2 percent in 2004 to 15 percent in 2012. A third case presents a sharp contrast to Costa Rica. Nicaraguans' expression of triple *dissatisfaction* (at 7 percent) had not changed significantly, though triple *satisfaction* rose from 13 percent in 2004 to 20 percent in 2012. Despite Nicaragua's extreme poverty, the Sandinista government was doing the region's best job of pleasing its citizens on economic and institutional performance. It was doing so while the main opposition Liberal family of political parties had effectively collapsed after losing to the FSLN in successive national elections.

Assuming that these patterns matter, our findings strongly suggest more risk of instability or public disloyalty to democracy, especially in Honduras, than in the other countries. Costa Ricans have not turned openly against their government or abandoned democratic values, but the latter have eroded somewhat while both diffuse and specific institutional support have eroded. Meanwhile, outside and domestic critics of the Ortega administration have harshly evaluated the Nicaraguan government, but Nicaraguan citizens appear increasingly contented with it.

What other attitudes and behaviors do triply disgruntled citizens hold? Compared to other more satisfied citizens, those who are triply dissatisfied protest somewhat more and express more support for confrontational political tactics. They also state less support for democracy, basic participation rights, and tolerance of dissenters' rights. All of these traits could encourage antidemocratic demagogues to challenge democracy. However, our data for 2012 continue to reveal a balancing finding that we observed for 2008—the triply dissatisfied engage somewhat less in politics than do more-satisfied citizens. They vote less and engage in party and campaign activism and civil society.[50] As of 2012, despite their less democratic views, the multi-disgruntled of Central America

FIGURE 9.1 Protest Participation Over Time, 2004–2012

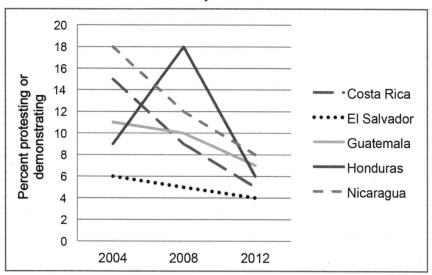

SOURCE: The AmericasBarometer by the Latin American Public Opinion Project (LAPOP), www.LapopSurveys.org.

were not more politically active than their more economically satisfied, institutionally supportive, and more democratically inclined fellow citizens.

CONCLUSIONS

Early in the twenty-first century, most Central Americans were behaving in ways necessary to and consistent with democracy by participating in politics in diverse arenas. However, certain values supportive of democracy had eroded since the previous edition of this book. Although a strong majority of Central Americans supported basic democratic participation rights and repudiated authoritarian rule in 2012, support for strongman rule and confrontational political methods had increased over 2008 levels. Meanwhile diffuse system support, support for participation rights, and tolerance of regime critics had declined significantly. These findings leave us with some concerns about democracy in the region.

Central Americans held important and in some cases growing reservations about their polities. Overall, their commitment to basic participation rights remained steady and high between 2004 and 2012, while their willingness to embrace a hypothetical coup declined. In contrast, their support for unelected leadership, though still low, rose between 2004 and 2012, while their tolerance for dissenters and support for specific national institutions declined notably. Diffuse support declined; it nonetheless remained in positive territory in four countries, though falling into negative territory in Honduras. Popular evaluation of specific institutions declined sharply in Costa Rica and Honduras while rising in El Salvador and Nicaragua. Support for confrontational political tactics rose, but support for rebellion remained stable across the region in the period covered by our surveys.

These regional trends notwithstanding, the values of Hondurans clearly deviated on the low end from regional average democratic norms and legitimacy evaluations. As Honduras vividly demonstrated with its coup in 2009, the actions and attitudes of citizens interact with complex national and international environments in shaping democratic consolidation. Hondurans' support for democracy and their political system in 2012 had deteriorated further from already low levels in 2008.

Despite their country's performance advantages, and to the surprise of many observers, Costa Ricans sank more deeply into unhappiness with their system's performance as their leaders and parties stumbled. This apparently came to a head in the 2014 Costa Rican election, in which the Citizen Action Party won the presidency for its first time, and the incumbent and long dominant National Liberation Party lost five seats in the Legislative Assembly (see Chapter 4). Meanwhile, Nicaraguans became more satisfied with their political system and rallied around its institutions under an increasingly dominant FSLN.

Central Americans, no strangers to previous bad regimes and economic turmoil, appeared willing to extend their rulers only so much rope. Significant minorities expressed hypothetical willingness to opt for protest and rebellion should their governments badly violate the social contract. Citizen support for their regimes in 2012 was strongest among Nicaraguans rather than Costa Ricans, who had previously expressed the highest evaluations. Hondurans remained by far the most simultaneously dissatisfied with institutions and economic performance and the least committed to democracy. Moreover, Hondurans were less tolerant and comparatively supportive of political confrontation and rebellion. This would alarm us more, but these very same multiply disgruntled citizens proved less active in politics than their more satisfied fellows. Thus in 2012 as before, the triply dissatisfied—19 percent of Central Americans—continued to offer mainly a latent rather than an active threat to system stability

Challenges to poorly consolidated democratic regimes tend to arise among elites—those who hold political, institutional, or economic power. In Honduras, for example, President Zelaya's efforts to consult the people about whether to promote reform of the country's constitution led him to actions judged illegal by the courts and the Supreme Electoral Tribunal. Zelaya's opponents in the armed forces and the National Congress then responded with unconstitutional procedures to oust and exile him. Because elites are the wild card in democratic consolidation, one cannot easily predict whether increased public disaffection or turmoil would threaten representative democracy as it now exists in each Central American nation.

Given this partly discouraging panorama of public opinion, what might these countries' rulers or even outsiders do to strengthen the prospects for democratic stability in Central America, especially in the cases more at risk? What actions might increase political support for these regimes? The larger contextual factors—especially the economies—are difficult for governments to manipulate in the short or medium term. Honduras and Nicaragua remain truly poor in real terms. Their disadvantages relative to the region's other three nations, and especially to the larger world economy, have actually widened in recent decades.

On the positive side, however, several factors are more malleable for local actors. Willing power holders could promote increased comity among political elites and greater accord on democratic rules of the political game. If accomplished, this could increase political stability and lower political risk. Indeed, such precedents helped found Costa Rican democracy. Peace accords in Guatemala, El Salvador, and Nicaragua bridged great chasms among elites to forge new democracies. Honduran political elites, on the other hand, have failed spectacularly to consolidate such a settlement on democratic rules, and institutions there continue to lose public support. Future efforts to refurbish Honduran democracy would require presently warring elites to advance an inter-elite democratic consensus. Costa Rica is experiencing something of the same problem, albeit public support is eroding from a higher starting point than in Honduras. Still, Costa Rican political elites might well propose several constitutional reforms that could ameliorate public disaffection.[51]

Our research has demonstrated the corrosive effect of crime and political corruption. Governments could, if they would, enact legal reforms and prosecute bribe takers. This would improve the economic climates, attract greater domestic and foreign investment, and undoubtedly win approval from citizens. Reducing political repression by improving police training and curtailing acts of official violence and repression could boost political support in the middle term by reducing fear and encouraging greater participation. Building or maintaining high-quality election systems and rules would also likely increase specific and diffuse support for political institutions. Election system quality and changes in the early 2000s were mixed. El Salvador and Guatemala improved their election systems and experienced 15 percent increases in turnout in their most recent presidential elections. Nicaragua's election system has deteriorated under increasingly partisan administrations; presidential election turnout has fallen over six points since 1990.[52] Obviously, efforts to improve election quality and reduce crime and corruption could strengthen citizen political support for civilian democratic regimes over time. Such measures were arguably at least partly within the reach of local leaders and could help each country move toward democratic consolidation.

The potential for progress toward democratic consolidation thus rests heavily on national elites as we write this. Election of a leftist president of El Salvador for the first time in 2009 and the direction of change in its citizens' attitudes and legitimacy norms seems to be moving El Salvador toward democratic consolidation, though the rhetoric of the ARENA candidates following the second round of the 2014 election was a point of concern. Nicaraguans have increased their support for institutions and political tolerance under the FSLN-led government. Nicaraguan political elites outside the ruling party, in deep disarray, express fury about the system. In Guatemala, other than increasing election turnout, prospects appear modest for ongoing political and economic progress and a further consolidation of democracy among political and economic elites. The protracted erosion of Costa Ricans' system evaluations and more recently their democratic attitudes are very worrying in the region's premier democracy. In Honduras consolidation prospects seem very poor indeed.

That leaves us with two critical questions: First, could and would national elites give the region's citizens enough economic progress and reform that the people would continue to support their fledgling democracies and not opt again to rebel? As argued repeatedly in the preceding chapters and in Chapter 10, after decades of US promotion of repression that blocked democracy, the international community eventually came together to encourage Central American regimes to adopt "low-intensity" democracy (formal electoral civilian regimes) as the Cold War waned. At the same time, however, external actors led by the United States promoted new economic policies that limited Central American governments' abilities to promote economic development with equity. Neoliberalism stripped governments of many tools to promote social welfare or invest in human capital. Thus, even if local ruling elites were willing to promote equitable development—as they had sometimes done in Costa Rica, Nicaragua, and even Honduras—neoliberalism had reduced their ability to make such choices.

The political pendulum in Latin America swung to the left with the election of several center-left governments, driven by popular frustration with such neoliberal policies. In Central America this frustration contributed to Manuel Zelaya's emergence as a populist advocate for the poor during his coup-truncated term. Nicaraguans in 2006 and Salvadorans in 2009 elected leftist governments more committed to addressing the needs of the poor. Venezuela's late president Hugo Chávez shared his country's oil wealth as foreign aid and encouraged a state-centric development model and repudiation of neoliberalism in Central America. Chávez's death in 2013 and subsequent political turmoil under his successor Nicolás Maduro called into question the stability of Venezuelan economic aid to Central America.

A second critical question is how might Central American citizens respond, through their attitudes and participation, to poor economic performance, to increased inequality, or to increasing poverty? (All these problems, recall, helped mobilize Central American unrest in the 1970s and 1980s.) At this writing, Central Americans showed somewhat flagging enthusiasm for democracy, and some expressed willingness or approval for confrontational and violent political tactics. Protests of neoliberal policies and their effects took place throughout the isthmus in the late 1990s and early 2000s. The 2008 recession was mild in Central America which, along with Venezuelan economic aid, may have bought regional leaders some time and political space. The region's economic fortunes will undoubtedly continue to fluctuate with global economic forces. The region's political future and democratic consolidation will depend heavily on how its citizens and leaders react to the vicissitudes of the world economy and powerful international actors.

RECOMMENDED READINGS AND RESOURCES

Booth, John A. 1998. *Costa Rica: Quest for Democracy*. Boulder, CO: Westview Press.

———. 2007. "Political Parties in Costa Rica: Sustaining Democratic Stability in a Latin American Context." In Paul Webb and Stephen White, eds. *Party Politics in New Democracies*. Oxford: Oxford University Press.

Booth, John A., and Patricia Bayer Richard. 1996. "Repression, Participation, and Democratic Norms in Urban Central America." *American Journal of Political Science* 40 (4):1205–1232.

———. 1998. "Civil Society, Political Capital, and Democratization in Central America." *Journal of Politics* 60 (August):780–800.

———. 2015. *Latin American Political Culture: Public Opinion and Democracy*. Washington, DC: Congressional Quarterly Press.

Booth, John A., and Mitchell A. Seligson. 1995. *Elections and Democracy in Central America Revisited*. Chapel Hill: University of North Carolina Press.

———. 2009. *The Legitimacy Puzzle in Latin America: Political Support and Democracy in Eight Nations*. Cambridge: Cambridge University Press.

Dahl, Robert A. 1998. *On Democracy*. New Haven, CT: Yale University Press.

Diamond, Larry, Juan J. Linz, and Seymour Martin Lipset. 1989. *Democracy in Developing Countries*. Volume 4: *Latin America*. Boulder, CO: Lynne Rienner Publishers.

Drake, Paul. 2009. *Between Tyranny and Anarchy: A History of Democracy in Latin America, 1800–2006*. Stanford, CA: Stanford University Press.

Hume, Mo. 2013. "El Salvador." In Diego Sánchez-Ancochea and Salvador Martí i Puig, eds. *Handbook of Central American Governance*. London: Routledge.

Huntington, Samuel. 1991. *The Third Wave: Democratization in the Late Twentieth Century.* Norman: University of Oklahoma Press.

Latin American Public Opinion Project (LAPOP). 2004–2013. Nashville, TN: Vanderbilt University Press. http://www.vanderbilt.edu/lapop/.

Pateman, Carole. 1970. *Participation and Democratic Theory.* Cambridge: Cambridge University Press.

Peeler, John A. 2004. *Building Democracy in Latin America.* Boulder, CO: Lynne Rienner Publishers.

Seligson, Mitchell A. 2002. "Trouble in Paradise: The Impact of the Erosion of System Support in Costa Rica, 1978–1999." *Latin America Research Review* 37 (1):160–185.

Seligson, Mitchell A., and John A. Booth. 1993. "Political Culture and Regime Type: Evidence from Nicaragua and Costa Rica." *Journal of Politics* 55 (August): 777–792.

Smith, Peter H. 2005. *Democracy in Latin America: Political Change in Comparative Perspective.* Oxford: Oxford University Press.

Webb, Paul, and Stephen White, eds. 2007. *Political Parties in New Democracies.* Oxford: Oxford University Press.

NOTES

1. Aristotle, *Politics (Aristotle's Politics)*, Richard Robinson, trans. (Oxford: Clarendon Press, 1962); Carl Cohen, *Democracy* (New York: Free Press, 1971); Robert A. Dahl, *On Democracy* (New Haven, CT: Yale University Press, 1998); John Stuart Mill, *Considerations on Representative Government* (Indianapolis, IN: Bobbs-Merrill, 1958); Carole Pateman, *Participation and Democratic Theory* (Cambridge: Cambridge University Press, 1970); and David Held, *Models of Democracy*, 3rd ed. (Stanford, CA: Stanford University Press, 2006). Works especially emphasizing democracy and democratization in Latin America include John A. Booth and Mitchell A. Seligson, *The Legitimacy Puzzle in Latin America: Political Support and Democracy in Eight Nations* (Cambridge: Cambridge University Press, 2009); John A. Booth, "Introduction. Elections and Democracy in Central America: A Framework for Analysis," in Mitchell A. Seligson and John A. Booth, eds., *Elections and Democracy in Central America, Revisited* (Chapel Hill: University of North Carolina Press, 1995); Larry Diamond, Juan Linz, Jonathan Hartlyn, and Seymour Martin Lipset, eds., *Democracy in Developing Countries: Latin America* (Boulder, CO: Lynne Rienner Publishers, 1999); Paul Drake, *Between Tyranny and Anarchy: A History of Democracy in Latin America, 1800–2006* (Stanford, CA: Stanford University Press, 2009); John A. Peeler, *Building Democracy in Latin America* (Boulder, CO: Lynne Rienner Publishers, 2004); and Peter H. Smith, *Democracy in Latin America: Political Change in Comparative Perspective* (Oxford: Oxford University Press, 2005).

2. The attitudes and behaviors of elites and influential foreign actors may also influence democratic consolidation. When elites share a broad consensus on democratic

rules of the political game it strengthens democracy by reducing disruptive challenges to the system. Hegemonic powers, neighboring countries, significant donors of foreign aid, and international organizations who prefer democratic rules of the game can impose costs that make it harder for local actors to abandon democratic institutions. They may also pressure local actors so as to imperil democracy. On democratic consolidation see Samuel Huntington, *The Third Wave: Democratization in the Late Twentieth Century* (Norman: University of Oklahoma Press, 1991); and Larry Jay Diamond, *Developing Democracy: Toward Consolidation* (Baltimore, MD: Johns Hopkins University Press, 1999). Peter Smith's *Democracy in Latin America* provides a cautionary note concerning the consolidation and quality of Latin American Democracy.

3. Mitchell A. Seligson and John A. Booth, "Political Culture and Regime Type: Evidence from Nicaragua and Costa Rica," *Journal of Politics* 55 (August 1993), pp. 777–792.

4. John A. Booth and Patricia Bayer Richard, *Latin American Political Culture Public Opinion and Democracy* (Washington, DC: Congressional Quarterly Press, 2015); John A. Booth and Patricia Bayer Richard, "Civil Society, Political Capital, and Democratization in Central America," *Journal of Politics* 60 (August 1998), pp. 780–800; John A. Booth and Patricia Bayer Richard, "Civil Society and Political Context in Central America," *American Behavioral Scientist* 42 (September 1998), pp. 33–46; and John A. Booth and Patricia Bayer Richard, "Repression, Participation, and Democratic Norms in Urban Central America," *American Journal of Political Science* 40:4 (November 1996), pp. 1205–1232; Seligson and Booth, "Political Culture and Regime Type."

5. Booth and Seligson, *The Legitimacy Puzzle in Latin America*, Ch. 8.

6. The 2012 and previous years' survey data were collected by research teams from Latin American countries under the auspices of the Americas Barometer of the Latin American Public Opinion Project (LAPOP), directed by Mitchell A. Seligson of Vanderbilt University. Each nation was surveyed using a large core of identical survey items. National probability samples of approximately 1,500 respondents were interviewed from each nation. Respondents were selected using stratified national sampling frames, with respondent clusters within sampling units chosen with their probability of selection proportionate to size. In the results reported here, each national sample size is weighted to 1,500 respondents, for a regional sample of 7,500. Respondents were voting-age citizens of each country. The authors thank the Latin American Public Opinion Project (LAPOP) and its major supporters for the data.

7. US Census Bureau, Voting and Registration Detailed Tables (2012), Table 1. Reported Voting and Registration, by Sex and Single Years of Age: November 2012. http://www.census.gov/hhes/www/socdemo/voting/publications/p20/2012/tables .html, accessed September 23, 2013.

8. The early 1990s surveys cited here were of urban residents only. Our comparisons between the 1990s and either 2004 or 2012 data here and elsewhere in the chapter are made for comparable urban populations. However, when we compare

2004 and later data we refer to national samples. The data for previous surveys also came from the LAPOP/Americas Barometer at Vanderbilt (see *Understanding Central America,* 4th and 5th eds., Ch. 9, and the LAPOP Web site for extended explanation and acknowledgments). In general, the sampling methodology from the early 1990s closely resembles that of the 2012 surveys. Items compared across surveys are identically worded.

9. These are the results of a multiple regression analysis using voter registration as the dependent variable with the following independent predictors: sex, age, age squared, educational attainment, standard of living, size of one's community of residence, and evaluations of regime economic performance, overall economic performance, and institutional support. Country dummies were included to control for specific national effects (Costa Rica, as the oldest democracy and most prosperous country, was excluded as the reference case). To conserve space, the full results are not shown.

10. The unweighted average voter turnout rate in the most recent presidential election through 2012 for Central America was 64 percent. Actual turnout data come from the International Institute for Democracy and Electoral Assistance (IDEA), Voter Turnout Database, presidential election turnout calculations by country, http://www.idea.int/vt/index.cfm, accessed September 23, 2013.

11. Ibid.

12. Results of a multiple regression analysis of voter registration using as dependent variables sex, age, age squared, educational attainment, standard of living, size of one's community of residence, evaluations of government economic management, overall national economic performance, and institutional support. Country dummies were included to control for specific national effects with Costa Rica as the reference case. To conserve space, the full results are not shown.

13. The early 1990s surveys consisted of an urban sample only. Again, our comparisons with the 2004 data here are for the comparable urban populations.

14. See International Institute for Democracy and Electoral Assistance (IDEA), Voter Turnout Database for all official results.

15. John A. Booth, "Political Parties in Costa Rica: Sustaining Democratic Stability in a Latin American Context," in Paul Webb and Stephen White, eds., *Party Politics in New Democracies* (Oxford: Oxford University Press, 2007).

16. Surveys from the 1990s and 2004 revealed that Central Americans had generally low confidence in parties, but there had been some change by 2012. On a 1.0 (very low) to 7.0 (very high) self-evaluation of one's "trust in parties," the following mean scores—all below the scale midpoint of 4.0—were obtained by country from our 2012 survey: Costa Rica 2.9, El Salvador 3.1, Guatemala 3.0, Hondurans 3.2, and Nicaragua 2.5. Costa Ricans, Salvadorans, and Nicaraguans reported slightly less trust in political parties than in 2004, while Guatemalans and Hondurans reported slightly more.

17. Results of a multiple regression analysis using frequency of attendance at political party meetings as the dependent variable, and as predictor variables sex, age, age

squared, educational attainment, standard of living, size of one's community of residence, evaluations of government economic management, overall national economic performance, and institutional support. Country dummies were included to control for specific national effects with Costa Rica excluded. The full results are not shown to conserve space.

18. Regional average citizen confidence in parties (on a 0 to 100 scale) remained low at 35 in 2012, statistically unchanged from 2004. Confidence in parties declined in Costa Rica (down four points to 31 out of 100) and in El Salvador (down eight points to 32). Confidence in parties rose in Guatemala (up seven points to 36 out of 100) and in Nicaragua (up 11 points to 40). Confidence in elections regionwide fell five points out of 100 from 2004 to 2012. In Nicaragua trust in elections rose seven points despite repeated problems with election administration. Elsewhere the trend of confidence in elections was markedly down, especially in Costa Rica (11 points out of 100), El Salvador (down 11 points), and Honduras (down seven points out of 100 since 2004).

19. Results of a multiple regression analysis using party and campaign activism (the average of persuading others how to vote, party meeting attendance, and campaign activity) as the dependent variable, and as predictor variables sex, age, age squared, educational attainment, standard of living, size of one's community of residence, evaluations of government economic management, overall national economic performance, and institutional support. Country dummies were included to control for specific national effects with Costa Rica excluded. The full results are not shown to conserve space.

20. John A. Booth and Patricia Bayer Richard, "Untangling Social and Political Capital in Latin American Democracies," *Latin American Politics and Society* 54:3 (September 2012): 33–64; Booth and Richard, "Civil Society and Political Context in Central America"; and Booth and Richard, "Repression, Participation, and Democratic Norms in Urban Central America."

21. The Honduran National Human Rights Commission in 2007 surveyed Hondurans' experiences with crime. It reported that 65 percent of Hondurans said they had quit going out at night for fear of violence, 44 percent curtailed their use of public transportation, and 43 percent had stopped visiting family and friends. See Borge y Asociados, *Encuesta Nacional de Opinión Pública: Seguridad Ciudadana* (Tegucigalpa, Honduras: Comisionado Nacional de los Derechos Humanos, August 2007), http://www.conadeh.hn/documentos.htm, accessed June 10, 2009.

22. We compared these 2012 data to those from a similar Central American survey from the early 1990s and discovered that Central Americans everywhere but Nicaragua reported big increases (dozens of percentage points) in involvement in church-related groups. This may stem from a widely observed growth of evangelical Protestant proselytism and the formation of myriad church congregations in the 1990s.

23. Results of a multiple regression analysis using overall group activism (the average church-related, school-related, and business-professional group activism) as the

dependent variable, and as predictor variables sex, age, age squared, educational attainment, standard of living, size of one's community of residence, evaluations of government economic management, overall national economic performance, and institutional support. Country dummies were included to control for specific national effects with Costa Rica excluded. The full results are not shown to conserve space.

24. These results are not comparable to those reported in the fourth edition of *Understanding Central America* because the question wording in 2004 for both items was "Have you ever contacted _____?" whereas in 2012 it was "Have you contacted _____ within the last twelve months?" The broader question for 2004 elicited higher reported rates of contacting officials.

25. Results of a multiple regression analysis using an index of contacting both local officials and legislators, and with sex, age, age squared, educational attainment, standard of living, size of one's community of residence, evaluations of regime legitimacy with respect to the economy, local government, political actors (the executive branch), and support for the democratic regime, as well as country dummies to control for specific national effects (Costa Rica was the excluded reference case). Age squared and squared terms for the five legitimacy variables were also included. Results not shown to conserve space.

26. Costa Rican governments typically respond to protests with study and policy change; see John A. Booth, *Costa Rica: Quest for Democracy* (Boulder, CO: Westview Press, 1998).

27. Results of a multiple regression analysis using protesting as the dependent variable, and as predictor variables sex, age, age squared, educational attainment, standard of living, size of one's community of residence, evaluations of government economic management, overall national economic performance, and institutional support. Country dummies were included to control for specific national effects (Costa Rica excluded). The full results are not shown to conserve space.

28. This pattern of U-shaped legitimacy-participation relationships confirms the findings of Booth and Seligson in *The Legitimacy Puzzle in Central America* (Ch. 5), who analyzed the same 2004 data set examined for our five countries, plus Mexico, Panama, and Colombia, and a 2002 data set for Costa Rica.

29. John A. Booth and Patricia Bayer Richard, *Latin American Political Culture:- Public Opinion and Democracy.*

30. Seligson and Booth, "Political Culture and Regime Type."

31. Results of a multiple regression analysis using the item on support for a strong, unelected leader as the dependent variable, and as independent variables sex, age, age squared, educational attainment, standard of living, size of one's community of residence, perceived safety of one's neighborhood from crime, corruption victimization, crime victimization, several political participation variables, and various legitimacy norms. The results are not shown to conserve space.

32. Results of a multiple regression analysis using the index of coup justification under certain hypothetical circumstances as the dependent variable, and as independent variables sex, age, age squared, educational attainment, standard of living, size of one's community of residence, perceived safety of one's neighborhood from crime, corruption victimization, crime victimization, several political participation variables, and various legitimacy norms. The results are not shown to conserve space.

33. Results of a multiple regression analysis using an index of support for basic political participation rights as the dependent variable, and as independent variables sex, age, age squared, educational attainment, standard of living, size of one's community of residence, perceived safety of one's neighborhood from crime, corruption victimization, crime victimization, several political participation variables, and various legitimacy norms. The results are not shown to conserve space.

34. Results of a multiple regression analysis using an index of support for basic political participation rights as the dependent variable, and as independent variables sex, age, age squared, educational attainment, standard of living, size of one's community of residence, perceived safety of one's neighborhood from crime, corruption victimization, crime victimization, several political participation variables, and various legitimacy norms. The results are not shown to conserve space.

35. Michael W. Foley, "Laying the Groundwork: The Struggle for Civil Society in El Salvador," *Journal of Interamerican Studies and World Affairs* 38 (1996), pp. 67–104.

36. Again, the data compared between the early 1990s and 2004 are for urban samples only.

37. Booth and Richard, *Latin American Political Culture: Public Opinion and Democracy.* The results reported here come from a multiple regression analysis using an index of support confrontational political methods as the dependent variable, and as independent variables.

38. Results of a multiple regression analysis using an item asking the level of the respondent's approval for armed rebellion against an elected government as the dependent variable, and as independent variables sex, age, age squared, educational attainment, standard of living, size of one's community of residence, perceived safety of one's neighborhood from crime, corruption victimization, crime victimization, several political participation variables, and various legitimacy norms. The results are not shown to conserve space.

39. Because it has no national armed forces, Costa Rica was excluded from this calculation for the military only.

40. Mitchell A. Seligson, "Trouble in Paradise: The Impact of the Erosion of System Support in Costa Rica, 1978–1979," *Latin American Research Review* 37 (No. 1, 2002), pp. 160–185; Fulton Armstrong, "Costa Rica: Losing Faith in Democratic Institutions?" AULA Blog, Center for Latin American and Latino Studies, American University, http://aulablog.net/2013/11/11/costa-rica-losing-faith-in-democratic-institutions/, accessed November 15, 2013.

41. These two measures in 2012 correlated with each other positively (Pearson's r = 0.48), indicating that the more corruption citizens experience, the more they and others perceive it to be a problem.

42. The correlation (Pearson's r) between crime victimization and the perception of insecurity in one's own neighborhood for 2012 is 0.18. Experiencing crime breeds a fear of crime among victims.

43. For example, see Booth and Seligson, *The Legitimacy Puzzle*.

44. Results of a multiple regression analysis using the index of evaluation of economic performance as the dependent variable. Independent variables were sex, age, educational attainment, standard of living, size of one's community of residence, corruption victimization, perceived corruption, crime victimization, perceived level of personal insecurity, evaluation of the nation's human rights performance, evaluation of the incumbent president, and the overall system performance variable described in note 50. Results are omitted to conserve space.

45. Because of the high intercorrelation (they vary similarly) of the four political-economic context variables in Table 9.3 they cannot be employed together in a multiple regression analysis. We therefore standardized GDP per capita, the combined democracy measure, the Political Terror Scale, and the functioning of government index and combined them into a single measure of system performance that equally weights each of these components. This system performance variable may be employed in a multiple regression analysis. We also reran this analysis using only GDP per capita in 2007 in place of the system performance measure to confirm that the economic variable mattered; the results were virtually identical to the analysis using overall system performance.

46. In analysis of the 2012 results we found a positive contribution of both context measures to economic evaluations; *Understanding Central America*, 5th ed., p. 202.

47. Results of a multiple regression analysis using the index of diffuse support for the political system as the dependent variable. Independent variables were sex, age, educational attainment, standard of living, size of one's community of residence, corruption victimization, perceived corruption, crime victimization, perceived level of personal insecurity, evaluation of national economic performance, evaluation of the incumbent president, and the overall system performance variable. Results are omitted to conserve space.

48. Results of a multiple regression analysis using the index of support for specific institutions as the dependent variable. Independent variables were sex, age, age squared, educational attainment, standard of living, size of one's community of residence, corruption victimization, perceived corruption, crime victimization, perceived level of personal insecurity, evaluation of national economic performance, evaluation of the incumbent president, evaluation of political actors, and the overall system performance variable. Results not shown to conserve space.

49. Booth and Seligson, *The Legitimacy Puzzle in Latin America*, Table 8.2.

50. See *Understanding Central America*, 5th ed., Figure 9.1.

51. Constitutional revision in Central America typically requires a two-thirds supermajority vote of the national legislature (60 percent in Nicaragua) for partial constitutional reforms. See the Political Database of the Americas, Center for Latin American Studies, Georgetown University, "Comparative Constitutional Studies," http://pdba.georgetown.edu/Comp/comparative.html, accessed November 15, 2013.

52. International Institute for Democracy and Electoral Assistance, Voter Turnout, Presidential, http://www.idea.int/vt/countryview.cfm?id=-1#pres, accessed November 13, 2013.

10

POWER, DEMOCRACY, AND US POLICY IN CENTRAL AMERICA

CENTRAL AMERICAN POLITICS DERIVE IN PART FROM EACH COUNTRY'S independent evolution, but the United States also exerts great influence. US proximity and the gross disparities in population and wealth between the region's major hegemon and its tiny neighbors have long allowed US policy to shape the region, sometimes to Central Americans' detriment. Washington's Cold War–era definition of its interests in Central America and its strategies for achieving them were short-termed, reactive, and excessively concerned with stability. The US effort to contain leftist influence and insurgency from the 1960s through the 1990s intensified national conflicts. By the mid-1990s civil wars had killed over 300,000 people (mainly civilians), nearly ruined regional economies, displaced millions, and left countless others jobless, orphaned, or physically or psychologically maimed. While by no means the only cause of the Central American tragedy, US policy contributed importantly to its onset and evolution.

The Cold War between the United States and the Soviets ended in 1990, and Central America's revolutionary-counterrevolutionary conflicts ended in 1996. US fears of Communist-inspired uprisings and subversion accordingly waned, and the United States scaled back its intervention in the region.

Nevertheless, Washington's policy in the region in the late 1990s and early 2000s remained interventionist, still informed by the ideological framework that shaped US Cold War intervention. The particular tools of US involvement in Central America changed more than the underlying policy itself.

Although the tactics of US policy toward the isthmus have evolved, overall US objectives have remained remarkably constant. US governments have always sought to protect US economic and security interests. This has entailed keeping as much control as possible over Central American events and policies to reduce perceived security threats and while maximizing economic interests. Even in times of lofty rhetoric about good neighborliness, the Alliance for Progress, human rights, or democracy, US policies consistently focused on maintaining political stability and influencing regional governments. Concerned about the Cuban revolution, President Kennedy promoted the Alliance for Progress to encourage economic development and democracy in Latin America. He simultaneously increased US military assistance throughout the region. US military aid under Presidents Kennedy, Johnson, and Nixon, intended to assist Latin American armed forces contain Communism, also helped them topple democratic regimes and worsened human rights abuses. Ironically, the presence of US-backed, rights-abusing dictatorships helped spark insurgencies in Central America from the 1960s throughout the 1980s.

US involvement in the isthmus diminished after 1990, and Central America virtually vanished from the news. Washington, however, has continued to promote US security and economic interests by keeping leftist politicians out of power, and by aggressively promoting economic policies and development models that conform to US interests.

THE PROBLEM OF POWER

Power is the basic currency of politics. Simply put, groups within a given polity generally receive benefit from the prevailing political regime in rough proportion to the amount of power they can bring to bear on that regime. The powerful receive the most; the powerless, little or nothing. Charles W. Anderson argued that the traditional "power contenders" in Latin American society—the Church, the military, the rural and urban economic elites— allow new groups to enter and receive benefits from the political system only when these groups demonstrate their own "power capabilities."[1] We showed in Chapter 2 that regime changes in Central America—especially struggles for democratization—have involved conflict and the reconfiguration of relationships among traditional power contenders and newer groups from the working, middle, and even upper classes.

Power capabilities vary from group to group. The Catholic Church exercises authority through its belief systems and moral suasion. The military holds much of the means of violent coercion. Economic elites use their wealth to influence policy and institutions. In contrast, lower-class groups have scant resources but can sometimes wield influence by organizing, striking, protesting, and voting. But normally the majority of Central American peasants, urban and rural workers, and slum dwellers lack sufficient organization and resources to give them real power capabilities. During the Cold War, when such groups attempted to develop power through organization, existing power holders called them subversives and "Communists" and violently repressed them. Because Central America's poor majorities held little power, policy makers usually ignored their plight. Previous chapters have shown, country by country, how this generated popular grievances, and how some regimes suppressed these grievances and thus made violence the people's last recourse.

Great power disparities between the small privileged upper class and its emerging middle-class allies and the underprivileged, impoverished majority generated the Central American crisis of the late twentieth century. As we noted in earlier chapters, power relationships in the five countries had deep historical roots. It is no accident that Costa Rica, with the most egalitarian society, and Honduras—an economic backwater that never developed a cohesive, exploitative national elite—were least affected by turmoil. It is also no surprise that Guatemala, El Salvador, and Nicaragua, the countries with the greatest historically rooted power disparities, experienced the region's highest levels of violence. Their elites, long accustomed to their lopsided power advantage, resisted sharing power and making policies to promote the genuine development of all sectors of society.

DEMOCRACY

Democracy provides a base of legitimacy for contemporary governments, and most regimes today claim to be democratic. The term *democracy*, however, is contested and its meaning debated. Socialist theorists usually stress distributive economic and social criteria, whereas those from the industrially developed West tend to emphasize procedural rules. In the United States, one definition with which few would quarrel is that democracy is "government of, by, and for the people." However simple this definition may sound, it sets forth two principles fundamental to effective democracy: first, that the system should be as participatory as possible, and, second, that it should facilitate general well-being.[2]

In the 1980s the United States promoted civilian rule and elections in Central America. When these appeared Washington proclaimed the birth of "democracy" in its client states, Guatemala, El Salvador, and Honduras, but condemned its alleged absence in revolutionary Nicaragua. Only in 1990, when the besieged Nicaraguan people elected the US-backed Violeta Barrios de Chamorro president, did Washington finally recognized Nicaragua as democratic. Closer inspection, however, makes this US interpretation difficult to sustain.[3] All four countries held nationwide, internationally observed elections. Observers pronounced elections in three countries—excluding El Salvador's in the 1980s—to be procedurally clean. But democracy requires much more than simply holding procedurally correct elections or establishing formal civilian rule. A critical issue is popular participation in elections and in other political affairs.

The elections in Guatemala in 1985 and 1990 as well as those in El Salvador in 1982, 1984, 1988, 1989, and 1991 took place under conditions of state-sponsored terror that had taken tens of thousands of lives and had disarticulated most mass-based civic and political organizations. Independent or critical media outlets were nonexistent. Repression confined most citizen participation in formal national politics to voting. Tiny minorities of center and right-wing parties nominated candidates and campaigned. Repression kept turnout low. In Nicaragua in 1984 and 1990, in contrast, there was no program of state-sponsored terror. Organizations representing the poor majority had been encouraged to develop, grow, and make demands on government. Opposition parties and elite interest groups openly participated in politics. International human rights organizations concurred that the systematized torture, murder, and disappearance of political opponents, widespread and institutionalized in Guatemala and El Salvador, were absent in Nicaragua. Though important rightists boycotted the 1984 Nicaraguan election, three parties on the FSLN's right and three on their left challenged the Sandinistas. Nicaragua's anti-regime media (including *La Prensa* and Radio Católica), though partly censored, carried an anti-Sandinista message to the voters. The six participating opposition parties enjoyed extensive, uncensored free access to state-sponsored radio and television.

One may also question the US application of the term *democracy* in Central America during the Cold War by asking: Were there governments "for the people"? In whose interest did they rule? The Sandinista revolution made efforts to deliver benefits to the people. By 1984, even its critics credited the government with "significant gains against illiteracy and disease."[4] Nicaragua also promoted agrarian reform, housing, social security, and the status of women. Eventually the US-backed Contra war forced the diversion of public spending away from social welfare and to the military budget. By the 1990 election most social programs had been sharply reduced, and the country was mobilized for war. Nicaragua's disastrous economic and political situation in 1990 led its citizens to use the democratic election system established by the revolutionary regime to vote the FSLN out of office and end the revolution.

Thus the Sandinista handover to the opposition in 1990 flowed from democratic rules of the game already in place and confirmed Nicaragua's transition to a civilian democratic regime in 1987.

In El Salvador and Guatemala, in contrast, the process of regime change toward democracy during the last decade of the Cold War proceeded differently. In each, the reformist military regime that overthrew the military-authoritarian regime acted with so much violent repression that many observers detected no meaningful transformation of the political systems. When each country's reformist military regime ceded rule to a transitional civilian government, skepticism abounded about how much real power these elected civilian rulers had while their militaries still held veto power over key matters. Civilian politicians, however, gradually gained independence from the armed forces as the Cold War faded, and formerly excluded power contenders were eventually allowed to take part. Honduras followed a similar path of gradual transition to democracy, albeit without a civil war or such intense repression.

Eventually all four countries established elected civilian regimes under pressure from the United States, but the quality of their democracies still remained to be determined as this was written. Some argue that not only must formal rules of democracy and repression-free popular participation exist but, more important, qualitative and socioeconomic foundations must also exist. To truly participate and thus influence decisions in a formally democratic country, the poor majority needs socioeconomic well-being and the fundamental human and political resources it provides. By the late 1990s Nicaragua, El Salvador, Guatemala, and Honduras all had formal civilian democracies, but poverty and maldistributed income and wealth left poor citizens largely without the socioeconomic requisites of an effective democracy.

Critics have accordingly tagged the four new democracies of Central America as "low-intensity democracies" or "polyarchies" to distinguish them from more egalitarian regimes of rule "by the people and for the people."[5] The rankings on comparative democracy indexes (see Figure 2.1) for Nicaragua, El Salvador, Guatemala, and Honduras confirm the mediocre performance of these formally democratic regimes. Thus elites—albeit including a broader circle of power contenders than in the 1970s—continue to dominate the polities and poorly meet democracy's basic norms even under formally elected civilian regimes.

MOBILIZATION

Following World War II, awareness grew that something was seriously wrong in Latin America. Those who viewed mass poverty as rooted in an extremely unequal distribution of power began advocating a greater diffusion of power.

In the 1940s and 1950s, social democratic and Christian democratic parties talked of "penetrating" the masses, of creating and fortifying party-oriented labor, peasant, and neighborhood organizations that would unify and express mass interests. Catholic educators such as Brazil's Paulo Freire argued that mass empowerment would require the emergence of a socially, politically, and linguistically literate citizenry. Followers of these teachings began promoting adult-education consciousness-raising programs in which poor people examined and questioned their social conditions.[6]

Jolted by the Cuban revolution in 1959, the United States at first supported reform in Latin America with programs like the Alliance for Progress (to promote economic growth) and the Peace Corps (to promote community development by mobilizing, educating, and empowering poor people to solve their own problems). For a while, thousands of idealistic US citizens worked with Latin America's poor and promoted collective self-help programs. Others promoted popular participation and mass mobilization. The US Agency for International Development (USAID) encouraged Central American governments to develop hundreds of community-action and improvement programs and cooperatives. Ultimately local and US-sponsored mobilization caused a surge of democratic participation by ordinary Central Americans. Soon, however, some Central American elites viewed this mobilization by the poor as a threat. They chided Peace Corps volunteers for associating with "Communists"—that is, the poor engaged in community action. Eventually, when the central governments complained to US diplomats, the Nixon administration terminated Peace Corps community-action programs. Thus keeping good relations with pro-US regimes mattered more to Washington than promoting popular participation and democratization.

The Latin American Catholic Church promoted the most extensive mobilization in the hemisphere in the 1960s. Beginning in the 1950s, Church figures such as Dom Helder Câmara of Brazil promoted "liberation theology," which called for social justice and uplifting the oppressed majority. By the end of that decade and the beginning of the next, they found a powerful ally in the Vatican as Pope John XXIII undertook his *aggiornamento,* or updating, of the Catholic Church. Part of this process, as expressed by the Second Vatican Council, was to focus on the problems of Latin America, by then the largest single segment of world Catholicism. This, in turn, stimulated Latin American Catholics to engage in deeper examination of the human problems of their region.

The apex of such concern came at the Second General Conference of Latin American Bishops at Medellín, Colombia, in 1968. Focusing on poverty and exploitation in Latin America, the bishops used a form of structural analysis not unlike the "dependency" explanation we discussed in Chapter 2.[7] They argued that Catholic clergy should make a "preferential option for the poor" by

GRASSROOTS MOBILIZATION. A protest march in San José, Costa Rica (photo by John Booth). Adult education in Nicaragua as depicted in a revolutionary mural (photo by Thomas Walker).

promoting Christian base communities (*comunidades eclesiales de base*, CEBs). In these grassroots organizations people of all classes would discuss the social problems of their community or country in light of the social gospel. In addition, natural community leaders or lay "delegates of the word" would be trained to preach the social gospel and act as community organizers.[8]

The Medellín bishops' conference deeply affected Latin America, especially Central America. Perhaps to the astonishment of many conservative bishops who had perfunctorily signed the high-sounding Medellín declarations, thousands of priests and nuns—and even a few bishops—began implementing these ideas almost immediately. By the 1970s, newly created CEBs were promoting extensive grassroots mobilization in the region's four northern countries. Tens of thousands of poor people were learning that, as human beings made in the image of God, they had rights to fair treatment, dignity, and justice from their governments and employers. Though the objectives and tactics of the CEBs were nonviolent, elite-dominated governments predictably viewed them as highly subversive. Again the label "Communist" was applied and, eventually, tens of thousands of Catholics, including dozens of priests and nuns and even one archbishop, died in the resulting repression.

By the mid- to late 1970s, social mobilization had become widespread throughout northern Central America. Peasants had joined unions and created cooperative organizations concerned with production and marketing. Urban workers had expanded the labor movement. Teachers, medical personnel, students, and women became more organized and active. As we noted in Chapter 8, the Honduran regime chose to accommodate or only mildly repress mobilization. Such relative moderation is probably the major reason why Honduras avoided open insurrection. In Somoza's Nicaragua, and in Guatemala and El Salvador, however, the more entrenched elites chose violent demobilization of new popular demands rather than accommodation. State repression prompted responding violence as increasing numbers opted for insurrection. In Nicaragua, mobilization, responding repression, and insurrection ultimately led to a revolutionary coalition victory in 1979. In Guatemala and El Salvador, state-sponsored terrorism (with especially heavy US material support—see Appendix, Table A.3) curtailed or reversed civilian mobilization and stalemated rebels.

The mobilization that had brought the rebel victory in Nicaragua continued under the revolutionary government thereafter. Prior to the victory, Catholics from the Christian base movement had joined with nationalist Marxists from the FSLN and others to organize a variety of grassroots organizations (see Chapter 5). After 1979 the CEB movement continued and other grassroots organizations emerged among farmers and ranchers. A 1984 estimate put between 700,000 and 800,000 Nicaraguan citizens—around half of all adults—in such organizations.[9]

Grassroots organizations defended the revolution, promoted political socialization, mobilized volunteers to carry out social programs, and provided venues for political participation, activities that ordinary people had never before experienced. The local organizations held internal elections, discussed local needs, organized to solve them, petitioned their government for everything from material and financial support to major changes in government policy, and named representatives to the planning boards of government economic and social service entities.[10] Sometimes petty corruption and abuse of power occurred, but overall the groups gave many ordinary Nicaraguan citizens their first experience of meaningful political participation.

The Sandinista-led government also used education to advance participation and democracy. Borrowing the techniques of Paulo Freire and using tens of thousands of volunteers, the revolutionary government undertook a basic literacy crusade its first year in power. The drive lowered rates of adult illiteracy and won Nicaragua a United Nations prize. For several years thereafter, the government sought to maintain and increase literacy and generally improve the educational level of all Nicaraguans. This not only built workforce skills but socialized Nicaraguans to support the revolution. A central motive for promoting education was to "empower" the people—to create a citizenry capable of intelligent self-government.[11]

THE ROOTS OF US POLICY IN CENTRAL AMERICA

At least until the end of the Cold War, the United States had certain legitimate, and widely consensual, security interests in Central America. Most agreed that it was in the interest of the United States that no Soviet bases, troops, advanced weapons, or nuclear arms be present in the isthmus, and that no country in the region form a military alliance with the Soviet Union. It was and remains in the interest of the United States that Central American societies enjoy sufficient prosperity, democracy, and political stability that their citizens not emigrate massively. Similarly, Central American nations needed peace among themselves, and mutually balanced and appropriately sized military forces. An arms race or intraregional conflict might have caused a war in Central America, sparked US military intervention there, or threatened the security of the Panama Canal or important trade routes. However, many critics of US policy in Central America believe that US actions during the Cold War actually harmed rather than advanced these interests. In order to understand how this came about, we must review the roots of US policy.

US interests in Central America have evolved over time and have sometimes been subject to intense debate within the United States. During the nineteenth century, encouraging trade, coping with massive British naval power, and transit across the isthmus dominated US concerns. As US sea power supplanted British dominance in the late nineteenth century and as the United States rapidly industrialized, the desire to establish and control a trans-isthmian canal led to US intervention in Panama in 1903. Once canal construction and operation were under way, the United States used troops in Panama and Nicaragua to assure a continuing canal monopoly and protect the canal itself. American diplomats (sometimes assisted by the US marines) aggressively promoted US business and geopolitical interests throughout Central America in the early twentieth century. During World War II, the United

States protected the Panama Canal from Axis interference through cooperative security arrangements with regional governments.

During the Cold War, US interests in Central America remained focused on economic and security concerns. Containing Soviet-inspired Communism was the major objective driving US policy. Despite the boom brought about by the Central American Common Market in the 1960s, US investments in Central America remained modest compared to those in most other parts of the world. Nevertheless, promotion of a "healthy business climate" in Central America also heavily influenced US policy choices.

Washington viewed popular mobilization in Central America after 1960 as problematic. Although a cause for hope for millions of poor people and a true step toward democracy, mobilization especially worried some of Central America's entrenched elites who responded with state terror to discourage participation. Hearkening to their cries of "Communist subversion," Washington joined the fray. The US government—whose citizens tenaciously defend their own right to participate in civic and interest organizations—allied itself with the privileged minority in Central America in its campaign against participatory mobilization. US policy in the region perhaps responded more to domestic political fears, misperceptions, and rhetoric in the United States and the fears of local elites than to the reality of the situation in the isthmus.

As a capitalist country, the United States promoted capitalism and protected US business interests at home and abroad. Policy makers in the White House, State Department, and Congress usually formulated national security—especially in Central America and the Caribbean—as much in business and trade terms as along military and geostrategic lines. From the early twentieth century on, the impulse to contain this "threat of Communism" motivated conservative politicians and cowed their critics. After World War II, and especially after the Cuban revolution, the fear of Soviet-inspired Communism in our backyard shaped US policy in Central America. Reformers were usually viewed as incompatible with US interests because American politicians feared being accused of "losing ground" to Communism. Thus even US leaders sympathetic to socioeconomic reform and democracy supported demobilization of Central American reformers whose demands were labeled "subversive" by Central American elites or by interested US observers.[12]

Much of the US preoccupation with Communism in Central America, however, was ill-founded and inappropriate.[13] (We examine Communism in Central America below). Ill-advised or not, most administrations from the 1940s through the 1980s strongly believed that Communism threatened. They transmitted this concern to Latin American military establishments as part of a doctrine of national security that justified a systematic and widespread demobilization campaign in Central America.

As taught in war colleges and military training centers around the hemisphere, the doctrine of national security was a product of both US anti-Communism and Latin American elaboration. It originated in an elaborate national security apparatus (i.e., CIA, National Security Council) created in the United States in the late 1940s. In 1950, National Security Council document NSC-68 described an expanding Communist menace and urged huge increases in military expenditures. Even though George Kennan, the originator of the concept of containment of Communism, by then felt that the threat described in NSC-68 was exaggerated, it nevertheless guided US behavior in the early Cold War. Its ideas spread to Latin America through US training programs for virtually all of the military establishments of the hemisphere.

Latin America in the 1950s and 1960s provided fertile ground for these Cold War security concepts. Though local Communist parties were weak and there were few, if any, external threats to the security of any of the elite-based governments, the privileged classes and their military allies found it convenient to portray popular mobilization and protest as subversive and part of a Moscow-controlled plot. In this setting, national security ideas from the United States were quickly adapted and refined into a fully fledged ideology, complete with training centers, native military philosophers, literature, and annual meetings of the Latin American Anti-Communist Confederation. The ideology was geopolitical, viewing national and international politics as a zero-sum game between Communism and the "free world." Whether in foreign or domestic affairs, a loss of territory, allegiance, or influence for one side was seen as a gain for the other. Internal politics became a battlefield. Social, economic, and political justice became largely irrelevant or seen as a point of entry for threatening ideological influences.

The national security doctrine was inherently elitist. It held the military uniquely capable of understanding the national good and, therefore, having the right to run the state and make decisions for society as a whole if military leaders judged that civilian politicians were performing poorly. The doctrine directly equated democracy with a visceral anti-Communism. Accordingly, strange as it may seem, the harshly authoritarian anti-Communist "national security states" created under this ideology were often described by their apologists as "democratic."

All opposition to national security states—and most forms of civilian organization except those on the right—were viewed as subversive and "Communist" or "Communist-inspired." Brutal demobilization and atomization of civilian society were accepted as appropriate. US personnel on occasion actively encouraged their Latin American colleagues to use what they euphemistically called "counterterror" (the widespread use of extralegal arrest, torture, and murder to quiet so-called subversive groups).[14] Most Latin American militaries and police received technical and material assistance and training including counterterror techniques. It is not surprising, therefore, that the tactics of torture, murder, and disappearance employed by security forces and government-sponsored death squads were similar from country to country.[15]

By the late 1960s and early 1970s, the USAID's benignly titled Office of Public Safety had close links to the security forces of Brazil, Uruguay, and Guatemala, countries with radical demobilization programs using death squads, torture, murder, and disappearance.[16] In the early 1970s these links became a public scandal in the United States and throughout the world. The US Congress investigated the links between American government programs and state-sponsored terror in Latin America. In 1974, Congress formally terminated US police and internal security aid programs and ordered the Department of State to submit yearly reports on the human rights performance of all countries to which the US government supplied aid. But these measures did not solve the problem. In practice, State Department human rights reports seemed to be influenced and colored more by the status quo–oriented policy goals of Washington than by the objective reality of the countries supposedly being described.[17] And though some of the most objectionable US links were discreetly terminated, state-sponsored terror and direct or indirect US material aid continued to rights-violating regimes and forces. Starting in 1982, the Reagan administration began successfully petitioning an increasingly red-baited Congress to make exceptions to the 1974 prohibition against US assistance to the security forces of El Salvador, Guatemala, and Honduras.

COMMUNISM IN CENTRAL AMERICA

Because so much US policy turned on the question of Communism in Central America, we must explore its meaning and influence. Most Central American insurgents and many of the area's intellectuals found Marxist and, in some cases, Leninist analysis useful in understanding the reality around them. Nevertheless, it is misleading to equate the intellectual acceptance of those analytical tools with a commitment to a Communist agenda or political subservience to the Soviet-oriented international Communist movement. Most Central Americans were too pragmatic and nationalistic to accept such control. Indeed, Soviet-oriented Communist parties fared poorly in Central America. Communists, socialists, and anarchists—many of them European exiles—influenced Central American intellectual life and labor movements in the early twentieth century. The Communists, followers of Karl Marx, received a boost over their leftist competitors because of the Soviet revolution in Russia. Although always targets of repression, Communists gained leadership roles in Central American labor movements in the 1930s. The Soviet alliance with the West during World War II gave the region's tiny Communist parties and their more successful unions a brief political opening in the early 1940s. Although repression of the left resumed in most countries after 1945, brief exceptions occurred in Costa Rica in the 1940s and Guatemala in the early 1950s, where Communist elements were junior partners with more conservative parties in government coalitions. Communist parties generally fared poorly because Soviets limited local parties' flexibility to pursue national solutions. The Stalin-Hitler pact of 1939 discredited Communists in Central America and elsewhere. Soviet insistence in later years that Latin American Communists seek accommodation with local dictators further tarnished their already poor image. Moscow so restrained local Communist parties that, in the 1960s, less-patient advocates of sociopolitical reform resigned in disgust and emulated Castro's successful insurgency.

Throughout most of their histories, therefore, local nationalists—including most other Marxists—mistrusted the small, Moscow-oriented Communist parties of Central America. Most Central American revolutionaries and intellectuals remember that the Cuban Communist Party, faithful to Soviet orders to peacefully coexist with Fulgencio Batista, opposed Fidel Castro until just before the rebel victory. In Costa Rica, the local Communist Party, the region's largest, backed the presidencies of Rafael Calderón Guardia (1940 to 1944) and Teodoro Picado Michalski (1944 to 1948). When Calderón Guardia and his allies won the 1948 election, the opposition claimed fraud and started a successful rebellion led by anti-Communist social democratic forces. Thereafter the Costa Rican Communists never won more than five of the 57 seats in the Legislative Assembly, and after the mid-1980s their influence eventually faded to nil.

In Nicaragua the Communist-led labor movement collaborated with the Somoza dictatorship in the 1940s. The founders of the FSLN broke away from the pro-Soviet Nicaraguan Socialist Party because it offered no solutions to Nicaragua's problems. Only just before the FSLN victory did the local Communists join the rebel cause. In Nicaragua after the rebel victory, no Moscow-oriented Communist Party played more than a peripheral role in the new government. In the election of 1984, Nicaragua's three Communist parties, which had lambasted the FSLN for allegedly selling out the revolution, garnered only 3.8 percent of the total vote.[18] After 1984, Nicaragua's traditional Communists remained opposed to the FSLN. In El Salvador, local Communists joined the insurrectionary effort just shortly before the would-be "final offensive" of late 1980 and early 1981.

In summary, during the Cold War traditional Central American Communist parties exercised their greatest influence on labor movements and in limited periods of participation in government in Costa Rica and Guatemala. However, at their strongest they remained weak, unpopular, opposed to revolution, and subservient to Moscow.

Central America's Marxist revolutionary movements were more complex than the region's traditional Communist parties. Most of the principal leaders of Nicaragua's FSLN, El Salvador's FMLN, and Guatemala's URNG were Marxist-Leninists. They shared socialism's predilection for distributive justice as an answer for unjust societies. Their revolutionary strategy followed Castro's in Cuba—guerrilla warfare against the regime and its armed forces, supplemented by tactical alliances with other social and political forces. Marxist-Leninist rebels, as we noted earlier, gained popular support largely because of the repressiveness of the regimes of Nicaragua, El Salvador, and Guatemala. In Nicaragua, the Sandinistas built their support base and broad coalition as the most viable alternative for those brutally repressed by the Somoza regime. Intense governmental repression blocked moderate, centrist options for redress of grievances in El Salvador and Guatemala and drove many into Marxist-led guerrilla movements.

Marxist-Leninist rebels regarded Cuba as a friend and ally and received some Cuban aid in their struggles. Soviet and Eastern bloc assistance to insurgents was limited, in keeping with Moscow's skepticism about their chances for success. Once the Sandinistas won power in Nicaragua, however, their links to the Soviet bloc became overtly friendly and Moscow became more cooperative. After the West refused to provide Nicaraguan military assistance in 1980, and correctly anticipating increased American hostility, the Sandinistas turned to Cuban and Soviet arms and advice for reorganizing their security forces.[19] As US antagonism mounted in the early and mid-1980s, Nicaragua rapidly strengthened its links to the Eastern bloc to counter an expected invasion, fend off the Contras, and replace embargoed Western aid, trade, and credit.[20]

Despite such links, the Sandinistas remained pragmatic in most policies. Instead of imposing Soviet-style Stalinist centralism and one-party political monopoly of the revolution (as Castro did in Cuba), they promoted a mixed economy and retained political pluralism. Although the Sandinistas never hid that they found parts of Marxist and Leninist analysis useful, their social, economic, and political policies revealed them to be pragmatic and nationalists, not orthodox Communists.

Nicaragua's critics highlighted the Sandinista government's friendly relationship with the socialist bloc, but that link should be put in perspective. Nicaragua increased its ties not only to the Eastern bloc but also to many non-Communist regimes. Nicaragua increased trade, aid, and diplomatic relations with governments as disparate as those of Brazil, Canada, Chile, France, Libya, the People's Republic of China, the Scandinavian countries, and Spain. Although Nicaragua frequently voted with the USSR in the United Nations, it sometimes abstained (e.g., on votes on Afghanistan and the Korean Airlines shoot-down) or voted against the USSR on important UN issues (e.g., the matter of sending a peacekeeping force to Lebanon). Nicaragua's UN voting record from 1979 through 1985 revealed that, although Nicaragua often voted against US positions and with the USSR, it agreed almost as often with most Latin American countries, especially with Mexico.[21] Although Nicaragua eventually relied almost exclusively on the socialist bloc for military supplies, the Sandinistas had first asked the United States to help standardize its military equipment. In spite of the Pentagon's endorsement of that Nicaraguan proposal, the Carter administration—facing a conservative, Cold War–embracing Ronald Reagan in the 1980 election campaign—chose the politically safe option of rejecting that request.[22]

Like the Sandinistas, other Central American insurgents appeared to be Marxist-Leninists with respect to revolutionary strategy, but pragmatic and nationalistic in concrete policy matters. They recognized that US influence in the isthmus would probably doom any purely Communist regime or government, especially one that allowed Soviet troops or missiles within its borders. Moreover, by the 1980s evidence of the failure of Stalinist political and economic centralism abounded. To assume that the Sandinistas or Central America's other Marxist rebels would ape failed systems was unrealistic.

Although the United States had been intensely worried about Communism in Central America for decades, its concerns now appear overblown. Communist parties were weak. Marxist-Leninist guerrillas had not prospered in Honduras and Costa Rica, where regimes were not excessively repressive. The excessive American concern about Communism produced misguided, counterproductive policies—the ugliest of which was to assist repressive regimes in their campaigns of demobilization.

DEMOBILIZATION IN CENTRAL AMERICA

Despite some death squad activity in Honduras in the early 1980s, systematic mass demobilization programs occurred largely where traditional elites were the most powerful and entrenched—Guatemala, El Salvador, and Nicaragua under the Somozas. In Guatemala and El Salvador, demobilization took the form of state-sponsored terror. In Nicaragua it came as state-sponsored terror prior to the Sandinista victory of 1979 and US-sponsored Contra terror from 1981 onward. Whatever the form, the objective remained constant—to atomize and make docile the ordinary citizenry of Central America. This would facilitate rule by traditional, conservative, pro-US elites or, where necessary, their replacement with friendly, if ineffective, reform-oriented moderates.

Demobilization—or at least the US link to it—lasted longest and was most brutal in Guatemala.[23] It commenced with the US-sponsored overthrow of elected reformist president Jacobo Arbenz in 1954. Scant hours after Carlos Castillo Armas was imposed as president, a mysterious Committee Against

Communism—comprised of CIA personnel—seized Guatemalan government, political party, and union documents and began compiling the so-called Black List. Before the year was out, the names of an estimated 70,000 individuals connected with the former government or with grassroots or political organizations from that era were included on the list of suspected Communists. That August, the Castillo Armas government issued a Law Against Communism, which declared, among other things, that anyone included on the "register," as it was formally called, was thenceforth banned from public employment and subject to indefinite imprisonment without trial.

Although this register ultimately became a death list, this took some time because the Arévalo and Arbenz governments had partially succeeded in training the Guatemalan security forces to respect human rights. However, in the ensuing decade the US government became increasingly involved in Guatemalan affairs, blocking a return to democracy in the early 1960s and providing ever-escalating doses of security assistance, advice, and training. Meanwhile, previously nonviolent politicians, frustrated by the closing of the democratic option, turned to open rebellion. By the late 1960s, the insurgents and the opposition in general were labeled "terrorists" and a program of state-sponsored "counterterror" was begun. Featuring the torture, murder, and disappearance of thousands of suspected Communist subversives, this demobilization program was carried out directly by uniformed security forces and indirectly by government-sanctioned death squads.

By the early 1970s, the rural areas had been "pacified." Terror now moved to the cities as General Carlos Arana Osorio, former coordinator of the rural pacification effort and now president, began eliminating alleged subversives (e.g., party leaders, intellectuals, media persons, and labor organizers) among the urban population. The mid-1970s brought a period of eerie calm. But corrupt military officers soon began taking over traditional indigenous lands. Peaceful protests were met with violence, and the whole cycle began again. Many indigenous people came to support reemerging guerrilla groups, and the regime responded with more rural terror, particularly in the early 1980s.

From 1977 through the mid-1980s, the United States formally suspended military aid to Guatemala because of human rights abuses. However, the aid cutoff proved more symbolic than real (see Appendix, Table A.3). US military training continued, and under the Reagan administration, some US material aid to the Guatemalan military, previously banned, was relabeled nonmilitary and resumed. What is more, Israel—the biggest recipient of US aid in the world—took up much of the slack as a supplier of military equipment and training to the Guatemalans during this period.[24]

The demobilization campaign of the late 1970s failed to eradicate leftist rebels. Growing corruption in the regime and deepening economic difficulties led to a 1982 coup and a "reformist" military government. Its first leader,

General Efraín Ríos Montt, sharply increased violent demobilization, but the economy eroded further, and some of the military's allies distanced themselves from the regime. Military leaders then ousted Ríos Montt, replaced him with General Oscar Humberto Mejía Victores, and decided to return nominal control of the executive and legislative branches to civilians. Washington approved the armed forces' plan to formally transfer power to civilians and supported the 1985 election and resulting civilian transitional regime. The Reagan administration, frustrated by the Congress' refusal to authorize funds for direct military aid to Guatemala's military regimes, viewed switching to the elected civilian president, Vinicio Cerezo, as a cosmetic change that would ease Washington's providing military and economic assistance to Guatemala.

For two presidential terms, the civilian transitional regime in Guatemala slowly progressed toward controlling the armed forces, ending the civil war, and reducing the demobilization campaign. Before taking office, moderate Vinicio Cerezo had to promise not to prosecute military personnel for human rights violations. Rights abuses continued, but no prosecutions occurred and Cerezo refused to allow the International Red Cross to open a Guatemalan office. Powerful economic groups blocked proposed socioeconomic reforms, and some business interests conspired unsuccessfully with rightist military radicals to overthrow the regime. Elected in 1990, Conservative president Jorge Serrano Elías made little progress on social problems, human rights abuses, or peace talks with the rebels. Serrano then attempted the disastrous self-coup of 1993, causing Congress and the judiciary to oust him from office. The resolution of this constitutional crisis strengthened the hands of those seeking peace and deeper democracy. Serrano's replacement, Ramiro de León Carpio, advanced the peace talks. Elected in 1995, de León's successor, Alvaro Arzú, completed peace negotiations, began curbing the military, and instituted a more inclusive, formal civilian democratic regime.

El Salvador, too, suffered a process of demobilization in the 1970s and 1980s in which the United States played a major role. Demobilization was nothing new there. The military, acting on behalf of the elite, perpetrated tremendous violence against poor people in the early 1930s when the world depression had set off local mass-based reform pressures. The resulting "slaughter" *(la Matanza)* took the lives of around 30,000 people. But the violence of the late twentieth century achieved new levels of carnage estimated by 1988 as at least 70,000 dead and 500,000 displaced.[25]

The demobilization campaign answered an unusual burst of popular mobilization in the early to mid-1970s. At first demobilization by presidents Arturo Molina and Humberto Romero occurred at moderate but well-publicized levels. International criticism, however, led the Carter administration to suspend most US military assistance. When revolutionaries overthrew Anastasio Somoza in neighboring Nicaragua, alarm swept Washington. President

Carter quickly decided to resume military aid to El Salvador lest it become the next country to "fall." This apparent policy reversal could be sold to the US Congress only if a civilian-military, reformist government were to come to power. Washington viewed the most acceptable civilians as the Christian Democrats.[26] Reformist elements in the armed forces, private sector, and opposition parties who shared Washington's desire to block a revolutionary outcome began plotting against General Romero.

The coup d'état took place on October 15, 1979. The civilians on the first junta and in the government were Social Democrats, Christian Democrats, and unaffiliated moderates, but the junta changed rapidly. Conservative interests blocked the reformists, and human rights abuses by the military actually increased. Within three months several civilians resigned from the junta in protest. The junta replaced them with individuals from the conservative wing of the Christian Democratic movement. Military hard-liners soon replaced moderate officers.

American military aid to El Salvador resumed after the coup. Despite fanfare about moderation and reform, torture, murder, and disappearances soared far above levels under the previous military governments.[27] In February 1980, US chargé d'affaires James Cheek met with Christian Democrats in the government and urged that El Salvador institute what he called "a clean counter-insurgency war" that would give the armed forces greater leeway against suspected subversives. Though some Christian Democrats resisted, Cheek's suggestions were implemented in March through Decree 155, which imposed a state of siege and gave the military draconian powers over civilians.[28] Throughout the remaining Carter administration and for several years into Reagan's, security forces systematically dismantled grassroots party and interest organizations and trampled human rights. US officials publicly blamed the tens of thousands of killings first on "violence of the right and the left" and later on "right-wing death squads." The government and even the military were falsely depicted in the United States as composed of moderates earnestly trying to control violence.

Congress eventually pressured El Salvador and the White House to reduce the shocking human rights abuses in El Salvador. In 1982 and 1983, with congressional approval for further military aid in the balance, the Reagan administration sent emissaries to San Salvador to pressure the government and military to curtail the killings.[29] As a result, for the next several years— although the aerial bombardment of civilian populations in rebel-controlled areas actually escalated—the death squad killings declined. But by then, the demobilization had largely succeeded. The leaders and many members of most grassroots party and interest organizations to the left of the Christian Democrats had been killed, driven underground, or forced into exile. The two opposition newspapers had been terrorized into extinction. The martyrdom of Archbishop Romero and numerous clergy and lay activists had cowed the Catholic Church into a much less critical posture.

News of the Salvadoran reformist military's bloody record in the early 1980s made continued economic and military aid from the US Congress progressively less certain. President Reagan then pressured El Salvador to move toward an elected, constitutional government. The junta called an election in 1982 for a constituent assembly to draft a new constitution. With terror at its apogee, parties of the extreme right won a majority of seats in the Constituent Assembly. US pressure brought a slackening in the violence, and Washington essentially forced the rightist dominated Constituent Assembly to appoint a moderate figurehead, Alvaro Magaña, as interim president. In 1984, with terror somewhat curtailed, Salvadorans cast their presidential vote for the US-funded and endorsed center-right Christian Democratic candidate, José Napoleón Duarte, a popular reformist ex-mayor of San Salvador. This ushered in a civilian transitional regime, but one that for years had limited power over public policy. Duarte's ability to rule and promote reforms was hamstrung by the constitution written by the rightist-dominated Constituent Assembly and by the overweening power of the armed forces.

By the time of the 1988 legislative elections, President Duarte was dying of cancer and his administration had proven itself corrupt. After the Esquipulas peace accord in August 1987, death squad terror again escalated as the Salvadoran right attempted to sabotage its implementation. Not surprisingly, voters in the 1988 and 1991 legislative and 1989 presidential elections abandoned the Christian Democrats and moved sharply to the right.

Nicaragua suffered demobilization both before and after the revolutionary victory of 1979. The Somoza regime conducted one wave from 1975 through July 1979. US-backed Contras carried out the second wave from 1981 through mid-1990. Together, these campaigns took nearly 81,000 lives, around 50,000 in the earlier period and almost 31,000 in the latter. Though some of these deaths were of combatants, most were civilians.

The barbarity of the Somoza regime's efforts to pacify Nicaragua and perpetuate itself in power is well documented.[30] Worth mentioning, however, is the close relationship that existed between the US government and Somoza's National Guard. In 1979 the Guard had more American-trained personnel than any other military in Latin America, not just proportionally, but absolutely.[31] US military aid and the training of Nicaraguan military personnel ceased fully only after Guard massacres of civilians in several cities in September 1978. As in Guatemala, Israel immediately picked up the slack by supplying the Guard with automatic weapons and other equipment. American military attachés remained in Nicaragua until months before Somoza fell, and helped spirit many of Somoza's officers into exile after the rebel victory.

The Reagan administration chose the Contras as its instrument to demobilize Nicaragua under the revolution. This counterrevolutionary force of remnants of the National Guard, first organized by agents of the Argentine military soon after the Sandinista victory, received a big infusion of funds from President Reagan's National Security Decision Directive 17 in November 1981. Although youths who had never served in Somoza's National Guard eventually made up the majority of the lower ranks, Contra officers were mostly ex-Guard officers.[32] The United States manipulated and funded the Contras from the early 1980s on. Revolutionary agrarian policies and military recruitment alienated enough peasants to turn the Contras into a strong social movement. This deeply worried the revolutionary government and armed forces.[33]

The demobilization tactics employed by the counterrevolutionaries and their US backers evolved. At first, some in the CIA believed the Contras could serve as authentic and ultimately successful guerrillas. However, when the Contras in their first two years employed crude terrorist tactics, the CIA commissioned its famous manual for Contra officers, *Psychological Operations in Guerrilla Warfare*.[34] Although criticized in the United States for cold-blooded instructions on selective assassination of government officials and suggested hiring of professional gunmen to create martyrs from among the opposition at antigovernment rallies, the document's overall thrust was relatively pragmatic. It sought to teach the Contras to focus their terror narrowly and intelligently. Selective assassination was advocated, but the Contras should not terrorize the population and should behave respectfully enough to win a civilian base to help them isolate and defeat the Sandinistas.

Some Contra units apparently followed the tactically sound CIA advice. Pockets of civilian support developed in remote, lightly populated central departments of Boaco and Chontales and in the north. But the Contras mostly failed to achieve such discipline and behaved brutally.[35] This brutality coupled with their widespread image within Nicaragua as US mercenaries and direct descendants of Somoza's hated Guardia Nacional. By the mid-1980s most informed observers recognized that the Contras could never rally enough popular support to overthrow the government.

Although the Contras grew in numbers in the mid-1980s as they recruited increasingly disgruntled peasants, their military accomplishments remained limited. The Contras forced the Sandinista army to improvise its own counterinsurgency strategy, which prevented the rebels from taking or holding territory. The military buildup, however, eventually disrupted the economy and undermined support for the government. As CIA awareness of the Contras' limitations grew, their tactics changed to employ terror and sabotage to disrupt the economy, government, and society. Contra units attacked rural social service infrastructure such as schools, health clinics, day-care centers, and food-program storage facilities; economic infrastructure such as cooperative or

SOCIOPOLITICAL DEMOBILIZATION. Scene at a Somoza National Guard body dump on the outskirts of Managua in the summer of 1979 (photo courtesy of *Barricada*).

state farms, bridges, power lines; cooperative or grassroots organizations; and persons connected to such infrastructure or organizations. Among the nearly 31,000 Nicaraguans killed in the Contra war were 130 teachers, 40 medical personnel, and 152 technicians.[36] The Contras planted antitank mines on rural roads, killing and mutilating hundreds. This tactic aimed to undermine the rural economy and alienate people from the government. Meanwhile, forcing heavy defense spending would undermine social services, cause inflation, and seed urban popular discontent.

The Contra terror of the late 1980s bore fruit. Social services were curtailed, or eliminated in some remote areas. Agricultural output declined, the economy soured, and inflation shot up. Membership in grassroots organizations, which had climbed through 1984, stagnated in 1985 and 1986, and then declined in 1987 and 1988 as economic dissatisfaction rose and making ends meet became ever harder. Opposition protests and union resistance to austerity programs grew in 1986–1987, and the government began to repress its critics and opponents and curtailed civil liberties.

By the February 1990 national elections, the US-sponsored program of demobilization had so undercut the Sandinistas' legitimacy and intimidated the populace that the victory of the US-endorsed candidate, Violeta Barrios de Chamorro, was all but inevitable. No doubt a plurality of those who voted for Chamorro had opposed the revolution all along. Even in the comparatively good times of 1984, the opposition had received nearly one-third of the vote. But other Chamorro voters were citizens who quit supporting the Sandinistas as they watched government programs deteriorate and the economy collapse in the late 1980s. Finally, another segment was people who, although they favored the revolution, were simply unwilling to face the punishment the United States had signaled would continue should the FSLN win. Typical of this group was a generally pro-Sandinista woman who, on the day following the election, was berated by an army veteran for having betrayed the Fatherland in voting for UNO. She was the mother of two draft-age boys, and she responded indignantly that she was not going to sacrifice her boys "for the fucking Fatherland!"[37] The latter two blocs of votes, which very likely provided the winning margin for UNO, appear to have been a product of US policy.

US POLICY IN THE POST–COLD WAR PERIOD

The end of the Cold War in 1989–1990 dramatically altered US foreign policy. Since the Soviet Union and the socialist bloc no longer appeared to threaten US interests, Washington could begin responding to Central American reality on its own terms. Accordingly, the United States immediately reversed its policy toward the civil wars in El Salvador and Guatemala. UN-backed efforts at achieving negotiated settlements between guerrilla forces and the governments of those countries—long opposed by the United States—were now enthusiastically endorsed. In Nicaragua, though Cold War policies lingered a while longer, President Bill Clinton eventually appointed a new US ambassador, John Maisto, who quickly observed that it was time for the United States to leave the "hangups of the Cold War" behind and treat all civilian forces in that country—including the Sandinistas—as legitimate.[38]

The post–Cold War shift in US policy toward the region greatly facilitated negotiated peace settlements in El Salvador (1992) and Guatemala (1996) and the various intra-elite accords on modifying the rules of the political game that took place in Nicaragua in the mid-1990s. This helped broker civilian-democratic regimes and bolstered prospects for their consolidation in all three war-ravaged countries. In 1994, the Summit of the Americas set a new agenda for hemispheric relations by focusing on such issues as the genuine promotion of democracy, sustainable development, and regional trade. The Clinton administration embraced a policy of engagement rather than interference, even apologizing for the US role in the Guatemalan civil war. But this less interventionist and more cooperative approach ended abruptly under the administration of George W. Bush. The rehabilitation of several Cold War–era ideologues instrumental in Reagan administration policies in Central America signaled a regression in policy.[39] Rather than emphasizing the promotion and support of democracy in Central America, the new Bush administration subverted it by interfering and manipulating elections in Nicaragua (2001, 2006) and El Salvador (2004). The June 2009 coup in Honduras offered insight into how the new Obama administration would manage crises in the region. President Barack Obama stated that the coup was illegal and a "terrible precedent."[40] In response to the coup, the United States suspended $16.5 million in military aid, supported Honduras' suspension from the Organization of American States, revoked visas for the coup leaders, and demanded that Zelaya be returned to power. The Obama administration's response was criticized as weak by regional leaders. However, US diplomats in late October 2009 actively promoted an arrangement that would have allowed Zelaya to finish his term if Congress approved.[41]

President Obama visited Central America twice, in 2011 and 2013. His 2011 visit to El Salvador focused largely on security. In 2013, his visit included a broader agenda. His public remarks at a Central American Integration System (SICA) meeting in San José, attended by the region's presidents, addressed investing in infrastructure, energy, and security. He stressed inclusion in developing human capital, particularly of women, girls, and indigenous persons.[42] President Obama made no mention of immigration reform, which the SICA presidents had pressed him on during their meeting with him at the 2009 Summit of the Americas meeting. At the beginning of his second term, Obama appointed Senator John Kerry secretary of state. As a senator, Kerry vociferously opposed Reagan-era policies in the region. In line with these views, in a speech before the Organization of American States in November 2013, Kerry declared, "The era of the Monroe Doctrine is over." Although the statement was greeted with applause, it seemed unlikely that any significant policy shift would be forthcoming.

Other aspects of US policy, however, did not change with the end of the Cold War. Principal among them was the promotion of a strongly capitalist economic model. Using heavily American-influenced international lending agencies—the International Monetary Fund, the World Bank, the Inter-American Development Bank—to wield both carrot and stick,

Washington insisted on harsh "structural adjustment" policies, which, though they resulted in overall growth, also concentrated income and hurt the poor majority. By the late 1990s, the dynamic contradictions began emerging between income-concentrating neoliberalism and the consolidation of civilian democracy—both promoted by the United States.

The necessity to secure the US economic agenda in the region resulted in the support of "low-intensity democracy," which emphasizes the election of "favorable" candidates over the democratic process. Using economic and diplomatic intimidation, the Bush administration sought to affect electoral outcomes in Nicaragua, El Salvador, and, to a lesser extent, Guatemala, by recasting the Latin American left (formerly labeled "Communists") as "terrorists." This is what Robinson calls the "promotion of polyarchy" in US policy, which is intended to make the region "safe" and "available" for capital.[43] The result is a form of democracy that is defined by electoral competition among elites, the neutralization or demobilization of mass movements, and the subordination of politics to global capital. With few exceptions, these policies have benefited local elites and global capital rather than the average citizen.

CAFTA and the Economy. One key element of the US economic agenda in the region was the creation of a free-trade zone. In 1989 the first Bush administration proposed a hemispheric free-trade area. In 1994 the North American Free Trade Agreement (NAFTA) became the first of what was hoped to be a series of free-trade agreements throughout the Americas. Discussions for a free-trade zone between the second Bush administration and the five Central American countries began in 2001. In early 2002 the Bush administration announced negotiations for a Central American Free Trade Agreement (CAFTA), which would take the place of the Caribbean Basin Initiative (CBI).[44]

CAFTA would give American firms increased access to the Central American market by reducing tariff barriers and removing investment barriers.[45] Lower investment barriers would allow US companies to compete for the provision of public services, part of the IDB's prescription for reforming the public sector.[46] This topic was a major sticking point in the negotiations between the United States and Costa Rica, specifically over its telecommunications and insurance sectors. While the other Central American countries had zealously pursued privatization policies from the late 1990s onward, Costa Rica, responding to domestic pressure, had not privatized any of its state-owned industries since 1995. After protests and a strike by public employees, Costa Rica withdrew for a while from CAFTA talks over US insistence that it open these sectors. However, the Costa Rican government ultimately said it would consider such policies. Like NAFTA, the agreement also would further reduce state autonomy by allowing US corporations to sue their host countries over "unfair" regulations.[47] There was also some disagreement over protection for key commodities, particularly US sugar and textile subsidies that could result in dumping (selling excess commodities at below-market prices in order to suppress real-market prices, a violation of international trade norms), and intellectual property rights as they pertained to access to generic drugs.[48] The agreement was signed by the five Central American countries and the United States in May 2004, but ratification did not go as quickly or smoothly as anticipated.

The US Congress passed CAFTA in 2005 by a narrow margin. Central Americans had little enthusiasm for the agreement. Farmers, workers, small business, civil society, and center-left political parties vocally opposed the trade agreement. Objections to the agreement included sovereignty and constitutionality, the inability of local agricultural products to compete against subsidized US agricultural products, exploitation of labor, and environmental degradation.[49] Opposition to CAFTA drew US attention, as Deputy Secretary of State Robert Zoellick pressed the agreement to the region's governments.[50] Others in the Bush administration vilified CAFTA opponents. In a May 2005 speech before the Council of the Americas, US commerce secretary Carlos Gutierrez referred to CAFTA's opponents as "the same opponents of democracy and freedom of 20 years ago," a sentiment widely echoed in the region's conservative press.[51]

El Salvador was the first country to pass CAFTA in March 2006, without popular consultation. Guatemala, Honduras, and Nicaragua similarly ratified the agreement in the following months. The governments also had to ratify several international conventions regarding collective bargaining, the right to strike, and other labor codes.[52] As noted, Costa Ricans objected most to CAFTA, but in October 2007 approved it by referendum in the region's only popular vote on the issue.

As we wrote this in 2014 it was too early to assess the impact of CAFTA (which went into effect in some countries as late as 2009). Early indications revealed an initial surge in trade and investment. The 2009 recession had a negative impact on both, though there were signs of recovery by 2011.[53] That said, many concerns about the costs and benefits of the agreement remained. Average wages in the region remained low[54] while the cost of living continued to rise. This made it impossible for full-time maquila workers to earn a wage above poverty levels.

The United States introduced other economic initiatives into the region. The Millennium Challenge Corporation (MCC), a US aid agency established in 2004, operated in El Salvador, Honduras, and Nicaragua. Typical programs focused on infrastructure, education, and good governance. Good governance was also a criterion for funding, though there was concern that it was selectively applied. The United States terminated funds to Nicaragua (about $62 million) following allegations of fraud in the 2008 municipal elections. In contrast, funding (about $10 million) was only temporarily halted following the 2009 coup in Honduras.[55] El Salvador was also one of four countries worldwide to participate in the US Partnership for Growth initiative, which focused on generating growth by engaging local constituencies in planning and transparency exercises. But the program also gave the United States a significant role in determining Salvadoran policy. The United States required El Salvador to pass a law on public-private partnerships, cowritten by the United States, the IMF, and the Funes administration, before agreeing to a second distribution of MCC funds.[56]

Emigration and Remittances. The Comprehensive Immigration Reform Act of 2007 (S. 1348) proposed major changes to US immigration policy. The bill, which ultimately failed, addressed border security, a temporary worker's program, and a path to citizenship for undocumented immigrants. It also proposed to restrict the number of unskilled immigrants through a merit system that favored skilled laborers. Central Americans reacted negatively to proposed immigration reform by the United States. Although President Obama pledged to address immigration reform at the beginning of his first term, attempts at comprehensive reform remained stalled in early 2014. Moreover, President Obama continued the deportation policies of his predecessor. President George W. Bush's administration deported approximately 2 million immigrants during his two terms. Obama deported 1.5 million immigrants during his first term alone, a significant rate increase.[57] Approximately 18 percent of those deported in 2011 were Central Americans.[58]

Yet hundreds of thousands of Central Americans continued to make the perilous journey through Mexico to *El Norte*, most in search of work. Migration and remittances have provided important safety valves for Central American governments long incapable of generating sufficient economic growth or employment for their citizens. (This is not, of course, an easy task for these countries, given their positions in the international economic system.) According to the 2010 US Census there were approximately 4 million Central Americans living in the United States, although the number was likely higher. According to US Census data, the Central America population in the United States increased by 137 percent between 2000 and 2010. Central Americans were 7.9 percent of US Hispanics. The biggest increases came from the three northern-triangle countries: the Guatemalan population grew by over 670,000 people (an increase of 180 percent), the Honduran population by 415,000 people (up 191 percent), and the Salvadoran population by almost 1 million (a 152 percent increase).[59] Salvadorans remained the largest Central American immigrant group and became the third largest Latino group; between 1.8 and 2 million Salvadorans were living in the United States by the end of 2013. The Salvadoran presence in the United States was so significant that Salvadorans refer to the United States as "Departamento 15" (the country is formally divided into fourteen departments).

Coffee and bananas were once the foundations of Central American economies, but by the 1990s migrants to the United States had become the new monocrop. Remittances (money sent home by workers abroad and often called *migradolares*) had become a vital part of the Central American economies.[60] In 2001 Central Americans sent home US$3.6 billion in remittances, more than foreign direct investment or official external development assistance.[61] By 2008 remittances grew to US$12.5 billion. Remittance growth was most dramatic in El Salvador, Guatemala, and Honduras. El Salvador's remittances nearly doubled from US$1.9 billion in 2001 to US$3.8 billion in 2008, Honduras' quintupled from US$460 million to US$2.7 billion, and Guatemala's increased eightfold from US$584 million to US$4.3 billion in 2008. In El Salvador, Honduras, and Nicaragua remittances averaged 18 to 20 percent of GDP, and they made up about 13 percent of Guatemala's GDP. Remittances were lower in Costa Rica than its neighbors, but it too experienced a US$80 million increase in 2001 to US$624 million in 2008. Although remittances declined for all countries in the region in 2009, they recovered or exceeded their 2008 levels by 2011.[62] These citizen-to-citizen transfers mitigated some of the costs associated with neoliberal policies by providing "income" to both the urban and rural poor. The growing reliance on remittances resulted in the growing number of Central America–linked hometown associations (HTAs), long popular with Mexican, Dominican, and other migrant communities.[63] Salvadorans used their role as remitters to underscore their demands for voting rights for nationals living abroad, a fight they won for the 2014 elections.[64]

These remittances were made possible, of course, by the steady migration flow from Central America to the United States. Hundreds of thousands of Central Americans (mostly Salvadoran) were in the United States on temporary protected status (TPS), having fled civil wars (El Salvador, Nicaragua) or natural disasters (Honduras and Nicaragua after Mitch, El Salvador after the 2001 earthquakes).[65] Should TPS end when the current extensions were to expire in 2015, migrants would be forced to return to their home countries, and the economic impact would be devastating. Not surprisingly, regional presidents, such as Maduro and Saca, visited the United States shortly after their inaugurations seeking the renewal of TPS for their populations. President Saca visited the United States again after the extension was announced, visiting Salvadoran communities and urging them to reregister as part of a TPS education and registration campaign by the Salvadoran embassy.[66]

Remittances and TPS provided a lever for US manipulation of El Salvador's 2004 presidential elections.[67] ARENA's campaign claimed that an FMLN victory would have a significant impact on remittances from Salvadorans living in the United States, which exceeded US$2 billion in 2002. This idea was reinforced by comments from three US congressmen five days before the election to the effect that an FMLN victory should lead to a review of the TPS of Salvadorans and a restriction on remittances.[68] The unequivocal message was that an FMLN victory would threaten remittances. When ARENA used the same message in its 2009 campaign, though, voters did not find it persuasive enough to keep ARENA in power.

The dependence on the renewal of TPS, as well as a continued reliance on US economic assistance, led some Central American countries to provide military support to the US "war on terror," in particular to the war in Iraq. In 2003 El Salvador, Nicaragua, and Honduras (the three Central American countries that enjoyed TPS for their populations in the United States) joined the US war by sending troops to Iraq. Guatemala's President Berger initially pledged to commit troops, but quickly rescinded the offer in the face of widespread opposition to the plan. Even Costa Rica (with no formal army) joined the "coalition of the willing" by declaring its support for the war. However, Costa Rica's courts later forced withdrawal of even this symbolic support because it violated the nation's statutory posture of international neutrality. By early 2004, only El Salvador remained in Iraq.[69] El Salvador finally removed its troops in February 2009.

Security. In the Latin American context, the US "war on drugs" became intertwined with the "war on terror." That was easy because the Revolutionary Armed Force of Colombia (Fuerza Armada Revolucionaria de Colombia, FARC) was known to tax production of all goods produced within its area of control. But FARC's involvement, though it was less active in the narcotics trade than Colombia's rightist paramilitary forces, allowed the United States to label it (and by extension guerrillas and former guerrillas elsewhere) as "narcoterrorist."

Central America was an important route for the transshipment of cocaine, and the United States enlisted the aid of regional governments in its counternarcotics policies. The result of the growing American effort to contain narcotics transshipments was a partial remilitarization of the isthmus in the form of increased US military aid.[70] In 2000 the United States established its own anti-narcotics military base, or Forward Operating Location (FOL), in El Salvador.[71] Additionally, there were a number of US DEA operations in the region that focused on intelligence, training, and interdiction. Under Operation Central Skies, the United States provided army helicopters, police and security training, logistics support, and personnel to local security forces in Costa Rica, El Salvador, Guatemala, and Honduras. Increasing political and economic pressure was applied to Central American states to cooperate in the American "war on drugs," going so far as to "decertify" Guatemala (a US declaration of that country's non-cooperation and withholding of certain assistance) following a dramatic decline in narcotics seizures there. Growing instability in Mexico and the encroachment of the drug war into the southwestern United States had become a major security issue for the United States by 2006. In 2007 the United States announced the Mérida Initiative, a three-year, $1.6 billion program targeting drug trafficking, organized crime, and gangs in Mexico and Central

America. In 2008 Congress approved $65 million for programs in Central America that included drug interdiction, public security, capacity building, and the rule of law.[72] There was some indication that the crackdown on cartels in Mexico, which received significantly more funding, had displaced their operations southward into Guatemala and Honduras. Some analysts claim the Mérida initiative was an outgrowth of the 2005 Security and Prosperity Partnership, which was an extension of NAFTA. Accordingly the goal of the Mérida Initiative was to "securitize" economic integration in the region to protect trade relations and guard against the potential bad effects of free trade (such as turning to other means of income due to rising unemployment).[73]

The plan ultimately evolved into the Central America Regional Security Initiative (CARSI), which focused on counter-narcotics and law enforcement, strengthening institutions, and prevention strategies.[74] Although the approach was more holistic than previous initiatives, it was not successful at reducing violence in the region. Critics argued that too much of the budget—two-thirds of funds between 2008 and 2011—was dedicated to anti-narcotics efforts and law enforcement, and that the dispersal of funds had been slow.[75] Furthermore, the US emphasis on the militarization of policing and security policy in the region seemed increasingly at odds with the evolving policy preferences of regional governments. El Salvador's gang truce, which may or may not be successful in reducing long-term violence and insecurity, was met with a tepid response by the United States. Regional presidents increasingly called on the United States to address demand reduction, especially as it was revealed that 80 percent of the cocaine destined for the United States passed through Central America.[76] Guatemala's Otto Perez Molina, a right-wing president by any measure, and later Costa Rica's Laura Chinchilla advocated for a dialogue on drug decriminalization and legalization, adding to the discourse that the US War on Drugs had run its course.

Gangs. Added to all this, Central America's recent problem with gangs was another curiously transnational phenomenon. During the 1970s and 1980s tens of thousands of Central Americans fled their homelands due to bloody and repressive civil wars. Many of them emigrated to the United States, often settling in urban areas such as Los Angeles, California. Out of place and threatened by preexisting Latino gangs, Central Americans either joined gangs or formed new ones of their own. Salvadorans created rival gangs, including the now notorious Mara Salvatrucha (MS-13). By the 1980s, US gangs were making the transition from turf wars to market wars due to the introduction of cocaine. Gang members engaged in numerous criminal activities, including extortion, kidnapping, drug trafficking, prostitution, murder, and human trafficking.[77] By the early 1990s, changes in American immigration policy led to the repatriation of Central American inmates to their homelands. The United States began deporting gang members in the early 1990s, including at least 1,000 Salvadorans who were sent back following the Los Angeles riots.[78] In 1992 the US Immigration and Naturalization Service (INS) established the Violent Gang Task Force, the same year in which MS-13 established itself in El Salvador, mixing with existing youth gangs in the country. The Illegal Immigration Reform and Immigrant Responsibility Act of 1995 (IIRIRA) targeted immigrants, regardless of legal status, with criminal records. Between 1994 and 1997, 11,235 Salvadorans, Guatemalans, and Hondurans with criminal records were deported.[79] The deportations contributed to the region's rising crime rates and the growth of gangs.

This new gang activity greatly aggravated Central America's crime wave, particularly in El Salvador, Guatemala, and Honduras. Gangs were responsible for countless murders (many of them quite brutal), kidnappings, and robberies and engaged in drug trafficking and human smuggling. In response El Salvador, Guatemala, and Honduras passed controversial anti-gang laws, and in 2004 all but Costa Rica signed an agreement to coordinate anti-gang measures and share arrest warrants. The US "war on terror" coincided nicely with the Central American "war on gangs." Indeed, a *Washington Times* story claimed that an al Qaeda leader met with leaders of Mara Salvatrucha in Honduras.[80] Although officials from Central American countries later disputed the story, there was little doubt that some recognized the opportunity to militarize the war on gangs under the guise of the US war on terror.[81] El Salvador, Guatemala, and Honduras sent military forces into the street to battle gangs, endangering the recently developed balance between new civilian police forces and the old style of military-dominated internal security. The policies were ineffective and merely forced the gangs underground.[82] By 2010 gang violence, increasingly intertwined with drug trafficking, organized crime, and homicides, was spiraling out of control in the northern triangle. The regional homicide rate was 41 per 100,000, though it was much higher in El Salvador and more than double that in Honduras. Citizens were increasingly dislocated due to the violence. The number of US asylum requests based on regional violence increased dramatically as a result.[83] In 2012, the United States added MS-13 to its list of transnational criminal organizations, which would allow the government to target its financial assets.[84]

CONCLUSIONS

US policy in Central America during the Cold War was not only destructive and ill-advised but, more important, counterproductive to the interests of both the United States and those of the peoples of the isthmus. Responding more to domestic political pressures in the United States and to outmoded conceptions of security and economic interests than to the concrete reality of Central America, it jousted with a vastly overblown threat of Communism for more than four decades. As a result, the United States sided with a tiny and exploitative elite in demobilizing strategies that took the lives of over 300,000 people. Furthermore, American policy did violence to both the concept and the practice of democracy in the region. Power and democracy go hand in hand. As long as US-advised military forces used counterterror to quiet and exclude from the political arena a wide spectrum of civil society, the transition to civilian democratic regime types was made impossible.

The end of the Cold War facilitated peace and democracy in the region. The US imperative shifted from fighting Communism to promoting the so-called Washington Consensus and democratization. Although there was support for democratic transitions in the 1990s, evidence clearly demonstrates Washington's preference for "low-intensity democracy." The emerging war on the terrorism-drug-gang nexus created a climate of insecurity that further endangered the region's democracies, all in an attempt to make the region safe for investment. Such policy threatened to create externally oriented democracies, which serve the needs of the US policy makers and international capital rather than those of the Central American people.

The Obama administration struck a new tone in the region on some key issues, but underperformed in some respects. The profession of neutrality in the region's elections constituted a dramatic departure from the policy of the previous administration. The United States eased travel restrictions to Cuba and expressed a preference for dialogue with Cuba and Venezuela, which also signaled a positive shift in policy. US opposition to the June 2009 Honduran coup and resulting de facto government indicated a reinvigorated US commitment to constitutional democracy in the hemisphere, although Washington's response was more tepid than some had hoped. It also revealed a US Latin American policy at least momentarily freed from a persistent tendency toward knee-jerk ideological anti-leftism prevalent during the previous six decades. Still there were some areas of continuity, including Obama's stated belief that market-based economies generate prosperity. His failure to pass comprehensive immigration reform during his first term, while simultaneously increasing deportations, disappointed many in the region. Finally, although the approach to regional security was more comprehensive than that of the previous administration, the emphasis on militarization did little to decrease violence and potentially undermined democracy and respect for human rights.

RECOMMENDED READINGS AND RESOURCES

Coatsworth, John. 1994. *Central America and the United States: The Clients and the Colossus*. New York: Twayne.

Dominguez, Jorge. 1998. *International Security and Democracy: Latin America and the Caribbean in the Post–Cold War Era*. Pittsburgh, PA: University of Pittsburgh Press.

García, María Cristina. 2006. *Seeking Refuge: Central American Migration to Mexico, the United States, and Canada*. Berkeley: University of California Press.

Hamilton, Nora. 2001. *Seeking Community in Global City: Guatemalans and Salvadorans in Los Angeles*. Philadelphia: University of Pennsylvania Press.

Hunt, Sarah. 2013. "The Role of International Financial Institutions in Central America." In Diego Sánchez-Ancochea and Salvador Martí i Puig, eds. *Handbook of Central American Governance*. London: Routledge.

Menjívar, Cecilia. 2000. *Fragmented Ties: Salvadoran Immigrant Networks in America*. Berkeley: University of California Press.

Nazario, Sonia. 2007. *Enrique's Journey*. New York: Random House.

Palmer, David Scott. 2006. *US Relations with Latin America During the Clinton Years: Opportunities Lost or Opportunities Squandered?* Gainesville: University Press of Florida.

Pastor, Robert. 2001. *Exiting the Whirlpool: US Foreign Policy Toward Latin America and the Caribbean*. Boulder, CO: Westview Press.

Perla, Héctor, Salvador Martí i Puig, and Danny Burridge. 2013. "Central America's Relations with the United States of America." In Diego Sánchez-Ancochea and Salvador Martí i Puig, eds. *Handbook of Central American Governance*. London: Routledge.

Robinson, William I. 2003. *Central America, Social Change, and Globalization*. London: Verso.

Rojas Aravena, Francisco Pedro Caldenty del Pozo. 20013. "Central America's Relations with Latin America." In Diego Sánchez-Ancochea and Salvador Martí i Puig, eds. *Handbook of Central American Governance*. London: Routledge.

Rosenberg, Mark B., and Luis G. Solís. 2007. *The United States and Central America: Geopolitical Realities and Regional Fragility*. New York: Routledge.

Notes

1. Charles W. Anderson, "The Latin American Political System," in his *Politics and Economic Change in Latin America: The Governing of Restless Nations* (New York: Van Nostrand Reinhold, 1967), pp. 87–114.

2. See Robert A. Dahl, *A Preface to Democratic Theory* (Chicago: University of Chicago Press, 1956); E. E. Schattschneider, *The Semisovereign People: A Realist's View of Democracy in America* (New York: Holt, Rinehart, and Winston, 1960).

3. See, for instance, John A. Booth and Mitchell A. Seligson, eds., *Elections and Democracy in Central America* (Chapel Hill: University of North Carolina Press, 1989).

4. National Bipartisan Commission on Central America, *Report of the National Bipartisan Commission on Central America* (Washington, DC: National Bipartisan Commission on Central America, 1984), p. 30.

5. William I. Robinson, *Promoting Polyarchy: Globalization, US Intervention, and Hegemony* (Cambridge: Cambridge University Press, 1996); and William I. Robinson,

Transnational Conflicts: Central America, Social Change, and Globalization (London: Verso, 2003).

6. Paulo Freire, *The Pedagogy of the Oppressed* (New York: Herder and Herder, 1968).

7. Second General Conference of Latin American Bishops, *The Church and the Present-Day Transformation of Latin America in the Light of the Council* (Washington, DC: United States Catholic Conference, 1973).

8. For more information about the changing Catholic Church, see Edward L. Cleary, *Crisis and Change: The Church in Latin America Today* (Maryknoll, NY: Orbis Books, 1985).

9. Estimate of US Embassy, Managua, June 25, 1985, to coauthor Thomas Walker.

10. For more information about mobilization in Nicaragua, see Luis Serra, "The Grass-Roots Organizations," in Thomas W. Walker, ed., *Nicaragua: The First Five Years* (New York: Praeger, 1985), pp. 65–89; or Gary Ruchwarger, *People in Power: Forging a Grassroots Democracy in Nicaragua* (Granby, MA: Bergin and Garvey Publishers, 1987).

11. See Deborah Barndt, "Popular Education," in Walker, ed., *Nicaragua: The First Five Years*, pp. 317–345.

12. The only Central American country in which some popular mobilization and socioeconomic reform has succeeded with US support is Costa Rica, where the social-democratic reformers of the National Liberation Party were associated with a political movement that ousted Communists from power in 1948.

13. For an illuminating discussion of the nature of the US policy maker's perception of a Communist threat in Latin America, see Lars Schoultz, "Communism," in his *National Security and United States Policy Toward Latin America* (Princeton, NJ: Princeton University Press, 1987), pp. 106–139.

14. Tayacán, *Psychological Operations in Guerrilla Warfare: The CIA's Nicaragua Manual*, prepared by the Central Intelligence Agency (New York: Vintage Books, 1985); US Department of Defense (DOD), "Fact Sheet Concerning Training Manuals Containing Materials Inconsistent with US Policy" (Washington, DC: DOD, September 1996).

15. Michael McClintock, *The American Connection,* Volume 1: *State Terror and Popular Resistance in El Salvador* (London: Zed Books, 1985), p. 47.

16. See Michael Klare, *War Without End* (New York: Alfred A. Knopf, 1972), Ch. 9.

17. Americas Watch, *Review of the Department of State's Country Reports on Human Rights Practices for 1982: An Assessment* (New York: Americas Watch, February 1983), pp. 1–9, 37–46, 55–61, 63–70. The report stated, for instance, that "a special effort appears to have been made to exculpate current leaders considered friends of the United States—such as . . . President Ríos Montt of Guatemala" (p. 5).

18. Latin American Studies Association, *The Electoral Process in Nicaragua: Domestic and International Influences* (Austin, TX: LASA, 1984), p. 17.

19. For detailed discussion and documentation, see Thomas W. Walker, "The Armed Forces," in Walker, ed., *Revolution and Counterrevolution in Nicaragua* (Boulder, CO: Westview Press, 1991).

20. John A. Booth and Thomas W. Walker, *Understanding Central America*, 3rd ed. (Boulder, Colo.: Westview Press, 1999), Appendix, Table A.9.

21. Mary B. Vanderlaan, *Revolution and Foreign Policy in Nicaragua* (Boulder, CO: Westview Press, 1986), p. 322.

22. Excerpts from State Department and Pentagon, Congressional Presentation Document, Security Assistance Programs, FY 1981, as reproduced in Robert Matthews, "The Limits of Friendship: Nicaragua and the West," *NACLA Report on the Americas* 19, No. 3 (May–June 1985), p. 24.

23. Michael McClintock, *The American Connection*, Volume 2: *State Terror and Popular Resistance in Guatemala* (London: Zed Books, 1985), pp. 32–33. This volume is also a source of documentation for the general observations in the next two paragraphs. For additional information about demobilization in Guatemala see Tom Barry and Deb Preusch, *The Soft War: The Uses and Abuses of U.S. Economic Aid in Central America* (New York: Grove Press, 1988).

24. Andrew and Leslie Cockburn, *Dangerous Liaisons: The Inside Story of the U.S. Israeli Covert Relationship* (New York: HarperCollins, 1991), p. 218; Leslie H. Gelb, "Israelis Said to Step Up Role as Arms Suppliers to Latins," *New York Times*, December 17, 1982, p. A.11; George Black, "Israeli Connection: Not Just Guns for Guatemala," *NACLA Report on the Americas* 17, No. 3 (May–June 1983), pp. 43–44; Benjamin Beit-Hallahmi, *The Israeli Connection: Who Israel Arms and Why* (New York: Pantheon Books, 1987), p. 78; Philip Taubman, "Israel Said to Aid Latin Aims of U.S.," *New York Times*, July 21, 1983, p. A4. The authors thank Richard E. Clinton Jr. for his research in this matter.

25. Lindsey Gruson, "Terror's Toll Builds Again in El Salvador," *New York Times*, December 20, 1988, p. 1.

26. On August 2, 1979, less than two weeks after the Sandinista victory in Nicaragua, coauthor Walker was one of three academics to deliver short presentations on "Central America after the Sandinista Victory" at a dinner seminar hosted by CIA Director Stansfield Turner in his executive dining room. Walker agreed to participate only on the understanding that he would deliver a sharp criticism of prior US policy in the region. Turner's first six words to the group were "There can be no more Nicaraguas." After the academic presentations, the assembled CIA, Pentagon, and Department of State personnel lapsed into a remarkably uninhibited discussion in which they identified El Salvador as the next possible "Nicaragua" and came to a consensus as to what type of regime could obviate such a, for them, worst-case scenario.

27. See McClintock, *The American Connection*, Volume 1.

28. For a good description and documentation of the role of James Cheek, see Tommie Sue Montgomery, *Revolution in El Salvador: Origins and Evolution*, 2nd ed. (Boulder, CO: Westview Press, 1995), Ch. 7.

29. For material on US officials' efforts to persuade El Salvador to improve its human rights performance, see "El Salvador," *Mesoamérica*, November 1982, p. 6; "El Salvador," *Mesoamérica*, October 1983, p. 6; "El Salvador," *Mesoamérica*, November 1983, p. 6; "El Salvador," *Mesoamérica*, December 1983, pp. 5–6; and "Reagan Says Death Squads Hinder Fight," *Miami Herald*, December 21, 1983, p. 18A.

30. Organization of American States, *Report on the Situation of Human Rights in Nicaragua: Findings of the "On-site" Observation in the Republic of Nicaragua, October 3–12, 1978* (Washington, DC: General Secretariat of the OAS, 1978).

31. Richard L. Millett, *Guardians of the Dynasty: A History of the U.S.-Created Guardia Nacional de Nicaragua and the Somoza Family* (Maryknoll, NY: Orbis Press, 1977), p. 252.

32. Arms Control and Foreign Policy Caucus, the US House of Representatives, "Who Are the Contras?" *Congressional Record* 131, 48 (Daily Edition, April 23, 1985, H2335). The head of the Contras was a former Guard officer, Enrique Bermúdez.

33. Booth's interview with Dora María Téllez, former FSLN guerrilla and former minister of health in the revolutionary government, Managua, June 30, 1998.

34. Tayacán [the CIA], *Operaciones sicológicas en guerra de guerrillas* [1983]. This was later translated and published commercially as *Psychological Operations in Guerrilla Warfare: The CIA's Nicaragua Manual.*

35. The documentation of Contra brutality is massive. The numerous reports of Americas Watch are good sources. Others are Reed Brody, *Contra Terror in Nicaragua, Report of a Fact-Finding Mission: September 1984–January 1985* (Boston: South End Press, 1985); and Christopher Dickey, *With the Contras: A Reporter in the Wilds of Nicaragua* (New York: Simon and Schuster, 1985).

36. Data from the Nicaraguan Ministry of the Presidency, January 1990.

37. From an argument overheard by members of the Latin American Studies Association Commission to Observe the 1990 Election on February 26, 1990, in Managua.

38. As quoted in Thomas W. Walker, "The 1994 Research Seminar in Nicaragua," *LASA Forum* 25, No. 3 (Fall 1994), p. 14.

39. Among key Reagan-era Central America policy team players rehabilitated by George W. Bush was John D. Negroponte, former ambassador to Honduras (1981 to 1985), who worked as US liaison to Nicaragua's contras. Bush appointed him ambassador to the United Nations, then ambassador to Iraq, and in early 2005, as national intelligence director. Elliott Abrams was a Reagan-era assistant secretary of state for inter-American affairs who worked with the illegal Iran-Contra scheme and in 1991 pleaded guilty to two counts of illegally withholding information from Congress. Pardoned in 1992 by outgoing president George H. W. Bush, Abrams was appointed senior director for democracy, human rights, and international operations of President George W. Bush's National Security Council. Cuban-American Otto Reich headed the Reagan-era State Department's Office of Public Diplomacy, which

manufactured anti-Sandinista and pro-Contra propaganda. George W. Bush named Reich the Department of State's assistant secretary of state for Western Hemisphere affairs on a recess appointment after Congress refused to confirm him for a regular appointment. See *Central America and Mexico Report,* "Elliott Abrams Appointed to NSC," 2001, Vol. 3, rtfcam.org/report/volume_21/No_3/article_3.htm, accessed on January 5, 2005; and CNN.com, *Inside Politics,* January 11, 2002, http://archives.cnn.com/2002/ALLPOLITICS/01/11/recess.appointments/, accessed January 5, 2005.

40. Arshad Mohammed and David Alexander, "Obama Says Coup in Honduras Is Illegal," Reuters, June 29, 2009, http://www.reuters.com/article/topNews/idUKTRE 55S5J220090629?sp=true.

41. Ginger Thompson, "Senator Fears Letter Sends Wrong Signal on Honduras," *New York Times,* August 7, 2009; Michael Fox, "Honduras and Washington: A Few Contradictions," *NACLA Report on the Americas,* August 3, 2009, https://nacla.org /node/6052.

42. Remarks by the President at a Working Dinner with SICA Leaders, May 3, 2013, http://www.whitehouse.gov/the-press-office/2013/05/04/remarks-president -working-dinner-sica-leaders.

43. William I. Robinson, "Polyarchy: Coercion's New Face in Latin America," *NACLA Report on the Americas,* November/December 2000, pp. 42–48.

44. The CBI, a trade liberalization policy of the United States for nations of the Caribbean area, was initially established by the United States in 1983 to assist economies with duty-free access for most of their goods to the US market. It sought to promote economic development and, consistent with neoliberalism, export diversification.

45. See the full text of the agreement at ustr.gov/Trade_Agreements/Bilateral /DR-CAFTA/DR-CAFTA_Final_Texts/Section_Index.html, accessed January 5, 2005.

46. Beatrice Edwards, "IDB Plan to Sell the Public Sector: The Cure or the Ill?" *NACLA Report on the Americas,* January/February 2003, pp. 13–19.

47. Ibid. See Article 20 and relevant subsections.

48. On generic drugs, see Latin American Database, "Congress, Kerry, Could Kill CAFTA," *NotiCen* 9, No. 21 (June 3, 2004); Latin American Database, "El Salvador First to Ratify CAFTA, But Followers May be Few," *NotiCen* 10, No. 1 (January 6, 2004).

49. See Mark B. Rosenberg and Luis G. Solís, *The United States and Central America: Geopolitical Realities and Regional Fragility* (New York: Routledge, 2007), Ch. 4.

50. Ibid.

51. "US Employs Cold War Rhetoric to Discredit CAFTA Opponents," *Central America Report* 3230 (August 2, 2005).

52. For a thorough discussion of CAFTA and worker's rights, see Washington Office on Latin America (WOLA), *DR-CAFTA and Worker's Rights: Moving from Paper to Practice* (Washington, DC: WOLA, May 2009).

53. J. F. Hornbeck, "The Dominican Republic–Central America–United States Free Trade Agreement (CAFTA-DR): Developments in Trade and Investment,"

Congressional Research Service (April 9, 2012), https://www.fas.org/sgp/crs/row/R42468.pdf.

54. Ibid., Table A-10.

55. Tim Rogers, "Honduras Becomes Poster Child for the U.S. Millennium Challenge Corporation," *The Tico Times* (September 30, 2010), http://www.ticotimes.net/Region/Nicaragua/Honduras-Becomes-Poster-Child-for-the-U.S.-Millennium-Challenge-Corporation-_Friday-October-01-2010.

56. Lily Moodey, "P3 Legislation in El Salvador: An Aggressive Reassertion of Neoliberal Economics?" Council on Hemispheric Affairs (August 7, 2013), http://www.coha.org/p3-legislation-in-el-salvador-an-aggressive-reassertion-of-neoliberal-economics/.

57. Suzy Khimm, "Obama Is Deporting Immigrants Faster Than Bush. Republicans Don't Think That's Enough," *Washington Post*, August 27, 2012, http://www.washingtonpost.com/blogs/wonkblog/wp/2012/08/27/obama-is-deporting-more-immigrants-than-bush-republicans-dont-think-thats-enough/.

58. US Department of Homeland Security, *Yearbook of Immigration Statistics: 2011* (Washington, DC: US Department of Homeland Security, Office of Immigration Statistics, 2012), http://www.dhs.gov/sites/default/files/publications/immigration-statistics/yearbook/2011/ois_yb_2011.pdf.

59. Sharon R. Ennis, Merarys Rios-Vargas, and Nora G. Albert, "The Hispanic Population: 2010," US Census Briefs, May 2011, http://www.census.gov/prod/cen2010/briefs/c2010br-04.pdf

60. See Robinson, *Transnational Conflicts*, pp. 203–209.

61. Inter-American Dialogue, *All in the Family: Latin America's Most Important International Flow, Report of the Inter-American Dialogue Task Force on Remittances* (Washington, DC., January 2004), pp. 3–4.

62. Rene Maldonado and Maria Luisa Hayem, "Remittances to Latin America and the Caribbean 2012: Differing Behavior Across Subregions," Multilateral Investment Fund, Inter-American Development Bank, Washington, DC, 2013, http://idbdocs.iadb.org/wsdocs/getDocument.aspx?DOCNUM=37735715.

63. For more on Hometown Associations, see Manuel Orozco and Eugenia García-Zanello, "Hometown Associations, Transnationalism, Philanthropy and Development," *Brown Journal of World Affairs* 15, 2 (Spring–Summer 2009), pp. 1–17.

64. Organizations such as Salvadoreños en el Mundo (Salvadorans in the World, SEEM) pressed for the right to vote via absentee ballot for more than 3 million Salvadorans living outside of the country.

65. TPS was extended until September 2006 for Salvadorans on January 6, 2005. Approximately 248,282 Salvadorans were eligible. US Department of Homeland Security, US Citizenship and Immigration Services Press Release, "DHS Announces 18-Month Extension of Temporary Protected Status (TPS) for Nationals of El Salvador," http://uscigov/graphics/publicaffairs/newsrels/elsal_2005_01_06.pdf, accessed January 8, 2005. Nearly 82,000 Hondurans and 4,300 Nicaraguans were

also granted extensions until July 2006. US Department of Homeland Security, US Citizenship and Immigration Services Press Release, "DHS Announces 18-Month Extension of Temporary Protected Status (TPS) for Nationals of Honduras and Nicaragua," October 29, 2004 (revised November 2, 2004), http://uscis.gov/graphics /publicaffairs/newsrels/Hon_Nica_TPS_04_11_01.pdf, accessed January 8, 2005.

66. Mary Beth Sheridan, "Salvadoran President Hails U.S. Work Plan: Immigrants Urged to Renew Benefits," *Washington Post*, January 9, 2005, page C01.

67. This section is derived from a paper by coauthor Christine J. Wade, "Play It Again, Uncle Sam: The Role of the United States in Latin American Elections," presented at the 2004 Meeting of the Latin American Studies Association, Las Vegas, NV, October 7–9, 2004.

68. In particular see "Disturbing Statement out of El Salvador," *Congressional Record*, March 17, 2004, pp. E394–E395; "El Salvador," *Congressional Record*, March 17, 2004, p. E402; and "Election in El Salvador," *Congressional Record*, March 17, 2004, p. E389.

69. The troops were a part of the Spanish-led Plus Ultra brigade. When Spanish troops withdrew in the summer of 2004, Honduras and Nicaragua followed suit.

70. See Adam Isacson, Joy Olson, and Lisa Haugaard, *Blurring the Lines: Trends in U.S. Military Programs with Latin America,* a joint publication by Latin American Working Group Education Fund, the Center for International Policy, and the Washington Office on Latin America, Washington, DC, 2004, http://wola.org/military /blurringthelinesfinal.pdf.

71. Dean Brackley, "Yanquis Return to El Salvador," *NACLA Report on the Americas* 34, No. 3 (November–December 2000), pp. 20–21.

72. Colleen W. Cook, Rebecca G. Rush, and Claire Ribando Seelke, "Merida Initiative: Proposed U.S. Anti-Crime and Counterdrug Assistance for Mexico and Central America," CRS Report for Congress, June 3, 2008, http://www.wilsoncenter .org/news/docs/06.03.08%20CRS%20Report.pdf.

73. Susan Fitzpatrick Behrens, "Plan Mexico and Central American Migration," *NACLA Report on the Americas*, January 12, 2009, https://nacla.org/node/5406; Laura Carlsen, "A Primer on *Plan Mexico*," Americas Policy Program Special Report (Washington, DC: Center for International Policy, May 5, 2008), http://americas.irc-online .org/am/5204.

74. U.S. Department of State, "The Central America Regional Security Initiative: A Shared Partnership," April 25, 2013, http://www.state.gov/p/wha/rls/fs/2013 /208592.htm.

75. Statement of Michael Shifter before the Committee on Foreign Affairs, Subcommittee on the Western Hemisphere, "Regional Security Cooperation: An Examination of the Central America Regional Security Initiative (CARSI) and the Caribbean Basin Security Initiative (CBSI)," June 19, 2013, http://thedialogue.org /PublicationFiles/ShifterCARSICBSICongressionaltestimonyFINAL.pdf.

76. United Nations Office on Drugs and Crime, "Transnational Organized Crime in Central America and the Caribbean: A Threat Assessment," UNODC, September 2012, http://www.unodc.org/documents/data-and-analysis/Studies/TOC_Central _America_and_the_Caribbean_english.pdf.

77. For more on Central American gangs see Washington Office on Latin America (WOLA), *Youth Gangs in Central America: Issues in Human Rights, Effective Policing, and Prevention* (Washington, DC: WOLA, 2006); Ana Arana, "How the Street Gangs Took Central America," *Foreign Affairs* (May/June 2005), pp. 98–110; Donna DeCesare, "Deporting America's Gang Culture," *Mother Jones* (July–August 1999), pp. 44–51.

78. Margaret H. Taylor and T. Alexander Aleinikoff, *Deportation of Criminal Aliens: A Global Perspective* (Washington, DC: Inter-American Dialogue, 1998).

79. Jerry Seper, "Al Qaeda Seek Ties to Local Gangs," *Washington Times*, September 28, 2004.

80. Latin American Database, "Strangely Circular Saga of Terrorism Disproved," *NotiCen,* October 14, 2004.

81. See Washington Office on Latin America, *Youth Gangs in Central America.*

82. President Barack Obama, press conference, June 23, 2009.

83. Fox News Latino, "Central Americans Seeking Asylum Quadrupled in Last Five Years" (July 17, 2013).

84. Hannah Stone, "US Defends Blacklisting of Salvador Street Gang," *Insight Crime* (November 29, 2012), http://www.insightcrime.org/news-analysis/us -defends-blacklisting-of-salvador-street-gang-ms13.

REFLECTIONS AND PROJECTIONS

WE NOW REFLECT ON SOME OF THE PATTERNS EMERGING FROM OUR examination of Central America over the last several decades and consider the region's possible future. Years of studying Central American politics, however, have taught us that it is far easier to sum up than to predict. We freely admit that our individual and joint writings—like those of most other observers over the years—contain many faulty predictions.

REFLECTIONS: REPRESSION, MOBILIZATION, AND DEMOCRATIC TRANSITION

The Crises

Central America's crises over the latter half of the twentieth century arose from several factors: (1) centuries of socioeconomic formation; (2) rapid economic growth in the 1960s followed by a sharp downturn in the mid-1970s; (3) elite and government intransigence in the face of mobilization driven by the economic crisis; and (4) Cold War politics and the behavior of the United States. We disagreed with the Kissinger Commission report of 1984, which argued that the violent upheavals of the 1970s and 1980s occurred mainly because of Soviet bloc and Cuban meddling in "our backyard."[1]

The early social and economic formation of the five major Central American countries powerfully shaped the crises and process we have examined.

Colonial Guatemala, El Salvador, and Nicaragua developed relatively strong, largely Hispanic ruling classes, which exploited the majority nonwhite, largely indigenous masses to produce primary export products. Inequality and repression were established from the start. Both political and economic pressures encouraged violent, military-dominated polities. In the other two countries, less exploitative systems developed, but for different reasons. In Costa Rica, native peoples were either killed or driven out of the central highlands, leaving practically no racially distinct underclass to exploit. Moreover, divisions among elites were minor, so civilian rather than military government became the Costa Rican norm, and brief instances of military rule were aberrations. Honduras, on the other hand, the poorest part of the region, never really developed the powerful, self-confident, and exploitative elite minority of its three immediate neighbors.

These differing social formations by the twentieth century had conditioned the governing elites of these five countries to respond differently to local sociopolitical crises.[2] Honduran and Costa Rican elites acted with relative moderation and accommodation whereas those of Guatemala, El Salvador, and Nicaragua exhibited intransigence and employed violent repression. Where accommodation or even mere co-optation prevailed, as was frequently the case in Honduras, social peace was preserved. Where intransigence and repression ruled the day, insurgent forces emerged, gained legitimacy, and either toppled the government (Nicaragua) or waged protracted civil wars (Guatemala and El Salvador).

At this juncture US interference actually exacerbated a problem it sought to solve. Seized by inflated Cold War fears of Soviet penetration into Central America, the United States misinterpreted mobilizing popular demands for social justice and democracy. Listening almost exclusively to the voices of an intransigent local elite and a foreign-policy establishment deeply suspicious of the left, Washington rallied to the trumpets of anti-Communism. Thus, in the 1950s—at the height of McCarthyism at home—the CIA helped overthrow Guatemala's first socially progressive democracy. US aid beefed up the military and police of all four local dictatorships and trained local militaries to implement repression and counterinsurgency. This began in Guatemala and Nicaragua in the 1960s, in El Salvador in the 1970s, and in Honduras in the 1980s. Faced with increasingly violent intransigence and no democratic avenues of redress, guerrilla movements formed and expanded—first in Guatemala and Nicaragua, then in El Salvador, and still later in Honduras.[3] We believe that, had local dictatorships been less protected by US arms, less encouraged by American support, and more constructively responsive to the demands of mobilized civil society and the needs of the suffering majority, accommodation might have obviated the conversion of opposition and mobilized demand making into insurrectionary movements.

Central America's Unique Patterns of Transition

Central America provides a remarkable laboratory for the study of democratic transition because it experienced several types of regime change. Of the five countries, Honduras—with its fragile state and divided elite—historically oscillated between military and civilian rule. The Carter administration pressed Honduras to become more democratic, and its top military officers grew keenly aware of the Nicaraguan revolution next door and the rising institutional cost to the military of remaining in power. Honduras thus moved quickly from military-authoritarian through reformist-military to transitional civilian democratic regimes in the early 1980s. This coincided with the Reagan administration's choice of Honduras as its staging ground for attacks on the Nicaraguan revolution and Salvadoran insurgency. Ironically, in the early 1980s repression by certain military units escalated dramatically while the elected government took a backseat to the US-supported military. But such extremism diverged from national character, and by the mid-1980s the military curtailed its own excesses.

The early and tentative years of the Honduran transitional civilian democratic regime in the 1980s became a full—but unconsolidated—civilian democracy by 1996 when civilians reformed and exerted greater control over the military. This status quo proved unstable in mid-2009 when a constitutional crisis in Honduras turned suddenly into a coup d'état. After assisting Congress and the Supreme Court in deposing President Manuel Zelaya and immediately exiling him, the armed forces returned to their barracks. Strong international pressure on the de facto interim regime sought Honduras' return to electoral democracy by restoring Zelaya to office for the remainder of his term. Honduras' Congress, architects of the coup, blocked an internationally brokered deal to restore Zelaya to office. The regularly scheduled election took place, and Porfirio Lobo became president in January 2010.

We continue to view post-coup Honduras as a semi-democracy despite the election. President Lobo moved the military back into internal security activity, and repression of political demonstrators, media, and opposition remained high. The Supreme Court blocked prosecution of the generals involved in the 2009 coup, and Congress in 2012 replaced four of the five Supreme Court justices because they overruled a police reform law. Having engineered a more pliant Court, Honduras' Congress passed new laws that undermined due process for public employees and denied citizens' rights to challenge the constitutionality of laws. In the controversial 2013 election, the National Party retained the presidency with only 37 percent of the vote, and the new LIBRE party of Xiomara Castro and deposed president Manuel Zelaya lost and immediately challenged the results. All these underscore Honduras' inter-elite turmoil and lack of agreement on democratic rules of the game.

Costa Rica's democratic transition during the first half of the twentieth century came a half century before its neighbors in the isthmus. Several factors contributed: inauguration of extensive education in the late nineteenth century; expansion of working-class organizations and other civil society during the 1930s; a tradition of civilian rule and elections—albeit elitist and often fraudulently manipulated; and a split in the ruling *cafetalero* elite in the 1940s. An unstable alliance between the organized working class and one elite faction culminated in the brief civil war of 1948 led by middle-class insurgents. Though the rebels prevailed, they lacked the strength to rule without cooperation from some *cafetalero* elite factions and the forbearance of the working class. The resolution of this stalemate involved the constitutional revision of 1949 that retained the social reforms of the ousted government and gave the presidency over to the bourgeois party allied with the rebels in 1949. This laid the foundation for an effective accord among political elites in the early 1950s that ensured a continuing and successful civilian democratic regime.

Although buffeted by the turmoil and violence that convulsed the region in the 1970s and 1980s, Costa Rica maintained its stability and democratic practices throughout with accommodation of opposition, good human rights performance, and public policy that improved middle- and working-class living standards. More recently intermittent economic problems, the imposition of neoliberalism, and party modernization upended the party system, splitting the National Liberation Party, elevating and then destroying the United Social Christian Party, and introducing several competitive new parties. Realignments among the political elite and serial corruption scandals have probably not undermined elites' consensus on democratic rules of the game. Despite their growing prosperity, Costa Rican citizens express growing dissatisfaction with their institutions and leaders and somewhat lower democratic norms. The regime remains consolidated civilian democratic, but warrants careful observation.

In the other three countries transitions from dictatorship in the 1970s to democracy in the 1980s and 1990s occurred at gunpoint. In each country economic strains in the 1970s led to opposition and popular mobilization for change, to which each government responded with violent intransigence. Nicaragua, El Salvador, and Guatemala in the 1970s offered no viable option to insurrection.

In Nicaragua, the FSLN overthrew the Somoza dictatorship in 1979 and began the revolution. Moderate in comparison to other Marxist-led regimes, the Sandinistas moved the Nicaraguan revolution from de facto rule with wide grassroots democratic participation under FSLN leadership (1979–1984) to an elected civilian-led revolutionary transitional government (1984–1987). From 1979 to 1987 the multiclass forces that had allied to topple the old regime divided. Ideological factions and class forces struggled to establish political space for themselves either within the unusually inclusive framework of the revolutionary coalition or outside it entirely. Those who broke away and joined the Contra war received extensive US backing. The Sandinistas and others who remained within the evolving revolutionary framework struggled to design institutions that would accommodate working- and middle-class interests without provoking a pro-Contra invasion by the United States. Promulgation of a new constitution in 1987 provided the institutional framework for civilian democratic rule. By 1990, the economic and political damage of the Contra war, US-orchestrated economic strangulation, and aspects of revolutionary policy had deeply polarized and beggared the country. Nicaraguans of all classes availed themselves of the election to eject the Sandinistas and end the revolution and Contra war by electing Violeta Barrios de Chamorro.

Guatemala and El Salvador passed from military-authoritarian regimes through military reformist regimes and civilian transitional regimes and ultimately to civilian democracy by way of civil war and elaborately negotiated peace settlements. Although they originally hoped to defeat their respective dictatorships and establish revolutionary regimes, both the FMLN of El Salvador (by 1982) and the URNG of Guatemala (by 1986) had discarded that objective as unrealistic. They had witnessed US policy toward the revolutionary government of Nicaragua and had become convinced, in the words of Rubén Zamora (the leader of the Salvadoran FMLN's political ally), that outright "victory would be ashes in our mouths."[4] The United States, and hence, its two client governments, would resist negotiated settlements until after the end of the Cold War. Meanwhile, the United States and key elites in El Salvador and Guatemala, including the armed forces, pursued a moderating and gradualist strategy of using elections and transition to nominally civilian government to enhance governmental legitimacy and deny rebels a broader coalition. With the Cold War and the Nicaraguan revolution over, Washington and local actors eventually accepted peace agreements similar to those envisioned by the guerrillas a decade earlier. Thus civilian democratic regimes emerged from decades of violent conflict, with former rebels included in the political arena and newly restrained militaries.

The legacy of "transition at gunpoint," as seen in Nicaragua, El Salvador, and Guatemala, appears mixed. On the one hand, all three countries now had at least formally democratic political institutions, and civil and political conditions were far better than those that had existed prior to the onset of guerrilla activity. In addition, because grassroots participation contributed to all three transitions, subsequent democratic regimes would feature increased political participation by ordinary citizens and their organizations.

Central America's transitions to democracy also had certain negative aspects. As in all civil wars, the fratricidal slaughter of the 1970s and 1980s and accompanying personal loss and black propaganda left deep polarization and partisan hatred that affected civil politics for years to come. New political-economic elites who emerged as leaders in the new regimes skillfully manipulated these divisions and fears to distract citizens from their class interests and thus to undermine the influence of the political left in elections. ARENA in El Salvador and the Liberals in Nicaragua invoked fears of lost remittances and other punishments by the United States to help them win several elections. That tactic, however, failed in Nicaragua in 2006 and 2011 when the fractious Liberals failed to produce a consensus candidate to run against the FSLN's Daniel Ortega. The Sandinistas won the presidency again with little more than a third of the vote in 2006 but almost double that in 2011. In El Salvador ARENA's ability to play the fear card had apparently exhausted itself in 2009 when the FMLN fielded a moderate presidential candidate, Mauricio Funes, but the strategy was resurrected for the 2014 elections. ARENA's fear campaign almost closed the FMLN's double-digit advantage going into the second round election.

Crime became a grievous and growing problem of the new democracies. Aggravating conditions included the rapid demobilization of tens of thousands of government and insurgent fighters in all three countries, abundant arms left over from the conflicts, and police reforms that cashiered large numbers of officers in Guatemala and El Salvador. These factors drove high levels of armed criminal delinquency—and sporadic renewed insurgency in Nicaragua—that threatened individual and public security. In Guatemala and El Salvador the new or reformed police agencies created by the peace accords could not cope with surging violent crime, much of it originating from former police officers and security agencies. Honduras and El Salvador also developed nasty urban gang problems as the United States deported immigrants back to their native countries. Deportees who had grown up in US cities and became involved with street gangs there replicated the criminal gangs in Central America. Finally, the narcotics-trafficking cartels of Latin America infiltrated and corrupted the police and armed forces, particularly in Guatemala and Honduras. As we wrote this in 2014, crime in the form of gangs, carjackings, armed assaults, murders, timber theft, police corruption, and drug trafficking remained grave problems in several countries. El Salvador, Guatemala, and Honduras had some of the highest homicide rates in the world. Weak security forces and justice institutions, often suborned by criminals, lacked the capacity and will to address major organized crime. *Mano dura* responses to gang crime proved ineffectual and generated a horrific surge of human rights abuse in the first decade of the 2000s.

Finally, the legacy of bitter competition between the United States and the three revolutionary movements during the 1970s and 1980s played a role in post–Cold War politics in Central America. For instance, in the 1996 Nicaraguan election, when the gap in the polls between conservative Arnoldo

Alemán and his FSLN opponent Daniel Ortega suddenly narrowed, the US State Department made repeated statements indicating Washington's disapproval of Ortega. The United States also applied similar pressure against Ortega's candidacy in the 2001 and 2006 Nicaraguan presidential elections.[5] US officials overtly expressed their preference that El Salvador's FMLN lose the 2004 presidential elections. These efforts by the United States failed to prevent Ortega's election to the presidency in Nicaragua in 2006 and again in 2011. In the case of El Salvador, the United States pledged neutrality and promised to respect the results of presidential elections in 2009 and 2014, both of which were won by the FMLN.

By 2013 our assessment of these three cases divides. The Liberal-Sandinista pact between Arnoldo Alemán and Daniel Ortega set Nicaragua on a path that appears to lead away from civilian democracy. The pact and changed electoral rules quickly excluded small parties from participation in governance. The two major parties, rather than neutral technocrats, took control of elections and eroded their quality. Controversial court rulings lifted the constitutional prohibition against presidential re-election. The effective collapse of the Liberals and the FSLN's landslide re-election in 2011 set legislative conditions for extended one-party dominance that some observers believe resembles Hugo Chávez's Venezuela or Mexico under the Institutional Revolutionary Party rule from 1929 to 2000. In 2014 the Sandinistas affirmed a set of constitutional amendments that further solidified FSLN power. The government was also making efforts to improve popular living standards with distributive programs and to involve citizens in local government policy making. We now tentatively classify the Nicaraguan regime as a semi-democracy, but its evolution continues.

In contrast, Guatemala and El Salvador persist as civilian democratic regimes. We believe El Salvador has made more progress toward consolidation than Guatemala. The latter failed to enact constitutional reforms to bring the badly underrepresented indigenous population more strongly into the government. Recent events in both countries to address crimes committed during the civil wars may further democratic consolidation and support the reconciliation of deeply divided societies. That said, both countries continue to suffer from endemic corruption and high levels of violence that undermine both the functioning and quality of democracy.

PROJECTIONS: PROSPECTS FOR DEMOCRATIC CONSOLIDATION
The External Setting

Let us consider Central America's prospects for democratic consolidation. Most theories on this subject focus on domestic considerations that promote or impede consolidation. In Central America, however, we see little sense in discussing such factors as if these countries existed in a vacuum. Central America's international environment, particularly the behavior of the United States, has long affected local regime types. This should not surprise anyone. The United States emerged from World War II as the world's most powerful nation and by the end of the twentieth century had become the world's only superpower. Washington exercised tremendous influence over the tiny nearby Central American republics through its diplomacy, assistance, willingness to project military power into the region, ties to regional militaries, and effective veto power over the decisions of such critically important international lenders as the International Monetary Fund, the World Bank, and the Inter-American Development Bank.

Although most US policy makers throughout the twentieth century would have probably preferred democratic forms of government,[6] this preference frequently took a backseat to American economic and security interests. Security trumped democracy, especially during the Cold War when the impulse to contain perceived Communist threats overwhelmed US scruples about Central American dictators.[7] Even when the Reagan and first Bush administrations pushed for the election of civilian governments in El Salvador and Guatemala, they kept supporting local militaries whose counterterrorism campaigns against a wide spectrum of civil society made such elections far from democratic. Until the Cold War ended, the United States also delayed negotiated settlements that would have allowed greater civil rights and fuller democracy. With the Cold War over in the 1990s, the United States reversed policy—promoting peace settlements and much freer and democratic politics. For example, US aid helped finance and technically assist Nicaragua's 1996 election. That said, US officials continued trying to discourage the election of leftist candidates well into the 2000s. Cold War habits lingered in American policy in the region.

New centers of international influence within Latin America have developed in recent decades. Mexico and Brazil emerged as very important economic and political actors. The Organization of American States (OAS), once dependably subservient to US preferences, actually came to adopt policies reflecting Latin American countries' interests. One dramatic example of this was the vote of the OAS in 2009 to invite Cuba to rejoin the organization, a position long opposed by the United States. (Cuba has declined.) Another important new hemispheric player has been Venezuela under the late president Hugo Chávez. Venezuela has used its oil and oil revenues to sway influence counter to those of the United States in the region. For instance, Chávez has provided energy and economic assistance to oil-poor Nicaragua, Guatemala, Honduras, and some municipalities in El Salvador. All three countries became members of the Venezuela-promoted organization Bolivarian Alliance for Latin America and the Caribbean (Alianza Bolivariana para las Américas, ALBA), though Honduras withdrew in 2010 following the 2009 coup. When the Obama administration announced a US$62 million cut in its aid to Nicaragua in June 2009, Venezuela responded by pledging $50 million to replace the lost American funds.[8] Venezuela has provided foreign assistance, in some cases greater than aid from the United States, to states and municipalities governed by parties of the left in an effort to counterbalance US influence in the region.

At this writing the United States still plays a major role in Central American nations, but other significant players also seek to influence events and sometimes counterbalance American policy. The Obama administration's policies on immigration, aid, and narcotics interdiction have remained similar to those of his predecessor. To the extent that Venezuela and other Latin American countries might differ with the United States on policy and back those differences with foreign aid, we believe some Central American leaders have felt less constrained by US preferences than when US policy and aid were virtually the only pressures brought to bear. The Sandinista government conducted deeply flawed and much-criticized municipal elections in November 2008 despite US objections. More recently the Nicaraguan legislature approved constitutional reforms that increased presidential power and the FSLN's hold on the Nicaraguan polity.

Venezuelan assistance to Manuel Zelaya in Honduras may have emboldened antidemocratic elites on both sides of the constitutional crisis and coup of 2009. Zelaya's opponents charged that the minimum-wage increase and his effort to conduct the poll to measure popular desire for constitutional reform were from the Chávez playbook. They decided to disrupt the constitutional order and rid themselves of Zelaya before he could move too far in the direction they feared.

We now examine domestic components of democratic consolidation—both in theory and in the concrete reality of Central America in the 2010s.

Internal Factors

By the end of the twentieth century, all the Central American nations had elected, civilian, constitutional regimes, a circumstance that would have seemed inconceivable as recently as 1980. In each newly democratized nation, power had changed hands through peaceful elections among civilian candidates several times. This remarkable change from authoritarian to civilian democratic regimes aroused much interest among scholars.[9] As we have so frequently argued in the preceding pages, Central America's old (Costa Rica) and new (all the rest) civilian democratic regimes all faced difficult political and economic challenges. The new democracies, in particular, stood at a critical juncture where their political actors had to work to conserve their fledgling democratic regimes from powerful and often unpredictable forces—and sometimes failed.

Practically speaking the preservation of democracy in Central America would require the four newer democratic regimes to devise predictable and widely acceptable political structures and processes more like those that existed in Costa Rica since the 1950s. These would need to be able to sustain citizen participation and protect individual political rights that guarantee civil society participation. This process of preserving the new democracies of the isthmus is *democratic consolidation*.[10]

Students of democratic consolidation identify several important consolidation factors. Among the most important is (1) an *elite settlement*, a consensus among a broad array of elites (the leadership of major social, economic, and political forces) to accept and accommodate each other's participation in the political game, to accept democratic procedures, and to allow the mass public and civil society to take part in politics.[11] Such accords, typically shaped by what Larry Diamond and Juan Linz call "founding democratic leadership,"[12] may derive from explicit pacts among elites or may simply evolve over time. These settlements must allow for some evolution so the regime can adjust to change and accommodate new power contenders.[13]

Another important element of consolidation is (2) an *autonomous civil society* (political participation and organized interest activity). Especially in matters of economic policy making, civil-society engagement helps communicate citizens' needs to government and restrain state power. Among other factors believed to promote consolidation are (3) a mass culture of support for democratic norms; (4) strong but moderate political parties; (5) a strong legislature; (6) a strong and effective government; (7) a small military that is allegiant to civilian leadership; (8) some deconcentration of wealth or amelioration of poverty; (9) moderate economic growth; and (10) as noted above, the support of important external actors.[14]

To evaluate each of these ten points for all five Central American countries would necessitate another volume and exceeds this chapter's scope. Nevertheless, a brief review of some issues will illuminate the prospects for democratic consolidation in Central America.

Prospects

We need not detain ourselves much longer with foreign actors' influence. As long as US foreign policy both values and reinforces democracy in Central America, it will exert pressure for (but not assure) local elites to play by democratic rules. Unfortunately, some trends here are not positive. For example, from the 1990s on several administrations in Washington interfered in elections in El Salvador and Nicaragua to discourage voting for parties of the once-revolutionary left. US endorsement of, and suspected involvement in, the abortive coup d'état against Venezuela's constitutionally elected late populist Hugo Chávez in 2002 and its active role in the removal of popularly elected Haitian president Jean-Bertrand Aristide in 2004 stood squarely at odds with America's avowed commitment to democratic and constitutional order in Latin America. At the beginning of the Obama administration observers waited to see whether the United States would continue to support democratic rules of the game in Latin America, and if so how energetic the support would be. Although the Obama administration reversed the Bush administration's policy of open attempts to manipulate electoral outcomes, one might question whether the administration overcorrected in some respects. US condemnation of the coup was tepid, and more pressure could have been placed on the government to reinstate Zelaya. Recognition of the Lobo government signaled that the United States was more interested in putting the issue to rest than supporting democracy. Continued flows of military aid to governments for fighting crime also had potential to undermine democratic institutions. Secretary of State John Kerry's declaration of the end of the Monroe Doctrine, while welcomed by regional leaders, seemed out of touch with already waning US influence in Latin America.

Since the 1980s other key outside actors of lesser (but growing) influence than the United States have also encouraged democracy in Central America, and several of these, including most European countries and the Catholic Church, favored and contributed in various ways to democratization and democratic consolidation. Central America's Latin American neighbors—many new democracies themselves—used diplomacy to promote Central American peace and democracy during the 1980s when direct armed intervention in the isthmus by the United States seemed likely. Most Latin American governments appeared likely to continue to prefer civilian democracy. Several Andean regimes, most notably Venezuela, Bolivia, and Ecuador, had altered democratic institutions to strengthen their presidencies, weaken checks and balances, and move toward a participatory populist-democratic model during the 2000s. Multiple democratic breakdowns (or movements toward a left-populist model) in Latin America could weaken regional support for electoral democracy in the isthmus and might encourage antidemocratic actors or further backsliding away from electoral democratic regimes in Central America. Brazil and Mexico have supported continued democracy and offered moderate alternatives to (if not the generous foreign aid of) the example of Venezuela.

Elite Settlement. Had there emerged broadly inclusive inter-elite agreements about democratic rules of the game? Costa Rica's elite settlement had been in place for decades, a cornerstone of that nation's political stability. Progress toward elite settlement elsewhere was somewhat less certain. In the late 1980s John Peeler, an expert on Costa Rica's elite settlement and on democratization, expressed doubt about the progress toward democratic elite settlements in the other countries of the isthmus.[15] Since then, however, several specific accords and pacts have been signed among formerly warring elites in Nicaragua (ending the Contra war in 1990), El Salvador (the 1992 peace accord), and Guatemala (the 1996 peace accord). Governments and their armed opponents agreed to nominally democratic political rules, formerly excluded players were allowed into the legal political arena, clean elections were held, and power has subsequently transferred peaceably from incumbents to victorious opponents several times in every country. Peeler's assessment of Central American formal electoral democracies in the early 2000s became more optimistic; he noted that the newer isthmian democracies had achieved both of his democratic stabilization criteria and at least one of two of his consolidation criteria.[16]

On the negative side, in Nicaragua, broken government promises and economic hard times led former combatants—ex-Contra and ex-army alike—for several years to return to arms in small-scale insurgency and banditry. Ex-combatant violence, however, has largely vanished. In El Salvador and Guatemala periodic assassinations of human rights activists and candidates for office clearly revealed that some political actors wished to intimidate some players or even destabilize the democratic regimes. Similar violence also took place in Honduras. There, of course, the illegal and unconstitutional behavior of diverse elite protagonists in the 2009 constitutional crisis and coup demonstrated beyond any doubt the absence of a broad elite consensus on democratic rules of the game.

Although the courts blocked the efforts of former military dictator Efraín Ríos Montt to return to Guatemala's presidency in 1999, Ríos Montt nevertheless won a congressional seat and was elected majority leader of the Congress for a term. In 2009 sensational charges surfaced that Guatemalan president Alvaro Colom conspired in the assassination of an attorney investigating government corruption and in two related assassinations. Investigation proved the charges were false, part of an attempt to cut short his presidency. Leaving the merits of any accusations aside, these incidents demonstrated a lack of commitment to democracy and the rule of law by parts of Guatemala's political elite.

In Nicaragua, the 1999 pact between Sandinista leader Daniel Ortega and President Arnoldo Alemán, plus later actions by the Supreme Court of Justice and the Supreme Electoral Council had deleterious effects over the next several years. Small parties were squeezed out of the system, leaving the FSLN and Liberals dominant. An ensuing Liberal schism cost Nicaragua's Liberals two successive election drubbings by Ortega and ultimately collapsed public support for Liberal parties. Election administration and election quality deteriorated. The FSLN captured a supermajority in the Assembly in 2011's elections. Thus FSLN-proposed constitutional reforms passed in 2014 sharply increased presidential power. Ultimately, therefore, the Faustian bargain of the Alemán-Ortega pact and the subsequent erosion of election quality and concentration of power in a single party calls into question Nicaraguan elites' commitment to democratic rules of the political game.

The Honduran coup d'état of 2009 revealed how little commitment Honduran political and economic elites held to democracy. President Zelaya's effort to poll Hondurans was not unconstitutional per se, but Congress and courts and election authorities outlawed it. Unbowed, Zelaya pressed forward. The Supreme Court then ordered Zelaya's arrest for violating the law and its rulings, an action within its constitutional scope. The army exceeded its authority and violated the constitution by exiling Zelaya instead. Led by a foe of Zelaya, Congress accepted a forged Zelaya resignation letter and replaced Zelaya with his nemesis, Roberto Micheletti. Elected government resumed in 2012 on its constitutional schedule, but the turmoil set off by the coup barely abated over the next four years. The protests of the coup and after brought militarization of the police, rampant human rights abuses, and suppression of opposition. Zelaya's supporters organized a new party headed by his wife Xiomara Castro for the 2013 election. Having divided the Liberal base, however, Castro lost the election and unsuccessfully challenged the results. In short, the protracted Honduran political drama demonstrates elite disregard for democratic rules of the game.

Levels of repression and political terror in the four newer Central American democracies remained at middling or higher levels into the 2010s, contrasting with Costa Rica's minimal repression (see Figure 2.2). Democracy and civil liberties scores for these four countries also remained problematically low by standards for electoral democracies (see Figure 2.1) and again notably worse than in Costa Rica.

In summary, although many Central American elites played by democratic rules in the early 2000s, there remained doubts and pockets of resistance that became clear from the end of that decade forward. Elites had not controlled rights violations—indeed, they had increased in response to soaring crime rates. Some elites had never demonstrated clear commitment to democratic rules and others appeared to be moving away from them. We may not know for some years whether Honduran elites will come to trust each other and accept democracy as the only political game, as elites had in Costa Rica's smoothly cooperative settlement. The FMLN's 2009 victory and transfer of power in El Salvador represented progress there, but ARENA's response to the 2014 results threatened to undermine democratic institutions. On balance, however, at this writing middle-run prospects for democratic elite settlements across the region appeared only moderate. The Honduran case was very troubling and Nicaragua's was becoming problematic. We consider the outlook for elite accord on democracy less encouraging than we did in either our fourth or fifth edition of this book.

Civil Society and Participation. How much autonomous civil society and political participation had developed in Central America? Turning first to political participation, surveys from the early 1990s, 2004, and 2008 in all Central American nations (Chapter 9) reported a wealth of voting and registration, electioneering, contacting of public officials, organizational activism, and communal self-help in all five nations. The range and breadth of citizen political activity was remarkable, especially given the history of turbulence in some countries. Indeed, in the early 1990s, the factor that most curtailed participation was high national levels of repression. Because repression declined somewhat following peace accords and resulting military and police reforms, we expected citizen participation to increase after formal democratization. From 2004 to 2008 we found that participation of various types increased in Guatemala and El Salvador, suggesting a payoff from reduced repression and increased democracy there. By 2012 Guatemalans became the most engaged citizens, especially excelling in civil-society arenas of group activism and community improvement. Nicaraguan participation also rose notably over prior surveys. In contrast, participation has declined steadily in Costa Rica, the oldest and best-established democracy in the region. Overall, Costa Ricans were the least-active citizens in the region.

Focusing on civil society, there was consistent evidence over time that activism within organizations increased Central Americans' support for democracy and political activity. Patterns of civil society activism within the region changed over time. In the early 1990s, higher national levels of civil society activism associated with higher levels of democracy within the region.[17] In 2008, however, the opposite proved true in Central America. As repression declined from the 1990s to the 2000s, civil society activism generally increased in countries where it had previously been lower (Guatemala and El Salvador), but those countries had lower democracy scores in 2008. Meanwhile Honduras' civil society level plunged because of crime. By 2012 Hondurans' civil society activism recovered 10 percentage points over 2008. Civil society activism rose in Guatemala (highest in the region) and Nicaragua (a close second), but declined markedly in Costa Rica.

These studies of participation and civil society provide a mixed result for democratic consolidation in Central America. Central Americans in 2008 were active in diverse organizations, with considerable variation by group type among the nations. Some trends were found in civil society activism between the early 1990s and 2004. Civil society activism fell sharply in Nicaragua in the late 1980s and after the 1990 FSLN electoral defeat, despite the Sandinista government's history of mobilizing support through organizations, but had recovered by 2012 as the FSLN stepped up its mobilization activities once again.[18] Over the 1991–2004 period, during which repression declined in the four newer democracies, engagement in church-related groups rose sharply everywhere but Nicaragua. From 2004 to 2008 the trends reversed, with church-group involvement declining modestly in three countries, falling sharply in Honduras, and increasing modestly in Nicaragua. By 2012 church-related group participation went up over 2008 everywhere but Costa Rica, where it fell 5 percentage points, and Nicaragua, where it remained unchanged. Involvement in school groups and activism in professional and business groups declined in most of the region from the 1990s to 2008. We suspect this rather broad demobilization trend across Central America from the 1990s through the first decade of the 2000s indicated that civil society activism cooled as political conflict subsided. As of 2012, the regional decline in business and school groups ended, but there were important local changes. Costa Ricans reported much less school-related engagement and a bit less business-professional group engagement. Nicaraguans and Hondurans in 2012 reported large increases in school-related activity over 2008.

The 2012 surveys revealed that women, those with higher system support, older and wealthier citizens, and residents of smaller communities were more active in civil society. Residents of the four nations with weaker democratic performance were more active in civil society than Costa Ricans. Costa Ricans, blessed with a better-performing system, had less recourse to interest group activity than other Central Americans. This contrast indicates how vital civil society activity remained to Central America's democratic future.

Public Attitudes and Culture. Did the broad general public of Central America support democratic rules of the game? In the early 1990s, high levels of repression reduced popular support for democratic liberties. Thus the subsequent waning of state repression might lead one to expect that, other things equal, citizen support for democratic liberties would increase. The surveys just mentioned explored citizen support for various kinds of participation and for citizens' rights and liberties. In summary, large majorities of Central Americans favored democratic liberties in the early 1990s, in 2004, and in 2008 (Chapter 9). However, democratic norms had declined slightly across time from the early 1990s to 2008. Tolerance of regime critics declined from 2004 to 2012. Other attitudes revealed mixed trends. Support for coups declined markedly over this eight-year span; we view this as positive. In contrast, preference for a strongman-type leader increased; the shift is a troubling shift, but only 24 percent expressed this view in 2012.

Guatemalans and Hondurans had the region's lowest levels of general democratic norms in 2012. Hondurans and Salvadorans expressed the lowest tolerance for regime critics. Support for confrontational political methods rose everywhere except Honduras between the early 1990s and 2004, likely due to diminished repression, and then remained stable in 2008. Support for confrontational methods increased across the region in 2012. One Central American in six supported the violent overthrow of an elected government in 2012, unchanged from 2004 and 2008. Local changes from 2008 to 2012 stood out, however, particularly large increases in Guatemala and Honduras.

Regionwide, Central Americans' evaluations of governmental legitimacy went down from 2008 to 2012. Diffuse or general support for political systems barely broke into the positive end of the scale in 2012, a several-point decline after a modest increase between 2004 and 2008. Only Nicaraguans' diffuse support remained stable from 2008 to 2012, and theirs was the region's highest. Costa Ricans' and Hondurans' general system support fell off sharply. Support for nine specific institutions (courts, legislature, and parties, etc.) in 2012 fell below the scale midpoint and was essentially unchanged from 2008. In 2008 only Costa Ricans had a net positive evaluation of their national institutions' performance, but their evaluations had slid into negative territory in 2012. Nicaraguans' specific institutional support rose considerably over 2008, as did El Salvadorans', leaving them tied for the highest support in 2012 (both just above the scale midpoint). Hondurans' evaluations of specific institutions were strongly negative, not surprising considering the 2009 coup and subsequent turmoil there.

The Honduran case warrants special emphasis in light of the events of 2009. In 2012, Hondurans expressed the weakest support for democracy and for their institutions (as in 2008). Their support for rebellion and coups, however, had declined sharply from 2008 after experiencing the coup. The Honduran mass public, of course, did not overthrow president Zelaya in June 2009. However, the public's comparative ambivalence about democracy likely just before it may have encouraged—and certainly placed little restraint on—the actions of the antidemocratic elites who unconstitutionally ousted an elected president. Hondurans' support for confrontational political tactics remained the same in 2012 as in 2008, suggesting a high probability of continued protest.

Based on these patterns, only Nicaragua manifested consolidating popular support for its political institutions. The Costa Rican institutions retained positive general support, but specific institutions had lost the support of a majority. The broad pattern here for the region is weakened democratic norms and lower system support, with Nicaragua moving in the opposite direction from the other four. It is cause for concern for democratic consolidation that such poor evaluations appeared well after regime change to democracy. Higher levels of system support were driven by better perceptions of economic performance and of presidential performance. Living in larger cities and experiencing corruption lowered diffuse support. The absence of demographic influences revealed attitudes of institutional support to be broadly spread across Central American publics rather than skewed toward one class population segment.

Party Systems. To what extent did Central America approach the model of other stable democracies in having two strong but moderate (ideologically centrist) political parties? Costa Rica for decades came closest with its dominant main parties—the social democratic PLN and the moderate conservative PUSC—which regularly traded ruling power. The PLN fared poorly in the 1998 and especially the 2002 elections, raising concerns that it might collapse. However, major corruption scandals then engulfed two successive Social Christian Unity Party presidents in the early 2000s. In the 2006 election it was the PUSC that virtually collapsed. It was supplanted by the new Citizen Action Party (PAC), a centrist party led by many former PLN leaders. In 2006 the PLN recovered sufficiently to win Oscar Arias the presidency, a performance repeated for Laura Chinchilla in 2010, but its candidate astonished the nation by withdrawing from the runoff election. Costa Ricans expressed the region's lowest evaluation of their political parties in 2012, a fact that no doubt contributed to the continuing instability in the party system.

Honduras' center-right National Party and the center-left Liberal Party between them effectively dominated the political arena for decades and beginning in the 1990s traded ruling power through elections. Hondurans in 2008 gave their parties the highest evaluation in the region, but that evaluation fell to the second lowest in 2012. By 2013, however, the Honduran two-party system was experiencing sharp stress. The insurgent LIBRE party, linked to deposed president Manuel Zelaya and probably taking votes from the Liberal Party (PLH), captured many more votes than the PLH. To what extent this reflected feuding within the PLH or a major shift in party alignment remained to be seen at this writing. Honduras' two-party system may be falling apart.

Two other countries had strong parties, but they were more ideologically polarized than centrist. El Salvador's ARENA, once on the far right, moderated somewhat after the mid-1980s and dominated the presidency and legislature from the Cristiani administration (1988) through its defeat by the FMLN in 2009. The Salvadoran Christian Democratic Party declined and virtually vanished by the 1990s. On the Salvadoran left was the former guerrilla-insurgent coalition, FMLN, which had joined the legal political struggle. The FMLN made large gains in legislative and city council elections in from the mid-1990s into the 2000s. In 2008, 24 percent of Salvadorans identified with the FMLN, and 13 percent with ARENA. The FMLN had finally defeated ARENA in the historic 2009 presidential election. This event gave El Salvador its first peaceful turnover of the presidency by an incumbent party to an opposition party since the 1992 peace accord. A split within ARENA following the 2009 elections resulted in the creation of the new GANA party, led by former president Saca. In 2012 ARENA's share of party identifiers slipped to 12 percent, while the FMLN's dropped sharply to only 14 percent. Seven of ten Salvadorans reported no party identification.[19]

In Nicaragua the FSLN moderated its leftist stances in the early 1990s and remained relatively strong. Despite losing three successive national elections (1990, 1996, and 2001), the FSLN frequently captured mayoral offices, including that of the capital Managua as in 2004. The Liberal Alliance, in 1996, had reconstituted a strong Liberal coalition and succeeded itself in power in 2001. Election law "reforms" implemented by the FSLN and Liberals under the so-called *Pacto* between Daniel Ortega and Arnoldo Alemán tilted the playing field steeply against other Nicaraguan parties, keeping them tiny, personalistic, and fractious. In 2006 the deeply divided Liberal movement split and nominated two candidates for president. This allowed perennial FSLN nominee Ortega to win the presidency with a scant 38 percent of the vote. Back in power and emboldened by Venezuela's Hugo Chávez's financial contributions, Ortega appeared to have moved the FSLN ideologically leftward—if only in rhetoric. In 2008 the FSLN had only 19 percent voter identification; all of the Liberal factions combined had very slightly less than the Sandinistas. Nearly 60 percent of Nicaraguans claimed to identify with no party at all. By 2012, following Daniel Ortega's re-election as president, 45 percent reported FSLN sympathy, only 8 percent for all Liberal factions combined, and half the population admitted no party identification.[20] The FSLN enjoyed a very strong base, but Nicaragua's Liberals were in deep trouble and no other opposition party appeared viable.

Guatemala had a nearly kaleidoscopic collection of several small and medium-sized ideological or personalistic parties of varying ages. The Christian Democrats of Guatemala, once a strong, centrist voice, failed to consolidate their electoral leadership. Vinicio Cerezo's presidency declined badly thereafter. PAN won the 1995 election in a runoff. PAN subsequently fared poorly in presidential races, losing in 1999 with Oscar Berger as its candidate. Berger won the presidency in 2003 but as the candidate of a coalition GANA. In the 2007 election Alvaro Colom's UNE led the first round and won the runoff. GANA finished a distant third. In 2011 the Patriotic Party (PP) led in the first round with ten parties competing, then won the runoff. The former revolutionary left's parties have performed very poorly since the 1996 peace agreement. In step with this ever-changing party spectrum, in 2008 only 15 percent of Guatemalans would identify themselves with a political party; the value fell to 11 percent in 2012. In 2009 UNE enjoyed the greatest support at 9.2 percent; by 2012 the Patriot Party was first with 8 percent.[21] At this writing, Guatemala's party system remains the most fragmented in the region.

In summary, for decades Costa Rica and Honduras clearly met the two-party, centrist model held up as useful by consolidation theory, but both appeared to evolve by 2013 into multiparty systems. Nicaragua had by 2011 effectively become a one-party dominant system. El Salvador had two strong parties and other very small parties, but appeared to be developing into a system of two dominant-but-polarized parties. The ex-guerrilla organizations FSLN and FMLN have survived and in the late 2000s prospered with presidential victories. Guatemala's system is based on ephemeral parties that rise around an individual over two elections; the second-ranked candidate in one election becomes the victor in the next, with the party per se changing. To the extent that the two-party centrist model might contribute to democratic consolidation, Costa Rica and Honduras appear to be moving away from this model even as El Salvador moves toward it. Nicaragua has moved toward a single dominant-party system, while Guatemala retains a highly fractious system. Most of these tendencies, except for El Salvador, do not offer the near-term prospect of a stabilizing two-party centrist system.

Armed Forces. To what extent were the region's militaries small and loyal to civilian rule? In the Central American isthmus as recently as 1990 this question was risible, but by the late 1990s there had been significant progress. In 1990, only one government approached the criterion of having a small and allegiant military—Costa Rica had dismantled its army in 1949. All the other countries had large armies swollen by war (or by US aid, in Honduras). After 1990 change came rapidly. After settling the Contra war in 1990, the new Nicaraguan government reduced the size of its military by 80 percent, civilianized the police, passed a new military code, and professionalized and renamed the army (now the Nicaraguan Army). Nicaraguan military behavior after 1990 suggested a willingness to accept civilian control. With the end of the Salvadoran and Guatemalan civil wars the armies of both countries underwent substantial force cuts and came under increased civilian influence. Top officers were retired and reassigned. In a troubling trend, Guatemala's military became somewhat resurgent in national politics during the early 2000s. In the mid-1990s the long truculent Honduran military submitted to reforms that included abolition of the draft, reassignment of officers, and civilianization of the police. For a while it seemed the old joke about Honduras had become passé—that the capital city should be called "Tegucigolpe" because of the frequency of military coups (*golpe* is Spanish for "coup").

No one familiar with the history of Central America's militaries could be wholly sanguine about their prospects for obedience to their civilian governments. But when we wrote our third and fourth editions of this book the armies of the isthmus were out of power. They had discredited themselves by their past abuses and poor performance as rulers, and lacked the former financial and political support of the United States. Expert observers of the regions' armed forces reported trends that were mostly encouraging for democracy (Guatemala possibly excepted) as the twenty-first century ended its first decade.[22] Central American militaries had become smaller, less human rights abusive, and more cooperative with civilian officials. Ruhl called the reduced political power of the area's armies "a great achievement for the region" and characterized the status quo in all four as falling between "democratic control" and "conditional subordination" to civilian authorities.[23] We viewed these changes as a positive omen for democratic consolidation.

Then came the giant step backward by the Honduran military when it ex-iled president Zelaya in 2009. It was "Tegucigolpe" once again. At this writing the military, rather than taking over the whole government as on several prior occasions, left power in the hands of the civilian coup participants (the Con-gress). The military's reluctance to rule left the constitution no less flagrantly violated, but at least civilians remained in power. The armed forces increased their participation in domestic security from the coup forward. These events strongly suggest that a healthy skepticism remained in order about regional armed forces' commitment to democracy and obedience to civilian rule. The Honduran coup of 2009 demonstrated that military reform and obedience to constitutional rule were clearly perishable.

Globalized Economies and Democracy

We have focused most of our attention on Central America's transformed po-litical regimes, but must also emphasize how the region's economies changed in the 1980s and 1990s in ways that will shape Central America's future for decades to come. From the 1970s forward, civil war, energy price increases, deteriorating terms of trade, excessive external borrowing, and the collapse of the Central American Common Market bedeviled the region's economies. In varying degrees, each at some time faced or experienced severe economic crisis and required international help. In exchange for the international credit required to prevent economic ruin, the United States, the World Bank, and the International Monetary Fund exacted fundamental economic transfor-mations. Under this intense outside pressure, and with the collaboration of modernizing local capitalists, all Central American countries eventually altered their economic models to embrace neoliberalism.

Scholars disagree about the effect of neoliberal economic policies in Latin America. Kaufman and Segura-Ubiergo have reported that trade openness and integration into global markets, canons of the neoliberal economic model, "had a consistently negative effect on the aggregate social spending" and that democracies with such neoliberal policies tended to protect social security pro-grams but spend less on health and education. Their analysis included data from three Central American countries, but ended in 1997.[24] Avelino, Brown, and Hunter studied a slightly larger number of Latin American cases, includ-ing all the Central American nations, for a slightly longer period. They found that democracies spent more on human-capital formation, not less, and that trade openness was associated with more education and social security spend-ing.[25] Portes and Hoffman examined the evolution of the class structures of Latin America between the end of the import-substitution industrialization model and the implementation of the neoliberal model, including specific analyses of Costa Rica, Honduras, and El Salvador. They reported increased income inequality, greater concentration of wealth among the wealthiest 10 percent, and a decline in public-sector employment, among other effects. These forced new survival strategies among middle and lower classes, including micro-entrepreneurship, violent crime, and migration abroad for work.[26] Hoffman and Centeno argued that Latin America's very high inequality arose in part from the region's position in the global economy, internal colonialism, and underdeveloped state structures.[27] Finally, Weyland considered the impact of neoliberalism on democracy in Latin America. He concluded that while openness to global pressures discouraged elites from rejecting democracy, it simultaneously undermined unions and leftist parties who speak for workers, depressed political participation, and weakened government accountability.[28]

We have shown that the neoliberal economic reforms pressed upon Central America reduced government spending on social welfare, education, and infrastructure, at least in the short term (although some recovery has occurred more recently). Governments streamlined payrolls, reduced budget deficits, privatized publicly owned corporations and services, curtailed regulatory efforts, and generally reduced the state's role in their economies. They slashed tariffs and import quotas to open up Central American economies to foreign goods and investment, aggressively promoted nontraditional exports, and sought national advantage in the international economy in tourism and as suppliers of cheap labor for light manufacturing and assembly plants. These nearly revolutionary reforms brought some new investment from within and from abroad and contributed to economic recovery in some countries. Neoliberalism advanced the economic fortunes of the local capitalists who took advantage of the new openings to the world capitalist economy and the reforms their international lending allies demanded. And with the aid of their external allies these economic actors gained new political power in the emerging civilian democratic regimes of the region. The new openness of the region's economies to the world undermined local manufacturing. New assembly plants had to compete in a global economy, which exerted relentless downward pressure on wages in those industries and left them vulnerable to relocation to the next cheaper labor market to develop. The prospect for continued foreign investment in assembly plants remained very uncertain, as Africa and Haiti could offer even lower-wage environments. The deterioration of the welfare of the poor majority of Central Americans seemed increasingly likely. Since the fifth edition we have seen some reduction of poverty, but this appears to come from broad economic recovery rather than redistribution of system benefits toward the poor.

Neoliberalism's effects on social and political systems were mixed. Positive political effects include the external pressure that dissuaded Guatemalan institutions from succumbing to the self-coup by President Serrano in 1993, thus preserving constitutional rule. And international actors facilitated peace settlements in Nicaragua, El Salvador, and Guatemala, and contributed to the democratization of the latter two. Negative effects were numerous. Neo-liberalism shrank the capacity of Central American governments to improve the general welfare of their citizens, promote economic growth, and invest in human capital. Governments with international financial monitors and exter-nally imposed structural adjustment agreements found themselves with more unemployed citizens who earned relatively lower average wages, and fewer government resources to redistribute income or ameliorate poverty. Govern-ments thus had fewer tools with which to promote their citizens' general welfare. Social pathologies such as urban gangs, narcotics use and trafficking, prostitution and sex tourism, violent crime, and public corruption increased across the region in the 1990s and 2000s. Trimmed-down states and under-funded and ill-trained police found themselves unable to respond effectively to these growing problems.[29]

One recent trend suggests renewed efforts by governments to address pov-erty and related problems, albeit to different degrees. Between 2005 and 2011 or 2012, all five countries increased social spending despite the 2008–2009 re-cession. The increases were, in descending order of greater spending on social programs as a percentage of GDP: Costa Rica's rose from 17.3 percent to 22.9 percent, Honduras' from 11.2 to 13.0 percent, Nicaragua's from 11.2 to 13.0 percent, El Salvador's from 12.0 to 13.0 percent, and Guatemala's from 7.6 to 8.1 percent. We see no clear pattern here by ruling-party ideology, but Costa Rica and Honduras somewhat fit the amelioration strategies they followed during the 1970s and 1980s.[30]

These pernicious political and economic trends, derived from Central America's traditional economic weaknesses, its elites' scant enthusiasm for reform, and the effects of neoliberal economic policies, appeared likely to have negative effects on democracy in the region. Our data have shown some demobilization of civil society engagement and election participation in the region, though we cannot link them directly to the effects of the neoliberal model. Flawed by their poor human rights performances, the democracies that emerged from regime transformation in Central America were widely and rightly criticized, and their citizens evaluated their institutions poorly. In one sense, neoliberalism's economic effects appeared certain to continue to limit some Central Americans' capacity to participate effectively in politics because so many lacked and might never gain the resources or human capital required to influence public decisions. Central American nations, operating leanly and meanly under the rules of the global economy, would lack both the resources and the will to lift up their citizens and improve their life chances. Recent evidence shows improved education spending, health, and life expectancy sta-tistics, so the discouraging trends have abated somewhat. As we write this, neoliberalism is well entrenched, but some politicians have worked against its premises as recovering economies allow. Deeper democracy has not flourished in the region, and trends in several countries are worrying. We do not yet know whether the low-intensity democracy encouraged by neoliberalism might remain the best that Central Americans outside of Costa Rica can expect for many decades to come.

CONCLUSIONS

On balance, then, we see both negative and positive signs for the consolidation of formal civilian democracies in Central America during the twenty-first century's first decade. In political terms, collectively the citizens of the isthmus enjoyed more human rights and greater political freedom than in prior decades. Central Americans' preference for democracy over dictatorship and democratic norms has eroded in recent years, but not collapsed. Political elites in some countries have followed formal democratic rules, but in others they have not. External actors have continued to support democratic regimes, but their attention to it has fluctuated and sometimes flagged. The great experiment of the Nicaraguan revolution—a regime that pushed for much more participatory democracy and greater social justice than the polities that survived it—had failed under a combination of fierce US pressure and its own errors. Nicaragua has moved partway back to its traditions of caudillo-style leadership and electoral impropriety.

Critics derided the new democracies of Central America as "low-intensity" or "light" democracies, and there was merit to the criticism. Formal democratic rules and procedures in a socioeconomic context of enormous inequality and widespread poverty would provide the legions of poor and unorganized Central Americans little influence over public policy. The great neoliberal economic experiment imposed upon the region by international actors, in the middle run, exacerbated inequality and poverty. Thus the only long-run hope for increased resources for the poor majority under neoliberal development models—and thus for increased popular political power and the deepening of democracy— appeared to be for the economies of the region to produce sustained and rapid growth. Some progress has occurred, but realistic prospects for such growth appeared to range from modest in somewhat stronger economies (Costa Rica and El Salvador) to grim in the nearly prostrate Honduras and Nicaragua. Fortunately, the recession that braked the world economy sharply in 2009 had only short-term effects in Central America and growth has resumed.

The legitimacy of specific political institutions across Central America is low and, outside of Nicaragua, eroding as we write this. Yet such poor performance evaluations of the governments do not constitute a "legitimacy crisis" as such. Formal democracy with low repression provides intensely dissatisfied citizens opportunities to work for change within their systems. Indeed, evidence exists that those with low legitimacy norms increased their participation within the system but protested less. Except for Honduras, the numbers of the most-dissatisfied and least-democratic citizens—a potential reservoir of support for antidemocratic elites, or of protest and rebellion—remained small. The multi-disgruntled were not much more active in politics than the region's more-satisfied citizens. In Honduras, however, the multi-disgruntled were sufficiently numerous—35 percent in 2012—to arouse concern. Popular commitment to democracy there was also notably weaker than elsewhere. The Honduran coup of 2009 and subsequent violent mass protests on both sides demonstrate the risks of a multi-dissatisfied and polarized citizenry.

We do not expect mass publics to overthrow democracy anywhere in the region. That is certainly not what happened in Honduras in 2009. Instead, large groups of multi-disgruntled populations could tempt and provide a reservoir of support for antidemocratic elites who might work to undermine democracy. In 2012 one Central American in four, up from one in five just four years earlier, preferred "a strong leader who does not need to be elected." Authoritarian attitudes were stronger and democratic attitudes weaker in Honduras than elsewhere in the region in 2008 and had become weaker still in 2012. Over a third of the populace could support a coup under certain hypothetical circumstances. These data suggest very little in Honduran public opinion that might restrain antidemocratic elites.

There was also a prospect of protest, which could either sustain or undermine democracy. Only one in sixteen Central Americans reported taking part in protests in the year before our 2012 surveys, down considerably from 2008. In 2012 one Central American in four approved of confrontational political methods including protest (a big increase over 2008), and one in six approved of armed rebellion against an elected government. Protest or political turmoil can offer a pretext for antidemocratic elites to disrupt the democratic order. In the aftermath of the Honduran coup, protests by supporters of both sides intensified political conflict, justified the ensuing governments' suppression of civil liberties, and brought repression by the security forces.

Thus, what Central America, aside from Costa Rica, had achieved as we write this is low-intensity democracy with very modest prospects for achieving government of, by, and for the people. Interestingly, Nicaraguans in 2012 were happier than Costa Ricans with their political system, though it was formally less democratic. Central Americans still marginally embraced the idea of democracy, but most evaluated their systems' performance harshly. After backsliding into semi-democracy in 2009, Honduras has showed little prospect for recovery to even low-intensity democracy as we write this. Consolidation of democracy in Honduras has stagnated or regressed.

On the other hand, low-intensity democracy was, we believe, better than no democracy at all, especially in one regard well known to all Central Americans. At least 300,000 lost their lives to authoritarian repression during the decades-long struggle for formal democracy. Whether democratic or semi-democratic, civilian governments—especially with curtailed militaries—intimidate, imprison, maim, and kill much less than do military regimes. Under Central America's democratic and semi-democratic civilian regimes, fewer will suffer the repression experienced under dictatorial or military regimes. Inequalities and economic limitations notwithstanding, citizens who may organize, contact officials, vote, and protest can defend and pursue their interests more effectively than those who cannot. In the traumatic 1970s, 1980s, and 1990s, millions of ordinary Central Americans won the right to become protagonists in their own political reality. This right remains, but its survival everywhere appears less certain than upon our last evaluation.

RECOMMENDED READINGS AND RESOURCES

Booth, John A., and Mitchell A. Seligson. 1998. *The Legitimacy Puzzle in Latin America: Political Support and Democracy in Eight Nations.* Cambridge: Cambridge University Press.

Hoffman, Kelly, and Miguel Angel Centeno. 2003. "The Lopsided Continent: Inequality in Latin America." *Annual Review of Sociology* 29 (2003):363–390.

Mahoney, James. 2001. *The Legacies of Liberalism: Path Dependence and Political Regimes in Central America.* Baltimore, MD: Johns Hopkins University Press.

Paris, Roland. 2002. *At War's End: Building Peace After Civil Conflict.* Cambridge: Cambridge University Press.

Peeler, John. 2004. *Building Democracy in Latin America.* Boulder, CO: Lynne Rienner Publishers.

Portes, Alejandro, and Kelly Hoffman. 2003. "Latin American Class Structures: Their Composition and Change During the Neoliberal Era." *Latin American Research Review* 38 (1):41–82.

Sánchez-Ancochea, Diego, and Salvador Martí Puig, eds. 2013. *Handbook of Central American Governance.* London: Routledge.

Smith, William C., and Roberto Patricio Korzeniewicz, eds. 1997. *Politics, Social Change and Economic Restructuring in Latin America.* Miami, FL: North-South Center Press.

Walker, Thomas W., ed. 1997. *Nicaragua Without Illusions: Regime Transition and Structural Adjustment in the 1990s.* Wilmington, DE: Scholarly Resources.

Weyland, Kurt. 2004. "Neoliberalism and Democracy in Latin America: A Mixed Record." *Latin American Politics and Society* 46 (1):135–157.

NOTES

1. National Bipartisan Commission on Central America, *Report of the National Bipartisan Commission on Central America* (Washington, DC, 1984).

2. See also James Mahoney, *The Legacies of Liberalism: Path Dependence and Political Regimes in Central America* (Baltimore, MD: Johns Hopkins University

Press, 2001), for another view of how historical developments shaped the behavior of Central American regimes.

3. Costa Rica's 1948 civil war did not present a threat to the security concerns of the United States because the Communist-led unions were part of the government coalition overthrown by the insurgents; see John A. Booth, "Democratic Development in Costa Rica," *Democratization* 15, No. 4 (August 2008), pp. 714–732.

4. Rubén Zamora in an interview with the Presbyterian Task Force on Central America (UPCUSA) in Managua, in November 1982. Official spokespersons for the FMLN whom the Task Force also interviewed in Managua at that time agreed and went into detail about their intent to fight only until a negotiated settlement could be achieved. Thomas Walker, a member of the Task Force, was present at those meetings.

5. For more detail, see "Epilogue: The 1996 National Elections," in Thomas W. Walker, ed. *Nicaragua Without Illusions: Regime Transition and Structural Adjustment in the 1990s*, (Wilmington, DE: Scholarly Resources, 1997), pp. 306–307.

6. For an interesting attempt to interpret US policy making in regard to the first Somoza in this way, see Paul Coe Clarke Jr., *The United States and Somoza, 1933–1956: A Revisionist Look* (Westport, CT: Praeger Publishers, 1992).

7. The most articulate defense of the "practical" approach to regime types was made by Jeane J. Kirkpatrick in her article "Dictatorships and Double Standards," *Commentary* 68 (November 1979), pp. 34–45. In it Kirkpatrick, who soon became President Reagan's first ambassador to the United Nations and major adviser on Latin American affairs, argued that it was better to support "traditional autocracies" than run the risk of Communist totalitarian regimes.

8. The United States took the action to express its displeasure with the apparent fraud in Nicaragua's November 2008 municipal elections. See "United States Slashes Aid to Nicaragua," *Latin American Herald Tribune*, June 16, 2009, http://www.laht.com/article.asp?/Articleid=337056&Categoryid=23558; and "Venezuela to Help Nicaragua After U.S. Rebuff," CNN.com, June 14, 2009, http://www.cnn com/2009/WORLD/americas/06/14/nicaragua.venezuela/index.html.

9. The literature on democratization in Central America includes John A. Booth and Mitchell A. Seligson, eds., *Elections and Democracy in Central America* (Chapel Hill: University of North Carolina Press, 1989); Mitchell A. Seligson and John A. Booth, eds., *Elections and Democracy in Central America, Revisited* (Chapel Hill: University of North Carolina Press, 1995); Deborah J. Yashar, *Demanding Democracy: Reform and Reaction in Costa Rica and Guatemala, 1870s–1950s* (Stanford, CA: Stanford University Press, 1997); John A. Booth, *Costa Rica: Quest for Democracy* (Boulder, CO: Westview Press, 1998); and Philip J. Williams and Knut Walter, *Militarization and Demilitarization in El Salvador's Transition to Democracy* (Pittsburgh, PA: University of Pittsburgh Press, 1997). Among the major sources on democratization in Latin America that also include studies or discussion of Central America are John Peeler, *Latin American Democracies* (Chapel Hill: University of North Carolina Press, 1985); Larry Diamond, Juan Linz, and Seymour Martin Lipset, eds., *Democracy in Devel-*

oping Countries, Volume 4: *Latin America* (Boulder, CO: Lynne Rienner Publishers, 1989); Guillermo O'Donnell, Philippe C. Schmitter, and Laurence Whitehead, eds. *Transitions from Authoritarian Rule: Latin America* (Baltimore, MD: Johns Hopkins University Press, 1986); James M. Malloy and Mitchell A. Seligson, eds., *Authoritarians and Democrats: Regime Transition in Latin America* (Pittsburgh, PA: University of Pittsburgh Press, 1987); Paul Drake and Eduardo Silva, eds., *Elections and Democratization in Latin America* (La Jolla, CA: Center for Iberian and Latin American Studies–Center for US-Mexican Studies, University of California–San Diego, 1986); and Dietrich Reuschemeyer, Evelyne Huber Stephens, and John D. Stephens, *Capitalist Development and Democracy* (Chicago: University of Chicago Press, 1992).

10. Michael Burton, Richard Gunther, and John Higley, "Introduction: Elite Transformations and Democratic Regimes," in John Higley and Richard Gunther, eds., *Elites and Democratic Consolidation in Latin America and Southern Europe* (Cambridge: Cambridge University Press, 1992, pp. 3–4), treat democratic consolidation somewhat differently than this—that is, as equivalent to, rather than merely including, an elite settlement: "A consolidated democracy is a regime that meets all the procedural criteria of democracy and also in which all politically significant groups accept established political institutions and adhere to democratic rules of the game" (p. 3).

11. See Peeler, *Latin American Democracies*; Burton et al., "Introduction: Elite Transformations . . . "; John A. Booth, "Elections and Democracy in Central America: A Framework for Analysis," in Booth and Seligson, eds., *Elections and Democracy*, pp. 19–21; and Mitchell A. Seligson and John A. Booth, "Political Culture and Regime Type: Evidence from Nicaragua and Costa Rica," *Journal of Politics* 55 (August 1993), pp. 777–792.

12. Larry Diamond and Juan J. Linz, "Introduction: Politics, Society and Democracy in Latin America," in Diamond, Linz, and Lipset, eds., *Democracy in Developing Countries,* Volume 4: *Latin America,* p. 15.

13. John A. Booth, "Toward Reconciliation and Democracy in Central America: Possible Roles for External Assistance," in Joaquín Roy, ed., *The Reconstruction of Central America: The Role of the European Community* (Coral Gables, FL: Iberian Studies Institute, University of Miami, European Community Research Institute, 1992), pp. 331–352; Diamond and Linz, "Introduction," pp. 10–17.

14. Diamond and Linz, "Introduction"; Samuel Huntington, *The Third Wave: Democratization in the Late Twentieth Century* (Norman: University of Oklahoma Press, 1991), pp. 208–316; Booth, "Elections and Democracy in Central America," pp. 16–21.

15. Peeler, *Latin American Democracies*; John Peeler, "Elites and Democracy in Central America," in Booth and Seligson, eds., *Elections and Democracy*; and John Peeler, "Autumn of the Oligarchs?" in Mitchell A. Seligson and John A. Booth, eds., *Elections and Democracy in Central America, Revisited* (Chapel Hill: University of North Carolina Press, 1995).

16. Guatemala and Honduras have had at least two peaceful presidential turnovers to opposition parties, but Peeler sees lingering threats to democratic institutions in both. El Salvador and Nicaragua have, Peeler contends, both eliminated significant threats to democracy, but neither had yet had two transitions to the opposition, by which he means to the former revolutionaries of the FSLN and FMLN. John Peeler, *Building Democracy in Latin America* (Boulder, CO: Lynne Rienner Publishers, 2004), pp. 126–127.

17. John A. Booth and Patricia Bayer Richard, "Repression, Participation, and Democratic Norms in Urban Central America," *American Journal of Political Science* 40 (1996), pp. 1205–1232; and John A. Booth and Patricia Bayer Richard, "Civil Society, Political Capital, and Democratization in Central America," *Journal of Politics* 60 (August 1998), pp. 780–800.

18. See John A. Booth and Patricia Bayer Richard, "Revolution's Legacy: Residual Effects on Nicaraguan Participation and Attitudes in Comparative Context," *Latin American Politics and Society* 48, No. 2 (Summer 2006).

19. LAPOP surveys 2008 and 2012, El Salvador.

20. LAPOP surveys 2008 and 2012, Nicaragua.

21. LAPOP surveys 2008 and 2012, Guatemala.

22. Mark Ruhl, "Curbing Central America's Militaries," *Journal of Democracy* 15 (July 2004), pp. 137–151.

23. Ibid. p. 148.

24. Robert R. Kaufman and Alex Segura-Ubiergo, "Globalization, Domestic Politics, and Social Spending in Latin America: A Time-Series Cross-Section Analysis, 1973–97," *World Politics* 53, No. 4 (2001), p. 553.

25. George Avelino, David S. Brown, and Wendy Hunter, "The Effects of Capital Mobility, Trade Openness, and Democracy on Social Spending in Latin America, 1980–1999," *American Journal of Political Science* 49, No. 3 (2005), pp. 625–641.

26. Alejandro Portes and Kelly Hoffman, "Latin American Class Structures: Their Composition and Change During the Neoliberal Era," *Latin American Research Review* 38, No. 1 (2003), pp. 41–82.

27. Kelly Hoffman and Miguel Angel Centeno, "The Lopsided Continent: Inequality in Latin America," *Annual Review of Sociology* 29 (2003), pp. 363–390.

28. Kurt Weyland, "Neoliberalism and Democracy in Latin America: A Mixed Record," *Latin American Politics and Society* 46, No. 1 (2004), pp. 135–157.

29. The application of neoliberal policies has proven detrimental to peace-building processes in Central America and elsewhere. See Roland Paris, *At War's End: Building Peace After Civil Conflict* (New York: Cambridge University Press, 2002).

30. Economic Commission for Latin America and the Caribbean, CEPALSTAT/ Data Bases, Government Social Spending, http://interwp.cepal.org/sisgen/Consulta Integrada.asp?idIndicador=134&idioma=e, accessed December 9, 2013.

APPENDIX

**TABLE A.1 Selected Economic Data for Central America,
by Country, 1960–2012**

	Costa Rica	El Salvador	Guatemala	Honduras	Nicaragua	Regional Means[a]
Gross Domestic Product (GDP)[b]						
1960	1,646	1,985	4,045	1,112	1,461	10,249
1970	2,932	3,437	6,911	1,905	2,849	18,034
1980	5,975	4,723	11,987	3,243	2,950	29,978
1990	6,313	6,334	12,923	3,985	2,587	32,143
2000	11,486	10,508	20,617	5,932	3,672	45,339
2010	15,596	11,185	24,080	6,580	4,011	62,327
2012	17,123	11,654	25,844	7,096	4,450	67,110
GDP per capita[c]						
1960	1,332	772	1,020	575	879	891
1970	1,694	958	1,373	725	1,388	1,207
1980	2,222	1,044	1,732	886	1,065	1,393
1990	2,094	1,210	1,404	775	663	1,209
2000	2,753	1,562	1,544	739	584	1,394
2010	3,548	1,804	1,676	906	690	1,627
2012	3,791	1,859	1,714	940	745	1,694
Percent change in GDP/capita						
1960–1970	27	24	31	26	58	35
1970–1980	31	9	26	22	-23	15
1980–1990	6	16	-18	-13	-38	-13
1990–2000	29	16	9	23	18	17
2000–2010	7	3	2	4	8	4
1990–2012	81	54	22	21	12	40
1960–2012	185	141	71	63	-15	90
Percentage[d] employed in agriculture						
1960	51	62	67	70	62	63[g]
1980	29	50	55	63	39	47[g]
2012	14	21	38	39	28	28[g]

(continues)

343

TABLE A.1 Selected Economic Data for Central America,
by Country, 1960–2012 *(continued)*

Percentage[d] employed in manufacturing						
c. 1950	11	11	12	6	11	10[g]
1983	16	14	15	13	15	15[g]
2012	22	20	14	21	19	19
Percentage of GDP from manufacturing						
1960	14	15	13	12	16	14[g]
1980	22	18	17	16	25	18[g]
2012	22	29	24	28	26	26[g]
Remittances as percentage of GDP						
1990	0.0	7.4	1.4	4.4	0.0	2.6[g]
2008	2.3	18.3	12.7	21.6	18.1	14.6
External debt[e]						
1980	2.7	.9	1.2	1.5	1.2	7.7[f]
1990	3.8	2.1	2.8	3.5	10.7	22.8[f]
2000	2.4	2.3	2.2	3.7	4.3	14.9[f]
2011	2.0	6.2	5.5	3.0	2.1	18.8[f]
Foreign debt as percentage of GDP						
1970	11.5	5.2	3.6	9.5	10.9	8.2[g]
1982	110.3	42.0	17.6	69.4	121.5	77.2[g]
1991	73.0	36.7	29.8	118.9	649.1	181.5[g]
2000	15.6	17.5	12.5	52.0	87.1	36.9[g]
2011	5.0	27.0	11.7	17.3	23.5	16.9[g]

[a]Weighted averages unless otherwise specified.
[b]In millions of 1986 US dollars; regional value is sum for all nations.
[c]In 1986 US dollars.
[d]Of economically active population.
[e]Disbursed total external debt, in billions of current US dollars.
[f]Sum of country totals.
[g]Unweighted mean.

SOURCES: John A. Booth and Thomas W. Walker, *Understanding Central America* (Boulder, CO: Westview Press, 1993), Table 2; Inter-American Development Bank, Economic and Social Progress in Latin America: Natural Resources. 1983 Report (Washington, DC, 1983), Tables 3 and 58; Inter-American Development Bank, Economic and Social Progress in Latin America: Science and Technology. 1988 Report (Washington, DC, 1988), Table E-1 and country tables; Inter-American Development Bank, Economic and Social Progress in Latin America: Natural Resources. 1994 Report (Baltimore, MD: Johns Hopkins University Press, 1994), Tables B-2, E-11, and country tables; Inter-American Development Bank, Economic and Social Progress in Latin America, 1997 Report: Latin America After a Decade of Reforms (Washington, DC: 1997), Tables B-1, B-2, B-10, E-1, and country profiles; Banco Interamericano del Desarrollo (Inter-American Development Bank), Situación económica y perspectivas: Istmo Centroamericano y República Dominicana (Washington, DC, May 2004), accessed January 6, 2005, iadb.org/regions /re2/SEPmayofinalMhung.pdf, pp. i–v; Economic Commission for Latin America and the Caribbean, Data Bases and Statistical Publications, Statistics and Indicators, accessed November 17, 2013, estadisticas.cepal.org/cepalstat/WEB_CEPALSTAT/estadisticasIndicadores.asp?idioma=i; U.S. Central Intelligence Agency, *The World Factbook* (Washington, DC: 1993), country reports, U.S. Central Intelligence Agency, *The World Factbook* (Washington, DC, 2004), accessed January 6, 2005, and U.S. Central Intelligence Agency, *The World Factbook* (Washington, DC, 2013), accessed November 17, 2013, cia.gov/cia/publications/factbook/, country reports.

TABLE A.2 Selected Social Data for Central America,
by Country, 1960–2013

	Costa Rica	El Salvador	Guatemala	Honduras	Nicaragua	Region[a]
Population (in millions)						
1960	1.2	2.6	4.0	1.9	1.5	11.2[b]
1980	2.3	4.5	6.9	3.7	2.8	20.2[b]
2003	4.2	6.6	12.3	7.0	5.3	35.4[b]
2013	4.9	6.3	15.4	8.1	6.1	40.1[b]
Population density estimate (persons/km²)						
1998	72.3	293.8	106.3	55.2	39.4	80.5
2013	94.1	295.2	139.4	71.4	46.2	132.7
Mean annual population growth rate (percent)						
1961–1970	3.4	3.4	2.8	3.1	3.2	3.3
1970–1980	2.8	2.3	2.8	3.4	3.0	3.0
1980–2003	3.6	2.0	3.4	3.9	3.9	3.2
2003–2013	1.7	-0.5	2.5	1.6	1.5	1.5
Percent indigenous population						
1978	1	2	60	2	2	14
2013[c]	1	4	41	4	4	12[d]
Percent Afro-origin population						
2012[c]	7	5	0	4	8	5[d]
Percent urban population						
1960	33	36	34	23	42	34
1996	49	48	42	49	74	50
2012	66	60	57	51	58	58
Percent literate						
1960	86	42	40	30	32	42
c. 2000	96	80	70	76	67	78
2013	96	85	76	85	78	84
Primary-school enrollment ratio						
1980	107	75	73	98	94	89
1990	101	81	78	108	94	92
c. 2002	108	112	103	106	105	107
c. 2012	94	94	93	97	92	94
University enrollment as percentage of university-age population						
c. 2001[c]	20	17	8	14	12	14
c. 2011	43	25	e	21	e	
Life expectancy at birth						
1980–1985	73	57	59	60	60	60
c. 2003	78	70	66	66	69	70
2013	78	74	72	71	72	73

(continues)

TABLE A.2 Selected Social Data for Central America,
by Country, 1960–2013 *(continued)*

Infant mortality/1,000 live births						
c. 1993	14	40	62	49	56	55
c. 2013	9	13	24	18	18	18[d]
Religious identification Catholic (percent)						
c. 1985	97	93	79	94	88	90
2012[c]	70	47	56	52	50	55
Religious self-identification Protestant/Evangelical (percent) 2012[c]						
c. 1985	3	4	6	3	8	5
2012[c]	23	39	38	38	40	36

[a]Unweighted average for region unless otherwise specified.
[b]Sum for region.
[c]Self-identified as belonging to this group, authors' analysis from 2012 AmericasBarometer surveys, www.LapopSurveys.org.
[d]Weighted average.
[e]Not available.
SOURCES: John A. Booth and Thomas W. Walker, *Understanding Central America* (Boulder, CO: Westview Press, 1993), Appendix, Table 3; Inter-American Development Bank, Economic and Social Progress in Latin America: Science and Technology. 1988 Report (Washington, DC, 1988), pp. 384, 408, 416, 440, 464; Inter-American Development Bank, Economic and Social Progress in Latin America, 1992 Report (Baltimore, MD: Johns Hopkins University Press, 1992), country tables; Inter-American Development Bank, Economic and Social Progress in Latin America: Natural Resources. 1994 Report (Baltimore, MD: Johns Hopkins University Press, 1994), country tables; Inter-American Development Bank, Economic and Social Progress in Latin America, 1997 Report: Latin America After a Decade of Reforms (Washington, DC: 1997), Tables A-1 and A2; Banco Interamericano del Desarrollo (Inter-American Development Bank), Situación económica y perspectivas: Istmo Centroamericano y República Dominicana (Washington, DC, May 2004), accessed January 6, 2005 at iadb.org/regions/re2/SEPmay; World Bank, Data, data.worldbank .org/country, accessed November 18, 2013; U.S. Central Intelligence Agency, The World Factbook (Washington, DC, 2013), accessed November 18, 2013, cia.gov/cia/publications/factbook/, country reports; and Economic Commission for Latin America and the Caribbean, Data Bases and Statistical Publications, Statistics and Indicators, estadisticas.cepal.org/cepalstat/WEB _CEPALSTAT/estadisticasIndicadores.asp?idioma=i, accessed November 18, 2013.

TABLE A.3 Mean Annual US Military Assistance and
Economic Assistance to Central America, 1946–1992

	Costa Rica	El Salvador	Guatemala	Honduras	Nicaragua	Region[a]
Military Assistance[b]						
Population (in millions)						
1946–1952	–	–	–	–	–	–
1953–1961	.01	.03	.19	.14	.24	.62
1962–1972	.16	.72	3.31	.90	2.36	7.45
1973–1976	.03	2.08	.83	2.23	.28	5.45
1977–1980	1.25	1.60	1.25	3.13	.85	6.98
1981–1984	3.95	98.85	.00	41.48	.00	144.28
1985–1988	3.93	112.78	5.20	57.73	.00	179.64
1989–1992	.10	63.10	2.35[c]	25.60	.00	91.15
Overall Mean 1946–1992	.83	23.86	1.63	12.38	.69	38.24
Economic Assistance[b]						
1953–1961	5.80	1.23	13.48	3.90	3.73	28.14
1962–1972	9.41	11.95	14.52	8.42	12.95	56.07
1973–1976	14.10	6.10	19.60	24.43	26.90	91.13
1977–1980	13.65	21.85	17.28	27.88	18.63	99.56
1981–1984	112.75	189.43	21.13	79.53	16.55	419.39
1985–1988	171.13	383.38	135.90	179.33	0.10	869.84
1989–1992	5.83	287.68	116.73	150.18	206.80	837.22
Overall Mean 1946–1992	36.48	78.72	32.73	42.06	26.83	216.83

[a]Includes only Costa Rica, El Salvador, Guatemala, Honduras, and Nicaragua.
[b]Millions of US dollars.
[c]The George H. W. Bush administration canceled Guatemala's 1990 military assistance of $3.3 million for human rights reasons. That left the aid delivered at less than originally appropriated for the period.
SOURCES: G. Pope Atkins, *Latin America in the International Political System* (New York: The Free Press, 1977), Tables D, E, and G. Pope Atkins, *Latin America in the International Political System* (Boulder, CO: Westview Press, 1989), Tables 10.2 and 10.4; and Office for Planning and Budgeting, US Agency for International Development, *U.S. Overseas Loans and Grants and Assistance from International Organizations: Obligations and Loan Authorizations*, July 1, 1945–September 30, 1992 (Washington, DC: Congressional Information Service, microfiche, 1993).

TABLE A.4 Central American Rebel Groups, 1959–1989

	Costa Rica	El Salvador	Guatemala	Honduras	Nicaragua
1959 1960				FMLH[a]	various groups[b] (1959–1961)
1961					FSLN
1962			MR-13 FAR, FGEI[c]		
1963					
1964					
1965					
1966					
1967					
1968					
1969					
1970	FPL				
1971			ORPA		
1972	ERP		EGP		
1973					
1974					
1975		FARN			
1976		PRTCS			
1977				PRTCH	FSLN splits[d]
1978			PGT-DN	MPL	
1979	La Familia	FAL			reunification of FSLN MPU-FPN[e]
1980	PRTC	FMLN[f]			
		FMLN- FDR[g]	MRP-Ixim		
1981			URNG[h]	FPR	
1982					
1983				DNU[i]	
1984					
1985					
1986					
1987					

(continues)

TABLE A.4 *(continued)*

	Costa Rica	El Salvador	Guatemala	Honduras	Nicaragua
1988					
1989				ERP-27	

*See List of Acronyms in the front matter of this volume.
[a]Only sporadically active through late 1979, when it resumed armed struggle.
[b]Of some 20 groups formed, only the FSLN survived beyond 1963.
[c]MR-13 disappeared after the late-1960s counterinsurgency campaign; the core of FAR survived to renew guerrilla activity in 1978; the core of FGEI survived counterinsurgency and helped form EGP.
[d]Under heavy counterinsurgency pressure, FSLN split into three factions with tactical differences.
[e]MPU-FPN coalitions linked broad-front political opposition with FSLN.
[f]MLN included all five Salvadoran guerrilla organizations.
[g]FMLN-FDR linked FMLN guerrillas with broad-front political opposition coalition.
[h]URNG linked the guerrilla groups EGP, FAR, ORPA, and the PGT-DN; MRP-Ixim not a member.
[i]DNU linked the MPL, FPR, and FMLH guerrilla organizations.

TABLE A.5 Comparative Data on Central Government Expenditures (percent of budget)

	Costa Rica 1978 1983	El Salvador 1984	Guatemala 1978 1984[a]	Honduras 1976	Nicaragua 1976
1. Defense	2.7 3.0	24.6	11.0 13.7	10.5	12.8
2. Education	24.5 19.4	15.5	13.0 12.7	20.7	16.9
3. Health	3.6 22.5	8.1	7.1 7.5	14.7	4.1
4. Social security/ welfare	28.3 14.5	3.7	4.1 3.9	4.7	19.9
5. Total percent on education, health, social security/ welfare (2 + 3 + 4)	56.3 56.3	27.3	24.2 24.1	40.1	40.9
6. Ratio of human services to defense (5:1)	21:1 19:1	1:1	2:1 2:1	4:1	3:1

[a]Slightly different budget breakdowns are used between Wilkie and Haber (1981) and Wilkie and Lorey (1987), on the one hand, and Inforpress Centroamericana (1985), on the other. The 1984 Guatemala data for the social security and welfare category on this measure are assumed to be the same as Inforpress' "labor" and "government" lines combined.
SOURCES: James W. Wilkie and Steven Haber, eds., *Statistical Abstract of Latin America, Volume 21* (Los Angeles: University of California at Los Angeles–University of California Latin American Center Publications, 1981), Table 2323; James W. Wilkie and David Lorey, eds., *Statistical Abstract of Latin America, Volume 25* (Los Angeles: University of California at Los Angeles–University of California Latin American Center Publications, 1987), Table 30; and Inforpress Centroamericana, *Central America Report*, 1985, p. 5.

TABLE A.6 Selected Presidential Election Results by
Percentage of Valid Vote, Central America.

Costa Rica, 1994–2014*								
	1994	1998	2002[a]	2002[b]	2006	2010	2014[a]	2014[b, c]
PLN	49.6	44.4	31.0	58.0	40.5	46.8	29.7	22.2
PUSC	47.5	46.9	38.5	42.0	3.4	3.9	6.0	
PAC			26.2		40.3	25.2	30.6	
PML		0.4	1.7		8.5	20.8	11.3	
Frente Amplio							17.3	
Total parties/ alliances competing	7	12	12		7	9	13	

*Constitution requires a minimum of 40 percent of the vote to avoid a runoff election.
[a]General election, first round (absolute majority required for victory).
[b]Runoff election.
[c]In 2014 the PLN candidate, Johnny Araya, withdrew from the runoff election several weeks before the final vote, essentially insuring victory for PAC candidate Luis Guillermo Solís.

El Salvador, 1994–2014							
	1994[a]	1994[b]	1999	2004	2009	2014[a]	2014[b]
ARENA	49.1	68.3	52.0	57.7	48.7	38.9	49.9
FMLN	25	31.7	39.0	35.6	51.3	48.9	50.1
PCN			3.8	2.7			
PDC	16.3		5.7	*			
CDU			7.5	3.9*			
MU						11.4	
Total parties/ alliances competing	9	2	7	4	2	5	2

[a]General election, first round (absolute majority required for victory).
[b]Runoff election.
*The CDU ran in coalition with the PDC in 2004.

(continues)

TABLE A.6 *(continued)*

Guatemala, 1999–2011

	1999[a]	1999[b]	2003[a]	2003[b]	2007[a]	2007[b]	2011[a]	2011[b]
FRG	47.7	68.2	19.3		7.3		49.9	
GANA			34.3	54.1	17.2			
PP					23.5	47.2	36.0	53.7
UNE			26.4	45.9	28.2	52.8		
PAN	30.3	31.8			2.6		2.8	
UCN					3.2		8.6	
LIDER							23.2	46.3
CREO							16.4	
Total parties/ alliances competing	11		11		14		10	

[a]General election, first round (absolute majority required for victory).
[b]Runoff election.

Honduras, 1993–2013*

	1993	1997	2001	2005	2009	2013
PLH	52.3	52.6	42.2	49.9	38.1	20.3
PN	40.7	42.8	52.2	46.2	56.6	36.8
LIBRE						28.8
PAC						13.6
Total parties/alliances competing	4	5	5	5	5	8

*The Honduran constitution provides for the election of the president by a "simple majority" (i.e., the largest number of votes).

Nicaragua, 1990–2011*

	1990	1996	2001	2006	2011
FSLN	40.3	37.8	43.0	38.1	
UNO	54.7				
PLC		51.1	55.5	26.2	
PCN			1.4	29.0	
MRS				6.4	5
Total parties/ alliances competing	10	22	3	5	5

*The Nicaraguan constitution provides for the election of the president by a "relative majority" of 40 percent. However, the Electoral Law (Law No. 331) further provides that a candidate can win with 35 percent if that candidate receives 5 percent more than the second place candidate; http://www.cse.gob.ni/index.php?s=8&&ley=1&&p=1.

TABLE A.7 Distribution of Legislative Seats Held Following
Selected Elections, Central American Countries*

Costa Rica. Distribution of Legislative Seats by Party, 1994–2010						
Party / year	1994	1998	2002	2006	2010	2014
PLN	28	23	17	25	23	18
PUSC	25	27	19	5	6	8
PAC			14	17	11	13
PML			6	6	9	4
Frente Amplio						9
Others	4	7	1	3	7	5

El Salvador. Distribution of Legislative Seats by Party, 1994–2012[a]							
Party / year	1994	1997	2000	2003	2006	2009	2012
ARENA	39	28	29	27	34	32	33
FMLN	21	27	31	31	32	35	31
PDC	18	10	5	5	6	5	
PCN	4	11	14	16	10	11	7
CDU	1	2	3	5			
CD					2	1	1
GANA							11
Others	1	6	2				1

[a]El Salvador holds legislative elections every three years.

Guatemala. Distribution of Legislative Seats by Party, 1995–2011					
Party / year	1995	1999	2003	2007	2011
UNE			30	52	
GANA			49a	37	
GANA-UNE					48
PP			a	29	56
FRG	21	63	41	14	1
EG				4	
PU			7	6	1
FDNG	6				
PAN	43	36	17	3	2
ANN		10	7		
UCN					14

(continues)

TABLE A.7 *(continued)*

Guatemala *(continued)*					
Party / year	1995	1999	2003	2007	2011
LIDER					14
CREO					12
Others	7	4	7	13	10

[a]In 2003 GANA and PP ran in coalition, along with two other parties. In 2011 GANA ran in coalition with UNE.

Honduras. Distribution of Legislative Seats by Party, 1993–2013						
Party / year	1993	1997*	2001	2005	2009	2013
PL	71	56	55	62	45	27
PN	55	60	61	55	71	48
LIBRE						37
PAC						13
Others	2	12	12	11	12	3

Nicaragua. Distribution of Legislative Seats by Party, 1990–2011[a]					
Party / year	1990	1996	2001	2006	2011
UNO	51				
FSLN	39	36	41	38	63
PLC			48	25	2
ALN-PC				22	
ALN		42			
PLI					27
MRS		1		5	
PCN		3	1		
Others		11			

[a]Losing presidential candidates who win a certain percentage of the vote also receive legislative seats, accounting for the deviation from the base number of 90 regular seats.

*SOURCES: These tables were compiled from data acquired from the respective countries' electoral tribunals, where available, and from the Political Database of the Americas website. Some variations in reporting of results were found among various other sources. It is important to consider in evaluating these data that seats won in elections may shift after the vote due to party defections, bloc voting, and alliance changes.

ABOUT THE AUTHORS

John A. Booth is Regents Professor Emeritus of Political Science at the University of North Texas. He is author of *The End and The Beginning: The Nicaraguan Revolution* and *Costa Rica: Quest for Democracy*, and coauthor of *The Legitimacy Puzzle in Latin America: Political Support and Democracy in Eight Nations* and *Latin American Political Culture: Public Opinion and Democracy*. His current research focuses on comparative political culture and behavior in Latin America.

Christine J. Wade is Associate Professor of Political Science and International Studies at Washington College. She is the coauthor of *A Revolução Salvadorenha* (Fundação Editora da UNESP) and the fifth edition of *Nicaragua: Living in the Shadow of The Eagle*. Her current research focuses on revolutionary movements in transition, peacebuilding, and postwar politics in El Salvador and Nicaragua.

Thomas W. Walker is Professor Emeritus of Political Science and Director Emeritus of the Latin American Studies Program at Ohio University. He is the author, coauthor, or editor of eleven books, most on Central America. The fifth edition of his *Nicaragua: Living in the Shadow of the Eagle* ,with Christine Wade as coauthor, appeared in 2011.

INDEX

Miskito Protectorate, 62
MLN. *See* National Liberation Movement
    (Movimiento de Liberación
    Nacional, MLN)
MLP. *See* Popular Liberation Movement
    (Movimiento de Liberación Popular,
    MLP)
MNR. *See* National Revolutionary
    Movement (Movimiento Nacional
    Revolucionario, MNR)
Mobilization, 279–283. *See also*
    Demobilization; Popular mobilization
Molina, Arturo Armando, 140, 143, 291
Monge, Luis Alberto, 80
Montealegre, Eduardo, 120, 122, 123
Moore, Barrington, 34
Morales, Evo, 223
Morales, Jaime, 119
Morazán Front for the Liberation of
    Honduras (FMLH), 216, 218
Mortality rates, 77
MPL. *See* Popular Movement for
    Liberation (Movimiento Popular de
    Liberación, MPL)
MS-13. *See* Mara Salvatrucha (MS-13)
Munguía Payés, David, 159
Murillo, Rosario, 121

Nasralla, Salvador, 228
National Advancement Party (PAN), 184,
    185, 332
National Assembly of Sandinistas, 31, 33,
    109, 113, 116, 117, 119, 120–123,
    126
National Association of Private Enterprises
    (Asociación Nacional de Empresas
    Privadas, ANEP), 146
National Conciliation Party (Partido de
    Conciliación Nacional, PCN), 139,
    157
National Democratic Organization
    (Organización Democrática
    Nacionalista, ORDEN), 143, 150
National Directorate of Unity (DNU), 216
Nationalist Republican Alliance Party
    (Alianza Republicana Nacionalista,
    ARENA), 147, 148, 150, 152–159,

161, 162, 163, 164, 190, 301–302,
    320, 327, 331
National Liberation Movement
    (Movimiento de Liberación Nacional,
    MLN), 175, 176, 178, 184
National Liberation Party (Partido de
    Liberacíon Nacional, PLN), 74, 75,
    78, 83–84, 85, 86, 87–89, 90, 243,
    262, 307n12, 318, 331
National Opposition Union (Unión
    Nacional Opositora, UNO), 102,
    113, 142
National Party (Partido Nacional, PN),
    211, 212, 215, 217, 218, 219, 221,
    223, 224, 226, 228–229, 317, 331
National Revolutionary Movement
    (Movimiento Nacional
    Revolucionario, MNR), 142, 146
National Union of Change (UCN), 194
National Unity of Hope (Unidad Nacional
    de la Esperanza, UNE), 188,
    191–192, 194, 332
Nation-states, regime change and, 37, 38
Navas, Zaira, 159
Negroponte, John D., 309n39
Neoliberalism, 3, 9, 28–29, 61–62, 264
    adoption of, 67
    Chamorro administration and, 114–115
    in Costa Rica, 72, 79–82
    democracy and, 334–337
    in El Salvador, 151, 152–153, 154
    in Guatemala, 186
    in Honduras, 219, 220, 229
New Guatemala Democratic Front
    (FDNG), 185, 186
Nicaragua
    Alemán-Ortega pact, 45, 118, 119,
        326–327, 332
    area of, 5
    capitalist factions of in 1960s and
        1970s, 100–101
    civil society and participation in,
        328–329
    communism in, 287
    conclusions regarding, 127–128
    contemporary politics of, 117–127
    demobilization in, 293–296, 295(photo)